THE EUROPEAN

COORDINATED

ECONOMY

CAPITALISM

SINCE

AND BEYOND

1945

BARRY EICHENGREEN

PRINCETON UNIVERSITY PRESS

PRINCETON AND OXFORD

Copyright © 2007 by Princeton University Press
Published by Princeton University Press, 41 William Street,
Princeton, New Jersey 08540
In the United Kingdom: Princeton University Press, 6 Oxford Street,
Woodstock, Oxfordshire OX20 1TW

All Rights Reserved

Fifth printing, and first paperback printing, 2008
Paperback ISBN: 978-0-691-13848-0

The Library of Congress has cataloged the cloth edition of this book as follows

Eichengreen, Barry J.
The European economy since 1945 : coordinated capitalism
and beyond / Barry Eichengreen.
p. cm. — (The Princeton economic history of the Western world)
Includes bibliographical references and index.
ISBN-13: 978-0-691-12710-1 (cloth : alk. paper)
ISBN-10: 0-691-12710-7 (cloth : alk. paper)
1. Europe—Economic conditions—1945– I. Title. II. Series.
HC240.E345   2006
330.94—dc22
2006010251

British Library Cataloging-in-Publication Data is available

This book has been composed in Goudy text with Impact
and Bank Gothic display

Printed on acid-free paper. ∞

press.princeton.edu

Printed in the United States of America

5   7   9   10   8   6

THE EUROPEAN

ECONOMY

SINCE

1945

THE PRINCETON ECONOMIC HISTORY OF THE WESTERN WORLD

Joel Mokyr, Editor

CONTENTS

CONTENTS

CONTENTS

FIGURES

Tables

PREFACE

This book was written at sunrise. Most of the work coincided with a home renovation project, making the best time for writing early in the morning, before the hammering began. It is an outgrowth of two previous projects. The first was the chapter on institutions and European economic growth commissioned by Nick Crafts and Gianni Toniolo for their volume *Economic Growth in Europe since 1945* (Cambridge University Press, 1996). It was in the context of writing that piece that I first experimented with the interpretation of corporatist institutions and European integration as solutions to the coordination problems that needed to be overcome in order to initiate and sustain economic growth. A seminar at the University of Lund organized in conjunction with this project enabled me to test these ideas and explore, with help from the authors of the other papers, how they might be applied to different European countries.

In 1997, I was invited by Mary Fulbrook to contribute a chapter on the economy to *Europe since 1945* (Oxford University Press, 2001), a volume in the Short Oxford History of Europe series. This allowed me to further develop my interpretation of the first post–World War II quarter century as a period of extensive growth and of Europe's growing economic difficulties as manifestations of the difficulty of making the transition from extensive to intensive growth. This chapter, the second precursor to the current book, was written during a sabbatical semester at the Center for Advanced Studies in the Behavioral Sciences, whose hospitality is acknowledged with thanks (no sawing and hammering there). This work was gratifying but also frustrating, given the impossibility of covering so much ground in fifty pages. That frustration was part of what convinced me of the need to treat the same issues at greater length.

Other scholars know much more than I about specific aspects of the terrain surveyed here. Olivier Blanchard, Francesco Caselli, Rui Esteves, Heather Gibson, Steve Nickell, and Leandro Prados provided help with data, for which I am grateful. I benefited from detailed readings of an earlier version of the manuscript by Andrea Boltho and Kevin O'Rourke. Valuable reactions on portions of the book were also provided by Anders Åsland, Frank Barry, Steve Broadberry, Christof Buchheim, Nick Crafts, Stanley Fischer, Michele Fratianni, Francesco Giavazzi, Robert Gordon, Patrick Honohan, Harold James, Peter Katzenstein, Joel Mokyr, Albrecht Ritschl, André Sapir, Pierre Sicsic, Hans-Werner Sinn, Peter Temin, Gianni Toniolo, Gabriel Tortella, and Brendan Walsh. Each of them had his own, often strongly held vision of how the post-1945 economic history of Europe should be written. I was not able to accommodate all of their views, although my discussion is no doubt more satisfactory for their advice. In part, my inability to elaborate their points reflects the limits of my own knowledge. But at the same time I was struck by the irreconcilable nature of the reactions of different readers. Evidently, Europe's post-1945 economic history means very different things to different observers. Although the interpretation here may not satisfy all readers, the existence of those differences makes the task of interpretation worthwhile.

In the same way that it has not been possible to represent every interpretation of Europe's economic experience in the second half of the twentieth century, I have not found it possible to recount the experience of every country. Rather than running through a litany of country cases, I have attempted to tell a thematic story, invoking country experiences as needed to motivate and elaborate those themes. Inevitably, this will leave some readers dissatisfied that their countries have not received the attention they deserve.

Although computers ease the production of a manuscript, they do not solve all technical problems. In Berkeley, Sibani Michael Bose helped to organize the book and much else, all the while stage managing theatrical productions and my office. Sudarat (Bo) Ananchotikul patiently assisted with the preparation of the charts and tables. Completing the book would not have been possible without their help.

At Princeton University Press, I am grateful to Peter Dougherty, whose added responsibilities have not diminished his enthusiasm for and attention to books in economics, to Linny Schenck, who guided the book through production, and to Madeleine Adams for an impeccable job of editing.

This book is dedicated to the two women in my life. My mother, Lucille Eichengreen, first took me to Europe more than forty years ago. My wife, Michelle Bricker, now takes me to Europe for pleasure and not just work—and shares with me much more.

ABBREVIATIONS

BDL	Bank deutscher Länder
Benelux	Belgium, Netherlands, and Luxembourg
CAP	Common Agricultural Policy
CDU	Christian Democratic Union
CEEC	Conference for European Economic Cooperation; or Central and Eastern European countries
CGIL	Italian Confederation of Labor
CMEA	Council on Mutual Economic Assistance
Cominform	Information Bureau of the Communist and Workers' Parties
CSC	Confédération des Syndicats Chrétiens
CSLB	Centrale Générale des Syndicats Liberaux de Belgique
DARPA	Defense Advanced Research Projects Agency
DGB	Deutscher Gewerkschaftsbund
ECB	European Central Bank
ECSC	European Coal and Steel Community
EDC	European Defense Community
EEC	European Economic Community
EFIM	Ente Partecipazioni e Finanziamento Industrie Manifatturiere
EFTA	European Free Trade Association
EMA	European Monetary Agreement
EMS	European Monetary System
EMU	economic and monetary union
ENI	Ente Nazionale Idrocarburi
EPU	European Payments Union
ERM	Exchange-Rate Mechanism

EU	European Union
FDES	Fonds de développement économique et social
FDI	foreign direct investment
FGTB	Fédération Générale du Travail de Belgique
FRG	Federal Republic of Germany
GATT	General Agreement of Tariffs and Trade
GDP	gross domestic product
GNP	gross national product
ICT	information and communications technology
ILO	International Labour Office
IMF	International Monetary Fund
INI	Instituto Nacional de Industria
IRI	Istituto per la Recostruzione Industriale
IT	information technology
LO	Landsorganisationen (Swedish Trace Union Confederation)
MRP	Mouvement Républicain Populaire
NATO	North Atlantic Treaty Organization
NEDC	National Economic Development Council
OECD	Organisation for Economic Co-operation and Development
OEEC	Organisation for European Economic Cooperation
ÖGB	Austrian Trade Union Federation
OPEC	Organization of Petroleum Exporting Countries
PBO	Publiekrechtelijke Bedrijfsorganisatie
PPP	purchasing power parity
PSBR	public-sector borrowing requirement
R&D	research and development
SAF	Swedish federation of employers associations
SEA	Single European Act
SEAT	Sociedad Española de Automóviles de Turismo
SGP	Stability and Growth Pact
SPD	Sozialdemokratische Partei Deutschlands
TFP	total factor productivity
TUC	Trades Union Congress
VSTF	Very-Short-Term Financing Facility

THE EUROPEAN

ECONOMY

SINCE

1945

- ONE -

INTRODUCTION

In the second half of the twentieth century, the lives of Europeans were transformed almost beyond recognition. In 1950, many of the continent's residents heated their homes with coal, cooled their food with ice, and lacked even rudimentary forms of indoor plumbing. Today, their lives are eased and enriched by natural-gas furnaces, electric refrigerators, and an array of electronic gadgets that boggles the mind. Gross domestic product per capita, what the income of a typical resident of Europe will buy, tripled in the second half of the twentieth century. The quality of life improved even more than suggested by this simple measure. Hours worked declined by one-third, providing an enormous increase in leisure time. Life expectancy lengthened as a result of improved nutrition and advances in medical science. To be sure, not all was sweetness and light. Unemployment rose. Tax burdens soared. Environmental degradation, political repression, and limits on consumer sovereignty were pervasive under the authoritarian regimes that dominated Eastern Europe for four decades after World War II. But by any objective standard, the last half century has left Europeans today enormously better off than their grandparents were fifty years ago.

Not all parts of the continent shared equally in this prosperity, of course, and not all portions of the last half century were characterized by equally rapid growth. Southern Europe grew faster than Northern Europe. Western Europe grew faster than Eastern Europe. Growth was slower after 1973 than before. This slowdown was most pronounced in Eastern Europe, where it culminated in a crisis of central planning that brought down not just the command economy but its authoritarian political superstructure as well. These are important qualifications, but they do not change the fact that the post–World War II period, and specifically the quarter century from 1948 to 1973, was a period of extraordinarily rapid change and a veritable golden age of economic growth.

What made possible the rapid economic growth of a continent that was devastated by World War II? Initially, Europe could grow rapidly simply by repairing wartime damage, rebuilding its capital stock, and redeploying men drafted into the wartime task of destroying output and productive capacity to the normal peacetime job of creating them. The rapid economic expansion of the early postwar years largely reflected this process of "catch-up growth."[1] The continent could then sustain its rapid growth by exploiting the backlog of new technologies developed between the two world wars but not yet put to commercial use. The 1920s and 1930s had been decades of instability and crisis, to be sure, but they were also a period of rapid technical change. Among other things, they saw the development of Lucite, Teflon, and nylon, improvements in the design of the internal combustion engine, and organizational changes such as the spread of assembly-line methods and modern personnel-management practices.[2] Most of these innovations were developed in the United States. But a depressed investment climate and then the disruptions of war made the 1930s and 1940s less than propitious times for Europe to emulate America's example. Consequently, by the end of World War II, the United States had opened up a huge lead in levels of output and productivity. But this also meant that there existed an extraordinary backlog of technological and organizational knowledge ready for Europe's commercial use. By licensing American technology, capitalizing on American produc-

---

[1] The term *catch-up* has been used in different ways in the literature on economic growth. It is used here to refer to the tendency of countries recovering from economic disruptions to catch up to their own potential levels of output.

[2] Similarly, World War II stimulated significant developments in computing, atomic energy, the production of jet engines and radar, and a variety of other fields, many of which also had considerable unexploited commercial potential.

ers' knowledge of mass-production methods, and adopting American personnel-management practices, Europe could close the gap. This aspect of growth in the second half of the twentieth century is known as "convergence," the tendency for levels of per capita income and productivity to converge toward those prevailing in the United States.[3]

For all these reasons, 1945 was a favorable jumping-off point for the European economy. Looking back on the extraordinary economic progress of the subsequent fifty years encourages a tendency to regard what followed as preordained. In fact, many things had to go right, and there was considerable uncertainty about whether they would. Catch-up, which entailed capital formation, the reallocation of labor, and the efficient use of these factors of production, required Europe to mobilize savings, finance investment, and maintain wages consistent with full employment and respectable profit rates. It required getting a range of complementary industries, each of which was necessary for the viability of the others, up and running simultaneously. Convergence required mechanisms for transferring to Europe and adapting to its circumstances the backlog of technological and organizational knowledge developed in the United States.

These were complex tasks. When we place ourselves in the position of contemporaries at the start of the period, as we will do in chapter 3, it becomes clear that any number of things could have gone wrong, as they had in the 1920s and 1930s.

That they did not go wrong now reflected the fact that Europe possessed a set of institutions singularly well suited to the task at hand. Catch-up was facilitated by solidaristic trade unions, cohesive employers associations, and growth-minded governments working together to mobilize savings, finance investment, and stabilize wages at levels consistent with full employment. The problem of getting a set of interdependent industries up and running simultaneously

---

[3] To be clear, there is also a literature on convergence within Europe (convergence of per capita incomes to the levels prevailing in, say, Germany or France). See, for example, Caselli and Tenreyro (2004). The bureaucracy of the European Union has developed its own terminology to denote this phenomenon, known as "cohesion."

was solved by extramarket mechanisms ranging from government planning agencies, state holding companies, and industrial conglomerates in Western Europe to wholesale nationalization and central direction of the economy in the East. The capacity expansion needed to efficiently operate these scale-intensive technologies was financed by patient banks in long-standing relationships with their industrial clients.

In a nutshell, then, opportunities for catch-up and convergence were realized because of the conformance, or more colloquially the "fit," between the structure of the Western European economy and the economic and technological imperatives of the day. The result was a period of exceptionally rapid growth from the end of World War II through the 1960s.

Critical to Western Europe's success was the security of private property rights and reliance on the price mechanism. But the rapid growth of the postwar golden age depended on more than just the free play of market forces; in addition it required a set of norms and conventions, some informal, others embodied in law, to coordinate the actions of the social partners and solve a set of problems that decentralized markets could not. Hence the "coordinated capitalism" of this book's title.

This codified set of norms and understandings—what economists mean when they refer to institutions—did not materialize overnight. To a large extent it was inherited from the past. It is not surprising that inherited institutions could be adapted to the needs of post–World War II growth, since the challenges of this period resembled those that had confronted Europe in earlier years. Modern industry had developed later on the continent than in Britain and the United States, at a time when the capital intensity of industrial technology was greater. These more demanding capital needs were met by great banks capable of mobilizing resources on a large scale.[4] As industrial production grew more complex and industrial sectors grew increasingly interdependent, it became more pressing to get a range of industries up and running simultaneously; hence the more

---

[4] This point, famously, is made by Gerschenkron (1962).

4

prominent role of the state.[5] Late-industrializing economies whose initial growth spurt depended as much on assimilating and adapting existing technologies as on pioneering new ones naturally developed systems of human capital formation emphasizing apprenticeship training and vocational skills as much as university education.[6] Thus, it was no coincidence that Europe had in place following World War II a set of institutions useful for relaxing the constraints on growth. It was also fortuitous that the inheritance was favorable, since these kinds of deeply embedded social institutions are slow to change.

Catch-up was similarly the forte of planned economies organized along Soviet lines. Bureaucrats decided how many factories to build, instructed state banks to mobilize the necessary resources, and limited consumption to what was left. They decided what foreign technologies to acquire, whether through licensing or industrial espionage. Because success measured in tons of steel production depended more on brute-force capital formation and the assimilation of standard technologies than on entrepreneurship and innovation, the centrally planned economies of Eastern Europe were able, initially at least, to perform tolerably well. The institutions of the command economy had severe limitations, as we will see, but they were best suited to the circumstances of catch-up growth.

Just as this inheritance of economic and social institutions contributed to the extraordinarily successful performance of the European economy in the third quarter of the twentieth century, it was equally part of the explanation for Europe's less satisfactory performance in the subsequent twenty-five years. As the early opportunities for catch-up and convergence were exhausted, the continent had to find other ways of sustaining its growth. It had to switch from growth based on brute-force capital accumulation and the acquisition of known technologies to growth based on increases in efficiency and internally generated innovation. This transition is some-

---

[5] This big-push approach to industrialization had already been emphasized by Rosenstein-Rodan (1943).

[6] A quick introduction to the literature on this subject is Sleight (1993).

times described as the shift from extensive to intensive growth. By *extensive growth* I mean growth based on capital formation and the existing stock of technological knowledge. It is the process of raising output by putting more people to work at familiar tasks and raising labor productivity by building more factories along the lines of existing factories.[7] *Intensive growth*, in contrast, means growth through innovation.[8] A larger share of the increase in output is accounted for by technical change, and less by the growth of factor inputs.[9]

Thus Europe, which had relied on extensive growth in the 1950s and 1960s, had no choice but to switch to intensive growth from the 1970s on. The problem was that institutions tailored to the needs of extensive growth were less suited to the challenges of intensive growth. Bank-based financial systems had been singularly effective at mobilizing resources for investment by existing enterprises using known technologies, but they were less conducive to growth in a period of heightened technological uncertainty. Now the role of finance was to take bets on competing technologies, something for which financial markets were better adapted.[10] The generous employment protections and heavy welfare-state charges that had given labor the security to accept the installation of mass-production technologies now became an obstacle to growth as new firms seeking to explore the viability of unfamiliar technologies became the agents of job creation and productivity improvement. Systems of worker co-determination, in which union representatives occupied seats on

---

[7] This is not to deny the existence of technical change but rather to emphasize the importance of capital formation—and the tendency for technological change to be embodied in new machinery and equipment—in this first phase of Europe's postwar growth. In economic models, the signature of extensive growth is a strongly rising capital–labor ratio such as that evident in the 1950s and 1960s, when Europe's capital stock grew at a rate of more than 5 percent a year while employment grew by about 1 percent. Extensive growth also took the form of shifting workers from agriculture to industry, where productivity was higher (thereby effectively augmenting the number of "efficiency units" of labor), while equipping them with prevailing levels of capital.

[8] Or at least more heavily through innovation.

[9] Some economists use these terms (*extensive* and *intensive growth*) differently, referring to the growth of gross domestic product (GDP) in the aggregate as extensive growth and the growth of GDP per capita as intensive growth. This is not their meaning here.

[10] These strengths and weaknesses of bank- and market-based financial systems are described in Allen and Gale (2000).

big firms' supervisory boards, had been ideal for helping labor to verify that owners were investing the profits resulting from its wage restraint but now discouraged bosses from taking the tough measures needed to restructure in preparation for the adoption of radical new technologies. State holding companies that had been engines of investment and technical progress were no longer efficient mechanisms for allocating resources in this new era of heightened technological uncertainty. They were increasingly captured by special interests and used to bail out loss-making firms and prop up declining industries.

Increasingly, then, the same institutions of coordinated capitalism that had worked to Europe's advantage in the age of extensive growth now posed obstacles to successful economic performance. In this sense, the continent's very success at exploiting the opportunities for catch-up and convergence after World War II doomed it to difficulties thereafter. And the durability and persistence of institutions, which had worked to Europe's advantage after World War II, were now less positive attributes than impediments to growth.

Eastern Europe manifested this problem in its most extreme form. The centrally planned economies were particularly inept at innovation, since new knowledge generally bubbles up from below rather than raining down from above. More than nearly any other activity, innovation responds to incentives, which were in chronic short supply in the command economies. This weakness of central planning came back to haunt the Eastern bloc once the party was over, the technological pantry was bare, and a premium was placed on innovation.

This, in bare-bones form, is the story told in this book. It is a way of understanding the golden age of growth that prevailed for twenty-five years after World War II and the subsequent slowdown. It explains how the average annual rate of growth of gross domestic product (GDP) per capita in Western Europe could have fallen by more than half between the 1950–1973 period and the 1973–2000 period.[11] It similarly explains why the deceleration between these

[11] Although Europeans reduced their hours worked after 1973, as discussed in chapter 12, causing the growth rate of GDP per hour worked to exceed the growth rate of GDP per

periods was even more dramatic in Eastern Europe and why the planned economies collapsed at the end of the 1980s. To be sure, no single explanation for these complex phenomena can possibly be complete. For example, Europe's growth deceleration was surely also affected by global factors beyond its control. It is revealing, though, that the rate of growth of output per hour declined more sharply in Europe than in the United States, which was affected by the same global forces. The exhaustion of the technological backlog and the difficulty of adapting inherited institutions to changed circumstances go a long way toward explaining this fact.

As these last sentences remind us, the story of Europe's postwar growth—indeed, the story of its growth over the entire second half of the twentieth century—cannot be told in isolation from developments in the rest of the world. This directs our attention to another aspect of the inheritance shaping growth in the third quarter of the twentieth century: the Great Power conflict. Countries falling within the ambit of the United States or the Soviet Union came under pressure to adopt the same form of economic and social organization as the power under whose security umbrella they sheltered. After a brief period of uncertainty, Western Europe was decisively propelled toward market capitalism and Eastern Europe toward state socialism. This choice became the single most important determinant of growth performance in the two halves of the European continent.

The nature of the conflict permitted Western Europe to free ride on the security system provided by the United States. Less defense spending allowed Western European countries to devote more government revenues and investment to private ends. In effect, the subsidiary role that Europe played in the Great Power conflict yielded a peace dividend that freed up resources for productive capital formation.[12] Eastern Europe was the recipient of an analogous

---

capita, the same was true in the earlier period, shorter hours being a corollary of higher living standards. Hence the growth rate of GDP per hour worked also fell, by roughly the same proportion.

[12] This leaves open the question of whether defense spending, and defense-related research and development in particular, had important commercial spin-offs. I return to this in chapter 9.

8

dividend; it imported energy and raw materials at submarket prices from the Soviet Union in return for the stationing of Soviet troops in the region.[13]

In addition, the Cold War provided an impetus for regional integration. The United States would not have acquiesced to the creation of a customs union of European nation-states capable of discriminating against American exports except for the priority it attached to building a bulwark against communism. And the Soviets would not have insisted so strongly on the integration of the Eastern bloc but for the example of Western Europe and the incompatibility of their own economy with those of Western European countries.

To be sure, European integration was never mainly a matter of external influence. This brings us to yet another aspect of the inheritance with implications for Europe's post–World War II experience. Europe inherited from the earlier period a deep and abiding strand of integrationist thought. To be sure, that Europe's national economies were deeply interdependent and that the fruits of their interdependence had been squandered in the first half of the twentieth century predisposed some toward the integrationist project. American influence also mattered, as noted earlier. Still, it is revealing of the predisposition toward regional integration that the postwar constitutions of France and Italy included clauses allowing for abrogating national sovereignty in favor of a supranational European authority. It is hard to imagine similar provisions in national constitutions in other parts of the world.

European integration was related to the wider process of globalization and was in turn driven by technological advances—such as high-speed road and rail transport, containerization, and, later, broadband and satellite telephony—that reduced the costs of transacting across borders. But integration went further and faster in Europe. In the 1950s, six European states put planning for their iron and steel industries under multinational control. In the 1960s, Europe became the first major region to create a full-fledged customs

---

[13] One can question, of course, whether it had much choice in the matter. See chapter 5.

union (a free trade area with a common external tariff). It built on this achievement by creating a single market in which barriers behind the border were dissolved by the mutual recognition of national regulations and the application of a single European competition policy, and then by establishing a single European currency, the euro, whose issuance was overseen by a transnational institution, the European Central Bank.

From an economic point of view, these were important achievements. They gave Western European governments confidence that German industrial capacity would be put to peaceful use, allowing ceilings on that country's industrial production to be lifted. They gave a boost to intra-European trade and encouraged restructuring along export-oriented lines. They exposed cosseted producers to the chill winds of competition and supported their efforts to navigate the transition from extensive to intensive growth. They enhanced the liquidity and efficiency of European financial markets. They helped to cement the economic and financial stability that stood in contrast to the disasters of the 1930s.

From a political standpoint, this achievement was still more remarkable. Barely five years after the conclusion of the deadliest war in modern history, irreconcilable enemies agreed to cede control of the coal and steel industries that were considered critical to their national security to a new transnational entity, the European Coal and Steel Community. Barely five years later, they agreed to surrender another key element of their national sovereignty, the ability to use trade policy to regulate the national economy. These were extraordinary accomplishments by any standard. Nothing analogous had occurred previously, either in Europe or elsewhere.[14]

The institutions of European integration were designed to solve a specific set of postwar problems. They were intended to lock Germany into Europe and ensure that the continent's largest producer of capital goods would apply its industrial might to peaceful uses.

---

[14] Compare, for example, East Asia, where it has taken more than a half century for the wounds of war to heal and for leaders, inspired in part by the European example, to begin taking the idea of regional integration seriously.

They were designed to lend legitimacy to national governments, freeing them to use their stabilizing and coordinating powers to stimulate the growth of productive capacity, since their destructive tendencies were now contained by the transnational structures of which they were part.[15] They fostered the international solidarity required by the Great Power conflict: the United States encouraged its Western European allies to forge closer economic and political ties, while the Soviet Union prohibited the participation of Eastern European countries that might have been tempted to collaborate in the integrationist initiatives of the West. In all these ways, the institutions of European integration formed another aspect of the coordinated capitalism that is the focus of this book.

In the 1970s and 1980s, efforts were made to adapt these institutions to the challenges created by the end of the postwar era and by the advent of a more competitive, innovation-intensive economy. The European Monetary System of 1979 responded to the breakdown of the Bretton Woods System of pegged exchange rates by instituting adjustable ones. The Single European Act of 1986, by integrating the product markets of the member states, made for a more competitive environment. In turn, competition ratcheted up the pressure to adapt, confronting firms with the need to change or die. The intensity of product market competition being especially important for explaining the speed of uptake of new technologies, information and communications technologies in particular, there is reason to think that product market competition has been especially beneficial for productivity in the recent period of intensive, innovation-based growth.[16] Creating more competitive and flexible capital and labor markets, another goal of the European project, was designed to make it easier for firms to undertake the necessary adjustments. This effort was more successful in the case of capital markets,

[15] See Milward (1992). The importance of European integration for relegitimizing state action and allowing economic growth to resume was particularly clear in the case of Germany, about whose renewed economic strength the rest of Europe would otherwise have had significant reservations (Berger and Ritschl 1995). For more on this, see chapter 6.

[16] See Organisation for Economic Co-operation and Development (2002) for discussion and evidence on this point.

11

where the advent of the euro created a truly pan-European financial market, than in the case of labor markets, where entrenched interests more successfully resisted change.[17] Still, and notwithstanding these caveats, Europe moved some way in the final quarter of the twentieth century toward the creation of more flexible and competitive markets in response to the pressure of integration.

Once more, however, there were limits to how effectively a set of inherited institutions could be adapted to changed circumstances. Simply encouraging the expansion of iron and steel production, liberalizing trade, or facilitating product market competition, tasks for which the institutions of European integration had been designed, was no longer enough now that it was necessary to fundamentally restructure the entire constellation of socioeconomic arrangements. Following earlier precedent, governments sought to make the European Union (EU) their agent for pushing through these changes. But such reforms were more invasive and therefore even more contentious than their predecessors. Those with a vested interest in existing arrangements naturally pushed back against pressure for reform and specifically against the EU's reformist influence. The fact that the EU's political dimension, which was needed to provide legitimacy for those making these difficult decisions, was less developed than its economic dimension now became more troubling. In addition, the end of the Cold War and the accession to the EU of the formerly "neutral" countries of Austria, Finland, and Sweden, followed by a long list of so-called transition economies, meant that the cozy decision-making rules of the Europe of the six founding members were no longer viable.

Committed federalists had always seen economic integration as a stepping-stone to political integration, but the vast majority of Europeans had resisted ceding sovereign national prerogatives to the European Commission (the European Community's protoexecutive branch) and the European Parliament. They rejected ambitious initiatives for developing the political dimension of their union, in

---

[17] Although, as we shall see, the euro did more to create a pan-European market in government securities than in intermediary services.

1954 with the French Assembly's rejection of the European Defense Community and the European Political Community, and in 2005 with French voters' rejection of the EU constitution.[18] As the fifty-plus years separating these events reveal, tension between the advantages of economic integration and reservations about political integration is an enduring characteristic of the European project. This tension did not prevent the European Community from being used to promote the recovery of heavy industry, the liberalization of trade, and the deregulation of product markets. But when more far-reaching and socially invasive reforms were required, a set of institutional arrangements whose economic dimension was more advanced than its political aspect became less effective. Again, a set of institutions tailored to the imperatives of postwar growth proved less suited to the circumstances of this later period, and adapting it to new conditions was no easy task. As a result, it was increasingly argued that the EU had become an obstacle rather than a facilitator of growth.

The Eastern European countries under the influence of the Soviet Union took an extended detour on their way to this destination. Following the breakup of the Council on Mutual Economic Assistance, their regional trade bloc, and of the Soviet Union itself, they sought to repair their historic ties with Western Europe, which now meant building links with the EU. They first joined the European Economic Area composed of the EU and its neighbors, a quasi free trade zone that exempted agricultural goods and the products of heavy industries, sectors that were politically sensitive in the West. From the start, however, the Eastern European countries' goal was to become members of the EU. Admission to the EU in 2004 of the first cohort of eight former East-bloc members symbolized their return to Europe. Qualifying required them to establish functioning democracies; through this channel the lure of EU membership played an important role in the development of their political sys-

---

[18] That France was the country putting the kibosh on these initiatives is revealing since, as we shall see, it was also the country most committed to the larger project of European integration.

13

tems. Admission to the club was further conditioned on economic reform. Indeed, the incentive to reform was the most tangible bene-fit of EU accession.

In Eastern and Western Europe alike, reforms remain incom-plete. Europe's markets are derided as "inflexible" and "rigid." Its generous welfare state is criticized as corrosive of effort. Its economy is dismissed as "stagnant." A population reluctant to embrace radical change is criticized as "complacent" and "unproductive." In a world of quicksilver markets and intense global competition, questions are increasingly being raised about the viability of the European model.

Are things really so dire? Is it really true that the European model has no future? Understanding the point to which Europe has come and answering these questions require going back to the start of the postwar period.

- TWO -

MAINSPRINGS OF GROWTH

This chapter takes a closer look at the facts to be explained. Table 2.1 presents an overview of Europe's economic growth from 1820 to 2000. Its figures for aggregate gross domestic product (GDP) show that Western Europe grew more than twice as fast from 1950 through 1973 as it did over the whole of the nineteenth and twentieth centuries.[1] The exceptional nature of the golden age is clear. The period 1973 through 2000, in contrast, was not atypical: the rate of growth of GDP in Western Europe, at 2.1 percent per annum, was the same as over the longer period. Figures for per capita GDP growth, in table 2.2, place the last quarter of the twentieth century in a slightly more favorable light but do not change the basic picture.[2]

The same broad patterns are evident in Peripheral Europe (Greece, Ireland, Portugal, Spain, and Turkey, so classified because they were relatively poor countries at the start of the golden age). In particular, table 2.2 shows the same tendency for the growth of per capita GDP to accelerate in 1950–1973 and fall back subsequently. These countries' relatively high rates of growth in both the third and fourth quarters of the twentieth century indicate their tendency to catch up with the Western European leaders.

---

[1] Following Maddison (2001), the first two decades of the nineteenth century are omitted, these having been dominated by the Napoleonic Wars, which create conceptual and measurement problems for such calculations. Given what most historians have characterized as slow growth in this period, adding it would only accentuate the exceptional nature of the period 1950–1973.

[2] Slower population growth rates, which translate into relatively faster per capita GDP growth rates, explain this difference in the picture painted by the two tables.

TABLE 2.1
Growth of gross domestic product, 1820–2000 (Average annual compound growth rate)

	1820–1870	1870–1913	1913–1950	1950–1973	1973–2000	**1820–2000**
Western Europe	1.7	2.1	1.1	4.5	2.1	**2.1**
Peripheral Europe	0.9	1.5	1.2	6.0	3.4	**2.1**
Eastern Europe	1.6	2.3	1.7	4.7	−0.2[a]	**2.2**[b]
World	0.9	2.1	1.8	4.8	3.0	**2.2**

Source: Maddison (2001).
Notes: Country groupings are made up of the countries enumerated in table 2.2.
[a] Average for 1973–1989.
[b] Average for 1820–1989.

In contrast, there is no such tendency in Eastern Europe.[3] By the middle of the twentieth century, this region had fallen behind not just the Western European core but also the Western European periphery.[4] As elsewhere, there was an acceleration after 1950. But there was no tendency to catch up to the Western European leaders; the growth of per capita GDP remained slower than in the West. Post-1973 performance was disastrous.

Another perspective is the comparison with the United States. Table 2.3 reminds us that Western European output and living standards fell significantly below those of the United States in the first half of the twentieth century. On the eve of the Great Depression, output per capita was less than two-thirds of U.S. levels.[5] In 1950, owing to the disruptions of World War II, Europe had fallen still

---

[3] Figures for this region must be treated especially cautiously, given questions about their accuracy, as explained at greater length in chapters 5 and 10. Still, the broad outlines are clear.

[4] The one episode of outperformance was the interwar period, but this was largely owing to the rapid growth imputed to the Soviet Union in the 1930s (see table 2.4). The accuracy of these estimates has been challenged, and in any case such figures should not be taken as a measure of the improvement in living standards and welfare, given Stalinist conditions.

[5] Whether there is evidence of Europe partially closing this gap in the 1930s depends on the measure used. If one considers output per hour worked, the gap actually widens further, consistent with the view that the 1930s was a technologically dynamic decade in the United States. That the two measures of labor productivity in table 2.3 move in opposite directions— Europe's output per person rises relative to that of the United States, but its output per hour worked falls—reflects the prevalence of work sharing and short hours in the United States in the 1930s (Bernanke 1985). This provides an interesting perspective on the contrast provided by output-per-hour and output-per-worker comparisons in the final decades of the twentieth century, as will be discussed later.

TABLE 2.2
Growth of real gross domestic product per capita, 1820–2000
(Average annual compound growth rate)

	1820–1870	1870–1913	1913–1950	1950–1973	1973–2000
Twelve Western European Countries					
Austria	0.7	1.5	0.2	4.9	2.2
Belgium	1.4	1.0	0.7	3.5	2.0
Denmark	0.9	1.6	1.6	3.1	1.9
Finland	0.8	1.4	1.9	4.3	2.2
France	0.8	1.5	1.1	4.0	1.7
Germany	1.1	1.6	0.3	5.0	1.6
Italy	0.6	1.3	0.8	5.0	2.1
Netherlands	1.1	0.9	1.1	3.4	1.9
Norway	0.5	1.3	2.1	3.2	2.9
Sweden	0.7	1.5	2.1	3.1	1.5
Switzerland	NA	1.5	2.1	3.1	0.7
United Kingdom	1.2	1.0	0.8	2.5	1.9
Regional average[a]	1.0	1.3	0.8	4.0	1.8
Five Countries of European Periphery					
Greece	NA	NA	0.5	6.2	1.7
Ireland	1.2	1.0	0.7	3.1	4.3
Portugal	NA	0.5	1.2	5.7	2.5
Spain	0.5	1.2	0.2	5.8	2.6
Turkey	NA	NA	0.8	3.3	2.4
Regional average[a]	0.7	1.1	0.5	5.1	2.5
Seven East European Countries					
Bulgaria	NA	NA	0.3	5.2	0.7[b]
Czechoslovakia	0.6	1.4	1.4	3.1	1.0[b]
Hungary	NA	1.2	0.5	3.6	0.9[b]
Poland	NA	NA	NA	3.4	0.3[b]
Romania	NA	NA	NA	4.8	0.6[b]
USSR	0.6	0.9	1.8	3.4	0.7[b]
Yugoslavia	NA	NA	1.0	4.4	1.6[b]
Regional average[a]	0.6	1.0	1.6	3.5	0.7[b]

Sources: Maddison (2001) and author's calculations.

Notes: [a] Weighted by period-average GDP. Regional averages exclude countries whose data are not available in the specified period. An exception is Ireland in the periods before 1938, for which Maddison uses U.K./British figures.

[b] Average for 1973–1989.

17

TABLE 2.3
Gross domestic product per capita and per hour, 1913–2003

	1913	1929	1938	1950	1973	2003
	GDP per capita as percentage of U.S. levels					
France	66	68	73	55	79	73
Germany	69	59	82	41	72	64
Italy	48	45	54	37	64	66
United Kingdom	93	80	102	73	72	72
EU-15 average	57	55	66	47	65	72
	GDP per hour as percentage of U.S. levels					
France	56	NA	NA	46	74	111
Germany[a]	59	NA	NA	32	79	98
Italy	42	NA	NA	35	78	100
United Kingdom	84	NA	NA	63	60	83
EU-15 average[b]	61	NA	NA	44	71	94

Sources: GDP per hour 1973–2003 is derived from Organisation for Economic Co-operation and Development (OECD), *National Accounts* (various years), and OECD *Labor Force Statistics* (various years). EU-15 data for 1973 are from data files provided by Olivier Blanchard (related to Blanchard 2004). EU-15 data for 2003 are from the OECD database. All other figures are from Maddison (2001).

Notes: [a] West Germany for 1950 and 1973.

[b] The following countries are excluded from the EU-15 average due to lack of data. 1913 and 1950: Greece, Ireland, and Spain; 1973: Greece, Luxembourg, and Portugal; 2003: Belgium and Luxembourg.

further behind. Although the golden age was global, the acceleration between 1950 and 1973 was even faster in Western Europe than in the United States. Hence, in this period Europe succeeded in eliminating about 40 percent of the initial post–World War II gap. This is why the golden age is commonly portrayed as a period when Western Europe converged toward the technological frontier defined by the United States.

For the period since 1973, one's image of Europe's relative economic performance depends on the brush used to paint the picture. If output and productivity are measured by GDP per capita, then the final quarter of the twentieth century appears as a period of relative stagnation. European GDP per capita in 2003 was still only 72 percent of U.S. levels, marginally higher than three decades earlier. The impression is different, however, when one considers GDP per hour worked, reflecting the shortening of the work year in Europe in the final quarter of the twentieth century. By this measure, European and U.S. productivity continued to converge through the early 1990s, when European GDP per worker-hour stabilized in the range of 90 to 95 percent of U.S. levels.

Table 2.2 also provides some useful information on the performance of individual Western European countries. Growth in the golden age was fastest in Germany, Austria, and Italy, reflecting the *Wirtschaftswunder* (Germany's postwar growth miracle), Austria's economic links to its larger Germanic neighbor, and Italy's success in shifting resources from agriculture to industry. It was slowest in the United Kingdom, a fact that by this time had already given rise to a literature on the country's economic failure. In Peripheral Europe, the golden age was bright in Greece, Spain, and Portugal but dim in Ireland, reflecting delay there in inaugurating the convergence process.

The growth of per capita output varied relatively little across Eastern Europe in the golden age, indicative of the strict regimentation of the Soviet bloc and the heavy hand of central planning.[6] Still, there are signs that it was slowest in the countries that started out with the highest levels of output per person (Czechoslovakia and the USSR) and fastest where output per capita was lowest (Bulgaria, Romania, and Yugoslavia).[7] Strong uniformity is also evident after 1973, notwithstanding variations in national reform programs. Not only is the post-1973 slowdown pronounced, in other words, but the stagnation is regionwide.

Further light can be shed by comparing the growth of output with the growth of physical capital, the growth of human capital, and technical change, as in table 2.4.[8] Relative to the United States,

---

[6] The revisions of the official statistics reported here should be taken with a grain of salt, since they may overstate economic performance by omitting the more slowly growing service sector and neglecting quality deterioration and disguised inflation. For more on this, see chapters 5 and 10. More generally, this is a reminder of the heroic nature of many of these estimates and the need to treat them skeptically.

[7] This suggests that growth in Eastern Europe was also characterized by the dual processes of catch-up and convergence discussed in the next section.

[8] Each of these variables is expressed in per worker terms. Details on the construction of these estimates can be found in the appendix. Unfortunately, the data needed for these calculations (at least for the entire period) are not available for the Eastern European countries.

the technological leader in 1950, we again see how all fifteen European countries converged to a greater or lesser extent in the second half of the century.[9] But the sources of this convergence varied. Throughout Europe, the physical capital stock per worker grew faster than in the United States, indicative of the importance of investment for economic growth. Average levels of human capital, derived here from average years of schooling, also grew more quickly in about two-thirds of the European countries. Technical change, similarly, was faster in about two-thirds of the European countries.[10] Here the outliers are the United Kingdom, where the recovery of productivity growth starting in the Thatcher years was not enough to overcome slow growth in the first three postwar decades, and Ireland, whose remarkable productivity performance in recent decades was enough to boost it to the head of the class.

Probing Deeper

The question is what deeper economic factors explain these patterns. The obvious place to start is with catch-up and convergence. *Catch-up* refers to the rapid growth achieved by reversing the loss of output and destruction of capacity caused by World War II.[11] At the end of the 1940s, capital stocks were below long-run equilibrium levels. Workers were unemployed owing to the general disorganization of the economy. European countries that had experienced wartime disruptions could grow fast by rebuilding the capital stock and expanding employment.

Or so goes the conventional wisdom. Actually, as early as 1947, only two years after the conclusion of hostilities, industrial production across Europe exceeded 1938 levels if Germany, where eco-

---

[9] In each European country, in other words, the growth of output per worker was faster than in the United States.

[10] But not necessarily the same ones in which average years of schooling grew faster than in the United States.

[11] A long line of studies links the acceleration of European growth following World War II to the scope for catch-up. Highlights from this body of work include Svennilson (1954), Lundberg (1968), Janossy (1972), and Abramovitz (1986).

TABLE 2.4
Average annual growth rate of output per worker and its
determinants, 1950–2000

Country	y	k	h	tfp
Austria	3.58	4.50	0.71	1.62
Belgium	2.66	3.25	0.69	1.12
Denmark	2.15	3.47	0.34	0.77
Finland	3.16	4.68	0.97	0.97
France	2.86	4.06	0.77	1.00
Germany	2.92	4.05	0.71	1.11
Greece	3.32	3.95	0.94	1.39
Ireland	3.77	3.17	0.62	2.31
Italy	3.52	3.34	0.86	1.85
Netherlands	2.19	2.92	0.76	0.71
Norway	2.50	3.05	0.44	1.19
Portugal	3.74	3.73	0.72	2.03
Spain	3.58	2.99	0.88	2.00
Sweden	1.93	3.36	0.67	0.37
United Kingdom	2.02	4.03	0.59	0.29
Memo item: United States	1.90	1.88	0.67	0.83

Source: See appendix.

Note: y = output per worker; k = physical capital per worker; h = human capital per worker; tfp = total factor productivity per worker.

nomic disorganization continued to prevail, is excluded from the comparison. By the end of 1948, industrial production including even Germany, which had completed its monetary reform and lifted most price controls, matched the levels of ten years earlier.

Nor had capital stocks fallen significantly from prewar levels. The lesson of strategic bombing was that as fast as air power destroyed productive capacity, the target country could repair and replace it. It is thus unsurprising that capital stocks and productive capacity were as high at the end of the 1940s as they had been ten years earlier.

But there was still scope for catch-up insofar as Europe had forgone eight years of normal growth of productive capacity and capital. Had Europe continued to grow between 1938 and 1946 at its customary 2.2 percent average annual compound rate, output and the capital stock would have been roughly 20 percent above prewar levels at the end of the 1940s. To the extent that investment had

21

been depressed by the turbulence of the 1920s and the slump of the 1930s, the gap relative to steady-state levels was larger still. This larger capital stock would have meant a higher capital–labor ratio and higher aggregate output. Thus, there was scope for rapid growth if Europe could now push its capital–labor ratio back up toward this higher steady-state trajectory.[12] In addition, unemployment rates ranged from 5 to 10 percent in many of these war-devastated economies, creating scope for rapid growth by putting the unemployed back to work. To some extent, then, the rapid growth of the golden age, especially at its beginning, represented a simple return to normalcy.

To be sure, normalcy, whether construed narrowly in terms of the steady-state capital–labor ratio or more broadly as the resumption of stability and growth, could not be taken for granted. Catch-up required higher than customary levels of investment. And higher levels of investment there were: a striking feature of the 1950s and 1960s is the rise in investment rates continent-wide.[13] Gross fixed investment as a share of GDP, excluding investment in housing, rose from 12 percent in France in the 1920s and 1930s, to 14 percent in the 1950s, and then 17 percent in the 1960s.[14] In Germany it rose from 11 percent in the 1920s and 1930s, to 17 percent in the 1950s, and then 18 percent in the 1960s. Even the United Kingdom experienced this shift, albeit from lower levels: gross fixed nonresidential investment rates there rose from 6 percent in the 1920s and 1930s, to 12 percent in the 1950s, and then 15 percent in the 1960s.[15]

---

[12] Thus, van der Wee (1986) shows that the negative correlation between the starting point in terms of technology and labor productivity (typically measured as initial per capita income) and the subsequent rate of growth was stronger during the golden age than in any previous period. The strength of this correlation can be interpreted as evidence of the "fit" between the technology and the economic structures of the time (see the discussion later in this chapter).

[13] This is the explanation for the golden age emphasized by Maddison (1991).

[14] Maddison (1991), table 2.3. Calculations for "the 1960s" cover the period through 1973, as is conventional.

[15] Relatively high investment rates are also evident in other European countries; see United Nations (1972), p. 14. No other Western European country had rates of fixed nonresidential investment as low as those of the United Kingdom in the 1950s (only Spain and Portugal came close).

All of this begs the question of what delivered high levels of investment in the postwar period and why Europe was not equally successful in translating capital accumulation into rapid growth after 1973. These are among the central questions for the remainder of this volume.

Convergence refers to the additional growth achieved by closing the efficiency gap that had opened up vis-à-vis the United States. By the end of the nineteenth century, the United States had assumed a significant lead in GDP per capita by harnessing its endowments of land and resources and pioneering mass-production methods. It had created a unified internal market on a scale unmatched anywhere in the world. This allowed it to develop the multidivisional corporation, an organizational form capable of exploiting economies of scale by ensuring that integrated producers had reliable supplies of raw materials and economical access to dispersed local markets.[16] By scaling up, American corporations cut production costs, leading to their emergence as world-class exporters and giving a further fillip to the development of the American system of mass production.

All this is evident in the gap in GDP per person between Europe and the United States, which rose from 25 percent in 1870 to more than 40 percent in 1913.[17] The gap widened further in the 1920s with the adoption of assembly-line methods (as epitomized by the motor vehicle industry, in which America captured an early lead) and the commercialization of new technologies (epitomized by radio, which diffused fastest in the United States). It then narrowed in the 1930s, owing to the exceptional severity of the American Depression, before widening again in the 1940s with the expansion of wartime capacity in the United States and further increases in the scale and mechanization of production.

By 1950, then, the gap between the technological leader and its European followers had grown to unprecedented size. Three decades of low investment had not been conducive to Europe's assimilation

---

[16] As emphasized in the influential account by Chandler (1990).

[17] To be sure, the abundance of land in the United States in the late nineteenth century also had something to do with this.

of mass-production methods, since many of these technological and organizational advances were embodied in machinery and equipment. Failure to negotiate a tariff truce in the 1920s and the ratcheting up of trade barriers in the 1930s, together with the difficulties of reconstructing international trade after World War II, had limited the market for firms contemplating investments in mass-production methods.

The bright side was that there now existed scope for rapid productivity growth if the technological backlog accumulated over the first half of the twentieth century could be successfully exploited. Doing so required freeing up exports and investment. The obstacles to investment were surmounted, as noted earlier. So too were the obstacles to trade. The growth of intra- and extra-European trade was one of the features of the 1950s and 1960s that stands in sharp contrast with the preceding decades. (See table 2.5.) Trade integration removed market size as a constraint on the adoption of new technologies. In practice, the Code of Liberalization of the Organisation for European Economic Cooperation (OEEC), the General Agreement on Tariffs and Trade (GATT), and the Common Market were powerful motors for the expansion of Europe's trade.[18] To be sure, this begs the question of why these arrangements were so successful. Neither the regional nor the multilateral approach to trade liberalization was new. Both had been tried between the wars, and both had failed disastrously.

Technology transfer proceeded apace. A growing share of technical progress was science based, facilitating the spread of new knowledge. Increasing amounts of generic knowledge were written down, speeding their diffusion via professional journals, conferences, and scholarly papers to which European scientists and academics had access. New communications technologies eased the dissemination of information. The internationalization of business deepened

[18] The role of the GATT has been contested, both historically and more recently. Irwin (1995) shows that the role of the GATT in the first postwar decade was to prevent countries from raising tariff barriers to offset the effects of removing quotas and exchange controls.

TABLE 2.5
Growth of intraregional and total exports, 1950–2002
(Average annual percentage growth rates)

	Intraregional exports		Total exports	
	1950–1973	*1974–2002*	*1950–1973*	*1974–2002*
Austria	14.2	10.8	13.2	10.4
Belgium-Luxembourg	13.5	8.5	12.1	8.8
Denmark	9.3	8.5	10.1	8.3
Finland	12.9	9.2	11.4	9.6
France	15.0	8.5	12.6	8.4
Germany	18.6	8.3	19.8	8.5
Greece	12.5	6.9	12.3	8.0
Ireland	9.6	13.4	10.5	14.1
Italy	15.9	9.1	13.8	9.3
Netherlands	14.5	8.8	13.4	8.8
Portugal	13.2	11.7	11.6	10.5
Spain	14.0	13.2	12.5	12.0
Sweden	11.8	7.2	11.2	7.5
United Kingdom	9.3	9.7	6.9	8.4
EU-15	13.2	9.6	12.2	9.5

Source: International Monetary Fund, *Direction of Trade Statistics* (1948–1980 and 1980–2003 versions).

commercial contacts. Multinational corporations such as the Ford Motor Company operated production facilities in multiple European countries. The U.S. government, for its part, did not attempt to stifle the dissemination of new technologies in order to husband its competitive advantage.[19] Instead it encouraged European officials, managers, and labor leaders to visit U.S. factories in conjunction with the Marshall Plan to see for themselves how production was organized on the shop floor.

Technology transfer requires that the acquiring economy have the capacity to assimilate foreign knowledge. Post–World War II Europe was singularly well positioned from this point of view. Levels of literacy and numeracy were similar to those in the United States. Europe possessed adequate stocks of engineers and technicians.[20]

---

[19] The notable exception, of course, was nuclear weapons technology.

[20] Increasingly so as the period progressed.

25

TABLE 2.6
Research and development indicators

	Number of qualified engineers and scientists in R&D (1967)	R&D expenditure as a percentage of GNP (1963)	Average annual growth of R&D at current prices (1963–1967)
Austria	2,401	0.3	28.0
Belgium	7,945	1.0	6.5
Germany	61,559	1.4	13.2[c]
France	49,224	1.6	17.9
Italy	27,755	0.6	11.3
Netherlands	20,500	1.9	15.9[c]
Spain	3,842[a]	0.2	19.2
Sweden	6,566[f]	1.4	9.3[c]
United Kingdom	53,865[g]	2.3	6.9[c]
United States	537,273	3.5	3.9[h]

Source: United Nations (1972), p. 100.

Note: Social sciences are in principle included, but are specifically excluded in Greece, Italy, Portugal, Sweden, the United Kingdom, and the United States.

[a] Includes humanities.   [e] 1964–1966.
[b] 1967.   [f] 1964.
[c] 1964–1967.   [g] 1965, Great Britain only.
[d] Full-time equivalents.   [h] 1963–1966.

(See table 2.6.) Technology transfer proceeded even more smoothly than these standard indicators would suggest because of the "fit" between the knowledge to be transferred and what might be called the European system of technology transfer. In the countries of continental Europe, education and training were heavily vocational. The majority of upper secondary students passed through vocational programs or apprenticeship training where they were schooled in the use of tools and equipment. Europe's educational system was thus tailored to a situation where the task was to assimilate existing techniques rather than to create new ones. It prepared workers for deciphering the blueprints and operator's manuals that accompanied the machinery and equipment embodying the advanced technologies of the time.[21] The principal exception was the United Kingdom, where higher education tended to be of a general nature and, not

---

[21] See, for example, Krueger and Kumar (2002). The United States, in contrast, emphasized general training, which was better suited to the more rapidly developing information technologies of the subsequent period. This is explored further later.

coincidentally, the convergence of productivity to U.S. levels proceeded more slowly.[22]

This is not to deny that technological advance also occurred in Europe itself. Basic research could be pursued in the research and development (R&D) labs of large European companies, where scientists and technicians elaborated advances in fundamental science inherited from the preceding period. Incremental innovation resulted from the observations and suggestions of skilled workers on the shop floor. Neither form of technological progress required easy entry by new firms or heavy investments on the frontier of science. This would change subsequently, however, when sustaining the rate of technical change required more radical innovation and consequently a more fluid economic environment.

Authors such as Charles Kindleberger, writing in the 1960s, also emphasized the growth of the labor force.[23] From 1947 through 1950, nearly one million persons of German and Polish ethnicity, many with extensive training and skills and of prime working age, moved from Eastern to Western Europe. In the 1950s, Western Europe's labor supply was augmented by additional ethnic German refugees from Central and Eastern Europe, French repatriates from Algeria, returning Dutch colonists from the former East Indies, and Southern European guest workers in Switzerland and France. Britain admitted 350,000 Irish workers between 1946 and 1959 and more than 540,000 Indians, Pakistanis, and West Indians between 1955 and 1968. Although the first members of the postwar baby boom generation started entering the labor market only in the late 1960s, immigration loosened labor market constraints in the meantime.

---

[22] Thus, in the 1950s, apprentices constituted only half as large a share of engineering industry employees in Britain as in Germany. See Broadberry and Wagner (1996). This difference was also historically rooted. The relatively less cohesive employers associations in Britain made for a greater danger of poaching of employees and therefore more reluctance on the part of firms to invest in training young workers. In addition, the countries of the continent were slower than Britain to complete the transition from handicraft to large-scale industry, and this relative slowness perpetuated the value attached to craft skills and the institutions that transmitted them. Finally, the earlier and stronger acceptance of publicly aided state education in countries such as France and Germany, a not entirely unrelated trend, worked in the same direction. See Sanderson (1994).

[23] The industrial labor force in particular. See Kindleberger (1967).

27

The modern industrial sector, which was the locus of learning effects and productivity spillovers, could grow rapidly by tapping these elastic labor supplies. With the consolidation of small farms and the adoption of new agricultural technologies, workers could move from Southern to Northern Europe and from farm to city without depressing food supplies. This permitted the industrial and service sectors to grow more rapidly than the economy as a whole. Because productivity was higher in industry than in agriculture, this process of labor reallocation added significantly to growth.[24] The elastic supplies of labor available to the modern industrial and service sectors minimized the threat that sharply rising wages would curtail profitability and choke off investment.[25] Given the dominance of mass-production technologies, which permitted tasks to be divided and conquered, the fact that much of this additional labor was unskilled was not a constraint on growth.

No sooner did contemporaries begin emphasizing these factors, however, than they began to dissolve. Unemployment declined as rapid growth sopped up idle labor. The Berlin Wall closed off the West German labor market from the east. In France, the rapid pace of structural change exhausted the supplies of unemployed labor previously made available by the agricultural sector. Other factors subduing labor militancy, such as memories of high unemployment in the 1930s, faded as older workers retired and a new generation entered the labor force.

Symbolic of labor's newfound militancy were the strikes and political demonstrations of the hot summer of 1968. With the breakdown of wage discipline, the share of profits in gross national product (GNP) began to fall. And with declining profits came de-

[24] Denison (1967) argues that this mechanism contributed as much as one percentage point per annum to European economic growth in this period, except in the United Kingdom, where agricultural employment had long before sunk to low levels. Three accounts emphasizing this factor are Broadberry (1997), Temin (2002) and Broadberry and Crafts (2003).

[25] Baily and Kirkegaard (2004) are skeptical of this point. They observe that real wages in fact rose strongly in countries such as Germany from their low starting point in the early 1950s. The rise in wages, however, was not out of line with the rise in labor productivity, enabling the profitability needed for investment to be sustained. For more details on the German case, see "Germany as Pacesetter" in chapter 4. This leaves open for the time being the question of what sustained this happy equilibrium, a question to which I return later.

clining investment, reflecting the reduction in the rate of return on new capital.

Another explanation for the relatively high investment rates of the first postwar quarter century is cyclical stability. Steady growth meant steady sales, heightening the profitability and attractiveness of investment. The standard deviation of real GDP growth averaged less than 1 percent in the 1960s in the fifteen Western European countries that subsequently became members of the EU, compared with 2 percent in the United States. (See table 2.7.) There was no economy-wide crisis like that of the 1930s leading to the collapse of demand, output, and profits. Indeed, there was not even a single serious recession from the beginning of the 1950s through the end of the 1960s.[26]

It is tempting to credit the Keynesian revolution for this new-found stability.[27] But in fact there was little active use of monetary policy. And given the lags in adjusting fiscal policy to economic conditions and the difficulty of tailoring spending by public enterprises to the cycle, fiscal impulses were often destabilizing.[28] Electoral considerations prompted procyclical fiscal actions in Germany in 1965, in France in 1968–1969, and in a number of European countries in the early 1970s. Fiscal policy worked best when left on auto-pilot, allowing automatic stabilizers to work.

Nor were the lessons of macroeconomics textbooks forgotten after 1973, when the business cycle returned. Those who ascribe the stability of the cycle before 1970 to macroeconomic policy, whether operating through discretionary adjustments or automatic stabilizers, thus must explain why cyclical instability resurfaced subsequently.[29]

---

[26] The drop in growth in the most severe interwar recession—in most cases, not surprisingly, that which set in after 1929—averaged 9.9 percentage points, implying that the growth rate fell to substantial negative numbers. Between 1950 and 1973, in contrast, European economies continued growing during their most serious slowdowns, if only by a relatively modest 0.5 percent. These figures are unweighted averages of data for ten European countries, based on Maddison (1991), table 4.1.

[27] As argued by Boltho (1989) and van der Wee (1986).

[28] See, for example, the discussion in Hansen (1969). Bispham and Boltho (1982) suggest, with some justification, that this negative assessment of fiscal policy should not be pushed too far. See the further discussion in chapters 4 and 7.

[29] Boltho (1989) suggests that macroeconomic policy worked to stabilize demand and output before the 1970s simply because households and firms believed that it would. The belief that the authorities possessed the capacity to stabilize demand, whether justified or not, itself

TABLE 2.7
Output and inflation stability, 1961–2000

	1951–1960	1961–1970	1971–1980	1981–1990	1992–2000
			United States		
Real GDP growth					
Average of annual rates	3.4	4.2	3.3	3.2	3.6
Standard deviation	2.9	2.0	2.5	2.2	0.6
Inflation					
Average inflation	2.1	2.8	7.9	4.7	2.6
Standard deviation of inflation	2.3	1.7	3.1	2.2	0.5
			EU-15		
Real GDP growth					
Average of annual rates	4.8	4.8	3.0	2.4	2.1
Standard deviation	1.4	0.9	1.7	1.2	1.1
Inflation					
Average inflation	3.6	3.9	10.8	6.7	2.4
Standard deviation of inflation	3.0	0.8	2.8	2.9	0.9

Sources: 1961–1970 from Independent High-Level Study Group (2003), p. 44; 1951–1960 constructed from Organisation for Economic Co-operation and Development, *National Accounts* (various years), and International Monetary Fund, *International Financial Statistics* (various years).

Note: GDP of unified Germany was first recorded in 1991; this is reflected in the last column.

One explanation is the growing incidence and severity of shocks. The early 1970s saw the breakdown of the Bretton Woods System of pegged but adjustable exchange rates. This was a shock to confidence and a threat to the growth of trade. The collapse of Bretton Woods cut loose the anchor provided by the dollar's peg to gold, planting seeds of doubt that inflation would remain moderate. European countries sought to replace Bretton Woods with a series of locally formed substitutes, the Snake in the Tunnel, the Snake in the Lake, and finally the European Monetary System, each now organized around the German deutschmark, which had emerged as the continent's strongest currency. But not until the 1980s did these efforts succeed in restoring a modicum of currency stability.

In addition, 1973 saw the first oil shock resulting from price increases by the Organization of Petroleum Exporting Countries

---

worked to buttress confidence and stabilize demand. "Bootstrap" equilibria of this sort are possible, but they are less plausible when they are based on expectations that are not well founded.

(OPEC) and curtailed production and an embargo on shipments of oil to the United States and the Netherlands by OPEC's Arab members, which inaugurated a period of generalized commodity price inflation. This supply shock was a challenge for a set of policy instruments designed to manage aggregate demand. The end of the decade then saw sharp interest rate hikes in the United States and the United Kingdom to rein in inflation, an indication of the failure of prior demand-management policies.

Implicit in this "shock-based" explanation for the post–1973 slowdown is the assumption that there had been no equally powerful disturbances in the third quarter of the twentieth century. At some level, clearly, this is too crude. There was the commodity price boom of the Korean War. There was the Suez Crisis in 1956 and the run on U.S. gold reserves on the eve of the 1960 presidential election. There were the imbalances created by the expansionary stance of U.S. fiscal policy during the Vietnam War. These disturbances were important, but they were small in comparison with those of subsequent years. Statistical studies point to an increase in the magnitude and dispersion of aggregate demand disturbances after the early 1970s.[30] To some extent, in other words, Europe may have simply been lucky in the 1950s and 1960s.

Yet one cannot avoid thinking that there was more to the golden age than a fortuitous absence of shocks. Nor can one simply take for granted the high investment, rapid export growth, and wage moderation of the period.

Institutional Foundations of the Golden Age

One explanation for the high investment, rapid export growth, and wage moderation that sustained the golden age is a set of institutions singularly well suited to the growth imperatives of the day. The interwar years had been marked by disruptive strikes and disputes over wages and work conditions. Excessive wage demands had stifled

---

[30] This is the finding of Bayoumi and Eichengreen (1994).

profitability, robbing firms of the incentive to invest.[31] European so-cieties now developed neocorporatist structures—tripartite govern-ing institutions involving government, management, and labor—to restrain wage growth and plow profits into investment.[32] Those arrangements were intended to prevent a repetition of earlier events. In this they succeeded: this time wage increases did not squeeze profitability. Labor unrest during the transition back to peacetime production was less: strike activity was only one-quarter as high in 1946–1950 as it had been in 1919–1924.[33]

Postwar governments supported the neocorporatist bargain. They asked unions to limit wage demands in order to make profits available for modernization and capacity expansion and provided assurances that labor would share fully in the eventual increase in incomes. The challenge was to reassure workers that management would in fact invest the profits that accrued as a result of their restraint. Skeptical that more investment, faster growth, and higher living standards would result from self-denial, labor hesitated to make the requisite sacrifices. The danger was that unions would pursue wage increases, management would pay out profits as dividends, and investment and growth would suffer, as they had in the interwar years.

The postwar period turned out differently because cooperation between capital and labor was cemented by a series of institutional bargains. A first set of institutions allowed the parties to monitor one another's compliance with the terms of their agreement. Ger-many's co-determination law, which placed worker representatives on the supervisory boards of large firms, is an example of this mecha-nism. Co-determination was introduced into the iron and steel in-dustry in 1951 and the rest of industry in 1952. The result was to place labor representatives on the supervisory boards of every joint stock company.[34] Works councils played an analogous information-

---

[31] Broadberry and Ritschl (1995) make this argument for both the United Kingdom and Germany in the 1920s and provide supporting evidence.

[32] Profits were important for investment because this was a period of financial repression and widespread liquidity constraints, which rendered retained earnings key for financing investment.

[33] See Boltho (2001).

[34] The 1952 law was replaced, twenty years later, by another one, which required that one-third of supervisory board members be labor representatives, and was then supplemented by the *Mitbestimmungsgesetz* of 1976, which required joint stock companies with more than two

disseminating role in small firms not subject to the co-determination law. By the late 1950s, more than one hundred large German firms had labor representatives on their supervisory boards. In German coal and steel companies, the workers appointed half of all supervisory board members as well as one member of the top management team. Other countries developed similar arrangements. In Austria, an analogous system of co-determination prevailed in nationalized industries, which accounted for perhaps 20 percent of employment, and was eventually extended to the rest of the economy. In the Netherlands, representatives of labor, management, and government worked together on PBOs (Publiekrechtelijke Bedrijfsorganisatie), reaching understandings on employment and investment policies. Norway established planning councils and production committees to promote worker participation in management decisions. In 1949, Sweden created the Cooperative Body for Increasing Exports and Production, also known as the "Thursday Club," where representatives of industry, trade unions, and government met to exchange information and views.

A second set of institutions created rewards and penalties to encourage cooperation. Austrian manufacturers were sold intermediate inputs at submarket prices from public enterprises in return for following the desired investment and dividend policies. The Swedish government regulated the payment of dividends by public companies.[35] The German government provided tax breaks for investment but not for firms paying out profits as dividends. Central banks helped to cement the bargain by pursuing low-interest-rate policies that encouraged firms to follow through on their investment commitments.

A parallel set of public programs bonded labor. In Belgium, the first postwar government adopted a social security scheme in return for labor's adherence to a 1944 social pact limiting wage increases. In return for the unions' promise of wage restraint, the Norwegian government offered legislation mandating paid vacations and lim-

---

thousand employees to appoint labor representatives as fully half of their supervisory board members.

[35] In addition, it invited corporations to place up to 40 percent of their profits into public accounts that could be accessed only with government approval, as discussed in chapter 4.

iting the length of the workweek. The Dutch government introduced unemployment insurance and old-age pensions, while extending social security coverage, as a quid pro quo for wage moderation. Starting in 1955, the Swedish government offered compulsory health insurance, an expanded system of disability insurance, and an array of retraining programs in return for labor's acquiescence to policies of wage restraint and solidarity. The Danish government offered an expanded system of sick pay in 1956, when the agreement to link wage increases to productivity negotiated during the reconstruction phase showed signs of breaking down.[36] The German government indexed retirement incomes to living standards in its 1957 pension reform. The Austrian government extended tax and social insurance concessions to labor in return for wage moderation. Italy mandated social security contributions by employers, albeit starting only in the 1960s, reflecting the extent to which its industry was still behind that of other European countries. Thus, many elements of the postwar social market economy originated in this period as part of the effort to more firmly bind capital and labor to cooperate.

But if wage restraint by one union resulted mainly in higher investment and employment growth elsewhere, since profits originating in any one sector could finance investment economy-wide, the incentive to defect from the agreement could prove irresistible. The solution was to coordinate wage bargains across firms and sectors. In Germany, the unions adopted a follow-the-leader approach. The metal workers' union went first, and other industrial unions took its wage settlement as the norm for increases. Elsewhere, bargaining was centralized in the hands of trade union federations and employers associations, and governments used their influence to harmonize the terms of the bargains reached by unions and employers at the branch level.

Swedish arrangements were prototypical. From the early 1950s, the SAF, the federation of employers associations, and the LO, the umbrella organization of blue-collar workers, met at the outset of the

---

[36] Johansen (1987), chapter 7. Old-age pensions followed in 1957.

annual wage round.[37] After they reached a framework agreement, negotiations between branch unions and employers commenced. These ratified or, more commonly, provided for limited modifications of the basic framework. The terms of the LO/SAF negotiation were designed to reconcile the workers' desire for wage increases with the restraint necessary to sustain profitability and employment. They provided a recognized norm for wage settlements. The state played a tacit role in these negotiations by signaling its view of appropriate wage increases given prevailing macroeconomic conditions and applying its seal of approval to the results. Through the first half of the 1960s, the LO/SAF norm guided even private white-collar and public-employee negotiations.[38] The SAF encouraged compliance by its member associations and individual employers by issuing warnings, chastising those who hesitated to comply, and threatening to fine employers who offered wage increases in excess of the authorized norm. The LO similarly enjoyed "considerable but not complete control" over its member unions, shop-floor negotiations, and wage developments through the 1950s.[39]

Internationally, the institutions of regional integration worked to solve a second set of coordination problems that hampered the reconstruction of Europe's trade. In 1947, the United Kingdom, responding to U.S. pressure, restored current-account convertibility (the right to convert domestic currency into foreign exchange for purposes related to international trade). Reserves immediately hemorrhaged out of the country and controls on merchandise transactions were reimposed after barely a month. This experience drove

[37] The first attempt to coordinate wage negotiations in this manner occurred in 1952, although efforts were not completely successful until 1956.

[38] The result was strong relative wage compression. Alexopoulos and Cohen (2003) argue that this was in fact the essential objective of centralized bargaining in Sweden. Upward pressure on the wages of less-skilled workers was designed, in their view, to force the exit of low-productivity firms and free up labor for employment in high-productivity firms such as Volvo and ESEA. This motivation is by no means incompatible with the one I emphasize, so long as the tendency to limit skilled–unskilled pay differentials is not corrosive of overall wage moderation.

[39] Olsson and Burns (1987), p. 189. The main limit on the LO's control—the tendency for branch unions and locals facing strong demand to negotiate exceptional increases in excess of the norm—manifested itself as "wage drift."

home the need for European countries to work together in opening their economies and to find a more gradual approach to restoring current-account convertibility. Given the difficulty of competing in U.S. markets, opening the current account meant gaining access to markets in neighboring European countries. Only to the extent that such markets were secured might producers earn the hard currency needed to purchase intermediate inputs and capital goods.

This meant that it was not feasible for governments to unilaterally open their economies. European countries had to move together down the road to current-account convertibility if they were to move that way at all. The European Payments Union (EPU), established in 1950, helped to coordinate their response. EPU members accepted the OEEC's Code of Liberalization, which committed them to remove import controls at a predetermined pace. Membership entitled a participating country to credits from its EPU partners with which to finance temporary trade deficits. This allowed governments to credibly commit to liberalization by obviating the need to roll back previous measures by more than limited amounts. The United States provided both political and financial support for this cooperative undertaking. It supplied start-up funding through the Marshall Plan and put aside fears that, if restrictions on intra-European trade were relaxed more quickly than restrictions on trade with the rest of the world, the agreement might result in de facto discrimination against U.S. exports.

The European Coal and Steel Community (ECSC), established in 1951, addressed the special problems of heavy industry. Coal and steel were the sinews of war; after three devastating wars between France and Germany in less than a century, it was seen as essential that the capacity of these industries be committed to peaceful use. Leadership came from France in the persons of the foreign minister Robert Schuman and his adviser Jean Monnet, but here too America lent critical support. In urging France and Germany to go ahead, the Truman administration put aside fears that the ECSC would be an anticompetitive cartel and that proceeding without the United Kingdom would shut that country out of Europe. Creating the ECSC entailed establishing a Joint High Authority to monitor production and investment decisions in the six founding member states.[40] In addition, the treaty provided for a Common Assembly as a political counterweight to the technocrats of the High Authority, a Council of Ministers through which governments could approve by qualified majority vote the proposals of the High Authority, and a High Court to adjudicate disputes between the High Authority and the contracting states. These arrangements clearly anticipated the European Commission, the European Parliament, the European Council, and the European Court of Law, all of which grew out of them after 1958.

More immediately, it is hard to imagine that France and other European countries would have agreed to lift ceilings on German industrial production, steel production in particular, without transnational oversight. Germany was at Europe's economic heart. It was the continent's principal producer of capital goods. Unless its economy was allowed to grow, recovery could not have been sustained in Western Europe.[41]

The most enduring transnational institution was the European Union (née European Community and European Economic Communities). At the most immediate level, the EU was important for sustaining the growth of Europe's trade. Over the second half of the twentieth century, intra-European trade grew even faster than Europe's trade with the rest of the world. In part this represented a reconstitution of the continent's "natural" trade pattern—that is, the tendency for European countries to trade disproportionately with their neighbors owing to low transport and communication costs. But it was no less important for this fact. The growth of trade allowed

[40] Thus, the ECSC was Europe's first effort to build a truly supranational institution and therefore was an important stepping-stone to the EU; see Gillingham (1991). Gillingham disputes the interpretation of Haas (1958), or at least of some of Haas's disciples, that the ECSC established an internal logic of spillovers through which this supranational initiative required supranational initiatives in other areas, creating an inexorable process of unification. He does acknowledge, however, that although there was nothing inevitable about it, the result of the process set afoot by the establishment of the ECSC was ultimately "the creation of a new political entity, Europe" (Gillingham 1991, p. 364).

[41] Not incidentally, Germany's steel capacity also figured importantly in America's strategic plans following the outbreak of the Korean War. This led the American high commissioner in Germany, John McCloy, to work hard to satisfy French preconditions for freeing up German steel production. See Killick (1997).

countries to restructure along export-oriented lines. By widening the extent of the market, it facilitated the adoption of U.S.-style mass-production methods. It admitted the chill winds of international competition, encouraging productivity growth. Europe after World War II thus provides a classic example of export-led growth.[42]

Under the circumstances, conditions that limited the growth of real wages limited the appreciation of real exchange rates.[43] Data for the 1950s, as in table 2.8, show that wholesale prices expressed in dollar terms were significantly below those of the United States, generally by one-quarter to one-half, relative to the benchmark levels of 1938. This was in contrast to the 1920s, when countries avoiding high inflation had attempted to push both prices and exchange rates back down to prewar levels, but prices had moved more slowly than currency values.[44] Hence, when they repegged their exchange rates in the mid-1920s, notorious problems of overvaluation had resulted.

After World War II, in contrast, undervaluation was the rule. The main exceptions were Belgium and France, which stabilized at levels that produced no improvement in competitiveness relative to 1938.[45] Revealingly, both countries lagged in terms of the growth of exports in the 1950s, in turn contributing to their disappointing growth performance. On the other hand, undervaluation and export growth were especially dramatic in Germany, reflecting the favorable rate at which the mark was stabilized in 1948 and further devaluation in 1949. This in fact was the general situation, notwithstanding counterexamples such as Belgium and France. And because wage and price inflation did not exceed the growth of labor productivity in the 1950s, the favorable competitive position tended to persist.

Competitive labor costs allowed Europe to shift resources into manufacturing, where learning effects and productivity spillovers

[42] See Beckerman (1962) for an early statement of this view.

[43] This is true as a matter of definition, since one way of expressing the real exchange rate is as the purchasing power of wages in terms of traded goods. To put the same point another way, because European production costs were low, European exchange rates were undervalued (*competitively valued* would be the more antiseptic term).

[44] In contrast, countries experiencing runaway inflation had had little choice about the level at which to peg, and high rates of inflation neutralized any tendency for prices to lag behind exchange rates. Such countries were neither significantly overvalued nor undervalued.

[45] And also Greece, whose experience is sufficiently distinct not to be considered here.

TABLE 2.8
Cost competitiveness after exchange-rate changes, 1947–1955
(1938 = 100)

	1947	1948	1949	1950	1951	1955
Austria	137	113	118	67	75	70
Belgium	143	138	132	115	117	115
Denmark	106	104	97	78	80	86
France	176	119	111	97	107	122
Germany	52	56	65	52	52	52
Italy	98	88	85	82	82	86
Netherlands	87	87	81	66	68	68
Norway	88	84	79	63	71	75
Sweden	104	104	94	72	83	86
Switzerland	100	96	96	94	91	91
United Kingdom	87	88	81	62	63	69
OEEC Europe	96	91	87	71	73	78

Source: Triffin (1957), p. 324.

Note: Figures are for wholesale prices expressed in dollar terms relative to the 1938 benchmark.

were strong. They allowed producers to lengthen production runs and exploit economies of scale and scope. They encouraged American multinationals to invest in Europe, providing a conduit for technology transfer. They produced the export earnings to finance purchases of imported capital goods embodying the latest technology. They generated the profits needed to make those investments attractive. By limiting the growth of consumption and promoting saving, they strengthened the current account and relaxed the balance-of-payments constraint.[46] The stability of exchange rates also kept interest rates low. With European interest rates linked to those in the United States, rapid growth did little to drive them up. And interest rates were of course an important factor in the cost of capital and therefore investment.

Thus, interpretations of Europe's growth as investment-led and export-led are two sides of the same coin. But this coin would not have had much currency in the absence of the institutions that facilitated the removal of barriers to trade.

[46] Recall that this was a period when portfolio capital flows and therefore access to external sources of finance for domestic investment (and for offsetting current-account deficits through capital inflows) were heavily controlled.

This interpretation can be extended in various directions. Domestically, the postwar period saw a political settlement that strengthened the hand of center-left and center-right parties. Reform of electoral institutions—raising the threshold that had to be reached to obtain parliamentary representation, for example—made it harder for splinter groups to gain a political foothold, reducing the danger that extremists would again disrupt the operation of the economy and in turn ensuring policy stability, which sustained investment. The neocorporatist bargain in which labor and capital accepted lower current incomes in return for higher future living standards was easier to sustain when there was little risk that some future government would renege on the agreement.

Internationally, the GATT system of trade liberalization and the Bretton Woods System of pegged but adjustable exchange rates encouraged the expansion of Europe's trade. The International Monetary Fund was established to lend support—and money—if dislocations arose along the way. By ensuring that trade with the rest of the world expanded along with intra-European trade, these institutions ensured that the net result of Europe's regional liberalization initiatives was mainly trade creation, not trade diversion.[47]

Institutions and History

This interpretation of the golden age is consistent with the emphasis that scholars place on the institutional foundations of economic growth.[48] Growth requires more than just markets, whose existence cannot in any case be taken for granted. It requires institutions capable of addressing coordination problems that cannot be solved at

[47] Trade diversion occurs when a regional or other preferential trade arrangement causes a country to import from a high-cost supplier with which it has such an arrangement instead of from a low-cost supplier in the rest of the world. It is least likely when the parties to the preferential agreement have relatively similar levels of development and productive structures (the European case) and when the reduction of trade barriers within the region is accompanied by the reduction of trade barriers with the rest of the world (the case under the GATT).

[48] Two classic references here are North (1990) and Acemoglu, Johnson, and Robinson (2001).

arm's length. In postwar Europe, this meant coordinating bargaining across sectors and coordinating trade liberalization across countries. It meant solving the time-consistency problem that created an incentive to renege on these agreements, rendering the parties to them reluctant to commit in the first place.

The question is why Europe developed a set of arrangements so well suited to these tasks. In part the answer lies in its history. Proponents of European integration could trace their antecedents back to Pierre Dubois, a jurist and diplomat in the French and English courts, who in 1306 proposed a permanent assemblage of European princes working to secure a lasting peace. The English Quaker William Penn had proposed a European parliament in 1693. Jeremy Bentham had advocated a European assembly, Jean-Jacques Rousseau a European federation, Henri de Saint-Simon a European monarch and a European parliament. The Pan-European Union, founded by the Austrian count Richard Coudenhove-Kalergi in 1923, lobbied for a European federation. This background predisposed the new postwar generation of statesmen toward European integration as a solution to the continent's economic and political problems.[49]

The immediate post–World War II context then shaped the response. One critical factor was the attitude of the United States. The United States had leverage because U.S. troops were still stationed in Europe and because of the Marshall Plan. The Truman Doctrine encouraged European integration in order to create a bulwark against the Soviet threat and to foster the European market for U.S. exports. U.S. officials reasoned by analogy with America's own history, in which integration and the economic convergence of North and South gradually eliminated conflicts that might lead to civil war. In response to the disastrous consequences of its pressure on the United Kingdom to restore current-account convertibility in

[49] In addition, it can be argued that the Nazis' forcible integration of Europe during the period of their wartime occupation provided an ironic demonstration of the efficiency of an integrated continental economy. The war also temporarily loosened economic ties between the metropolitan powers and their overseas dependencies and encouraged and legitimized independence movements in the colonies, reducing the viability of the imperial alternative.

1947, the United States provided 350 million dollars of Marshall Plan money for the EPU and encouraged the development of the ECSC, putting aside worries that regional initiatives could lead to a Fortress Europe.

On the European continent, where industrialization had begun later than in Britain, governments had always played an active role in helping to surmount the obstacles to modern economic growth and preventing countries from falling behind their industrial rivals with potentially dangerous security consequences. They had encouraged the development of banks such as the Crédit Foncier to meet the demanding capital requirements of late industrialization and to substitute for underdeveloped financial markets. They had pioneered social insurance to reconcile workers to the uncertainties of industrial labor. The insecurity and social tensions created by the spread of industrial capitalism were reflected not just in the Bismarckian welfare state but also in proposals in various countries to bring together society's organized interests in an effort to advance the common good. Bismarck himself had advocated the creation of an economic council (*Wirtschaftsrat*) to reconcile the interests of the social partners. Efforts to build institutions to free the continent's citizens from the tyranny of the market were encouraged by nineteenth-century Roman Catholic theology and twentieth-century Christian Democratic ideology.

Between 1914 and 1918, governments had brought together unions and management to negotiate economy-wide wage agreements and avert work stoppages that might have disrupted the war effort. Although these attempts to bring the unions into wartime planning did not prove durable, they set a precedent. The Russian Revolution further encouraged Western European governments to incorporate labor movements into processes for overseeing the operation of the economy, partly in order to head off more extreme solutions suggested by the more radical returning servicemen. Two symbols of this effort by Western European governments were the recognition of collective labor representation by a provision of the Treaty of Versailles and the early postwar creation of an International Labour Office (ILO) under the control of governments, employers associations, and union movements.

Eventually, some of the mechanisms for coordination that developed during World War I were rolled back. The postwar recession undermined labor's bargaining power, while schisms on the left divided labor over whether to support the Bolsheviks and pursue a nonparliamentary road to power. Nevertheless, labor was better organized than before World War I, and the expansion of the franchise gave parliamentary labor parties a louder voice in policy making. Their demands now being heard, the 1920s saw the continued growth of government spending on basic social services. In Weimar Germany, social transfers were raised to unprecedented levels as the government attempted to regain the electoral support of workers whose security had been undermined by hyperinflation. The Scandinavian countries, which had relatively high levels of enfranchisement and social affinity, similarly ramped up social spending.[50] The decade even saw what might be called experiments in indicative planning—with agents as unlikely as the Bank of England, which played a prominent role in the efforts to rationalize British industry.

The later corporatist experiments explicitly acknowledging the social role and contribution to decision-making processes of civic groups representing a range of interests—the Basic Agreement in Norway in 1935, the Peace Agreement in Switzerland in 1937, and the Main Agreement in Sweden in 1938—built on these earlier foundations.[51] These were efforts to arrange cooperative responses to the economic crisis of the 1930s. They reflected the recognition that resolving the crisis required coordinated adjustment in which currencies were devalued, wages were stabilized, and investment and profitability were restored.[52] Again, it is hard to imagine that Euro-

---

[50] On the role of enfranchisement and social affinity in these trends, see Lindert (2004).

[51] In other cases such as Britain, the social climate and inheritance were less hospitable to sustained development along these lines. Even there, however, there were attempts—albeit unsuccessful—to move in this direction; they included the Whitley Councils in the 1920s and the Mond-Turner talks in the 1930s.

[52] See, for example, the discussion of Sweden in Olsson and Burns (1987). To be sure, Norway, Switzerland, and Sweden were not typical of Europe; among other things, they were unusually small and open. This observation leads authors such as Katzenstein (1985) to argue that democratic corporatism found its firmest foothold in small, open economies most vulner-

pean societies would have responded in this way without the war-time precedent and the perception that the Depression was a crisis tantamount to war.

It is revealing that many of these corporatist pacts, particularly the most successful ones, originated in small countries, since it was small European countries that tended to develop the most highly articulated neocorporatist institutions after World War II. One interpretation of this is in terms of social affinity: corporatist compromises may simply be easiest to reach in small countries, where in an economic crisis everyone knows someone who is seriously affected. Small countries are also more vulnerable to security challenges, and an external threat is something that can help to make compromises work. In the Netherlands, a country with reason to worry about the prospect of Nazi invasion, the tripartite structure that evolved into the PBO after World War II was already contemplated in the final years of the 1930s as a device for encouraging national solidarity and increasing economic efficiency. In Sweden, a 1938 agreement between the LO and the SAF established a complex of rules and procedures governing strikes, lockouts, and the annulment of contracts. Although this agreement did not yet give the peak associations a role in wage negotiations, it acknowledged the status of organized labor and of the LO in particular. It encouraged the presumption that sectoral wage negotiations would be based on an economy-wide norm and the principle that industrial relations should be based on cooperation. In the 1930s, limited coordination was achieved through the development of a follow-the-leader arrangement similar to Germany's (discussed earlier), in which the powerful Swedish metal workers' union negotiated first, setting the wage norm for other branches. From there it was only one more step to norm-setting by peak associations after World War II.

In France, similarly, Popular Front policies originated as a response to the economic crisis and included protocorporatist elements. But the Popular Front, riven by internal divisions, proved

---

able to economic disruption, where small size encouraged a "we're-all-in-the-same-boat" mentality. See chapter 12.

unsuccessful in achieving the coordinated adjustment needed to initiate and sustain recovery. The unsatisfactory nature of this experience helps to explain why the neocorporatist response was pursued
less systematically in France after World War II than elsewhere in
Western Europe.

Nor is it possible to understand state corporatism—the use of
centralized negotiations under government control to regulate labor
and product markets in Franco's Spain, Mussolini's Italy, and Hitler's
Germany—in isolation from the economic crisis. These regimes had
their own unsavory motives, to be sure. They saw corporatist arrangements as a way of circumventing parliamentary decision making and suppressing democracy. They sought the centralization of
wage negotiations in order to strengthen their control over the
economy. Following the conclusion of hostilities, the Allies, finding
these structures convenient for their own efforts to regulate the
economies of countries they now occupied, chose to use rather than
dismantle them. In Germany, the American occupation authorities
authorized renewed union activity as early as September 1945, and
in June 1946 they permitted the establishment of trade union associations on a zonal basis.[53] Almost immediately, a twelve-member
trade union committee began to assist the *Landerrat* (the council
of state ministers) in formulating policies toward labor and social
insurance.

Throughout Europe, crises elicited this response because of the
existence of powerful collectivist predispositions. In light of the experience of the 1930s, insulating Europe's citizens from the instability of the market now became a paramount goal of socialist and
working-class parties. Further encouragement was lent by Marshall
Plan administrators who had seen the American economy take a
temporary corporatist turn under the National Industrial Recovery

---

[53] Policy in the British and French zones was broadly similar although there was more
hesitation to authorize the formation of centralized associations. But Britain's Labour government viewed giving workers a voice in the governance of industry as a priority. The British
therefore installed a "parity model" in the iron and steel industry of the Ruhr Valley, in which
the workers made up half of the members of the supervisory board in the iron and steel
industry, out of which grew the German co-determination legislation of 1951–1952. See chapter 3 for more on this.

Act.[54] And the need for government to supplement and stabilize the market was the general lesson drawn from the economic collapse of the 1930s. At the same time, more extreme elements—especially, on the left, Communist unionists and parties—opted for pragmatism and shared growth over ideology and revolution. In this they were encouraged by evidence of Moscow's authoritarianism, which sat uneasily with Western Europe's deep-seated democratic traditions, and by the political marginalization of communism that followed the advent of the Marshall Plan. Communist parties and unions subordinated their revolutionary aspirations to the national recovery effort. Their rhetoric was fiery, but they did not challenge the reality of a private-ownership economy.

This interpretation of the neocorporatist response as historically rooted is at odds with the influential views of Mancur Olson.[55] In Olson's theory, periods of rapid growth typically follow major disruptions, such as war, that clear away the inheritance of vested interests and restrictive institutional arrangements clogging the operation of the economic system. In Olson's model, it is the absence of a historical legacy rather than its existence that is the precondition for rapid growth.

However compelling this general theory of economic success, it is hard to see how it applies to postwar Europe. The war removed from the European scene neither France's influential farm lobby nor Germany's powerful unions, convenient though it may be to assume the opposite. An elaborate set of institutions that developed out of inherited arrangements continued to shape the interaction of such

[54] The First New Deal, adopted in response to the economic crisis of the 1930s, had some distinctively protocorporatist elements. It created industry-level planning boards with tripartite involvement of government, management, and labor that sought to stimulate investment and stabilize wages. (The New Dealers had their own definition of this last element because in the deflationary circumstances of the 1930s; stabilizing wages meant preventing their continued decline and even recovering some of the ground lost.) But the United States did not possess the strong labor movement or Christian Democratic tradition needed for these innovations to take root. Nonetheless, the same U.S. leaders who saw advantages in coordinated capitalism sought to transplant the model to postwar Europe and used the Marshall Plan to prepare the soil. See Maier (1978) and Hogan (1987).

[55] See Olson (1982) and, for an application to post–World War II European economic growth, Olson (1996).

46

interest groups. Significant wartime and postwar disruptions there surely were. But, in this case at least, institutional continuity more than institutional disruption provides the backdrop to economic recovery and growth.

These facts go some way toward explaining not just the historical origins of post–World War II institutional arrangements but also why those arrangements were well suited to the technological imperatives of the day. The institutional arrangements of the postwar period, from government involvement in labor/management negotiations to bank-dominated financial systems, can be seen as legacies of the process of institutional substitution emphasized by scholars such as Alexander Gerschenkron.[56] They were designed to exploit opportunities for catch-up via capital accumulation and for convergence via the importation of technology from abroad. The late nineteenth century, when these arrangements began to develop, was similarly a period of extensive growth. This made it feasible to adapt these arrangements to the circumstances of another period of extensive growth after World War II.[57]

The End of the Golden Age

Toward the end of the 1960s, output and productivity growth began to slow, and macroeconomic instability reared its ugly head. The question is why a set of arrangements that had been so conducive to growth and stability for a quarter century now produced less satisfactory results.

One answer points to the rise of the capital–labor ratio toward steady-state levels owing to Europe's success in building up its capital

---

[56] See Gerschenkron (1962).

[57] As at many points, Britain is a telling counterexample. The country's industrialization had begun in an earlier period when the capital requirements of manufacturing were more modest, obviating the need for a bank-centered financial system to mobilize large amounts of finance. There was no need for government to organize big-push industrialization, since the first industrial revolution was limited to a relatively small segment of the British economy. Labor, for its part, was organized on a craft- rather than industrial-union basis, appropriate for the technological imperatives of that earlier era.

stock after a long period of subpar investment, and to the exhaustion of elastic supplies of labor and hence to the disappearance of supernormal returns. (See figure 2.1.) Another answer, not entirely unrelated, emphasizes changes in the conditions making for a comfortable fit between the continent's institutions and its technological circumstances. The more efficiently the technological backlog was exploited, the less scope remained for fast growth through the old system of technology transfer. It became more difficult to grow by building more factories along the lines of existing factories and by purchasing blueprints, licenses, and operator's manuals from the United States. At this point, the same institutions that had played such a positive role in the preceding years became obstacles to growth. Sustaining growth now involved investing in new products and unproven technologies. In this brave new world, it became more difficult for government holding companies, planning commissions, and bureaucrats to identify high-return uses for funds. The bluntness of their incentives compared to those of private entrepreneurs became a liability. Growth requiring innovation, an education system that imparted vocational rather than general training made it hard for workers to accustom themselves to unfamiliar tasks and new forms of work organization. Industry-wide unions discouraged wage differentiation between enterprises operating under different conditions, erecting a barrier to new-firm formation. The compression of wage differentials between skilled and unskilled workers discouraged acquisition of the specialized knowledge essential for an innovation-based economy. High taxes on top incomes blunted the rewards for entrepreneurship and risk taking.

Almost simultaneously, the wage restraint that had supported profitability and investment for nearly two decades began to weaken. Attitudes changed with fading memories of unemployment in the 1930s and with the entry of a new generation of workers into the labor force. It is no coincidence that the late 1960s saw strikes, wage inflation, and a declining share of profits in national income, trends that produced lower investment rates after 1973. And with the collapse of the Bretton Woods System in 1971–1973, inflationary ex-

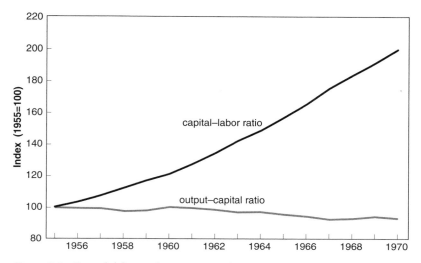

Figure 2.1. Capital–labor and output–capital ratios, 1955–1970. *Sources*: Organisation for Economic Co-operation and Development (OECD) (1983); OECD, *National Accounts* (various years); OECD, *Labor Force Statistics* (various years). *Note*: Figure shows aggregate series for four European countries: France, Germany, Italy, and the United Kingdom.

pectations lost their anchor. So long as European countries were committed to defending their exchange rates against the dollar, any acceleration of inflation (relative to that prevailing in the United States) had to be halted quickly. And so long as inflationary bursts were only temporary, workers had limited incentive to demand compensatory wage increases. By anchoring expectations, the Bretton Woods System thus moderated the impact of demand stimulus on inflation and wages. Because demand stimulus translated into increased output rather than being dissipated in inflation, the effectiveness of stabilization policy was enhanced.

But with the rise of capital mobility—itself a concomitant of the reconstruction of financial markets following the disruptions of the 1930s and World War II—the anchor began to drag. Unions began to worry that inflation, once ignited, would persist, since there was no longer a credible exchange-rate commitment to force governments to apply the brakes. Now Keynesian demand stimulus increased wage demands and inflation, not employment and growth.[58] Monetary and fiscal policies that now stimulated inflation rather than output lost much of their capacity to stabilize the economy.

Ultimately, these pressures, together with declining scope for catch-up and convergence, led to a slowdown in growth. This in turn weakened the incentive to adhere to the postwar bargain. The payoff in terms of higher future living standards that would result from current sacrifices depended on the economy-wide rate of growth. Consequently, as growth rates showed signs of falling, the agreement to trade wage restraint for investment proved harder to sustain.[59] To be sure, the coming of full employment across much of Europe by the late 1960s would have complicated efforts to maintain wage restraint under any circumstances. And the slowdown of growth as a factor corrosive to the postwar bargain provides a better explanation for the failure to restore wage restraint subsequently than for its initial breakdown, since the initial wage explosion started in 1968, whereas the slowdown in growth became apparent only three and more years later. Still, there is no question that the superimposition of these additional factors made the maintenance of wage restraint, profitability, and high investment more difficult still.

European countries responded with the now traditional treatment, deepening the involvement of government in the economy, extending the welfare state, and accelerating European integration. These responses were meant to reinforce wage moderation, subdue inflation, and stimulate exports and growth. Governments sought to extend the system of bonds, sanctions, and rewards with which they had supported the postwar social compact and helped to sustain wage and price stability for more than two decades. In return for a renewed commitment to wage restraint, unions were promised increased health and unemployment payments and were offered larger social security stipends.

[58] Evidence on the persistence of inflation and its impact on the economy is provided by Alogoskoufis and Smith (1991).
[59] Baily and Kirkegaard (2004) emphasize this argument.

But this strategy quickly encountered diminishing returns. The costs came in the form of growing public spending and a bloated state sector. They were evident in mounting debt problems. They manifested themselves as high tax rates and welfare-state policies that blunted the incentives for innovation and slowed the pace of labor reallocation. This was the period in which Europe's welfare state "overshot."[60] I will argue that such overshooting was no coincidence.

Sometimes problems breed their own solutions. In Europe, rising unemployment and slowing growth led first to experimentation with heterodox remedies. The failure of these experiments then led to policy consolidation, with Thatcher's disinflation in Britain, Mitterrand's turn away from state-led expansion in France, and fiscal retrenchment in Denmark and Ireland. The European Community responded in 1986 with the Single Market Program to intensify product market competition and in 1989 with plans for monetary unification. The 1990s then saw halting progress in the direction of fiscal consolidation and labor market reform. But these changes were gradual. Their slow pace was indicative of the deeply embedded nature of Europe's inherited institutions.[61]

---

[60] In the words of Lindbeck (1994).
[61] As documented by Saint-Paul (2004).

- THREE -

THE POSTWAR SITUATION

Although World War II was immensely destructive, its impact on productive capacity was surprisingly limited. To be sure, there was substantial destruction of transportation infrastructure, housing, power-generating capacity, and industrial equipment. But where roads and bridges had been damaged, they could be repaired quickly. The same was true of industrial capacity and power generation. The speed with which physical damage could be repaired was a lesson of the Allied experience with strategic bombing, the impact of which on enemy war production had been less than anticipated.[1] The aggregate numbers suggest that Europe's productive capital stock was roughly the same in 1947 as ten years earlier.[2] This is not to deny the existence of wartime setbacks; absent the war, the capital stock presumably would have continued to grow at 2 percent a year, resulting in levels perhaps 20 percent higher than prewar—and actual—by 1947. But neither does this suggest disastrous losses of productive capacity.

More important was that strategic bombing discouraged the adoption of mass-production methods that were already relatively far advanced in the United States. Mass producing aircraft and ships, as was done by the Ford Motor Company at the Willow Run plant and by Henry Kaiser in his mile-long assembly lines stretching back

---

[1] U.S. Department of State (1947), p. 31. See Ross (2003) for a recent study.
[2] In Germany, where there had been considerable wartime investment, it was actually higher. Abelschauser (1975), pp. 14–30.

from the docks of Richmond, California, presupposed an ability to deliver a continuous flow of inputs.[3] This was not possible when bridges and rail lines were being knocked out in nighttime bombing raids and factories had to be dispersed to smaller, camouflaged premises.[4] The war thus reinforced the existing divergence between the mass-production orientation of the United States and Europe's historical dependence on batch methods.

The war's most profound damage was to the economic and social system. The price mechanism as a means for allocating resources was largely in abeyance so long as governments continued to rely on rationing and price controls. Where producers had collaborated with enemy occupiers, as in the case of Louis Renault in France, their assets were seized and their companies nationalized, raising questions about who would run them in the future and how. Europe's trade had ground to a halt. Its capital markets remained inert. Governments depleted their reserves of dollars and gold, leaving them no means of financing imports from the United States. Banks drafted into the war effort had been forced to invest heavily in government bonds and now lacked the resources to resume normal peacetime lending. The future of the price system, the financial system, the trading system, and even the private property rights system was now fundamentally in doubt. As the Oxford don Thomas Balogh sweepingly put it, the war had "smashed the delicate balance of the nineteenth-century world economy and undermined the fundamental basis of Western European existence."[5]

The question was with what kind of new system postwar leaders and their followers would replace prewar arrangements. Inevitably, their response built on earlier foundations. There turned out to be considerable continuity between institutional developments in the first half of the twentieth century and the structures that postwar politicians and societies put in place after 1945. Balogh's assessment turned out to be too sweeping; the delicate balance of the nine-

---

[3] See, for example, Lane (1951). Overy (1995) notes that the Ford Motor Company produced more military equipment during the war than the country of Italy did.

[4] This is a theme of Overy (1995).

[5] Balogh (1949), p. 1.

teenth-century world may have been smashed, but not beyond repair. Below the surface, the foundations of Europe's earlier economic
and political achievements remained in place.

The conclusions drawn subsequently by analysts such as Mancur
Olson—that the war had created scope for faster growth by clearing
away old institutional impediments—were similarly misleading.[6] Although the war may have disturbed the earlier constellation of institutional arrangements and interest groups, it did not prevent them
from being rapidly reconstituted. All the war had done was to add
a bit of extra "play" to the system—some extra scope for adapting
old structures to new needs. Two wars in barely twenty-five years
had created a desire not to repeat past mistakes. Politicians therefore
sought to capitalize on the period of extraordinary politics following
the armistice by adapting inherited institutions to the new circumstances of the third quarter of the twentieth century and preventing
the outbreak of another devastating European war.

Reconstruction

Superficially, wartime destruction was extensive. In France, the inventory included 1.8 million buildings damaged, nearly one-quarter
beyond repair; 115 railroad stations severely damaged or destroyed;
more than 70 percent of locomotives damaged or removed; all major
canals, riverways, and ports unnavigable; nine of every ten motor
vehicles out of commission; and vast amounts of productive farm-
land transformed into dangerous minefields. In the Netherlands,
metal items of every sort, even church bells, had been seized and
exported to Germany. Eighty-five percent of Italy's merchant marine
had been destroyed, along with one-third of its railway capacity and
perhaps one-fifth of its industrial plant and equipment. In Germany,
20 percent of residential buildings—50 percent in the major cities—
was severely damaged. Ninety percent of the country's rail network

---

[6] See Olson (1996); also see "Institutions and History" in chapter 2.

was either blocked by wrecked rolling stock or rendered impassible by bomb damage to the tracks.

Although this destruction was extensive, it was uneven. In the north of Italy, where industry was heavily concentrated, most capacity survived the war intact.[7] Hydroelectric generating capacity, on which Italian industry depended for power, was in fact 16 percent higher in 1946 than before 1938. The capacity of the engineering industry was 30 percent higher. Roads, bridges, railways, and ports were extensively damaged, but these could be rapidly repaired. Even where factories had been dismantled, as in the case of the steelworks of Genoa, whose German-made machinery was carted off by German troops, the consequences could be reversed quickly. New machinery could be purchased with American help. Factories could be rapidly rebuilt. The results were not always aesthetic, but they were functional. Restoring the housing stock took longer but was less essential to the immediate resumption of production.

What was true for Italy was also true for other countries. At the conclusion of hostilities, industrial production was barely 40 percent of prewar levels in Belgium, France, and the Netherlands and less than 20 percent in Germany and Italy. But from this unenviable starting point it was possible to boost output quickly by putting people back to work. And work they did. Trade unionists and the left, extending even to Communist Party hardliners, approached postwar reconstruction as a national effort comparable to the resistance. "Produce, produce" and "Work hard first, then ask for concessions" were the slogans of the Confédération Générale du Travail in France.[8] Maurice Thorez of the French Communist Party, upon returning from wartime exile in Moscow, singled out production as the highest duty of the French worker. In Italy, Stakhanov squads of model workers were formed to encourage more intense effort.[9] Herbert Morrison spoke for the left-dominated Labour government

---

[7] German bombing had been concentrated in the south, where the Allies were expected to land. See de Cecco and Giavazzi (1993). A number of the other facts and observations in this paragraph are taken from this source.

[8] Ross (1982), p. 31.

[9] Armstrong, Glyn, and Harrison (1991), p. 55.

in Britain when he observed that "the battle for socialism is the battle for production."[10] Strike activity was all but absent in 1945–1946, reflecting Europeans' recognition that it was necessary to get the economy moving again (in contrast with the United States, where strike activity increased in 1946). In addition, radical unions and their political wings worried that disruptive labor action might drive the middle class into the arms of the right, making it more difficult for labor movements to achieve their political goals. Where the narrow base of radical movements meant that governing required the formation of coalitions, the military-style discipline imposed by labor unions and parties on their rank and file was designed to demonstrate that they could function as reliable partners.

The repair of transportation and communication facilities and labor's commitment to the battle for production facilitated rapid revival. As table 3.1 shows, already in 1947 industrial production continent-wide exceeded 1938 levels, if one excludes the western zones of occupied Germany. Compared to industry, agricultural output was slower to recover. Fields had to be plowed and planted; as always, farmwork had its own rhythms. Yet despite the cold winter of 1946–1947 and the dry summer that followed, agricultural output throughout Europe reached 80 percent of prewar levels by 1947–1948. At that point, workers and left-wing parties began questioning the need to subordinate their economic and political goals to the national recovery effort, and sporadic strikes began breaking out.

Conditions were most difficult in Germany. There was no rail, telephone, or mail service. Months passed before basic utilities such as electricity, gas, and water were restored. There was little factory production. The country was divided into four zones under the supervision of separate occupying powers. Internal trade remained difficult, given the Allies' reluctance to rebuild a railway system that had played a central role in Germany's mobilization for war. The Soviets, who occupied much of Germany's industrial heartland, saw the priority as dismantling factories and equipment and carting them

---

[10] Carew (1987), p. 22.

TABLE 3.1
Production in Western Europe (1938 = 100)

	1947	1949	1951	Percentage increase 1951 over 1947
Turkey	153	162	163	7
Sweden	142	157	172	21
Ireland	120	154	176	46
Denmark	119	143	160	35
Norway	115	135	153	33
United Kingdom	110	129	145	32
Belgium	106	122	143	33
Luxembourg	—	132	168	—
France	99	122	138	39
Netherlands	94	127	147	56
Italy	93	109	143	54
Greece	69	90	130	88
Austria	55	114	148	269
Germany (Federal Republic)	34	72	106	312
All countries participating in the Marshall Plan	**87**	**112**	**135**	**55**
All participating countries exclusive of Germany (Federal Republic)	105	130	145	37

Source: U.S. President, First Report to Congress on the Mutual Security Program (31 December 1951). Drawn from Brown and Opie (1953), p. 249.

off as reparations.[11] The intentions of the other occupying powers remained obscure even after the Morgenthau Plan to dismantle German industry was shelved in late 1944.[12] French plans called for a permanent Allied occupation, for detaching the country's industrial heartland, the Ruhr, and placing it under international control, and for transferring the steel-making region of the Saar to France. Directive 1067 of the U.S. Joint Chiefs of Staff, issued in 1945, forbade military administrators from "looking toward the economic rehabilitation of Germany" or taking steps "to maintain or strengthen the German economy" except to the extent that doing so was required

[11] Much of the civil industrial plant dismantled and shipped eastward as reparations turned out to be too advanced for Soviet use, and in some cases it was ultimately shipped back to the original owners.

[12] This refers to the plan for permanently dismantling a large share of German industry presented by U.S. Treasury Secretary Henry Morgenthau to Roosevelt and Churchill at the Quebec Conference in September 1944.

to prevent the spread of disease and unrest.[13] In March 1946, the Allies implemented a Level of Industry Plan to restrict German industrial output to one-half of prewar levels.

Not surprisingly, the uncertainty created by these measures discouraged investors from committing resources to industrial activity. In 1947, German industrial production was barely one-third of prewar levels, below even the ceilings imposed by the Level of Industry Plan. Agricultural production, or at least the portion that was marketed and recorded, fell from 70 percent of prewar levels in 1946–1947 to 58 percent in 1947–1948. During the war, the fertility of the soil had been maintained by the large number of livestock transferred from occupied regions; now, with such transfers going the other way, fertilizer was in short supply. In the spring of 1947, food rations in German cities fell to less than eight hundred calories a day. Workers used what little energy they possessed to forage for food and barter for coal. They sold light bulbs and copper wire pilfered from factories for whatever they could get. Physical survival depended increasingly on food aid from the United States and the United Kingdom.

This situation posed a dilemma for the Allies. Germany was the economic center of Europe. It supplied the capital goods needed for the recovery and growth of its neighbors. The Level of Industry Plan limited the production of machine tools to 10 percent of 1936 levels. The vision of U.S. Treasury Secretary Morgenthau and his fellow "pastoralizers" of a Germany that concentrated on farming and light manufacturing was incompatible with the need for a vibrant and prosperous European economy to provide a bulwark against the Soviet Union. Ultimately, the advent of the Cold War in 1946–1947 catalyzed a shift in U.S. thinking. It forced even the French to acknowledge that the Allies could not afford to dismantle German industry and that other means would have to be found to contain German might. But, reflecting the price that the Allies had paid to defeat the Nazis, this realization was slow in coming.

[13] U.S. Department of State (1947), pp. 155–156.

The Transition to Sustained Growth

A lesson widely drawn from the war was the importance of fixed investment, industrial investment in particular. The Allies and the Nazis had engaged in a deadly industrial race, success in which was measured in tons of steel and numbers of tanks, aircraft, and ships. Ultimately, the United States had tipped the balance by bringing to bear its own formidable industrial might. The key to restoring economic vitality after the war consequently came to be seen as repairing industrial capacity.[14] Growth and higher living standards were also shared goals around which governments could rally their supporters. And the United States had already indicated that it would insist on an open trading system, making it imperative for European countries to raise productivity in order to compete. "The psychology of 1945," as it has been called, attached priority to growth and specifically to industrial growth.[15] For all these reasons, growth became "an obsession."[16]

Consequently, recovery in the early postwar years was driven by spending on industrial capacity. Priority was given to heavy industry. Thus, the Monnet Plan, the ambitious modernization program rolled out by the French government in 1946, emphasized investment in transportation, energy, and iron and steel. It was implemented mainly through the provision of public funds on favorable terms from budgetary accounts such as the Modernization and Equipment Fund.[17] It assumed an ability to import large amounts of coal, intermediate inputs, and machinery.

But these ambitions soon ran up against feasibility constraints.[18] Europe itself produced only limited amounts of the capital goods that were essential inputs into this process because the occupying powers still restricted German production. Machinery and other in-

---

[14] And continued economic development was portrayed in terms synonymous with capital formation in general and industrial capital formation in particular. See Lewis (1954) for an influential statement of this view.

[15] Adams (1989), p. 47.

[16] In the words of van der Wee (1986).

[17] See "Next in Line" in chapter 4.

[18] This position is strongly argued by Milward (1984).

puts might also be purchased from the United States for hard currency. Unfortunately, Europe's balance-of-payments position had been weakened considerably by the war. Countries had sold off foreign assets to pay for national defense, so they now received less income from overseas investments. By 1947 they had exhausted their dollar and gold reserves and were forced to devote what was left to importing food. Exports, for their part, could be used to finance imported inputs only to a limited extent, imports having to come first to facilitate the expansion of capacity. And borrowing abroad was infeasible, given the uncertain political situation and memories of the disastrous performance of interwar loans. The extreme case was occupied Germany, where foreign trade, aside from compulsory exports of coal, timber, and scrap, was nonexistent.

The incompatibility of governments' postwar investment plans with the balance-of-payments constraint came to the fore in 1947, when they combined with a poor harvest to produce a European current-account deficit of 5 percent of GDP. Under other circumstances a deficit of this magnitude might not have created immediate sustainability problems, for there was reason to think that sooner or later economic growth would resume. As growth proceeded, investment ratios would decline toward customary levels, and savings would rise along with household incomes. Given sufficient time, the current-account deficit (the difference between investment and savings) would right itself. The problem in 1947 was that the immediate outlook for growth was clouded. And without growth, Europe's imbalances would not correct themselves.

In the meantime, finance for these imbalances remained uncertain. With exports still depressed, there was no way for Europe to generate the necessary financing on its own. And the lower the level of exports, the more worrisome the current-account deficit became. An external deficit of 5 percent of GDP is less alarming for an economy that exports one-third of GNP than for one that exports hardly anything at all. With the volume of exports still depressed, Europe's imports of goods and services exceeded exports by 65 percent. In other words, restoring balance to the external accounts would have required Europe to boost its exports by more than half.

Moreover, since trade was the slowest-growing component of national income, there was little scope for Europe to respond to the sudden curtailment of external financing by boosting its exports. Instead, eliminating the deficit required curtailing the demand for imports. Private consumption, which had already fallen below 1938 levels, might have to be compressed further, perhaps by an additional 10 percent, threatening social stability. Or investment would have to be reduced by one-fifth, jeopardizing the prospects for growth. This is why the external deficit and the danger that it might have to be eliminated caused such alarm.

The second obstacle to growth was price controls. In the environment of shortages that prevailed at the end of the war, many wartime controls were retained. They were now used to direct labor and raw materials as a way of maintaining the production of key commodities. Wages were frozen in order to insure that competition for labor did not draw manpower away from priority uses. Workers were permitted to take only jobs listed on government employment exchanges. To prevent price gouging and minimize unrest, the authorities froze the prices of food, fuel, clothing, and other essentials and rationed purchases. To prevent profiteers from exporting scarce goods, they embargoed foreign sales. They regulated the lending and investments of banks and forced those institutions to absorb the public sector's debt by investing deposits in government bonds, just as they had during the war. To prevent excess liquidity from spilling over into imports of luxury items and exhausting central banks' hard-currency reserves, they limited the movement of prices.

But so long as prices were frozen below equilibrium levels, producers had little incentive to bring their goods to market. Farmers stored their grain rather than selling it. As one of the architects of the Marshall Plan, Will Clayton, explained to the U.S. secretary of state, George Marshall, in 1947, although "French grain acreage [is] running 20–25% under pre-war, collection of production [is] very unsatisfactory—much of the grain is fed to cattle."[19] Farmers fattened their pigs and cows instead of slaughtering them. Shortages

[19] Quoted in Killick (1997), p. 69.

of bread and sugar led to rioting in Verdun and Les Mans. Unable to purchase consumer goods, workers spent time not at the factory but cultivating their garden plots and foraging in the countryside. Unable to purchase supplies, firms were reduced to producing their own inputs, at considerable cost. These problems were most severe in Germany, where the wages and prices fixed by the Nazis in 1936 continued to form the basis for the administered price structure of the Allied occupiers a decade later.[20] Firms produced only those goods that could be bartered for the products of other firms (in the so-called compensation trade), that were demanded by workers to supplement their wages and prevent them from leaving the firm, or that were required to qualify for additional allotments of raw materials.[21] Although black markets existed, prices were extraordinarily high since the risks of elicit transactions were still substantial in an occupied country.[22] One egg cost eight reichsmarks on the black market in Hamburg in 1948, which was roughly the wage paid a skilled worker for an eight-hour day.[23] Not surprisingly, absenteeism was rampant. Activity peaked on weekends when city dwellers took their household goods to the countryside to barter for grain and potatoes.

Shortages and price distortions grew worse the longer governments continued running deficits and printing money, widening the gap between black-market and controlled prices. Officials threatened those suspected of hoarding. The Ramadier government in France, for example, attacked speculators, those traditional French bugbears, for withholding stocks.

Decontrolling prices and allowing the market to operate thus required accepting that the war was finally over and the economy

[20] Giersch, Paque, and Schmieding (1992) describe the peculiar result in which essential goods that had been subject to the Nazis' prewar controls were in short supply, but exotic items that had not existed in the 1930s and therefore had not been subject to controls were widely available in the second half of the 1940s. In addition, the relative prices of basic agricultural and industrial goods were depressed—and shortages of them were particularly acute—because their controlled prices could be changed only by the Allied Control Authority itself, which was loath to act, whereas the producers of final goods could deal with more pliable German price controllers. Mendershausen (1949), p. 650.

[21] See Buchheim (1993b), p. 71n.

[22] In particular, substantial fines could be imposed under the provisions of the Control Council law of March 1947.

[23] Buchheim (1993a), p. 88.

could again be entrusted to market forces. That there was reluctance to move in this direction is not surprising. The market system had been in abeyance for the better part of a decade, and the last time it had been allowed to operate, in the 1930s, it had malfunctioned disastrously, culminating in the Great Depression. Communists and socialists, who did not accept the legitimacy of market outcomes, had formed the backbone of wartime resistance movements and were in a strong political position following the armistice. Moreover, so long as budgets remained in deficit and governments printed money to bridge the gap, decontrol implied inflation. It was not obvious to the working class that abundant supplies of essential goods at prices they could not afford were preferable to scarce supplies at affordable prices. Balancing budgets required tax increases and expenditure reductions. And in the fractious postwar political environment, no consensus prevailed on the composition of the requisite adjustments.

These observations point to a third fundamental obstacle to growth: policy uncertainty. Communists occupied important positions in the Italian and French governments. The French Communist Party won more than one-quarter of the votes cast in the three elections of 1945–1946. In the 1946 election for the Constituent Assembly, the Communists and the Socialists, then allied, won 40 percent of the popular vote. The Danish Communists proved popular in the first postwar elections, but the Social Democrats refused to share power with them, leading to a weak minority government incapable of implementing stabilization plans. There may have been few instances where Communist Parties made strong bids for state power, but their presence in or support for postwar coalitions heightened policy uncertainty. In Britain, the Labour government that came to power in 1945, which included a number of individuals of radical persuasion, embarked on an ambitious program of industrial nationalization. In Germany, the single largest political party, the Social Democratic Party (Sozialdemokratische Partei Deutschlands, SPD), advocated the nationalization of industry and the retention of price controls. Its leader, Kurt Schumacher, believed that the postwar period would be one of social revolution leading to the abolition of capitalism and the establishment of a socialist state.[24] The British installed Viktor Agartz, another prominent SPD leader and supporter of planning, state control, and centralization, as head of the German economic administration in their occupation zone. The socialization of industry was advocated even by the main opposition to the SPD, the Christian Democratic Union (CDU), an anticapitalist movement having developed among the Christian parties partly as a result of the need to compete for support and partly because capitalism had been associated with the rise of the Nazis. The Ahlen Program, endorsed by the leaders of the CDU in the British occupation zone, was at best ambivalent about the merits of the market.[25]

It was not clear that governments led by these individuals and parties would respect private property, shun the imposition of confiscatory taxes, and let the market work. Entrepreneurs therefore held off investing until they learned more about the status of private property. Investors held off purchasing securities until they knew more about how their dividends would be taxed. Banks hesitated to lend, not knowing whether their principal would be inflated away. Workers hesitated to invest in skills and training until they knew more about the structure of pay and employment.

Normalization and the Political Economy of the Marshall Plan

In retrospect, the solution to these problems was clear. Restocking the shelves required removing price controls. But to avoid igniting inflation, budgets had to be balanced and the excess of money and credit created by wartime governments had to be removed. Reduc-

---

[24] See Edinger (1965).

[25] The Ahlen Program condemned "the capitalist economic system" and called for nationalization of heavy industry, government economic planning, and worker participation in management, but it was also formulated in an attempt to block more ambitious SPD plans for extensive nationalization. The program was substantially prepared by Robert Pferdmenges, a Cologne banker and an adviser to Adenauer. See Nicholls (1994).

ing the pressure of demand would strengthen the balance of pay-ments, allowing private enterprise to import raw materials and inter-mediate inputs. But it would also slow the rate of growth and weaken support for the market system unless the reduction in public invest-ment was offset by a rise in private investment. This in turn required eliminating fears of confiscatory taxation and nationalization. And all of these required political consolidation that strengthened the hand of parties at the center of the political spectrum.

The basis for this normalization resided in Europe itself. For those of middle age, memories of the aftermath of World War I, when political fragmentation and polarization had led to repeated changes in government, militated in favor of moderation. Political extremism had been further discredited by the experience of the 1930s and the war. The absence of reparations on the same scale as after the earlier war also weakened the case for extremism as a pos-ture expedient for insisting on or resisting their payment. And once the Soviets revealed their true color by their actions in Eastern Eu-rope, the costs of government by coalition that included a party taking instructions from Moscow became clear. Finally, the United States, which after World War I had taken the first opportunity to withdraw from Europe and international entanglements generally, responded very differently after World War II, most famously with the Marshall Plan.

The Marshall Plan addressed each of the obstacles to postwar recovery. By providing thirteen billion dollars in U.S. government grants over four years, it relaxed the external constraint. Europe's trade deficit was 11.5 billion dollars from 1948 through 1950, a pe-riod during which U.S. grants were ten billion dollars.[26] The Mar-shall Plan thus solved the catch-22 of having to export in order to pay for imports but being unable to produce for export without first importing materials and machinery. It sustained Europe's strategy of investment-led growth and reconciled the need for investment finance with the insistence on higher living standards.

---

[26] It can be argued, not unreasonably, that European deficits had to be reduced to meet the financing constraint imposed by the Marshall Plan. In practice, the 1949 devaluations were important for squaring this circle, as explained later.

In addition, the Marshall Plan provided incentives to embrace the market. Countries accepting American aid had to sign bilateral pacts with the United States agreeing to decontrol prices, stabilize exchange rates, and balance budgets. In effect, they had to commit to putting in place the prerequisites for a functioning market economy. This reduced uncertainty about property rights, encouraging investment and initiative.

The Marshall Plan also helped governments to decontrol prices and restore the operation of the price mechanism by reducing inflationary pressure. In the absence of steps to balance the budget and reduce the pressure for money finance, decontrol would have simply led to inflation. Looking back, it is not obvious that open inflation would have been worse than the repressed inflation and shortages resulting from the operation of postwar price controls. But recalling the experience after World War I, when similar pressures had exploded into hyperinflation, contemporaries were not prepared to contemplate a real-time experiment. In Germany, where Ludwig Erhard's decontrol of prices raised the cost of living and provoked a rash of strikes in late 1948, the arrival of Marshall Plan funds gave the government leeway to offer concessions and avoid having to roll back its earlier liberalization measures. In France, Marshall Plan funds were used to defray the costs of public enterprises and retire public debt, thereby lightening the load on the fisc.[27] Directly and indirectly, Marshall aid limited the belt-tightening to which the public had to agree in order to bring national budgets into balance and permit the relaxation of controls.[28]

These observations point to another way in which the Marshall Plan mattered: it tipped the balance of political power toward centrist parties. U.S. officials such as Dean Acheson, the undersecretary and later secretary of state who shaped both the Truman Doctrine

[27] Esposito (1994) argues that the decision of some European governments to allocate Marshall Plan aid to the retirement of public debt indicates the inability of the United States to compel them to devote its aid and their own counterpart funds to U.S. commodity and merchandise exports and its inability to shape their industrial policies more generally. My interpretation suggests that, in the longer term, the decision to allocate aid to debt retirement was not such an unhappy outcome from the point of view of the United States.

[28] See Casella and Eichengreen (1993).

and the Marshall Plan, made clear their reluctance to favor Socialist governments with aid. The Marshall Plan strengthened the hand of political moderates who could cite the loss of U.S. grants as an additional cost of opposing their programs. They could cite the high levels of investment that the Marshall Plan helped finance as tangible evidence that political moderation would lead to higher living standards. In France, announcement of the Marshall Plan led the Mouvement Républicain Populaire (MRP), the Radicals, the Moderates, and some Socialists to ask whether a government with Communist partners could expect to receive significant amounts of U.S. aid. It convinced the Socialists in the Ramadier government that the United States was a more reliable supporter of French interests than the USSR was. In Belgium, Luxembourg, and Italy, the announcement of Marshall aid was quickly followed by the dismissal of Communist ministers from the government. In Denmark it was followed by a major setback for the Communists in the October 1947 elections. In Italy it helped the Christian Democrats gain a safe majority in Parliament in April 1948. In Germany it strengthened the hand of the CDU and its coalition partners, the Free Democrats, who squeaked by the Social Democrats in a close vote in 1949. The Marshall Plan thus had the effect of creating a split between Socialist and Communist parties, or at least of exploiting tendencies toward such a split, with the Socialists agreeing on the need to accept Marshall aid and the Communists under instructions from Moscow to reject it. The result was to marginalize the Communists.[29]

At the most fundamental level, the Marshall Plan defined the conflict between East and West as a choice between central planning and the market. As Klaus Hinrich Hennings has put it, "the Marshall Plan implied a private ownership economy, and thus in effect put an end to debates on other forms of economic organization."[30] To be sure, Europe would go on to develop its own form of

[29] In some of these cases political consolidation preceded the Marshall Plan, but Carew (1987) shows how even the anticipation of U.S. aid worked to strength the position of centrist parties.
[30] Referring to the German case. Hennings (1982), p. 478.

market capitalism, what was referred to as the mixed economy, the social welfare state, or the social market economy, in which the state played a role in regulating and even running industry, became deeply involved in wage negotiations and investment decisions, and extended a generous social safety net. But there was no doubt now that these initiatives would be superimposed on a private-ownership economy.

The Soviet Union was invited to participate in the Marshall Plan, although there are reasons to question the sincerity of the U.S. offer. In June 1947, Moscow sent a delegation headed by Vyacheslav Molotov to Paris to meet with representatives of the French and British governments and discuss a joint response to the U.S. offer, but the Russians walked out when told that they would have to share information about their economy and accept preconditions for the extension of aid. Czechoslovakia and Poland then attempted to accept the U.S. invitation but were overruled by Stalin. Thus, in the same way that the decision by the Americans, the British, and the French to go ahead with monetary reform in the three western zones of occupied Germany in 1948 without the participation of the Soviets marked the decisive division of that country, the decision to go ahead with the Marshall Plan decisively divided Europe.[31] Perhaps the intensification of the Cold War left no other choice. But the result was to place Western Europe firmly in the capitalist, market-oriented camp.

The response to price liberalization was immediate. Stores empty one day were overflowing the next as goods flooded out of hoards. Because workers now had goods to buy, absenteeism fell. These effects were most dramatic in West Germany, but they were seen throughout Europe. The sudden supply of materials from mines and farms provided industry with the inputs needed to expand production.

As budget deficits fell and printing of money slowed, external disequilibria were reduced. It became possible to lift import restrictions and for European economies more fully to exploit their com-

---

[31] On the German monetary reform, see the next section.

68

parative advantage in international markets. Of course, exporting required the ability first to import scarce production inputs, such as cotton, hides, and leather. Starting in 1948, the Marshall Plan also played a key role in relaxing this constraint.

A final effect of the Marshall Plan was to encourage European integration. American aid was contingent on agreement by the recipients on a collective strategy for using U.S. funds. The Marshall Planners saw their initiative as encouraging the formation of a "United States of Europe" whose close economic and political relations would make war unthinkable and which would constitute a united front against the Soviet Union. The process would start with the creation of the Conference for European Economic Cooperation (quickly renamed the Organisation for European Economic Cooperation, or OEEC), which would eventually evolve into a legislature for Europe and ultimately be followed by other complementary institutions, including an interstate commerce commission and a central bank.

More immediately, European integration was a way of reconciling France and other European countries to higher levels of German industrial production and of disarming those, including influential voices in the U.S. government, who insisted on pastoralizing the German economy. By locking Germany into Europe and promoting the development of institutions of shared governance, the Marshall Plan encouraged Paris to agree to the elimination of ceilings on German production. By substituting American aid, it enabled the French and other victors to drop their claim to German reparations. In the course of negotiating access to U.S. funds, Foreign Minister Georges Bidault was also forced to abandon France's insistence on autonomy for the Rhineland and Ruhr and accept the fusion of the British and American occupation zones. In this sense the Marshall Plan helped to set the stage for the creation of the West German state, negotiated at the Six-Power Conference in London in 1948.

Already in 1947, U.S. administrators such as the military governor of the American occupation zone in Germany and commander in chief of U.S. forces in Europe, General Lucius D. Clay, an engineer by profession, had seen the losses caused by directives forbidding measures to foster the recovery of the Germany economy and had begun surreptitiously disregarding their instructions. British administrators similarly backed away from their earlier commitment to the widespread nationalization of German enterprise. At the beginning of 1947, the two countries fused their administrative areas into a Bizone that offered more scope for rebuilding internal trade and production (since the British zone was heavily industrial while the American zone was more agricultural). They allowed the limited resumption of commercial exports from the Bizone, mainly raw materials and semifinished products at this early stage. By summer, they had modified the Level of Industry Plan to allow industrial production to rise to 1936 levels.[32] Except perhaps in France, the Cold War had rendered moot all ambitions to pastoralize the Germany economy.

In effect, then, the United States and Britain had already accepted the argument for Germany's economic normalization before the Marshall Plan. But it is hard to imagine that they would have moved further in this direction or that their initiatives would have succeeded in overcoming resistance in France and other countries had the Marshall Plan not created a larger political and economic structure into which to embed the German economy. "A Europe which includes Germany" was the solution of General Marshall and the U.S. administration.[33]

German Economic and Monetary Reform

Production in the Bizone and the French occupation zone was still running at just half of 1936 levels in mid-1948. Output was recovering more quickly in the Soviet zone, where compulsory labor and

---

[32] The actual behavior of output in this period is a matter of some dispute. The official statistics suggest that the growth of output had stalled by the summer of 1947, reflecting pervasive shortages and the breakdown of the monetary economy. Electricity consumption (which may better reflect production by small enterprises not captured by the official statistics) and inventory accumulation in anticipation of eventual monetary reform suggest some continued rise.

[33] This quotation from George Marshall is cited in James (1996), p. 75.

larger supplementary food rations for workers had at least temporary effects. Hence there were growing fears that Germany's failure to recover faster and to resume conventional levels of capital-goods production could choke off European recovery.

The Americans had hoped for a monetary reform for the whole of Germany, but their ambitions were frustrated by the Soviets. Moscow employed a variety of delaying tactics, notably demanding the right to print the new banknotes in Leipzig as well as at the Reich printing works in Berlin. This was enough to preclude an all-German reform, since allowing decentralized provision of the new currency—including by the one party with at best mixed incentives to see the project succeed—threatened to vitiate monetary control. Now the Western powers decided to go ahead on their own, despite the fact that doing so would constitute a definitive split between East and West Germany. The American government printed new banknotes in the United States and housed them in former Reichsbank buildings in Frankfurt. After first setting out the broad parameters of the monetary reform, in April 1948 the Allies constituted a German working group to fill in the blanks.[34] Ignoring German objections, they established an independent central bank, the Bank deutscher Länder (BDL), in the three western occupation zones. They armed Ludwig Erhard, the newly installed liberal-minded director of the Economic Administration, with a fiscal-reform plan that significantly reduced tax rates, especially in the lower brackets, to further encourage labor effort.

The need for monetary reform was a by-product of rationing and forced savings in the 1930s and during the war. Because consumer goods were rationed, households had stockpiled their earnings in the form of deposits, which their banks invested in public debt instruments, financing the Third Reich's budget deficits. Now this overhang of deposits (that is, the disproportionate share of money deposited in banks rather than spent) was eliminated by converting only limited

---

[34] The Allies rejected an alternative proposal, the Homburg Plan, submitted to them by the German authorities in April, making clear who controlled the broad parameters of the monetary reform.

numbers of reichsmarks into newly minted deutschmarks at a parity of one to one. The remaining cash and bank deposits of households were converted at a rate of ten to one, and the deposits of public authorities were canceled.[35] Debts were similarly scaled down by 90 percent. The Reich bonds of the commercial banks were converted into "equalization claims" bearing a 3 percent interest rate.[36]

With the monetary overhang thereby removed, decontrol could proceed. Erhard forced the issue by having his press secretary, Kuno Ockhardt, announce the end of controls on household items as well as cars, bicycles, tires, and agricultural machinery on the same day that the new currency was distributed—before obtaining the agreement of the occupying authorities.[37] Within a week he had removed price controls on most manufactures and many foodstuffs.[38]

The results were nothing short of miraculous. Absenteeism, after averaging nearly 15 percent over the preceding six months (the combination of low wages and shortages of consumer goods rendering paychecks all but irrelevant), fell to 10 percent in June and 6 percent in July. Industrial production rose by nearly 15 percent between June and July. By December 1948 it was up by more than 50 percent from midyear levels. The most dramatic increases were in sectors where price controls had been most severe, such as textiles, apparel, shoes, motor vehicles, and electrical equipment.[39]

Clearly, had ceilings and rationing remained in place, these measures would not have succeeded in restoring the incentive to

[35] Half of the resulting deutschmark balances were released immediately. The authorities held off deciding the fate of the blocked half, giving them room to tailor the reform to the needs of price stability. As it turned out, inflationary pressure was more intense than expected, as the velocity of circulation picked up in response to the restoration of confidence and the success of the monetary reform, and wages rose strongly (albeit from low levels), reflecting strong demand for labor. In the end, therefore, the blocked half was largely canceled or credited to special accounts earmarked for investment.

[36] To fill the resulting hole in their balance sheets, the banks were recapitalized by grants of deposits with the BDL.

[37] Mierzejewski (2004), pp. 69–70.

[38] In the Bizone, controls remained on a few key items such as essential foodstuffs, utilities, transportation, and rent.

[39] The least progress, correspondingly, was in sectors where controls remained, notably coal and iron ore (Giersch, Paque, and Schmieding 1992, p. 39).

produce. The contrasting experience of the French zone underscores the point; there, price controls and rationing were removed more slowly, and activity was slower to recover. But in the Bizone, with these obstacles removed, the *Wirtschaftswunder* could get under way. Since Germany was at the heart of the European economy, that heart could now beat more strongly.[40]

Obstacles to Integration

A healthy blood flow required that the heart be connected to the body by a network of arteries and veins. A further task was therefore to rebuild intra-European trade. The problem was that European currencies were inconvertible, meaning that they could not be changed into dollars or other foreign currencies without the permission of the issuing government.[41] Concerned to husband their precious hard currency for purchases from the United States, each European country limited such transactions, effectively restricting imports from its neighbors to the value of receipts in its currency obtained by exporting to that country.

In these circumstances, agreements between pairs of contracting countries were the only feasible way of organizing Europe's trade. The first such agreements had been signed in 1943 in London by the governments in exile of Belgium, the Netherlands, and Luxembourg. By the late 1940s, Europe's trade resembled a spaghetti bowl of more than two hundred bilateral arrangements.[42] Contracting governments agreed to lists of commodities for which they would issue licenses for imports from partner countries and specified the exchange rate at which those transactions would take place. The most restrictive arrangements preset both prices and quantities to ensure that trade would balance continuously. Where prices or quantities were allowed to vary, temporary deficits were financed by the

---

[40] For two statements of this argument, see Gimbel (1976) and Berger and Ritschl (1995).
[41] Except, that is, at unfavorable black-market rates.
[42] See Diebold (1952).

surplus partner up to a specified ceiling or "swing." Beyond that, quantitative restrictions were binding.

These limited credits were extended on the assumption that surpluses and deficits were temporary and reversible. The problem was that the pattern of bilateral imbalances showed no signs of reversing itself. Throughout much of Europe, inflation was still high in 1947–1948, reflecting chronic budget deficits and monetary overhangs.[43] Almost immediately, then, countries where inflation and demand were high exhausted their credits from countries that had completed their monetary reforms and brought inflation under control.

Ongoing imbalances also reflected the traditional pattern of intra-European settlements. The Netherlands customarily ran deficits with Belgium, for example, reflecting its dependence on imports of coal and steel from its neighbor to the south, and earned the hard currency needed to settle its accounts by exporting other commodities to countries such as Denmark. Now, however, the Netherlands was prevented from using the proceeds of its Danish sales to import industrial inputs from Belgium. Hence when the Netherlands exhausted its swing, Belgium refused to issue additional credits, forcing the Netherlands to halt all imports from Belgium.

The exhaustion of credits soon became a generalized problem. The recovery of intra-European trade, which had risen to 60 percent of 1938 levels by 1947, therefore threatened to shift into reverse.

The nature of the remedy, a multilateral clearing arrangement, was no mystery. Currencies acquired by exporting merchandise might then be used to pay for imports from any participating country. The only constraint was that each country's total imports and exports had to balance, or at least the imbalance could not exceed the country's credits from the clearing union as a whole.

This was not current-account convertibility; finance for imports of commodities and merchandise would still be limited to currency earned through current exports of commodities and merchandise.

<hr>

[43] The main places where it had been brought under control by this time were the Low Countries and Scandinavia. Italy had also stabilized early, in 1947 (see chapter 4).

And if a country fell into chronic deficit vis-à-vis the clearing union, it still would have to restrict its purchases by rationing import licenses. The United Kingdom had been plunged into the cold bath of current-account convertibility in 1947, when the United States had required it to restore current-account convertibility as a condition of the Anglo-American loan.[44] The result had been the rapid exhaustion of reserves, as residents and foreigners used every loophole to convert unwanted sterling balances into foreign merchandise or currency.[45] The United Kingdom had consequently been forced to suspend convertibility after only seven weeks. Unilateral convertibility clearly was not feasible in a world still riddled with financial imbalances, in which most countries continued to apply quantitative restraints. The lesson was that European countries would have to move more gradually—and together—down the road to current-account convertibility.

The result was the First Agreement on Multilateral Monetary Compensation negotiated by Belgium, Luxembourg, the Netherlands, France, and Italy in November 1947.[46] Impetus came from the U.S. Economic Cooperation Administration's Planning Group, led by Richard Bissell and Harlan Cleveland, who saw the reconstruction of intra-European trade as essential to economic recovery and political solidarity.[47] To ensure enthusiasm in the Planning Group and the Congress for the extension of Marshall Plan aid, in

[44] The United Kingdom obtained a loan of 3.75 billion dollars repayable over fifty years starting at the end of 1951 and bearing an interest rate of 2 percent. U.S. officials extracted a commitment to restore current-account convertibility as the quid pro quo for these concessionary terms.

[45] To be sure, special factors had contributed to the rapid exhaustion of the loan and thus to the run on sterling. The harsh winter of 1946–1947 had added to the demand for coal, while the adverse climatic conditions of both winter and spring had increased the country's dependence on imported grain. More generally, the recovery of production required the large-scale importation of raw materials, which could be processed into exportable products only with a lag. This tendency for the balance of payments first to deteriorate as a result of the economy's incipient recovery was also evident in Germany in 1950–1951 and also led to a balance-of-payments crisis, albeit one that could be handled very differently (see the discussion later in this chapter).

[46] A comprehensive analysis of the genesis of this agreement is Toniolo (2005).

[47] Dyson (1994), p. 62.

August 1947 Hervé Alphand, the head of France's delegation to the Conference for European Economic Cooperation (CEEC), issued an invitation for all CEEC countries to join France in a clearing union. Unfortunately, his invitation coincided with the sterling crisis, which left the United Kingdom in no mood to participate. This meant that the scope for settling balances multilaterally was limited. In addition, domestic imbalances were still extensive, and exchange rates had not yet been adjusted to sustainable levels. It was clear that the countries that had made the least progress would incur chronic deficits. Since the prospective surplus countries had no wish to be on the line for extensive credits, it is not surprising that the First Agreement included no provision for financing of temporary deficits.

A second attempt, the Agreement for Intra-European Payments and Compensations, negotiated in October 1948, was organized, again with U.S. impetus, through the newly formed OEEC, the consortium of Marshall Plan aid recipients. A notable difference from the First Agreement was that this one included the United Kingdom (as a member of the OEEC). But, again, only a small fraction of the participants' liabilities were canceled multilaterally. And, again, no credits were provided. The binding constraint on extension of credits was the dollar shortage, countries still being desperate for imports from the United States. Granting credits to trading partners threatened to absorb resources that might otherwise be used to earn dollars and purchase U.S. goods.

More fundamentally, the dollar gap reflected the inadequate competitiveness of the European economies. Compared to 1938, average hourly earnings adjusted for exchange rates had fallen relative to the United States, but productivity had fallen even further. The United States had not suffered extensive disruptions as a result of the war. While European capital stocks were roughly unchanged from 1938 levels, the U.S. capital stock was fully one-quarter higher. The United States had used its position as foundry for the Allied war effort to develop new technologies and to elaborate assembly-line methods. In light of the increase in U.S. labor productivity,

European costs of production were now too high. This rendered earning dollars difficult. Given the shortage of dollars, there was no willingness to extend credits in order to rebuild intra-European trade.[48]

The 1949 Devaluations

The solution came with the 1949 currency devaluations. When the U.S. economy entered a recession in 1949, Washington feared that Europe's balance of payments would weaken further and require additional Marshall Plan aid. The Truman administration, led by the Treasury, therefore added its voice to those pushing for devaluation. With this shove, Britain took the leap and other European governments followed. The devaluation of European currencies amounted to 53 percent for Austria and 30 percent for the Netherlands, Sweden, the United Kingdom, and the sterling area. Three outliers were Italy, which devalued by an unambitious 8 percent, Belgium, which devalued by only 13 percent, and France, which devalued by a relatively modest 22 percent. In these three countries, the improvement in competitiveness achieved vis-à-vis the United States through currency devaluation had largely evaporated within two years. The failure of these countries to adjust their currencies more fully was a major factor in their disappointing export growth in the 1950s.

Germany also devalued the deutschmark by a relatively modest 21 percent. The chancellor, Konrad Adenauer, had favored a larger change, but the French objected. The Americans, concerned to maintain French support for multilateralism, backed France's view. Problems of external balance, therefore, resurfaced in Germany within a year.

[48] To put the point another way: with virtually all European currencies overvalued against the dollar and thus vulnerable to eventual depreciation, countries refused to accumulate claims denominated in the currencies of their neighbors for fear of capital losses. Overvalued currencies also meant that countries had to retain severe quantitative restrictions on imports in order to avoid exhausting their remaining international reserves.

These exceptions notwithstanding, European competitiveness vis-à-vis the United States was enhanced by the realignment of currencies. Of the nearly forty billion dollars of current-account deficits that European countries ran against the United States in the first postwar decade, more than 90 percent was incurred in the first four years of reconstruction, that is, before currency devaluation. At the same time, the reluctance of governments to contemplate larger devaluations meant that the dollar gap was not eliminated. This reluctance was informed by the prevailing "elasticity pessimism," the contemporary name for the belief that even large exchange-rate changes could have only small effects.[49] Related to this were fears that larger devaluations would precipitate the breakdown of wage moderation if workers experienced serious erosion of their purchasing power. A sharp decline in real wages might stretch the postwar social compact to the breaking point. No one disputed that the mechanism by which currency depreciation strengthened competitiveness was by lowering the purchasing power of wages and the prices of exported goods.[50] There were reasons to fear that workers would not react favorably to even larger declines in their purchasing power. If labor then responded by demanding higher wages, the terms-of-trade effect would erode, dissipating the gain in export competitiveness. This led governments to limit the magnitude of devaluation.

In the absence of larger adjustments, Europe's balance of payments remained fragile. This prevented countries from liberalizing their trade and payments unilaterally. Instead they had to move together down the road of external liberalization. Marshall Plan administrators sought to address this problem by committing the recipients to liberalize their trade and by providing dollars that they might offer one another to finance temporary imbalances. Starting in October 1948, the United States sought to compel countries to pass on a portion of their Marshall aid to others with whom they ran bilateral surpluses in the form of "drawing rights," which the

---

[49] The seminal empirical contribution to the debate was Orcutt (1950). The phrase *elasticity pessimism* was coined by Machlup (1950).

[50] Equivalently, by engineering a deterioration in the devaluing country's terms of trade.

surplus countries naturally resisted. This arrangement also gave rise to moral hazard: it encouraged countries to expand their intra-European deficits in order to be able to request more so-called conditional aid.[51] Not surprisingly, intra-European imbalances quickly became binding again.

The next attempt to solve this problem was the Finebel Plan of February 1950, *Finebel* being a conflation of the names of the participating countries: France, Italy, the Netherlands, Belgium, and Luxembourg. Negotiators had in mind a multilateral payments union, the progressive elimination of import quotas, and eventually a cooperative agricultural policy. But notable by its absence was Germany, which France was still reluctant to include as a partner. Predictably, this rendered the scheme unattractive to the Netherlands, which relied heavily on the German market. The Finebel negotiations died in March 1950. If a solution to this problem was to be found, evidently it would have to be found at the pan-European level.

The European Payments Union

This recognition dovetailed with the U.S. vision of a European confederation numbering among its members not just France, Italy, and the Benelux countries (that is, Belgium, the Netherlands, and Luxembourg) but also the United Kingdom and Germany. Already in 1949 the United States had lobbied for the creation of a European Payments Union including all these countries and had offered 350 million dollars of Marshall Plan money toward its credits.[52] To render the arrangement palatable to Britain and France, Paul Hoffmann, the chief Marshall Plan administrator, scaled back earlier plans. In proposing an EPU to the members of the OEEC, he omitted all reference to supranational institutions, acknowledging that

[51] Triffin (1957), pp. 153–158.

[52] The U.S. Treasury Department, in contrast to the State Department, opposed the creation of the EPU, preferring to expand and strengthen the International Monetary Fund. This contrast underscores the close connection between the EPU and the Marshall Plan.

earlier State Department visions of a "United States of Europe" had been overambitious and negotiations to achieve them had only alienated the British, the French, the Dutch, and others. Still, the United Kingdom, leery of anything that smacked even vaguely of political integration, opposed the EPU until it saw that resisting would have very significant costs in terms of American goodwill. The French, reluctant as always to accept full participation by Germany, resisted until they saw that the rest of Europe was prepared to go ahead without them.

Since the EPU involved the entire group of Marshall Plan recipients, there was more scope for the multilateral cancellation of bilateral imbalances than in earlier, more geographically limited arrangements. Since it was funded by the Marshall Plan, the EPU provided significant credits for use in financing temporary deficits and aiding countries experiencing transitional difficulties. In turn these came packaged with mechanisms assuring the creditors that their loans would be repaid. When a member exhausted its quota, the EPU Managing Board, composed of independent experts reporting to the Council of the OEEC, met to advise the Council and recommend the adoption of corrective policies. The Managing Board could also authorize additional credits under exceptional circumstances. These discussions were generally initiated well before a country's quota was exhausted, and it was made clear that the provision of exceptional assistance was conditional on the country's early adoption of policies of adjustment. The fact that the EPU was capitalized with Marshall Plan money, putting at stake members' goodwill with the United States, gave the participating countries another reason to take their commitments seriously.

The EPU was rendered attractive to surplus countries by the fact that it was linked to the Code of Liberalization of the OEEC, which obliged members to eliminate measures discriminating against other participants. This pledge benefited countries in strong payment positions that had felt the brunt of discrimination and had been reluctant to extend credits to their multilateral clearing partners. Members further agreed to reduce trade barriers, initially by 50 percent.

Again, the liberalization of trade disproportionately benefited countries in strong export positions.

The impact of the EPU is evident in figure 3.1, which shows the volume of intra-OEEC transactions spiking up in 1951. Much of this increase was accounted for by Germany and Austria, as shown in figure 3.2. It was precisely this increase in German trade that would not have been possible without the EPU.[53] Foreign trade had been the principal category of transactions exempted from Erhard's liberalization in 1948. With the removal of half of Germany's quantitative restrictions in 1949, consumers could finally indulge their appetite for imported goods, and the relatively minor 1949 devaluation of the deutschmark did little to deter them. The outbreak of the Korean War in 1950 led to panic buying, fears of a Soviet attack on Western Europe having been fanned by U.S. statements that the North Korean attack was part of a coordinated Soviet effort. To be sure, the war in Korea created an upsurge in orders for German industry, which had regained its mantle as the leading European producer of capital goods. But there were lags between Germany's demand for imported inputs and its production of exports.[54] And because Germany's exports started from a lower level than its imports, even with both components of the trade balance growing strongly the current-account deficit still widened in absolute terms.[55]

As Germany's current account swung into deficit and the country exhausted its EPU quota, Europe's gold and dollar reserves, which had begun rising following the 1949 devaluations, started once more to fall. Denmark, the Netherlands, and Italy all depended on the German export market and hence feared a shock if Germany

---

[53] This point is made by Temin (1995), who similarly emphasizes the severe if temporary nature of German balance-of-payments problems in 1951 and the role of the EPU in solving them.

[54] The rise in commodity prices caused by the Korean War aggravated the problem. So too did the tendency for the German government to meet its 50 percent liberalization requirement by removing restrictions on imports of raw materials (thereby continuing to protect domestic producers of manufactures), which heightened the economy's dependence on imported inputs (Wallich 1955).

[55] Giersch, Paque, and Schmieding (1993), p. 17.

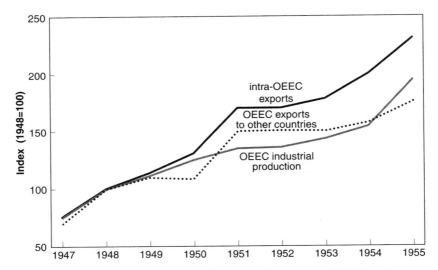

Figure 3.1. Organisation for European Economic Cooperation (OEEC) production and trade, 1947–1955. *Source*: Eichengreen (1994).

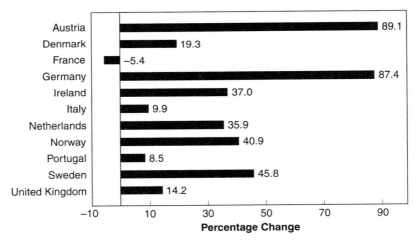

Figure 3.2. Change in intra-OEEC exports from selected European countries, 1950–1952. *Source*: International Monetary Fund, *Direction of Trade Statistics*, Historical, 1948–1980.

reverted to import controls.[56] If the Danes, the Dutch, and the Italians were forced to respond in kind, the volume of intra-European trade could implode. The German government might then be led to reimpose price and allocative controls, jeopardizing Erhard's market-oriented reforms.

The EPU quickly dispatched to Germany a delegation comprising the Swedish economist Per Jacobsson and the British civil servant Alec Cairncross. Jacobsson and Cairncross concluded that German problems could be surmounted without resort to controls if the economy were given time.[57] The EPU Managing Board therefore extended Germany an exceptional 120 million–dollar credit conditioned on macroeconomic and structural policies designed to bring the country's external accounts into balance. The German authorities agreed to maintain the prevailing exchange rate, abstain from government borrowing, and raise taxes. They increased turnover taxes to limit consumption and adjusted the structure of corporate and income taxation to limit investment. Reserve requirements on most banks were raised by 50 to 100 percent, and the discount rate was raised over the objections of Chancellor Adenauer, who feared that doing so might slow the progress of reconstruction.

The impact on Germany's balance of payments took some months to materialize. In March 1951 the authorities were authorized to reimpose quantitative restrictions but only on a temporary basis—that is, only in order to give other adjustment measures more time to work—and with the mediation of a committee of independent experts appointed by the OEEC Council to supervise the distribution of German import licenses. The BDL required companies purchasing inputs abroad to make 50 percent prepayment in foreign exchange. Erhard reluctantly restored additional items to the restricted list.

---

[56] They were not reassured by the fact that this was the response suggested by the Allied high commissioner in Germany, John McCloy, in a letter to Chancellor Konrad Adenauer. James (1996), p. 96.

[57] See Jacobsson and Cairncross (1950).

Everyone held their breath. After some months, Germany's external accounts swung into surplus. The trade deficit for the year fell to thirty million dollars, down from more than seven hundred million in 1950. Symbolic of this triumph, the Federal Republic subscribed to the General Agreement on Tariffs and Trade in October, and repaid the EPU loan five months ahead of schedule. By April 1952, more than three-quarters of all imports were again entering Germany duty free. A year later that ratio had risen to 90 percent.

These improvements were too rapid to be attributable entirely to the adjustments in macroeconomic policy, since monetary and fiscal measures take time to work. More fundamentally, the German balance of trade was already correcting itself, just as Jacobsson and Cairncross had forecast. Exports in the pipeline were now becoming available. This is not to deny that the EPU played an important role. In its absence, Germany would have had to reimpose more stringent import restrictions, forcing other countries to do likewise, or it would have had to devalue the deutschmark, which would have had a similar impact on other countries. The EPU reassured firms and households that no devaluation was in the offing, limiting panic purchases of imports to avoid subsequent price rises and helping to sustain investment. Germany's foreign customers and suppliers, who had delayed making payment for their purchases and had demanded advance payment for their sales, reverted to normal timing, moderating the pressure on the country's international accounts.

The Netherlands, which suffered a similar crisis partly as a result of the controls and restrictive macroeconomic measures to which Germany was forced to resort, negotiated a similar package. In return for an increase in its quota, the Dutch government adopted a range of restrictive monetary and fiscal measures. By the end of 1951, with the recovery of German output and demand, the Netherlands too had become a persistent creditor in the EPU.

Current-account convertibility—the removal of the exchange controls that countries used to bottle up the demand for imports—came only at the end of 1958. But as early as 1950–1951 it was clear that the EPU was working to solve the coordination problems that had prevented European countries from moving down the road of trade liberalization. Export-led growth would not have proceeded as quickly or continued as successfully in its absence. And the mechanism through which this goal was achieved—a transnational board of financial technocrats who reported not to national governments but to the OEEC—augured the role of regional integration in the long period of growth about to commence.

- FOUR -

DAWN OF THE GOLDEN AGE

If trade was one of the engines of Europe's growth in the 1950s, investment was the other. New technology, to be commercialized, had to be embodied in plant and equipment, which in turn required investment. Investment rates, including housing and infrastructure, ran more than one-quarter above those of the interwar years. Governments kept interest rates low and regulated the financial system to channel resources toward capital formation.

But countries varied enormously in the efficiency with which they deployed this additional capital. In Belgium the efficiency of investment was depressed by government programs that channeled resources into declining industries.[1] As a result, generating an additional percentage point of growth required devoting an additional 6 percent of national income to investment.[2] Norway devoted a large share of its investment to electrifying the north, an undertaking more important on political than on economic grounds. There, generating an additional percentage point of growth required devoting an extra 10 percent of national income to investment. Ireland force-fed investment to a declining agricultural sector and to infant industries in which the country lacked minimum efficient scale. Supporting an additional percentage point of growth required devoting an astonishing 14 percent of national income to investment, which is

---

[1] As described by Lamfalussy (1961).

[2] This estimate of the incremental capital–output ratio as well as those that follow are from United Nations (1962), chapter 2, p. 17.

what happens when you invest but do not grow and why the economic situation in Ireland came to be regarded as unsustainable.

More typically, investment in the amount of about 4 percent of GDP was required to generate an additional percentage point of growth. In Germany this figure (known to economists as the incremental capital–output ratio) was an even lower 3 percent. Of course, Germany was special. Industry concentrated on the production of capital goods that were in strong demand in the period of reconstruction.[3] Since recovery had been delayed until the final years of the 1940s, the country entered the 1950s with underused resources. And until the Berlin Wall went up in 1961, West Germany received a flood of immigrants from East Germany and the German-inhabited regions of Poland and Czechoslovakia.

A rapidly growing labor force moderated upward pressure on wages, which in turn allowed revenues to be plowed back into capital formation. So long as refugees from the German Democratic Republic (GDR) flooded into West Germany, there was a reserve army of labor standing at the ready. Unemployment remained in the high single digits until this influx was absorbed. Increases in labor costs were thereby limited even when the economy was expanding at breakneck speed. The same mechanism operated in the Netherlands with the return from the East Indies of Dutch settlers (some three hundred thousand, constituting 7 percent of the labor force) and in Switzerland with the importation of guest workers from Southern Europe. It operated in Italy and France with the movement of underemployed labor from agriculture to industry and services, thereby relieving supply-side pressure on the tertiary (administrative and service) sector.[4]

Table 4.1 shows the growth rate of output per worker in the 1950s, along with its determinants. Germany's leading position reflects the exceptionally rapid growth rate of capital input—faster than in any other European country—and the rapid growth of pro-

---

[3] By 1952, machinery, transportation equipment, and metals again accounted for half of German exports and more than 60 percent of German exports of manufactured goods (Buchheim 1993b, p. 80).

[4] This is the mechanism emphasized by Kaldor (1966) and Kindleberger (1967).

CHAPTER 4

TABLE 4.1
Annual growth rate of output per worker and its determinants,
1950–1960

Country	y	k	h	tfp
Austria	5.95	5.52	0.34	3.90
Belgium	2.97	4.50	0.45	1.19
Denmark	3.29	5.32	0.32	1.31
Finland	4.91	9.36	0.71	1.35
France	4.31	5.49	0.40	2.23
Germany	6.40	8.87	0.17	3.36
Greece	4.26	3.17	1.10	2.48
Ireland	2.77	1.01	0.15	2.34
Italy	5.89	3.94	0.56	4.21
Netherlands	3.98	5.29	0.32	2.02
Norway	3.02	5.45	0.29	1.03
Portugal	5.03	1.38	0.72	4.09
Spain	4.99	0.53	0.91	4.21
Sweden	2.96	6.90	0.14	0.59
United Kingdom	2.51	7.32	0.25	−0.07
Memo item: United States	1.92	0.40	0.81	1.24

Source: See appendix.
Note: y = output per worker; k = physical capital per worker; h = human capital per worker; *tfp* = total factor productivity per worker.

ductivity. Technical progress was also rapid in Austria, which shared initial conditions with Germany, and in Italy and Spain, reflecting their technological backwardness and scope for converging to technological best practice. Britain's poor performance reflects disappointing productivity growth and the slow rate of increase of educational attainment, whereas Ireland's poor performance results from the slow increase in both physical and human capital stocks.

Table 4.2 shows that the average worker was only half as productive in agriculture as in industry. The principal exceptions were Britain, where a century of free trade had forced farmers to rationalize their operations, and Denmark and the Benelux countries, which specialized in truck and dairy farming. Part of the explanation for the rapid productivity growth of this period was thus the shift of employment from low-productivity agriculture to high-productivity manufacturing and services.[5] The share of employment in agricul-

[5] As emphasized by Denison (1967) and Temin (2002) and noted in chapter 2.

TABLE 4.2

Output per person in agriculture, manufacturing, and services in Western countries, 1959 (Productivity in manufacturing = 100)

Country	Agriculture	Services
Belgium	84	66
Denmark	93	95
France	32	69
Italy	48	68
Netherlands	91	73
Portugal	37	80
United Kingdom	115	96
West Germany	42	84
Memo: United States	55	58

Source: United Nations (1962), p. 36.

ture fell by nine percentage points in Germany, eight points in Italy, and seven points in Norway in the course of the 1950s.[6] Although farmers were a powerful lobby and government protected their interests, the agricultural sector was still allowed to contract, in relative if not absolute terms.

Understanding Growth in the 1950s

Together, these observations provide a perspective on Europe's growth at the outset of the golden age. They suggest that an important determinant of growth was the starting point, which had three distinct but related dimensions. First was the extent of prior industrial development and the scope that now remained for boosting productivity and incomes by shifting workers from agriculture to industry and services. Second was the productivity gap and hence the scope for boosting incomes by converging toward technological best practice. Although the scope for such convergence was greatest in industries where the standardized products and mass-production

[6] Here again the United Kingdom was the exception. It having already largely completed the process of shedding agricultural labor, the share of employment in agriculture declined by only one percentage point over the course of the decade.

methods pioneered by the United States had yet to diffuse to Europe, opportunities existed for raising productivity by reorganizing operations and installing new technologies in the service sector as well.[7] Third was the extent of wartime disruption and therefore the scope for growing rapidly by making up lost ground.

A visual depiction of this is in figure 4.1, where each country's starting point, measured by income per person in 1950, is plotted against its annual average rate of growth over the subsequent decade.[8] Although there is a clear negative association, there is also considerable idiosyncratic national variation. For example, Germany performed better in the 1950s than can be explained by its starting point, while Ireland performed worse. Evidently, other factors were also at work.

One such factor was the structure of industrial relations. Neo-corporatist societies were more successful at limiting increases in unit labor costs and devoting resources to capital formation. They made growth a priority and were able to act accordingly. In contrast, societies lacking national unions, cohesive employers associations, and governments capable of harmonizing wage bargaining saw coordination break down as each craft- or industry-based union attempted to leapfrog the wage gains of others, and owners uncertain about the future paid out profits rather than plowing them into capacity expansion and modernization. Such countries, of which the United Kingdom and Ireland are examples, were characterized by low rates of investment and productivity growth.

[7] Europe lagged the United States in the standardization of services (financial services, for example), in the adoption of line-and-staff management systems (for railway transportation and other sectors where the coordination of activities was particularly important), and in the use of office machinery (telephones, typewriters, adding machines, vertical filing systems, and the like). These forms of office machinery had begun diffusing earlier, starting in the late nineteenth century, but their adoption remained more widespread in the 1950s in the United States than in Europe. In reality, of course, the technological and organizational changes described here are not so easily distinguished; the adoption of office machinery was typically the catalyst for the reorganization of tasks to facilitate a higher degree of worker specialization. On this see Broadberry and Ghosal (2002).

[8] With the average relationship superimposed. Note that we are now looking at income per capita, not income per worker (the growth rate on the vertical axis is also measured this way).

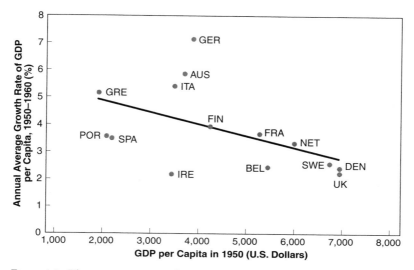

Figure 4.1. The starting point and growth in the 1950s. *Source*: Maddison (2001). *Note*: Gross domestic product per capita is expressed in 1990 U.S. dollars.

Another factor shaping growth was countries' ability to mobilize the entire range of industries needed to initiate the process of extensive growth.[9] To expand the capacity of the transportation equipment industry, for example, they needed reliable supplies of high-quality steel. Expanding the capacity of the steel industry in turn required reliable supplies of coal. But getting coal from the pit-head to the power plant in turn required transportation equipment (locomotives and railway rolling stock). In the absence of adequate installed capacity in all these industries, it was doubtful that any of them could thrive.

There were reasons to doubt that a decentralized market left to its own devices could coordinate investments in all these sectors. European countries were also constrained in their ability to import the missing elements from abroad, especially toward the beginning of the decade. Moreover, the absence of foreign competition, together with limited competition at home, rendered producers reluc-

---

[9] The interpretation here is similar to and partly inspired by the interpretation of industrialization experience in East Asia by Rodrik (1995), which in turn is beholden to the earlier work of Gerschenkron (1962) and Rosenstein-Rodan (1966).

tant to undertake dedicated investments for fear that they would be extorted by suppliers of essential inputs who would be able to use their market power to skim additional profits.

In these circumstances, industrial modernization required policies to coordinate a range of complementary investments, none of which would have been as profitable in the absence of the others. The Monnet Plan of 1948, under which the French authorities used their control of the banking system to direct credit toward particular industries, sought to stimulate complementary investments in coal, steel, electricity, cement, agricultural machinery, and transportation. In Italy this role was played by state-owned holding companies such as IRI and ENI, which enjoyed preferential access to credit and similarly undertook extensive investments in heavy industry and energy production. In Spain it was played by INI, a state holding company inherited from the 1940s. In Portugal this function was carried out by industrial conglomerates that were large enough to pursue investment projects in a number of different sectors simultaneously. In Sweden it was provided by the control of a wide range of industrial companies by the Wallenberg Group and the other so-called Fifteen Families.[10] In Austria, the government nationalized virtually all of the assets seized by the Germans after the *Anschluss* and by the Soviets during their wartime occupation, making the state the owner of the transportation, steel, chemical, engineering, and mining industries and creating one body capable of undertaking the relevant range of investments.

These, then, were alternative solutions to the same coordination problem, many of which involved government intervention. This intervention worked because the problem to be solved was no mystery. Initiating extensive growth required undertaking a constellation of complementary investments, mainly investments in mass-

[10] In the 1950s, as many as one in seven or eight Swedish industrial workers was employed in a company controlled by the Wallenberg brothers. For firms not under group control, the government facilitated information sharing and investment coordination by publishing periodic economic surveys that pooled information and assessed the compatibility of firms' investment plans. Benner (1997) provides a somewhat mixed evaluation of this aspect of public policy.

production industries pioneered previously by the United States. This was something that bureaucrats could do tolerably well.

Other countries addressed this problem less systematically and less successfully. For example, although nationalized sectors accounted for one-fifth of the British economy, in managing the public sector Britain adopted neither the ambitious planning strategy of France nor the free-market orientation of Germany. In the 1960s the government established the National Economic Development Office to draft a national investment strategy, but its plan remained on the shelves, the authorities lacking levers like those in France to direct the flow of credit.

Germany as Pacesetter

Initiating extensive growth required least in the way of intervention in Germany. The country already possessed the relevant range of industries, from coal and steel to transportation equipment and electrical machinery. Hence there was no need for an indicative plan or big push to get complementary industries up and running, since the entire range was already in place. The main thing needed now was a competitive environment in which producers could react to market opportunities—one in which they *had* to do so to survive.

One measure of the government's success in creating this environment was the low level of price–cost margins, which ran at only half the British level in the first half of the 1950s.[11] Small and medium-sized firms competed with legions of other small and medium-sized firms, requiring them to price aggressively and reduce costs regularly in order to survive. In turn this rendered German firms highly competitive on international markets. Exports rose from 9 percent of national income in 1950 to 19 percent in 1960. External conditions were propitious for German recovery. Investment demand was high throughout Europe, aiding German firms specializing in the production of capital goods. The Korean crisis stimulated the

---

[11] Data for 1954–1959 are from Crafts and Mills (2004), table 2.

demand for capital goods worldwide.[12] And just when Germany's expanding industrial sector began diversifying into the production of consumer goods, private consumption surged across Europe, reflecting rising incomes and in turn helping to sustain the growth of German exports. Rapid export growth in turn made investment profitable and attractive. Investment ran at nearly 25 percent of GDP, well in excess of the Western European average. Investment and exports were the fast-growing components of aggregate demand, and government and private consumption the slow-growing ones.[13]

The commitment to growth provided a focal point around which political parties and interest groups could coalesce. Politics still had a bad smell; by comparison, thrift and hard work were wholesome values. Memories of the abuse of power by the state led to political decentralization, encouraging healthy competition for investment by regional governments. "Ordo-liberalism," the ideology of minimal interference by government in the operation of the economy kept alive in the 1930s by academics such as Walter Eucken and his colleagues in the Freiburg School, now made a comeback in reaction against the Nazi era.[14] Economists such as Wilhelm Röpke and Alfred Müller-Armack provided the Free Democratic Party with ammunition in its fight against economic restrictions.[15] Germany thus dismantled price controls more rapidly and comprehensively than most European countries. Monetary and fiscal policies were sound and stable.[16] Bud-

---

[12] Notwithstanding its tendency also to drive up the prices of the primary inputs on which those same capital goods producers depended; see chapter 3.

[13] This was the general European pattern, but the German case was especially pronounced. Between 1950 and 1960, exports and private investment grew by 13.5 and 9.4 percent per year, respectively, while private consumption grew by 7.8 percent per year and government spending by 8.0 percent per year. Giersch, Paque, and Schmieding (1992), p. 63. The contrast in question was especially evident in the first half of the decade.

[14] Two reviews of the origins and content of ordo-liberalism are Nicholls (1994) and Labrousse and Weisz (2001).

[15] But not before the conclusion of a considerable period of uncertainty, as described in chapter 3.

[16] The German monetary authorities did in fact allow the money stock to rise by 16 percent per year between 1952 and 1960 to accommodate the rapid growth of money demand. Monetary policy was first used actively in the effort to fine-tune activity in the boom of 1955–1956, when the central bank tightened monetary conditions, and the slowdown of 1957–1958, when it tightened initially but then reversed course. Meanwhile, fiscal policy moved from strong surplus in the first half of the 1950s to close to balance in the second half of the decade,

get surpluses freed up resources for investment. Reductions in personal and corporate income taxes and the limited progressivity of marginal tax rates favored private saving.[17] The result was to channel additional resources into the metal-making and metal-using industries in which Germany had a comparative advantage and for whose products there was robust demand.

To be clear, the government by no means refrained from all intervention in the economy. There was the creation of the social market economy, notably the provision of unemployment insurance and public pensions, which gave workers the security and protection they needed to accept an intensely competitive market environment. There was public ownership in the transportation and utility sectors. The big power-generating companies received preferential access to the credits made available through Marshall Plan counterpart funds, and basic industries received favorable tax treatment on the depreciation of their investments. But once these immediate postwar bottlenecks, mainly in power generation, were loosened, public influence over investment decisions declined.[18] To be sure, the government continued to provide generous depreciation allowances for investment and a range of tax exemptions to encourage the retention of earnings, which (as intended) favored capital-intensive activities. But, beyond this, efforts to influence the composition of investment did not go. There were few attempts to save jobs of questionable viability, as in Belgium. There was no effort to build up industries critical for big-push industrialization, this being unnecessary given the relatively advanced state of the country's heavy industry.[19] The authorities allowed public investment in transportation,

reflecting the growth of defense and social spending. See Giersch, Paque, and Schmieding (1992).

[17] Marginal tax rates were reduced from 80 percent for top incomes in 1948 to 55 percent in 1955. These details remind us that statements about "lower" marginal tax rates are relative. Still, these formidable marginal rates were accompanied by a wide range of exemptions encouraging saving and investment.

[18] Buchheim (1993b), pp. 76–77.

[19] The Italian alternative of relying on state holding companies would not have been feasible in any case owing to the occupying powers' policies of deconcentration and the suspicions that would inevitably have been aroused by heavy state involvement in industry (Gramer 2004).

public utilities, and housing construction to conform to market signals rather than attempting to override them.[20]

Meanwhile there developed de facto coordination of wage negotiations by the country's unions, now organized along industrial lines, national in scope, and associated through an umbrella organization (the Deutscher Gewerkschaftsbund, or DGB).[21] In the country's cohesive employers associations they found willing partners. The metal workers went first, formulating their demands with an eye toward the anticipated reaction of other unions. Although the DGB was not directly involved in wage negotiations, it provided a forum for discussions among union leaders, and its researchers provided economic analyses to help frame the annual wage round. This enabled the metal workers to pick a level of wage increases appropriate for the economy as a whole and encouraged other unions to follow. Together with the influx of labor from the east, this delivered the wage moderation needed to sustain profitability and investment. In contrast to Britain, where unit labor costs rose by about 50 percent in the course of the 1950s, in Germany they barely budged.[22] It could be that wages lagged behind productivity because the unions did not fully anticipate the vigorous recovery of productivity and output.[23] But even if this is part of the explanation, it is hard to imagine that the unions would not have revised their expectations and adapted their behavior by the second half of the decade.[24]

Some would cite memories of high unemployment in the 1930s and the privation and inflation of the 1940s in explaining why labor

---

[20] Hennings (1982), pp. 484–485.

[21] The DGB had been founded in 1949.

[22] Unit labor costs in deutschmark terms rose by 2.2 percent per year in the 1950s, while real unit labor costs (unit labor costs in deutschmarks adjusted by the value-added deflator) fell by 0.9 percent per year.

[23] See, for example, Hennings (1982). Some commentators have also pointed to the behavior of asset prices to support the argument that it took some time for observers to realize that the economic miracle was real. Thus, not until the end of the 1950s did price–dividend ratios on German stock markets recover to pre-Depression and pre-hyperinflation levels—although this could have had as much to do with the low level from which they started as with any failure to appreciate the rapid pace of growth.

[24] Baily and Kirkegaard (2004) object to this characterization of the 1950s as a period of wage restraint, on the grounds that real wages rose robustly. This misses the point that real wages rose more slowly than productivity, allowing unit labor costs to decline and profitability and investment to be sustained at high levels.

was not more aggressive. Others would emphasize the unions' commitment to shared growth, including their willingness to share employment opportunities with newly arrived immigrants. Still, there
is no way that German labor could have acted on these impulses in
the absence of organizational arrangements capable of concerting its
wage demands.

Next in Line

Like Germany's, the industrial structure of the Netherlands was well
suited to the circumstances of the 1950s. The country specialized in
chemical and electrical industries whose products were in strong
demand and where technology was advancing with stimulus from
formal science.[25] But, in contrast to Germany, the rapid growth of
the Dutch economy cannot be ascribed to delayed recovery from
World War II. The government had carried out an early monetary
reform, cutting the money supply by two-thirds in 1945 and reducing
inflation to the low single digits.[26] Over the subsequent five years,
output rose by 10 percent per year, faster than anywhere else in
Western Europe.[27] To be sure, labor productivity had not recovered
fully by 1950. A backlog of attractive investment opportunities remained. But if the incompleteness of the country's recovery can explain why growth was unusually rapid in absolute terms, it cannot
explain why the Netherlands continued to outperform the Western
European average.

The roots of this success lay in the role of the country's neocorporatist institutions. The crisis of the 1930s had led to extensive
discussions between the Social Democrats, who moderated their socialist agenda in the interest of compromise, and progressive Catholics alienated from liberal ideology by years of economic depression.
During the occupation, the Nazis then used these social partners

---

[25] This favorable industrial structure also helps to explain why the country did well compared with Belgium, an obvious counterpart, which will be considered later in this chapter.

[26] Except in 1947–1948, when the inflation rate reaccelerated to 10 percent.

[27] This provides a sense of what would have been possible in Germany in the second half
of the 1940s in the absence of economic, financial, and political constraints.

as a mechanism for administering prices and allocating resources, regularizing their interaction. After the war, the Labor Foundation (Stichting van de Arbeid) was quickly established as a meeting place for union and employers organizations. The tripartite Social and Economic Council (Sociaal-Economische Raad), with members drawn one-third from trade unions, one-third from employers associations, and one-third from a pool of independent experts, was then created to provide a forum for the discussion of wages, investment, and social policies.

From there it was a small step to coordinating negotiations between the unions and employers organizations. Wage guidelines were issued by the Board of Government Mediators, which acted on behalf of the minister for social affairs.[28] The Social and Economic Council then advised the government on whether or not to authorize the proposed increase, and the collective agreement came into effect upon receiving the approval of the Board of Mediators. The process was repeated annually. In 1950, all of this was given a legislative foundation.

These arrangements delivered wage moderation and a high degree of flexibility. As a result of substantial devaluations in 1944 and 1949, the Netherlands started the decade with hourly labor costs only about 80 percent those of its principal European competitors. Labor cooperated in preserving the country's competitive position; thus, in 1951, when the Korean War drove up raw material prices, leading to a deterioration in the terms of trade, the unions agreed to a 5 percent cut in real wages in order to help sustain economic growth. Unit labor costs rose only two-thirds as much as the Western European average over the 1950s. The Netherlands thus emerged as a low-cost producer; the result was a surge of exports, which were the fastest growing component of aggregate demand. As late as 1960, wage labor costs were fully 20 percent below those prevailing in Belgium and Germany.[29]

---

[28] In practice those guidelines were developed jointly with the Foundation of Labor and were informed by the forecasts of the Central Planning Bureaus.

[29] Provoking complaints in those countries of unfair Dutch competition. See Visser and Hemerijck (1997), p. 93.

TABLE 4.3

Growth of gross domestic product and its components in the Netherlands, 1951–1973 (Average annual growth rates, constant prices)

	1951–1963	1963–1973
GDP	4.4	5.5
Private consumption	4.9	5.3
Government consumption	4.3	2.6
Private investment	6.1	7.4
Government investment	6.9	2.8
Exports	8.3	10.4
Imports	8.5	9.8

Source: van Zanden (1998), p. 135.

The resulting profits helped to underwrite investment, 60 to 80 percent of investment in industry being financed by retained earnings. Gross fixed nonresidential investment ran at 18 percent of GDP in the 1950s, higher even than in Germany. After exports, investment was the fastest growing component of GDP. (See table 4.3.) The government sharpened the incentive to allocate resources in this direction by levying higher taxes on dividends than on retained earnings. As in Germany, it interfered only modestly in the allocation of resources, limiting its industrial policies mainly to modernizing the electricity supply.[30]

Austria, another country that shared with Germany both a border and an inheritance of corporatist institutions, also grew strongly in the 1950s. A small economy with strong links to its neighbors and a substantial industrial base, it adapted smoothly to an environment where the dual motors for growth were exports and investment in industry. Prior to 1934, Austria had possessed a strong but ideologically divided union movement; now it placed its unions under a party-unaffiliated umbrella organization, the Austrian Trade Union

---

[30] In addition, the government extended subsidies to two companies where political pressure to do so was overwhelming. These were Hoogovens, the integrated steel producer, and Royal Dutch Soda, a newly founded chemicals firm. See van Zanden (1998), pp. 142–143. In addition, provincial and municipal governments provided financial assistance to a variety of local enterprises. Nonetheless, van Zanden concludes that when it came to specific measures, Dutch industrial policy was limited, and that government policies were largely subordinated to the market—the industrialization plans of the period 1949–1963 were far more important "in the public mind" than in practice.

Federation (Österreichischer Gewarkschaftsbund, or ÖGB). Social
Democrats shared the leading positions in government, starting with
the Grand Coalition of the immediate postwar years, and in management of nationalized industries, giving labor a stake in the stability
of both economic and political processes. On the employer side,
membership in the Austrian Economic Chamber was universal. Although bargaining took place between employers and sectoral
unions, the ÖGB and the Chamber exercised oversight, coordinating wage setting economy-wide. Throughout the 1950s, the unions
followed a policy of "deliberate wage restraint . . . designed to
strengthen Austrian exports in world markets."[31] Starting in 1957,
coordination was reinforced by a newly created Parity Commission,
with representatives from government, unions, and industry charged
with identifying appropriate levels for prices and wages. Although
the Parity Commission did not regulate wage setting, its recommendations provided a focal point for negotiations and strengthened the
oversight of ÖGB leadership over its constituent unions.

Another distinctive aspect of Austria's economic structure was
the fact that the social partners owned shares in the central bank.
In this period when there was a consensus favoring wage moderation
and high investment, the cooperation of the central bank helped to
cement the bargain. Interest rates were adjusted to reinforce incentives for investment, and the unions could have confidence that
price developments would be consistent with what they had expected when agreeing to the wage bargain.

France, a country whose performance was perceived as disappointing by contemporaries, is in fact a more ambiguous case. In
terms of the growth of aggregate GDP, it was squarely in the middle
of the European growth leagues. When one instead considers GDP
per capita, France's growth in the 1950s was surpassed only by that
of Germany, Austria, Italy, Switzerland, and Greece.[32] That the

---

[31] Katzenstein (1984), p. 39.

[32] The rankings in table 4.1, based on output per worker rather than output per capita,
differ in minor ways, but the implication is the same.

country's performance was not more favorable in aggregate terms was a function of the slow growth of its labor force, nothing more.[33] But this was cold comfort for a country with France's geopolitical ambitions, since the ability to project force abroad depended at least as much on aggregate as on per capita income growth. The comparison with Germany, which expanded nearly twice as fast in the aggregate, rendered the fact that GNP growth was not faster of even greater concern to French observers.

France also suffered from slow export growth and chronic reserve losses.[34] Inflation and the consequent deterioration in external competitiveness reflected the high level of demand applied by the government. In an effort to bottle up the pressure, the authorities deployed a panoply of exchange and trade controls, making France one of the most protected economies in the OEEC.[35] Responding to complaints from producers who found it hard to cope with import competition, the government regularly disregarded the OEEC's schedule for removing import quotas. In 1952 it reinstituted quotas in response to balance-of-payments difficulties.[36] In 1954 it began once more to remove quotas and relax currency restrictions; with Germany expanding its export share and moving toward currency convertibility, there was pressure to follow suit. But France did so only under the cover of a "special provisional compensatory tax" of 10 to 15 percent on most freed commodities, designed to protect producers from the import shock.

As a result, the openness ratio (exports plus imports as a share of GDP) remained unchanged between 1950 and 1959, a period of

[33] From 1946 through 1962, the economically active population grew by just 0.1 percent per year, far below the European average. The growth of the labor force then accelerated to 0.8 percent per year over the next fifteen years, reflecting the arrival of repatriates from Algeria and then entry into the labor market of the baby boom generation. See Sautter (1982).

[34] This competitiveness problem received official recognition in 1954 with the establishment of a national commission for the study of disparities between French and foreign prices.

[35] Lynch (1997), p. 128.

[36] The alternative would have been to raise taxes, but the bill proposing this was defeated in the National Assembly by the Communists and the Gaullists, forcing the government of Edgar Faure to resign.

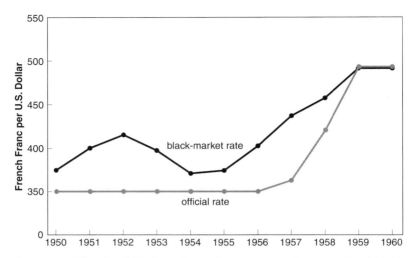

Figure 4.2. Official and black-market exchange rates in France, 1950–1960 (Annual average exchange rates). *Sources:* International Monetary Fund, *International Financial Statistics* (various years); Pick (various years).

strongly rising trade ratios in most other countries.[37] Many sectors remained only lightly touched by import competition. Even at the end of the decade, imports accounted for only 8 percent of domestic consumption of manufactured goods and for less than 5 percent in fully half of all manufacturing industries.[38]

But even these harsh trade restrictions could not contain the pressure on the balance of payments. The situation was again in contrast to Germany, whose external accounts were in strong surplus after 1951. Between 1955 and 1957, with government expenditure rising in response to the conflict in Algeria, France lost two-thirds of its foreign reserves. The franc's black-market exchange rate against the dollar ranged far above the official rate of 350.[39] (See figure 4.2.) Still

[37] The only other countries where this ratio failed to rise were the United Kingdom, Ireland, and Italy, for reasons described later.

[38] Outside manufacturing, the ratio was only a little higher, at 13 percent.

[39] The low black-market discount through the spring of 1951 reflected first the transitory effects of the 1949 devaluation and then the unusual strength of French industrial exports (largely steel products and chemicals) associated with Korean War demands. It was a purely temporary phenomenon.

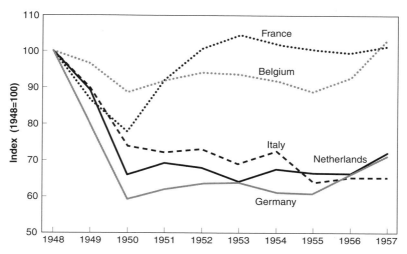

Figure 4.3. Unit labor cost indexes in U.S. dollars. *Source:* Eichengreen (1994), p. 63.

the authorities hesitated to devalue, invoking French *grandeur* and the disappointing results of the 1949 currency adjustment, when the upward movement of wages and prices had neutralized the change in relative prices after two years.[40] (See figure 4.3.)

Continuing reserve losses finally forced the authorities to devalue in 1957. But again the gains in competitiveness were dissipated quickly, reflecting the failure to adopt complementary policies. Although the government sought to encourage wage restraint, it had a well-known habit of surrendering to strike activity. The authorities had regularly conceded wage increases to buy labor peace, for example following the general strike of August 1953, perceived by some, in more than a little panic, as a "revolutionary situation."[41] An eighteen-month plan launched in 1954 had again sought to buy labor peace, this time by increasing wages by 10 percent. This fed

[40] Those with longer memories also recalled the disappointing results of the 1936 devaluation, whose impact on competitiveness had been neutralized even more quickly by increases in labor costs.

[41] *Economist* (15 August 1953), cited in Armstrong, Glyn, and Harrison (1991), p. 111.

inflation, since minimum wages and, indirectly, the entire wage structure had been indexed to inflation since 1952.[42] Thus, when the government devalued in 1957, workers had every reason to think that employers and the government would again accede to pressure for compensatory wage increases, as they in fact did.

At the root of these problems was the fragmentation of industrial relations. Worker representation was divided between a half dozen major unions with different ideological orientations and histories of mutual hostility. Strong political identification and ideological orientation meant that the unions could mobilize their members for strikes and demonstrations but could not compel them to cooperate with one another. Craft-based identities remained stronger than in countries with more large enterprises and more extensive urbanization. Even memories of the Paris Commune, in which twenty thousand workers had died, limited the government's capacity to encourage solidaristic behavior. For all these reasons, the coordination necessary to restrain wage growth was lacking. This meant inadequate international competitiveness, leading the government to rely on trade restrictions to maintain external balance, as a result of which the country did not share the benefits of export-led growth. Investment rates fell rather than rising in the first half of the 1950s, mirroring the fall in the share of profits in national income and the slow growth of the retained earnings on which firms relied for investment finance.[43]

Yet, despite all this, the rate of growth of output per worker was right at the European average. In part the explanation for why the economy did so well lies in the extent of wartime damage. Prewar levels of production were matched only in 1951. France thus started with significant underused capacity, including underused labor in agriculture. The country could grow simply by putting more people

[42] The indexation of minimum wages was also a factor in the reluctance of the authorities to adjust the exchange rate in response to the country's chronic balance-of-payments problems; they feared that any improvement in competitiveness obtained by changing the dollar rate would quickly be eroded by inflation.

[43] At the beginning of the 1950s, thirteen of thirty-seven French industries relied entirely on retained earnings for investment finance (Adams 1989, p. 69).

to work in the modern sector. Where production was concentrated in small, family-owned-and-operated firms that lacked the scale needed for adopting up-to-date technology, a little bit of rationalization and consolidation went a long way.

But to make investment worthwhile, capacity had to be adjusted in a range of up- and downstream industries. This constraint bound tightly in a period when dollars were scarce and balance-of-payments problems prevented bottlenecks from being loosened by importing raw materials and intermediate inputs. Producers were reluctant to undertake the requisite investments in the absence of assurances that other complementary investments would also take place. Given the absence of competing foreign suppliers, especially in the aftermath of the war, producers feared that suppliers would be able to charge whatever they wanted for essential inputs, vitiating the advantages of investment.

This coordination problem provided a rationale for indicative planning. This initiative was not without precedent; already under Vichy, observers had noted how shortages of energy had constrained the growth of the steel industry, which in turn constrained the growth of steel-using industries such as mechanical and electrical engineering. In response, that regime had created a Ministry of Industrial Production and an agency for allocating industrial products, the Office Central de Réparation des Produits Industriels, which acted on the basis of information provided by committees established at the industry level.[44] Inspired by this precedent, Charles de Gaulle, whose laissez-faire instincts were tempered by a belief in the need for a strong state, backed the establishment of a Planning Commissariat. Created by decree in January 1946 and led by Jean Monnet, the maverick businessman and diplomat who had spent much of the war in London arranging for the supply of U.S. matériel to the French and British armies, this new Commissariat soon devel-

---

[44] Lynch (1997), pp. 14–15. More generally, France had a considerable history of mixed enterprises, private enterprises in which the state held an equity investment or controlled the management. It had already taken a modest step toward a coordinated economy in 1924, establishing the National Economic Council, a consultative body of representatives of labor, management, and consumers.

oped into a force to be reckoned with. Charged with drafting a multiyear blueprint for reconstruction and modernization, Monnet's first plan, scheduled to run from 1947 through 1950 (but ultimately extended through 1952 so that it terminated together with Marshall aid), targeted for expansion the coal, steel, electricity, cement, agricultural machinery, and transportation industries.[45] Subsequent plans cast their net more widely while still focusing on basic industry. Planners quickly came to refer to the need to foster a "concerted economy" (*économie concertée*) in which the expansion of capacity in related industries was effectively coordinated.

To oversee the exercise, the Commissariat général du Plan was established under the Ministry of Economic Affairs. *Commissions verticals* dealt with relations between upstream and downstream industries, while *commissions horizontals* dealt with economy-wide issues such as supplies of energy and labor. Representatives of government and management (many of whom had graduated from the same *grandes écoles*) sat on these commissions together with union leaders and members of professional organizations. Their discussions served as a mechanism for encouraging firms in different sectors to move ahead with investment plans, the payoff to which depended on others moving ahead with similar plans at the same time. As van der Wee (1986) puts it, these efforts at coordination prevented supply bottlenecks from impeding the development of a new industrial structure. Or, in Hackett's words, planning "makes it possible to take an all-embracing view of the prospects of the economy and encourages the different sectors—public or private—to work to the same general outline of future developments"—to coordinate their decision making, in other words.[46]

The government used a variety of devices to encourage complementary investments, including the allocation of scarce raw materi-

---

[45] There was some irony in the fact that this ambitious plan, crafted by the soon-to-be father of the European Community, relied on reparations and obligatory German exports of coal to meet its targets. See Parsons (2003), p. 39.

[46] Hackett (1965), p. 16. McArthur and Scott adopt a more skeptical attitude toward the impact of planning, but they similarly speak of its role in inducing different firms and interest groups to "act in a coordinated fashion." McArthur and Scott (1969), p. 485.

als and permission for a company to use foreign exchange to purchase equipment abroad. Above all, control of credit enabled it to channel resources to favored sectors. In 1948, the Modernization and Equipment Fund (Fonds de modernisation et d'équipement) was created to make long-term loans to nationalized industries and funded with Marshall aid. The authorities extended special "productivity loans" at favorable interest rates. The four big nationalized banks were expected to win the approval of the Bank of France and the Commissariat before extending industrial loans. Firms were required to obtain the authorization of the Treasury, which consulted with the Planning Commissariat, before floating bonds. The government in turn guaranteed private placements of bonds by companies whose investments they sought to promote.

In the course of the 1950s, alternative channels developed for providing credit to industry, complicating these efforts at official control. The effectiveness of the plan now relied more on information sharing—on encouraging concerted action by firms with potential investments whose profitability depended on other firms' potential investments—than it did on control of credit. Planning provided information critical for decision making in a period when there did not exist freely functioning capital markets to transmit price signals and allow investors to hedge risks. The Bank of France, having been nationalized after the war, established the Service central de risques to gather information from the commercial banks about firms requesting large loans. This put the government in a position to criticize investment plans that it saw as diversionary or unwise. Business leaders pooled information on what was happening in their industries when meeting under the aegis of the Planning Commission, overcoming the obstacles to coordination posed by the absence of not just free capital markets but also basic census data.[47] As Estrin and Holmes put it, "Indicative planning is based on the notion that . . . the allocation of resources can be improved by pro-

---

[47] Shonfield (1965, p. 127) notes that "compared with almost any of the advanced industrial countries, including Germany, Sweden, and Holland, the French started off with a smaller quantity and poorer quality of statistical information."

viding individuals and firms with information about everyone else's behavior."[48] Such information was important for what Carré, Dubois, and Malinvaud refer to as "consistency among decisions influencing the medium future."[49]

Monnet himself saw the role for the Commissariat général du Plan as insulating policy from political influence. The advantage of vesting power in the hands of a few far-sighted technocrats lay in removing it from the hands of politicized ministries that otherwise would have brought about an even worse allocation of resources.[50] If the counterfactual is not market-led investment but an allocation of resources by ministers motivated by political considerations, then delegating power over this decision to a set of independent technocrats could have been efficiency-enhancing.

Still others argue that the plan functioned as a kind of insurance policy that reconciled the citizenry to the restoration of the market economy and the removal of restrictions on German production. France's experience with the market in the decade leading up to the war had not been a happy one. In the absence of effective intervention, the economic crisis of the 1930s had ground on for longer than virtually anywhere else. The Monnet Plan signaled that the authorities were now prepared to place a heavier stabilizing hand on the economic tiller. "The First Plan was more than a mere document

---

[48] Estrin and Holmes (1983), p. 7.

[49] Carré, Dubois, and Malinvaud (1975), p. 460. The authors go on to characterize the consistency of such decisions with longer-term implications as something on which the market can "provide little light" (in the absence, one should add, of freely functioning capital markets). In Sweden, the government undertook periodic long-term planning surveys, which similarly sought to pool information on the consistency of investment plans and facilitate coordination. Benner (1997, p. 96) quotes a passage from the 1956 survey making this point: "Within several large companies plans are now drawn up for production, investments etc. for the next five or ten years. . . . What is obvious is that planning in these different areas are [sic] mutually dependent. It seems to be valuable to compile these different plans, to investigate whether they are compatible, and as far as possible elucidate to what extent the claims made on society's total resources are fair in relation to their development, as far as this can be assessed. One of the most important purposes with a long-term survey of this kind is to fulfill this service function in relation to industry and various public activities."

[50] Monnet's biographer points in this direction when he writes of "the enormous difficulties that had to be overcome to keep to any long-term goals at all. Most of them were rooted in a regime for which weak government and short-term considerations were a way of life. To establish investment as a priority in such a system was an endless struggle." Duchêne (1994), p. 178.

outlining some hopes, or a collection of urgent investment pro-
grammes," as Sautter put it. "It was a shared belief that growth, productivity and the opening to the outside world would make possible
a non-zero sum game for all." In this way the Monnet Plan and
its successors "made the idea of an opening to foreign competition
acceptable to a country with deeply protectionist reflexes."[51] More
open economies tend to have larger governments, reflecting the role
of the public sector in providing insurance to those least able to
cope with the uncertain consequences of market competition.[52] The
adoption of the First Plan signaled the readiness of the French government to assume this responsibility.

Similarly, the Monnet Plan, by emphasizing the need to build
up capacity in coal, steel, cement, and other basic industries, reassured the citizens of France that their country would not again be
at the mercy of Germany's industrial might. In this way the Monnet
Plan complemented the Marshall Plan and the European Coal and
Steel Community. Steel, in particular, was associated with national
security.[53] The Monnet Plan, by increasing domestic supplies of steel
and other basic products, promised to enhance that security. In turn
this encouraged French acquiescence to the removal of ceilings on
German industrial production, creating a more favorable international environment for economic revival and growth. The initial
goal of the planners was to strengthen the country's military capacity
in order to prevent a recurrence of "the humiliation of 1940," the
disastrous defeat of the French army in the Second World War. The
First Plan followed on the heels of American announcements that
France's postwar security would be guaranteed by the United Nations and the atomic bomb, and not by a large-scale U.S. military
commitment in Europe, which convinced the French of the importance of reconstructing their economy faster than Germany's. This
explains the plan's concentration on heavy industry at the expense
of food processing, consumer goods, and housing.[54]

[51] Sautter (1982), p. 456.
[52] See the evidence in Rodrik (1998).
[53] The same was true in Eastern Europe, as discussed in chapter 5.
[54] See, for example, the discussion in Baum (1958), p. 37.

Giving indicative planning credit for France's positive economic performance in the 1950s is controversial, especially since government direction failed so miserably at other times and places. One should take care not to simply echo the self-congratulatory evaluations of the planners; as de Gaulle's adviser Jacques Rueff, himself a skeptic of planning, once put it, "planners are like the rooster who believes that his crowing causes the sun to rise." But there are good reasons why it makes sense to think that indicative planning worked well in this period. The direction of resources by civil servants was straightforward insofar as there was relatively little uncertainty about the most productive investments.[55] In their analysis of French planning, Estrin and Holmes make this point. "The French economy was relatively simple when indicative planning was introduced in 1946, so the planners could expect to have a large impact on the system as a whole by focusing attention on easily identifiable 'important' sectors. Moreover, the environmental path of the economy was relatively stable and predictable."[56]

But this extensive system of subsidies, concessionary loans, and cross indexation led to an overemphasis on heavy industry to the neglect of housing, agriculture, and consumer goods. It fed the tendency toward excessive public spending. Government, running persistent deficits partly as a result of its effort to finance investment by public enterprise, had a leg up in the competition with the private sector for funds. Not only was there the modernization and equipment fund, but other government agencies spent on infrastructure, housing, and rural development, and there was no appetite for paying taxes to foot the bill. (See table 4.4.)

By the end of the 1950s the French economy had become more complex and thus more difficult for bureaucrats to direct. Financial markets had begun to recover, providing other mechanisms for

[55] An account emphasizing the extent and importance of the technological backlog in the French case is Baum (1958).

[56] Estrin and Holmes (1983), p. 18. In this sense, the successes of indicative planning in France reflected many of the same factors accounting for the relatively successful performance of the even more heavily planned economies of Central and Eastern Europe in these same years. See the discussion in chapter 5.

TABLE 4.4

Central government budgetary expenditures and receipts, France, 1945–1954 (Billions of current francs)

	1945	1946	1947	1948	1949	1950	1951	1952	1953	1954
Operating expenditures of civil services	296	345	444	681	842	1,114	1,297	1,394	1,559	1,736
Total capital expenditures	52	165	239	578	828	832	755	809	859	312
of which:										
Equipment of civil services	14	43	70	98	150	121	140	145	179	⎫ 500
Economic and social investments	3	39	77	280	432	426	303	332	350	⎭
War damage and construction	35	83	92	200	246	285	312	332	330	312
Military expenditures	175	171	231	332	377	463	857	1,269	1,242	1,110
Deficit of special treasury accounts	—	—	—	—	—	—	—	70	62	55
Total expenditures	523	681	914	1,591	2,047	2,409	2,909	3,542	3,722	3,713
Total receipts	238	462	685	1,050	1,487	1,952	2,161	2,698	2,940	2,903
Budget deficit	285	219	229	541	560	457	748	844	782	810

Source: Baum (1958).

111

transmitting information relevant to investment decisions. Industrial statistics improved with the creation of INSEE (the French National Institute for Statistics and Economic Studies) and the establishment of the Commission des Comptes et des Budgets Économiques de la Nation and their production of national income accounts and related production and investment data.[57] Gradually the plan came to play a smaller role. The commitment to the market economy was then consolidated following de Gaulle's return to power in 1958 and his appointment of Antoine Pinay, a fiscal conservative, as finance minister. Once a second, more successful devaluation in 1958 loosened the balance-of-payments constraint, it became easier to import inputs, rendering it less essential that the entire range of complementary investments be undertaken at home. French industry had an increasingly broad range of suppliers, both domestically and abroad. And with the establishment of the European Economic Community (EEC), other mechanisms now existed for binding Germany into Europe.

Thus, even if the façade of planning was retained, the reality was scaled back. The Rueff Plan, adopted in conjunction with the 17.5 percent devaluation in 1958, imposed drastic cuts in subsidies, significantly increasing the prices of foodstuffs and other consumer goods. Income was allowed to shift toward profits, providing additional finance for investment. Depreciation allowances were adjusted to provide incentives for capital formation. The Rueff Plan was indicative, as it were, of France's rededication to market-led growth. It signaled that the country was now ready to join Europe in pursuing growth based on exports and investment.[58]

Italy, like France, had experienced two decades of protection by the end of World War II. Agriculture was specialized in the production of cereals because of Mussolini's policy of self-sufficiency, while

---

[57] A law of 7 June 1951 compelled private cooperation with this process by establishing the principle of obligatory, centralized, and confidential gathering of statistics.

[58] There was then a brief revival of interest in planning, reflecting hopes that more stable government would enhance the role of the state, leading to the preparation first of a two-year Interim Plan and then the Fourth Plan of 1962–1965. Interest in the exercise quickly dissipated, however. McArthur and Scott (1969) write of widespread "disillusionment" and "disappointment" on the part of the advocates of *planisme*.

industry was dominated by traditional branches such as food pro-cessing and textiles. Hence, few Italian industries were positioned to capitalize on export opportunities. The General Tariff that went into effect in July 1950 then imposed high import duties, averaging 24 percent. As a result of all this, exports contributed less to growth than in most of the other top performers prior to the advent of the EEC.[59] The share of exports in manufacturing value added rose by only 2 percent between 1951 and 1958. The openness ratio (imports plus exports as a share of GDP) fell between 1950 and 1959, some-thing that happened as well only in the United Kingdom and Ire-land, two notoriously poor performers in terms of trade.

To be sure, Italian leaders such as Alcide De Gasperi and Luigi Einaudi, prime minister and president, respectively, in the critical early postwar period, looked forward to the day when Italian industry could compete with Europe's leaders, By bringing the country into the European Coal and Steel Community in 1951, they signaled their intention of opening to Europe. And, already at the beginning of the decade, foreign markets mattered importantly for producers of certain products, including typewriters, refrigerators, washing machines, sewing machines, and automobiles. Usually these were the products of Italian companies that had acquired significant for-eign markets before the war and were now able to use their contacts and experience to reestablish a foreign presence: Fiat, Pirelli, and Olivetti were leading examples.[60] Notwithstanding their export sales, domestic demand played a larger role and export demand a smaller one than in Europe's other high-growth economies.[61]

[59] Of which Italy was a founding member, in 1958.

[60] In Fiat's case, many of these early post–World War II exports apparently were sold at a loss in an effort to build market share. This strategy was feasible because of the profits that could be made in the heavily protected domestic market. In the 1950s, import tariffs on motor vehicles averaged 40 percent, and even then imports were also subject to strict quota limits. The OEEC Code of Liberalization required the removal of quotas on most imports, as we have seen. Italy used the limited leeway it still possessed to impose quota restrictions mainly to protect the auto industry (along with motorcycles, printing machines, and selected agricul-tural products).

[61] Thus, real exports and investment grew at roughly the same pace between 1950 and 1960. In Germany, in contrast, exports grew almost twice as fast as investment. In the Nether-lands exports grew half again as fast.

In addition, industrial relations were less effectively coordinated than in Europe's other high-performing economies. When Mussolini established four labor confederations—covering industry, agriculture, commerce, and banking, respectively—to act as umbrella organizations for Italy's thirty-two national industry-based federations, the country's unions were only starting to emerge from an early period of heavy repression.[62] The Fascist union structure then collapsed at the end of World War II, leaving little on which to build. As Allen and Stevenson put it, "As with many other aspects of Italian life, there was a need to rebuild institutions that had not been operational for some twenty years and which, before then, had had a short history."[63]

The Italian Confederation of Labor (or CGIL), which built from the top down, quickly enrolled a large membership. But it possessed few well-organized local unions or experienced union leaders. The effort to create a national trade union confederation then came to grief in 1948, when first the Catholics, then the Social Democrats, and finally the anti-Catholic Republican groups all established their own confederations, leaving only the Communists in the old organization. Employers associations were thus forced to negotiate with rival union alliances, frustrating efforts to solve collective action problems.[64]

As the incapacity of the union confederations became apparent, plant-level bargaining led by locally elected factory councils became increasingly prevalent, decentralizing the process further. In Fiat's plants, these councils were typically led by members of the Communist Party, who were predisposed to disruptive action. To minimize the risk of workplace disruptions, the government acceded to requests for generous tariff protection on the grounds that this would enable companies to raise wages and thereby buy economic and social peace.[65] Thus, the inadequate coordination of wage bargaining

[62] The slow growth and late consolidation of the union movement in Italy can be understood as a concomitant of the country's relatively late industrialization (Horowitz 1963).

[63] Allen and Stevenson (1974), p. 132.

[64] In addition, the unions were unsuccessful at organizing recent migrants from the center and the south, who accounted for a growing share of unskilled and semiskilled industrial labor.

[65] Fauri (1996), p. 201.

and the slow growth of Italian exports were two sides of the same coin, just as coordination, wage restraint, and export growth went hand in hand in other countries.

All this makes it more than a little difficult to understand how Italy could have grown as rapidly as it did. To be sure, the country had undergone early and successful inflation stabilization in 1947 as a result of new reserve requirements on bank lending designed by Einaudi, then still minister of the budget. This facilitated reactivation of the price mechanism, giving the country a head start on reconstruction. Textile exports, which still accounted for 40 percent of Italian exports, were aided by labor problems in Britain and the temporary suspension of Japanese and German production. The outbreak of the Korean War then further stimulated the demand for exports. Italy also had the "advantage" of starting out behind. With 90 percent of firms employing five or fewer workers, industry had only begun to explore the use of mass-production methods. Fiat, among the technological leaders, had begun experimenting with assembly lines before World War II but without approaching the division of labor or levels of product standardization achieved by Ford. Considerable efficiency gains could now be reaped by installing conveyer belts and assembly lines in Italian factories and proceeding further in the direction of standardization.[66] Industries where American equipment and methods were now adopted *en masse*, with a strongly favorable impact on productivity, included petroleum refining, textiles, motorcycles, and, of course, automobiles.[67] Consistent with this observation, Italy was one of the European countries with the highest payoffs to investment in the 1950s, as measured by the incremental capital–output ratio.

[66] Much of this American equipment and machinery having been imported using funds and technical assistance from the Marshall Plan. In 1947, the U.S. Export-Import Bank loaned ten million dollars to Fiat to finance its purchase of new equipment, the main Fiat factory having suffered severe damage from bombing in 1942. The firm then obtained nearly thirty million dollars in Marshall Plan funds (more than any other Italian company) to purchase additional equipment in the United States. Fauri (1996), p. 178.

[67] The country had a surprisingly large stock of scientists and engineers, facilitating this process of technology transfer. Table 2.6 illustrates this for a slightly later period.

Moreover, nearly half of all employment was still in agriculture. An extensive land reform in 1950, when more than two million acres of land were compulsorily acquired from *latifondisti* and re-distributed to the landless, now encouraged more intensive cultivation. This allowed resources to be shifted from agriculture to industry and labor from south to north. Elastic supplies of labor fueled the growth of new industries producing and exporting consumer and producer durables. The famous instance was the migration of southern farm laborers to Turin, Fiat's home. Graphically portraying the income and productivity differentials motivating this migration, one commentator writes, "Southerners would arrive in rags, sleep on park benches or at the train station, and wait as long as it took to get a job in a Fiat plant."[68] In fact, the fall in the share of employment in agriculture, from 46 to 36 percent of total employment between 1951 and 1958, was matched by strongly rising employment shares not just in industry but also services, where productivity is harder to measure. Fiat and Turin, though important, were not the entire story.

Finally, the state holding companies occupying the industrial high ground helped to coordinate investment across the energy and industrial sectors, relaxing supply-side bottlenecks. These entities were another legacy of the country's history: the Istituto per la Ricostruzione Industriale (IRI), set up in 1933 to oversee the portfolio of companies previously managed by three troubled banks, brought under public control firms engaged in iron and steel production, metal working, shipbuilding, transportation, and banking.[69] IRI in turn spawned state holding companies such as the Ente Nazionale Idrocarburi (ENI) to invest in oil and gas supplies, natural gas deposits having been discovered in the Po Valley in the 1940s as a result of the efforts of Enrico Mattei, the headstrong entrepreneur given the unenviable task of closing down Mussolini's loss-making oil-

---

[68] Friedman (1988), p. 62.

[69] IRI subsequently enlarged and diversified its field of activity, becoming the second largest corporation in Europe in the 1960s. After years of criticism that it was less suitable to an environment of intensive growth, it was finally liquidated in 2000.

exploration industry, who then became the head of ENI.[70] Without ENI there would not have been enough energy to justify investment in the modernization of industrial capacity. And without IRI there would not have been enough investment in industry, in the steel industry in particular, to provide Italy's energy producers with the reliable demand needed to justify heavy investment in energy supplies and to ensure that downstream producers of machinery and motor vehicles had adequate supplies of high-quality steel.[71] As Shonfield has put it, "the management of IRI viewed itself as the guardian of a number of the key sectors of modern industry, on whose efficiency the performance of the rest of the Italian economy would depend. This was outstandingly true of steel, with more than half of the industry in IRI's hands. If the price of Italian steel was too high, or the quality below the best international standard, there would be little chance for Italy's engineering exports in world markets."[72]

State holding companies addressed these coordination problems in a manner analogous to indicative planning. They freed firms from hold-up problems that otherwise would have discouraged dedicated investments. Enjoying preferential access to credit from specialized banking institutions controlled by the state, the leading examples of which were Mediobanca and IMI, they accounted for 20 percent of all industrial investment in the 1950s.

As Italy converged toward the technological frontier, the direction of resources by bureaucrats became more problematic and the justification for public intervention in private decisions weakened. Opening to Europe and allowing producers to avail themselves of alternative sources of supply diminished the hold-up problems that

[70] ENI subsequently broadened its activities to engineering, chemicals, textiles, and nuclear energy. This earlier experience spawned the Ente Partecipazioni e Finanziamento Industrie Manifatturiere (EFIM) to create basic industries, such as nonferrous metals, that did not exist in Italy.

[71] Cement is another case in point. Without adequate energy it would not have paid to expand cement-producing capacity, but without additional cement-producing capacity it would not have paid to increase energy production. And short supplies of cement, in turn, would have slowed the development of the key construction industry.

[72] Shonfield (1965), p. 186.

would have discouraged investment in the absence of the state holding companies. The heavy hand of the state, and the clientelism
and restraints on competition that it bred, created growing problems. Policy and the investment activities of the state holding companies increasingly favored special regional and industrial interests
at the expense of economy-wide growth.[73]

But these were problems for the future. In the 1950s, these same
factors were invoked as explanations for what was increasingly referred to as the Italian Miracle.

The Laggards

Ireland, the United Kingdom, and Belgium brought up the rear of
the pack. These countries performed poorly both absolutely and relative to expectations (that is, relative to the cross-country trend
evident in figure 4.1).[74]

Ireland was the most dramatic outlier. The main obstacles to
growth were restrictive policies inherited from earlier years, starting
with the import tariffs put in place by the Fianna Fáil government
in the 1930s. This strategy was not inappropriate in a period when
trade was collapsing and there was no scope for export-led growth,
but it was less obviously attuned to the circumstances of the 1950s,
when trade was expanding strongly. And the strategy was particularly disadvantageous for a small country such as Ireland. Small size
prevented producers from achieving the scale necessary to cost-effi-
ciently supply the capital goods and manufactured components required by industry.[75] To the extent that inputs were imported, they

---

[73] The government published a ten-year plan for the development of southern Italy in 1950
and then the Vanoni Plan for the development of employment and income over the decade
1955–1964, which again gave priority to addressing regional economic problems.

[74] Denmark, Sweden, Portugal, and Spain might also be added to this list, in that their
growth rates were low and they lie below the regression line depicting the average relationship
between initial per capita GDP and subsequent growth. But Denmark and Sweden were outliers only to a minimal extent; their slower-than-average growth is largely explained by their
high initial per capita incomes. The Portuguese and Spanish cases are discussed in chapter 7.

[75] The government also closed off the other potential channel for technology, foreign direct
investment, through the Control of Manufactures Act.

were imported from Britain, no longer the technological leader.[76] The high import content of industrial production meant that, whenever manufacturing expanded, the economy ran up against balance-of-payments constraints.

Despite these problems, resistance to policy reform was strong. Protection for agriculture and traditional industry flowed from and came to be identified with Irish nationalism, since the years between the creation of a democratic Ireland in 1922 and enactment of the constitution in 1937 were a troubled time for international trade. Small landowners and domestic industries unable to withstand import competition were among those opposed to reform on self-interested grounds.[77] The political elite allied with these interests and with the tradition-bound Catholic Church to preserve the status quo. Antigrowth ideology was pervasive; the government even resisted investing in telephony and roads on the grounds that these were mere conveniences for the rich. At the end of the 1950s, Ireland had only 50 telephones per thousand population, compared to 150 in the United Kingdom and more than 400 in the United States. Getting one's friends to the head of the queue for installation was an important device supporting the prevailing system of clientelism.

From 1950 to 1960, Ireland's average annual compound rate of growth was only one-third of the Western European average. The incremental capital–output ratio, summarizing the efficiency, or more literally the inefficiency, of investment, was almost three times the European norm. Another blow was a severe recession in 1956, which was especially alarming given that the rest of Europe now appeared to be recession free.[78] The results were a deep downturn and a surge of emigration.[79]

[76] The country's few exports, predominantly agricultural, were also directed toward the slowly growing British market.

[77] See Garvin (2004).

[78] The causes of the recession were no mystery: the authorities had first mistakenly attempted to hold down interest rates in the face of an increase in bank rate in London, creating a payments deficit to which they then overreacted with a fiscal contraction. But this did not reassure Irish observers.

[79] In the decade ending in 1961, the population of Ireland dropped by four hundred thousand, until it was 5 percent below its level at the founding of the state in 1922. For an analysis of the mistaken policies of 1956 and their consequences, see Honohan and Ó Gráda (1998).

The question was what to do. One option was to continue supporting the traditional Irish values of rural life, agrarian employment, and industrial self-sufficiency even at the price of continuing
stagnation. The alternative was to break with the past and open the
economy to foreign trade and investment. Small farming would give
way to large-scale commercial agriculture. Foreign investment
would facilitate the acquisition of advanced technology and up-to-
date management techniques. The economy would then produce
more of what could be produced at low cost; high-cost sectors would
be driven out of business by import competition.

These ideas represented a radical break with the past, and there
was predictable resistance to an abrupt about-turn. Not only were
import-competing industries and small farmers opposed to the shift,
but many Irish were actually ambivalent about whether economic
development was a good thing. It was argued that preserving a "rural,
neo-Gaelic, Catholic Arcadia" was desirable on moral and social
grounds. Development that came at the expense of rural life and
traditional values and that emphasized unbridled capitalism over religious allegiance might come at too high a price. Some went on to
suggest that even had policy makers desired change there was little
they could do, the dominantly agricultural composition of output
and employment being an indelible fact of Irish economic life. Thus,
while the second half of the 1950s saw an intensification of reformist
rhetoric, reform in practice fell short.

The debate was then catalyzed by an influential report on the
economy published by the Department of Finance in 1958 and
largely written by the department's secretary, T. K. Whitaker. Re-
acting to the recession of 1955–1956 as much as the disappointing
long-term trend, Whitaker's report and the white paper based on it
had a startling pro-growth orientation. They provided the basis for
an influential group of politicians, civil servants, academics, businessmen, and trade unionists to begin breaking away from the constellation favoring isolationism and stasis.

To be sure, the white paper was reticent about free trade, saying
only that Ireland would eventually have to face up to prospect of

European integration.[80] Reflecting society's deeply ingrained bias toward traditional sectors, it devoted half of its twenty-four chapters to agriculture, forestry, fisheries, fertilizers, and "turf" (peat). As fundamental prerequisites for change, the events of the preceding decade were surely more important than Whitaker's report. Traditional policies had patently failed to deliver the goods. Especially when other parts of Europe surged ahead, those espousing traditional policies saw their hand significantly weakened. It was thus necessary for Irish nationalism to reinvent itself.[81] In addition, by the second half of the 1950s Irish leaders could see European integration coming. They welcomed the opportunity to shift the country's external relations away from the United Kingdom and toward Europe; opening and reform were prerequisites for this reorientation.

Still, the white paper mattered insofar as it reframed the debate as how to promote faster growth. By process of elimination, it pointed to greater export orientation as a logical policy response. Influential politicians such as Sean Lemass, the minister of industry and commerce for the better part of the preceding quarter century when the protectionist apparatus was put in place and now head of government, abruptly shifted sides. Supported by this progressive coalition, the government began implementing policies to rationalize the mix of goods produced for export and for domestic consumption. These allowed Ireland to begin attracting modest amounts of foreign direct investment (FDI). And they helped ready the country for membership in the European Free Trade Association (EFTA) and, ultimately, the European Community (EC).[82]

Given thirty years to work its effects, this combination of export orientation, FDI, and EC membership ignited an economic boom. But that was in the future; in the short run, the improvement was modest, reflecting the partial nature of reforms and the understand-

[80] On page 2 it stated, less than enthusiastically, that "sooner or later protection will have to go and the challenge of free trade accepted. There is no other choice for a country wishing to keep pace with the rest of Europe" (Whitaker 1958).

[81] In the words of Garvin (2004), p. 6.

[82] At this stage, actually applying for EEC membership was more problematic, given Ireland's long-standing policy of neutrality and its 1949 decision not to join the North Atlantic Treaty Organization (NATO).

able difficulty of coping with greater openness following an extended period of protection. Although growth accelerated in the 1960s and nonfarm employment started rising again, the country was able to begin closing the gap only relative to Europe's worst performers.

British economic performance in the 1950s was equally disappointing. It was cold comfort that the country's slow growth was in part explicable by initial conditions—that, unlike Ireland, Britain had been quick to restore full capacity utilization after the war. Similarly, per capita GDP being relatively high in 1950, there was less scope than elsewhere for growing rapidly by catching up to the technological leader. And there was less scope for boosting productivity simply by shifting labor from agriculture to industry, the share of employment in agriculture having already fallen to 5 percent.[83] Figure 4.1 suggests that these initial conditions go some way toward explaining the slow growth of the British economy. But they are not the entire story; that the United Kingdom lies below the average relationship between initial per capita income and subsequent growth in figure 4.1 is indicative of this fact. Having been at the head of the European class in GDP per capita in 1950, by 1960 the United Kingdom had been overtaken by Denmark and Sweden, and a number of other countries were snapping at its heels. Subsequently, it fell still further back in the per capita income leagues. Initial conditions can explain why countries with relatively low incomes succeed in closing the initial gap, but they cannot explain this overtaking.

At its root was the stagnation of total productivity growth evident in the last column of table 4.1. In seeking to explain it, observers noted how Britain's early industrialization bequeathed a decentralized system of industrial relations complicating the maintenance of wage moderation. To be sure, British officials, managers, and union leaders, like their counterparts in other countries, saw the

---

[83] Broadberry and Crafts (2003) calculate that a bit less than one-third of the shortfall in Britain's productivity growth relative to that of West Germany in the years 1950–1979 is attributable to this fact (one-quarter of the West German labor force still being employed in agriculture in 1950). One presumes that the largest effects were felt toward the beginning of the period, when the shift out of agriculture was largest.

need to moderate wages in order to finance investment and productivity growth. But this was easier said than done. Britain had emerged from World War II with 1,900 employers organizations active in industrial relations.[84] Fewer than one-sixth of these were national federations. Although many of the others were organized on an industrial basis, some were locals that dealt with only a section of an industry. Typically, they had only a weak allegiance to one of the two central associations, the Federation of British Industries and the British Employers' Confederation. Similarly, there were more than seven hundred separate trade unions.[85] Of these, only 186 were affiliated with the Trades Union Congress (TUC).[86] The TUC had little control over its affiliates, and those affiliates in turn exercised little control at the enterprise level, given overlapping jurisdictions and the failure to rationalize historical boundary lines. With workers negotiating at the enterprise and craft level, power devolved to the shop stewards, many of whom were political radicals with little interest in the broader implications of their decisions. As a result, the powers of the General Council of the TUC were limited to mobilizing mutual support in periods of industrial conflict.

Efforts to maintain wage restraint in order to finance high levels of investment had to overcome a free-rider problem, since any one union's concessions increased the profits available to stimulate investment and encourage employment growth not only in that sector but economy-wide. This was more difficult in a country with fragmented industrial relations. The result, predictably, was chronic pressure on wages. It also meant that the competitive real exchange rate obtained as a result of the 1949 devaluation did not remain competitive for long. And when the government sought to use fiscal policy to stimulate the economy, as it did when growth slowed, the United Kingdom, like Ireland, ran up against the balance-of-payments constraint. The authorities were then forced to reverse direction, repeatedly interrupting investment in the pattern known as

---

[84] Flanders (1952), p. 104.
[85] As of the end of 1950.
[86] Admittedly, some of these were federations of unions.

"stop-go."[87] Given the lags between the formulation of policy, the implementation of changes, and the impact of the effects, many of these fiscal initiatives were poorly timed.[88] And automatic fiscal stabilizers worked less powerfully to the extent that much public expenditure was devoted to nationalized enterprises whose budgets were impervious to cyclical conditions.[89] The resulting macroeconomic volatility reminded observers of the unstable 1920s and 1930s. It left firms reluctant to commit to investments in new technologies that took time to come to fruition.

Labor, for its part, resisted the introduction of new techniques that threatened traditional work pace and organization. In craft industries such as printing, unions continued to resist increases in work pace, the reorganization of tasks, and the introduction of new equipment. Even in industries, such as motor vehicle manufacturing, where it was impossible to resist the introduction of mass-production methods, workers imposed restrictions on manning and line speeds. Indeed, even in entirely new industries such as petrochemicals, the unions were able to impose restrictive practices regarding demarcation and overtime.[90] As a result, production runs were shorter than in Germany and the United States.[91] Manning levels were higher. Shipbuilding, which had pride of place in British history, was a prime case where restrictive practices led to loss of business.

The Conservative government of 1951–1955, rather than striving to cultivate labor's cooperation, caved in to demands from the unions in order to avoid provoking their hostility and rekindling the political unrest that had bedeviled the 1920s. Seeking to avoid strikes on the grounds that these would cast doubt on its ability to

[87] A classic instance of this occurred in 1955–1956. When the British economy slowed, the authorities stepped on the fiscal accelerator (notably the chancellor of the exchequer, R. A. Butler, in his April 1955 "pre-election budget"). In response to the pressure of demand, money wages rose by 7 percent in 1955 and 8 percent in 1956. A payments crisis followed (exacerbated by the outbreak of the Suez Crisis), forcing the government to step on the brakes and turn to the IMF for financial support.

[88] Hansen (1969) and Dow (1965) both suggest that British fiscal-policy initiatives were actually destabilizing on balance.

[89] United Nations (1962), chapter 6, p. 25.

[90] Gospel (1992), p. 131.

[91] See Pratten (1976).

deliver shared growth, the government became an engine of concession rather than change. And even when officials and employers sought labor's cooperation, they could identify no counterpart on the union side. In 1951–1952 the government sought union assent to a pro-growth program of wage restraint that would have tied wage increases to increases in production. The delegates to the TUC immediately rejected a recommendation by their General Council to consider the proposal. The same happened in 1957 when the unions rejected Chancellor Macmillan's attempt to coordinate economy-wide wage settlements. As Edelman and Fleming put it, "the only period of real wage restraint was from 1948 to 1950 and that was not attributable to any formal policy. . . . Thereafter restraint fell by the wayside, and has never again been made really effective on the trade union side."[92]

Management, meanwhile, had little incentive to push for restructuring. Pressure to perform was least in nationalized enterprise, and almost half of investment in the 1950s was in the public sector, where rates of return were predictably low.[93] While the dismal performance of productivity was especially evident in coal mining, it was nearly as bad in airlines and public utilities. Since nationalized sectors accounted for one-fifth of the British economy, this constituted a considerable impediment to growth. And in managing the public sector, Britain implemented neither the systematic planning approach of France nor the free-market orientation of Germany. There was nothing resembling an industrial plan or even effective steps to loosely coordinate investment in the various nationalized industries. Falling between two stools, the government's approach lacked coherence. A classic example was the railways, to which much public investment was devoted in the second half of the 1950s but without anything resembling a coherent strategy.

The private sector, meanwhile, was sheltered from the product-market competition felt in Germany and Europe's small open economies. Britain was slow to reorient its commercial relations away from

---

[92] Edelman and Fleming (1965), p. 290.
[93] United Nations (1962), chapter 6, p. 24.

the Empire. The imposition of tariffs and the acceptance of cartels in the 1930s—policies pursued in an effort to counter the fall in prices in the global Depression—now bequeathed a cozy environment cosseted from the chill winds of competition. Aggressive competition policy was seen as incompatible with the British approach to organizing the economy. Even overt collusion was not precluded until the adoption of the Restrictive Practices Act of 1956. The effects of these restrictive practices were evident in price–cost margins (which ran at more than twice German levels) and in the persistence of supernormal profits.[94] And where management underperformed, regulatory obstacles stood in the way of hostile takeovers.[95]

Not surprisingly, growth, especially export growth, was disappointing. Between 1955 and 1960, when performance could no longer be ascribed to the very different starting points bequeathed by wartime destruction and delayed recovery, Britain's exports increased by roughly 20 percent in value. Over the same period, West German exports increased by nearly 50 percent. The United Kingdom was not among the founders of the EEC. To be sure, Britain joined EFTA. But "the mutual reduction of tariffs within the European Free Trade Association did not carry the same threat of intensified competition in the British market as did the signing of the Treaty of Rome for the . . . members of the European Economic Community."[96] Given EFTA's small size, the prospects for trade were tied to the more slowly growing markets of the Commonwealth and the Empire. For better or worse, the British were reluctant to move from a Commonwealth to a European orientation. Meanwhile, the country's overseas commitments remained extensive. Defense spending absorbed 8 percent of GDP in the 1950s, in contrast to 4 percent in Germany. None of this made for a comfortable balance-of-payments position.

The situation was similar in Belgium. As a result of the country's early industrialization and ethno-linguistic divide, labor-market in-

[94] See Crafts and Mills (2004) and Geroski and Jacquemin (1988).

[95] On this, see Broadberry and Crafts (1990).

[96] United Nations (1962), chapter 6, p. 27. For more on the effects of the EEC and EFTA, see chapter 6.

stitutions were neither atomistic nor efficiently centralized. To be sure, there had been some movement toward greater centralization in the 1930s. A June 1936 strike involving 20 percent of the labor force had prompted the government, with the support of the Socialist Party, to convene a national labor conference that reached an agreement on standards for the length of the workweek and the recognition of unions in collective bargaining. Follow-up conferences were then held in the second half of the 1940s. But the proposals discussed in these ad hoc meetings were never acted on. Belgian industrial relations remained fragmented and uncoordinated, and pressure from the labor market remained intense.[97] In contrast with neighboring Holland, the government was little involved in wage negotiations. And, unlike much of the rest of Europe, where real wages were significantly below prewar levels in the second half of the 1940s, in Belgium they were pushed back up to 1938 levels as early as 1947–1948. All through the 1950s, unit labor costs in industry remained significantly above levels in Germany, the Netherlands, Italy, and other countries. (See figure 4.3.)

The problem was compounded by the small size of Belgium's 1949 devaluation. Whereas other countries devalued by 30 percent vis-à-vis the dollar, Belgium devalued by only 13 percent. Policy makers feared that larger reductions in the purchasing power of households would provoke a reaction.[98] This left less retained earnings for investment, which was lower than in the other countries of the European continent.[99] (See table 4.5.)

In addition, Belgium was still specialized in coal, steel, nonferrous metals, textiles, and glass, industries in which demand was stagnant and foreign competition was intense. In the short run this problem was papered over by strong demand from countries still undergoing reconstruction and seeking substitutes for capital goods

[97] Eventually, unionism consolidated into two large organizations, the Confederation des Syndicates Chrétiens (CSC) and Fédération Générale du Travail de Belgique (FGTB), along with a series of smaller professionally oriented unions and one small central organization, the Centrale Générale des Syndicats Liberaux de Belgique (CSLB). The CSC dominated in Flanders and the FGTB in Walloonia, although Flemish speakers dominated both organizations.

[98] See Bismans (1992), p. 475.

[99] Excepting only Portugal.

TABLE 4.5

Gross fixed nonresidential investment as a percentage of gross domestic product, 1951–2000

	1951–1960	1961–1973	1974–1987	1988–2000
Belgium	12.8[a]	15.9	13.9	14.9
Denmark	14.2	16.6	14.3	14.0
France	13.7	17.3	15.0	14.8
Germany	16.3	18.9	14.6	14.8
Italy	15.1	14.5	14.5	13.9
Netherlands	18.0	19.9	14.6	15.3
Spain	13.8[b]	16.9	15.3	17.8
United Kingdom	11.7	14.4	14.2	14.1

Source: Organisation for Economic Co-operation and Development, *National Accounts*.
Notes: [a] Average for 1953–1960.
[b] Average for 1954–1960.

not yet being supplied by Germany. There had been little wartime damage to industrial capacity, Belgium having been overrun by the German army and the latter then having withdrawn quickly following the breakdown of its defense lines in northern France. The authorities had also proceeded with an early monetary reform (even before the country had been fully liberated from German occupation) and had decontrolled most prices and imports at an early date.[100]

But with these advantages came costs. Plant and equipment were old. Output per worker could be raised by replacing them with newer models, as some producers did, but the low level of retained earnings depressed aggregate investment. Pressure to reorganize and import the latest American technologies was limited by the easy profits earned in the postwar restocking and re-equipment boom. Consequently, the growth of labor productivity remained below that of Germany, the Netherlands, and France. And any tendency to centralize and coordinate industrial relations under government auspices was weakened by the full employment that prevailed already at the end of the 1940s.

---

[100] Belgium was in the unusual position of being able to decontrol imports as a result of its large foreign-exchange reserves earned through exports of uranium and copper from the Congo and the extensive use of the port of Antwerp by the United States in the final months of the war. See van der Wee (1986), p. 38.

In the early 1950s, as competing suppliers, notably Germany, came back on line, Belgium's liabilities became apparent. The government made things more difficult by pouring resources into declining sectors such as textiles and farming. It extended subsidies to coal mining and used political rather than economic criteria to distribute orders for railway rolling stock. Its capacity to invest in infrastructure, education, and R&D was hamstrung by subsidies to special interests and transfer payments, which already moved the budget into deficit, anticipating a European tendency that would become more widely evident subsequently.

Toward the Golden Age

The 1950s is commonly seen as inaugurating an extraordinary quarter century of economic progress for Europe as a whole. It was possible for Europe to grow simply by repairing wartime damage and putting idle resources back to work. Output could be boosted by shifting labor from agriculture to industry, where its productivity was higher. Investment in the commercialization of American technology and the adoption of mass-production methods had an exceptional payoff. The impact of these favorable initial conditions was evident in the acceleration of growth virtually everywhere. Although the improvement in performance was not uniform, differences in response across European countries only underscore the importance of this same set of determinants, growth tending to be fastest where wartime disruptions were most extensive, where there was the most scope for shifting labor from agriculture and industry, and where there remained the largest gap in output and productivity relative to the technological leader.

But the institutional inheritance and the facility with which societies now adapted to the imperatives of extensive growth mattered to their ability to capitalize on these opportunities. Countries with strong peak associations and a history of corporatist cooperation were able to adapt their industrial relations systems to the need to moderate wages and reinvest profits. Those with a tradition of public–private sector collaboration were able to use indicative planning and state holding companies to coordinate the modernization of a range of up- and downstream industries. Those whose trade had been oriented toward Europe could now commit to the creation of the EEC to lend credibility and permanence to that export orientation. But not all European countries shared this inheritance. Consequently, they varied in how easily they adapted to the new circumstances of the 1950s.

By the end of the decade, the easy opportunities for growth had been played out. Wartime damage had been made good. Employment in agriculture had declined. American technologies that were easily transplanted to European soil had been successfully transferred. The 1960s would provide a test of whether this same set of arrangements could deliver high growth in what would turn out to be a more challenging environment.

- FIVE -

EASTERN EUROPE AND THE PLANNED ECONOMY

In Eastern Europe, just as in the continent's West, there was scope for rapid growth by making good the destruction wrought by World War II. Losses of GDP between 1938 and 1946 were even larger than in Western Europe, on the order of 50 percent in Yugoslavia and Poland, 40 percent in Hungary, and 25 percent in Czechoslovakia. But in most of these countries, with the exception of East Germany, national incomes were back up to prewar levels by 1950. Consequently, the scope for boosting output by repairing wartime damage cannot by itself explain the apparently rapid pace of post-1950 growth, just as in Western Europe.

Like the Western European periphery of Greece, Ireland, Portugal, and Spain, the economies of Central and Eastern Europe could grow quickly by virtue of starting out behind. Excepting parts of Czechoslovakia and what became the German Democratic Republic, the region had been made up of peasant societies before the war. Per capita GDP measured in purchasing power parities was less than one-quarter that of the United States in 1950 and barely 40 percent of the levels of the twelve principal Western European countries.[1] Living standards were behind even those of the Soviet Union.

As a corollary of its underdevelopment, the region was heavily agricultural. On the eve of World War II, only eastern Germany had

[1] Maddison (2001), p. 185.

a larger share of the labor force in industry than in agriculture. Aside from that part of Germany, only Czechoslovakia had much of an industrial base. This explains in part why leaders saw the expansion of industry as a logical way of fostering economic development and enhancing political security.

Unfortunately, few of the preconditions supporting rapid growth in the West had taken root in the East. There was little in the way of modern labor-market and financial institutions. A substantial fraction of investment in infrastructure and industry was foreign-financed, making the economy vulnerable to the foibles of international capital markets. Only in Czechoslovakia had multiparty democracy taken root between the wars or had there been thoroughgoing land reform.[2] In other countries, parliamentary democracy had dissolved into right-wing dictatorship, leaving in its wake little in the way of self-governing institutions.

Underdevelopment, inequality, arbitrary governance, and dependence on fickle foreign finance fueled doubts about the efficacy of the market system. The market economy had been further discredited by the Great Depression and National Socialism, whose rise was seen, rightly or wrongly, as resulting from the concentration of economic power and having been supported by big business.[3] The helplessness of Eastern European countries in the face of Germany's military might encouraged efforts to promote industrialization as self-protection, especially once the region was squeezed between the Soviet Union to the east and NATO troops to the west. In addition, the role of the communists in the resistance lent their arguments a veneer of legitimacy. Prominent among those arguments was the need to enhance national self-sufficiency and to overcome the obstacles to industrialization in the manner in which they had been overcome in the Soviet Union. These arguments for stronger state control were especially compelling in the economic and political chaos

---

[2] Across Eastern Europe as a whole, less than 1 percent of agricultural holdings accounted for more than 40 percent of the acreage.

[3] On the role of the Great Depression as a rationale for postwar planning in Central and Eastern Europe, see Brus and Laski (1989). On the role of the rise of National Socialism, see Roesler (1991) and, for a skeptical view, Turner (1985).

following the war. Thus, while acknowledging the overwhelming importance of the Soviet Union in political and economic developments east of the Iron Curtain, it is also important to recognize indigenous sources of this social turn.[4]

To be sure, the popular fronts that took power following the war included not just communists and socialists but also other parties, including parties dominated by property owners. Their leaders espoused mixed economic systems in which public and private ownership would coexist, although communist leaders naturally preferred a higher level of public ownership and greater central control. With only a bit of exaggeration, a parallel can be drawn with French indicative planning, in which the allocation of credit, rather than command, was used to guide resources toward priority uses.[5]

The question of whether this model would have been viable was rendered moot by the outbreak of the Cold War, which led Joseph Stalin to use the Information Bureau of the Communist and Workers' Parties (Cominform) to bring Eastern European politics into line. With Soviet support, Communist parties seized control using tactics ranging from electoral fraud to the intimidation, expulsion, and even execution of so-called collaborators. Coalition governments were purged of dissidents and transformed into monolithic structures under Communist control. The Catholic Church was suppressed. A much more rigid system of central planning than envisaged by most popular leaders was then put in place.

The Strategy of Central Planning

The central planning system was transplanted to Central and Eastern Europe in 1948–1949, the Soviet economy providing the model. Ownership of all major branches of industry was assumed by

---

[4] Berend (1996), pp. 12–13, similarly argues that the more prominent a wartime anti-Nazi resistance movement was, the greater its role in the formation of the postwar government. He also concludes that "one cannot deny the potential of self-determination, though it was indeed limited by great power politics."

[5] See Swain (1992), pp. 37–38.

the state.[6] Most private business was declared illegal, and strict limits were placed on the right of individuals to produce for the market. Commercial banks were replaced by Soviet-style single-channel banking made up of monobanks each with a specialized function (mobilizing saving, channeling resources into investment, financing foreign trade). Stock exchanges were closed and financial reporting practices were modified to meet the needs of the bureaucracy. Turnover taxes were imposed as the main source of government revenue. Laws were adopted limiting the ability of workers to leave an enterprise without the employer's approval and levying draconian penalties on anyone deviating from the prescriptions of the plan or interfering with its achievement. The task of rendering policy makers accountable to the people was accomplished, in theory, by consolidating the rule of the party—that is, by making the Communist Party the exclusive vehicle for expressing the preferences of the working class. In practice, of course, the party was beyond accountability.

Agriculture was collectivized starting with arable land and proceeding to livestock. This was the slowest part of the transformation owing to peasant hostility. Revealingly, at the time of Stalin's death in 1953, only Bulgaria had collectivized as much as 50 percent of its agricultural land. But the Communists were nothing if not persistent. Eventually, enforced collectivization proceeded virtually everywhere. With the exception of Poland and parts of Yugoslavia, where small private agriculture persisted, by the mid-1960s at least 90 percent of agricultural land had been collectivized across the greater part of Eastern Europe.[7]

---

[6] Widespread nationalization got under way first in Poland, where much industry had been German-owned. The state took over these and other enterprises under a law of 3 January 1946. Czechoslovakia, Yugoslavia, and Albania quickly followed. The exception to this trend was the Soviet occupation zone of Germany, which had not yet become the GDR. This late start on nationalization was then compounded by the labor uprising of 1953 (see the discussion later in this chapter), which caused the authorities to go slow. In the GDR, private and mixed private-and-state-owned enterprises therefore continued to coexist until the latter were finally nationalized in 1972. Up to that time, roughly one-third of the urban labor force in the GDR was still occupied in the private sector.

[7] See Marczewski (1974). Even there, however, the household plots of the members of collective farms continued to account for a substantial share of total agricultural production.

Starting with Yugoslavia in 1947 and Czechoslovakia and Bulgaria in 1949, each country inaugurated a five-year plan.[8] The planning commission, overseen by the Council of Ministers—by the party, in other words—used the concept of "material balances" to project changes in production. In practice this meant comparing prevailing levels of production of goods and services ("known resources") with the levels required to meet the targets of the plan ("known demand") using a fixed-coefficients input–output model. The planning commission formed a preliminary estimate of how much of each product was required to achieve "balance." These preliminary estimates were then passed down to the industrial ministries, typically four to seven in number, which developed more detailed plans for their subdivisions, the so-called industrial directorates. The industrial directorates drew up instructions for each of the enterprises under their command, and the enterprises in turn drew up provisional plans for their divisions and plants. The results were then passed back up to the planning office, which revised its projections of material balances in light of inconsistencies. The exercise was then repeated. In practice this cumbersome process was often completed only some months after the beginning of the year to which the plan ostensibly applied. The resulting documents could run many thousands of pages. Given its hierarchical structure, the system provided few channels for direct cross-sector sharing of information, much less for coordinating production.

That the planners relied on quantity rather than price targets is not surprising. Setting many thousands of prices would have been difficult under any circumstances, but the prospect was especially nightmarish in the turbulent conditions following the war. Marx's labor theory of value provided little guidance for price setting in practice, as the Soviets had learned to their chagrin. The authorities therefore resorted to rules of thumb, the main rule being to favor industry over agriculture and heavy industry over light industry. Prices were adjusted upward for industrial goods, capital goods in particular, and downward for agricultural products. These relative

[8] In Poland, the authorities opted for a six-year plan.

prices had their institutional counterparts: in Hungary, for example, the Ministry for Industrial Affairs was split into a Ministry for Heavy Industry and a Ministry for Light Industry.[9] It was no mystery which one was regarded as the higher priority.

This skewed structure reflected the desire of the planners to encourage heavy industry as the Soviets had done in the 1930s. From the start, the Soviet economy provided the template for industrialization throughout Central and Eastern Europe. The presumption was that if this strategy had worked in the Soviet Union, then it would work in Eastern Europe. The approach was also expedient insofar as it served military as well as economic purposes. In particular, with the outbreak of the Korean War, Stalin instructed party leaders to increase their targets for heavy industry still further.

This approach to economic development was also ideologically driven. Privileging heavy industry was justified in terms of Marx's model of primitive accumulation, as interpreted by Stalin, which implied that sustained growth required the output of producers' goods to expand faster than the output of consumers' goods. Agriculture, in this view, was simply a reservoir of primitive accumulation to be used to underwrite the expansion of industry.

Giving priority to heavy industry and in particular to the production of capital goods meant increasing the output of coal, iron, steel, and associated goods. It meant expanding capacity along established lines. More factories were built in the image of existing factories. More people were assigned to work in them. Economic growth "became dependent on a fix of ever greater inputs of labour and capital."[10] The approach was known as the "mobilization model" of growth, the idea being that savings, labor, and raw materials were to be mobilized in the cause of industrial development to the maximal extent possible, in an effort akin to war. Revealingly, the influential Polish economist Oscar Lange characterized strict central planning as a permanent war economy.[11]

---

[9] The split occurred in 1949.
[10] Aldcroft and Morewood (1995), p. 106.
[11] See Lange (1958).

TABLE 5.1
Sectoral composition of investment in Eastern Europe, 1953–1956
(Percentage of total investment)

	Industry			Agriculture		
	1953	1955	1956	1953	1955	1956
Albania[a]	50	41	54	10	18	10
Bulgaria	40	39	37	14	20	22
Czechoslovakia	42	39	37	11	14	15
East Germany	50	52	48	17	15	—
Hungary	48	41	46	6	11	—
Poland	52	43	44	10	15	17
Romania	57	57	55	7	14	10

Source: Brus (1986), table 24.2.
Note: [a] Figures in the first and fourth columns are for 1950.

This was extensive growth with a vengeance. Applying Western conventions and prices, Zauberman (1964) estimated that gross capital formation as a share of service-sector-inclusive GNP was as high as 44 percent in Czechoslovakia and 48 percent in Poland in 1953—extremes not matched again until the 1990s in East Asia.[12] U.N. estimates for the 1960s constructed on a similar basis put the ratio of gross investment to GNP at 35 percent for Eastern Europe, compared with 25 percent for Western Europe.[13] Higher rates of gross investment have been seen subsequently but they had not been seen before.

Of this investment, 40 to 60 percent was devoted to industry. Of that, the vast majority was dedicated to the heavy-industry complex. In contrast, only 15 percent of aggregate investment was allocated to agriculture.[14] (See table 5.1.) This was barely half the average in the Iberian peninsula and Southern Europe, the other

---

[12] Investment rates measured at Eastern European prices were not especially high, but the value of consumer goods was inflated by increases in turnover taxes, whereas investment goods were often valued at prices that reflected the subsidies received by final users. But even conservatively valued, as in the official statistics, the rate of growth of the capital stock was rapid, reflecting the low level from which it started.

[13] See Kornai (1992).

[14] These are estimates for the first half of the 1950s. Agriculture's share was slightly greater in Poland, given the continued prevalence of private farming. Construction, transportation, and other services accounted for the balance.

agriculture-intensive portions of the continent. A positive aspect of this strategy was that, with the output of the typical industrial worker valued at three times that of the typical agricultural worker, structural change in the form of the shift of resources out of agriculture and into industry and services promised to contribute even more to growth in Eastern Europe than in the West.[15] Nor did the mobilization of labor stop there. Once the reservoir of rural labor was drained, additional workers were mobilized by collectivizing agriculture, forcing women into the state and cooperative sectors, and even enlisting convict labor. Whereas employment expanded by 0.6 percent per year in the 1950s and 1960s in Western Europe, it grew by 1.7 percent per year in the East.[16] In Hungary, Poland, and Bulgaria, the entire increase in labor supply in the course of the 1950s went into sectors other than agriculture. This shift from agriculture to industry was especially dramatic in East Germany and Czechoslovakia, with agricultural employment falling by 20 percent.[17]

Workers were employed on multiple shifts, and even economically obsolete plant and equipment were kept going around the

[15] With the notable exception of the GDR, where the share of agriculture in employment had already sunk to Western European levels. Contemporary estimates by Rosenstein-Rodan (1943) suggested that as much as one-quarter of the agricultural labor force was in a situation of disguised unemployment and could be transferred to industry without hindering food production. Rosenstein-Rodan's estimates of rural unemployment were criticized subsequently, when food production did not expand as quickly as had been foreseen by the planners, for overstating the extent of the phenomenon. Note that this same mechanism was at work in Western Europe in the 1950s, as emphasized by Temin (2002) and analyzed in chapter 4.

[16] In addition, there was considerable growth in the stock of human capital. One respect in which the socialist economies nominally excelled was in the education of their residents. Investment in human capital responded to many of the same political and ideological imperatives as investment in physical capital. (Not incidentally, education could also be used as a mechanism for propagating party ideology.) Schooling was something that the state could organize, as it also did in the West. The state could train more instructors, build more classrooms, and enroll more students. By the early 1970s, the GDR had nearly 70 percent more teachers in proportion to its population than the Federal Republic did. Educational attainment rose impressively in many Eastern European countries, both primary education and the receipt of postgraduate and advanced degrees as well as vocational training. Unfortunately, the advantages of an educated labor force accrue mainly in a situation where workers can apply their knowledge and training in creative ways—that is, by responding to incentives. And incentives were in decidedly short supply in the centrally planned economies.

[17] Most of the absorption of peasants into nonagricultural employment was concentrated in the early postwar years; the process slowed in the second half of the decade. While much of the reallocation of labor was in the direction of industry, the service sector expanded as well, although it remained stunted by Western European standards.

clock. Theoreticians spoke of socialism as abolishing the "moral obsolescence" of capital, meaning that, in order to advance the cause, workers would be motivated to expend however much ingenuity and effort was needed to operate antiquated equipment. From the standpoint of the individuals required to work multiple shifts under unpleasant conditions using obsolete equipment, of course, the morality of this approach was not so clear-cut. Another way of putting the point is that from an economic perspective—not that anyone chose to adopt this—much of the supposed productivity gap between industry and agriculture was illusory. Not just the long hours and oppressive conditions under which industrial workers were required to labor but also the artificially high prices assigned to industrial goods exaggerated the gain in output that could be achieved by redeploying labor from agriculture to industry. Emphasizing heavy industry at the expense of textiles and food processing, which had been the only industrial sectors to develop indigenously prior to World War II, also closed off the route to modern economic growth running from light industry to heavy industry and from the production of consumer goods to the production of capital goods that had been followed by virtually every previous industrial economy, with the notable exception of the Soviet Union. Eastern European planners assumed that the economy could leap directly to the top of the technological ladder, to the production of sophisticated capital goods, instead of climbing up rung by rung. Ultimately, their grasp fell short of their reach.

Despite all this, governments reported impressive rates of growth of net material product, on the order of 6 percent per year in Hungary, 7 percent in Poland, and a credibility-straining 10 percent in East Germany and 11 percent in Bulgaria in the 1950s.[18] (See table 5.2.) The backlog of proven technologies and the fact of limited prior industrial development provided immediate scope for

[18] The U.N. Economic Commission for Europe constructed alternative measures, dubbed "physical indicators of global output," based on time series for a limited number of observable aspects of consumption and production. These suggested slightly higher growth rates for Hungary but lower ones for Poland and, not surprisingly, East Germany and Bulgaria. Maddison's (2001) estimates, as reported in chapter 2, suggest growth rates of 4.6 percent for Hungary, 4.7 for Poland, and 6.9 percent for Bulgaria in the 1950s.

TABLE 5.2
Average annual growth of net material product and gross industrial
output, 1951–1960

	Net material product		Gross industrial output	
	1951–1955	*1956–1960*	*1951–1955*	*1956–1960*
Bulgaria	12.3	9.7	13.7	15.9
Czechoslovakia	8.2	6.9	10.9	10.5
East Germany	13.1	7.2	13.7	8.7
Hungary	5.8	6.0	13.2	7.6
Poland	8.6	6.6	16.2	9.9
Romania	14.2	6.6	15.1	10.9

Source: Smith (1983), table 3.1.

raising production. The region's poorest countries reported the fastest rates of growth as they boosted investment rates from the low levels that had prevailed previously and imported foreign technology. All this suggested that convergence like that happening in the West was underway in the East as well.[19] By the late 1960s, roughly half of all output originated in the industrial sector. This was true even of the poor countries of the Balkans, where industry had been all but absent in the aftermath of World War II. If the objectives of the Soviet-type development strategy pursued in Eastern Europe in this period are taken as the rapid creation and expansion of the industrial base, then it must be acknowledged that these goals were achieved, albeit at a cost.

In part, that cost took the form of limiting consumption and underinvesting in housing, urban transit, and the provision of electricity and heat to the household sector. (With industry having first call on available energy supplies, urban power outages became a feature of everyday life.) In Hungary in the first half of the 1950s, even measured living standards compared unfavorably with those prevailing before the war. Elsewhere, the official statistics might indicate otherwise, but these were riddled with valuation problems. With

[19] A caution is that the recorded growth rates of the region's poorest countries, such as Bulgaria and Romania, may overstate the actual growth rate of production even more than elsewhere in the region insofar as such countries had been incompletely monetized in prior years and collectivization now brought the agricultural sector into the monetary sphere.

industry growing faster than agriculture, the high prices assigned to industrial goods exaggerated the weight attached to the economy's rapidly growing sectors. Working multiple shifts under difficult conditions hardly resulted in a high quality of life, even leaving aside the toll of deaths and suffering where terror was used to elicit effort. East German citizens visiting West Germany in the 1950s were aware that their economy's high recorded growth rates had not eliminated the gap in living standards. From the mid-1950s on, two hundred thousand annually chose not to return, influenced by this reality and by the attractions of freedom from political tyranny.

Against this background, signs of decelerating growth in the 1960s were alarming. The deterioration in growth performance was most obvious in the region's more advanced economies, Czechoslovakia and the GDR, where tight labor markets were becoming a constraint at the same time as in Western Europe. A fall in recorded output in Czechoslovakia in 1963 shattered assumptions of the "recession-proofness" of central planning. To some extent these events reflected exceptional factors, such as poor harvests, the effects on construction of a series of unusually harsh winters, and the rupture of trade links with China. The growth of national incomes in fact recovered in the second half of the 1960s when these transitory factors passed and increases in Soviet petroleum and iron ore capacity came on line, providing cheap inputs for Eastern European economies poorly endowed with these commodities. The planned economies then staggered through the 1970s with the help of resources obtained using the proceeds of loans extended by Western commercial banks, an innovation made possible by the new policy of détente and by the banks' need to find an outlet for their recycled petrodollars. These loans allowed Eastern Europe to run current-account deficits vis-à-vis the West and to import a new generation of technologically advanced capital goods. Imported technologies were compatible with the prevailing model of extensive growth; adopting them merely required workers, managers, and planners to repeat the process in which they had engaged after World War II. But although technology licensing boosted productivity for a time, it could not delay the day of reckoning indefinitely.

141

Problems of Central Planning

Even where unexploited opportunities provided immediate scope for expanding industrial production, Stalinist ideology led the planners to push the process too far. Central and Eastern Europe had been the continent's breadbasket; the region was endowed with rich agricultural land, providing a logic for why it should produce and export agricultural goods. Instead, agriculture was starved of resources. Czechoslovakia, Poland, and Yugoslavia managed to match prewar levels of grain production only at the end of the 1950s. As a result, foodstuffs were rationed, provoking chronic complaints by the household sector.

Even with a more favorable stance toward primary production, the cost and availability of industrial inputs would have been a problem, given the planners' emphasis on industry. Aside from Poland and Romania, the economies of the region were poorly endowed with energy and industrial raw materials. The steel works symbolic of socialist growth—which later came to be seen as symbols of mistaken policies—were voracious consumers of iron ore and fuel. Although some of these materials could be imported, trade was limited by the ethos of self-sufficiency and the fact that each Eastern European economy was attempting to industrialize along similar lines, meaning that there was no one with excess supplies to export.

Inefficient investment in heavy industry therefore dictated inefficient investment in coal and ore mining and energy generation. Hungary, for example, attempted to develop its low-grade coal deposits rather than importing energy from abroad. In the second half of the 1950s and first half of the 1960s, 40 percent of its industrial investment was devoted to fuel and energy programs.[20]

A corollary of this effort to transfer resources to heavy industry was neglect of the handicraft trades. While heavy industry expanded, towns and villages were deprived of blacksmiths, shoemakers, and tailors. Directing resources toward investment in heavy industry meant limiting those available for investment in housing. In

---

[20] Berend and Ranki (1986), p. 236.

conjunction with wartime destruction and rural–urban migration, the result was "a truly desperate situation" in which the little modern housing available was allocated on political grounds.[21] Thus, unlike in the West, where increases in output translated into commensurate improvements in living standards, in Eastern Europe living standards, insofar as they can be measured, improved to a much more limited extent. The bulk of what was produced by the industrial sector was used to satisfy industry's own demand for inputs.

Managers for their part followed a "minimax" strategy, seeking to minimize plan targets while maximizing the planned allocation of resources. They protected themselves against missing production targets by overordering raw materials, building excess capacity, and employing superfluous labor. Much of what these inputs were used to produce was poorly tailored to the needs of downstream users, since the incentive was to make what was easiest, given available inputs and targets, not to maximize anything resembling profits. The planners sought to elicit the managers' cooperation in maximizing the level and optimizing the mix of production. But the long distance and many hands involved in passing along information on the resources necessary to fulfill the plan's targets meant that the managers had a strategic advantage. They could speak more authoritatively about what happened on the shop floor, allowing them to inflate the capital, labor, and raw-material requirements of production and exaggerate capacity constraints.

In response, the planning committee and industrial ministries demanded more detailed information about production and issued more detailed instructions. They required reports on production and sales on a weekly and, eventually, a daily basis. But they were constrained by the accuracy and availability of the information for which they depended on enterprise managers. They could do nothing to shorten the intrinsic distance between the ministry and the plant or prevent managers from embellishing the facts. They sought to elicit more information about the enterprise's capacity by arbitrarily raising its targets and threatening dire consequences if these

---

[21] Brus (1986), p. 26.

were not met, but if production fell short, they could not be sure whether this reflected binding capacity constraints or strategic behavior. Taut planning, as the practice was known, also penalized the most efficient firms and encouraged them to push output beyond full capacity, often at visible cost in terms of product quality and the maintenance of plant and equipment. In turn, the planners' attempts at micromanagement created additional inefficiencies by encouraging even more devious responses at the enterprise level.

In the West, one manifestation of the rise in living standards was the growing variety of consumer goods delivered by the market economy. Under planning, in contrast, enterprises were given targets only for the volume of output; they reaped no reward for producing a wider range of goods. In the 1950s, the Hungarian footwear industry produced just sixteen types of shoes, not those types that were most desired by consumers but rather those that were easiest to fabricate.[22] Firms that had once undertaken production runs of no more than one or two thousand pairs of a particular style now aspired to produce twenty-five thousand pairs at a time, limiting variety. Enterprises producing crockery supplied no small pots and pans because output targets were specified in terms of weight, not number and variety. The planners responded with more detailed directives, which managers and workers then found new ways of evading. The system became more bureaucratic but no more efficient.

Many of these consumer goods were shoddy, quantity targets providing no reward for quality. In Hungary in 1951, 25 percent of the shoes sold on the domestic market were classified as substandard, an astonishing admission for an administrative apparatus not known for its forthrightness.[23] In the second half of the 1950s, public dissatisfaction and, in extreme cases, open revolt resulted in some reallocation of resources to consumer-goods sectors and in efforts to give managers a profit motive.[24] But the problem persisted.

---

[22] Aldcroft and Morewood (1995), p. 110.

[23] Swain (1992), p. 72.

[24] On these reform efforts in Hungary and other countries, see the discussion in the next section.

Above all, there was the challenge of eliciting effort. Socialist ideology went only so far in substituting for pecuniary compensation, which was in any case a blunt instrument where consumer goods were in short supply. Disenchantment with the socialist model mounted as it became evident that its shortcomings were systemic and irremediable. After 1953, the Romanian press no longer encouraged workers to exert Stakhanovite effort.[25] Threats and compulsion could force effort but not efficiency. The socialist system was notorious for "storming," for desperately boosting production in the last month of the quarter and the last quarter of the year, when a majority of the output mandated for the planning period was delivered so as to avoid punishment for missing targets. In practice, periods of wasteful inactivity were thus interspersed with short episodes of intense but inefficient effort.

Threats and compulsion were the ultimate incentive mechanism. As a leading Hungarian planner put it in 1952, "Strict measures must be taken to make the plan effective. Those breaking it must receive not only disciplinary punishment but, in more serious cases . . . must be brought to trial."[26] Everyone could predict the outcome of such trials. But with the thaw following Stalin's death, threats and compulsion became less effective. In Hungary the reformist leader Imre Nagy, formerly professor of agricultural economics at the Budapest University of Economics, committed to abolishing forced labor camps. Following Nikita Khrushchev's secret speech denouncing Stalinist terror at the Twentieth Congress of the Communist Party of the Soviet Union in 1956, similar reforms spread to other countries. It was now clear that compulsion, terror, and forced labor would be available—fortunately, it should be emphasized—to a more limited extent.

This left only more pay for more effort as an incentive mechanism. Piece rates therefore became the dominant mode of compensation. Conveniently, they could be seen as the true expression of the socialist principle of "to each according to his work," although

[25] Brus (1986), p. 63.
[26] Cited in Berend (1996), p. 77.

145

there was still the minor problem that the prices used to value that work were fundamentally arbitrary. Workers were aware, however, that increases in output would be met by reductions in piece rates as the authorities sought to devote resources to augmenting industrial capacity. This encouraged informal norms limiting effort that offset the official norm to work harder in order to advance the people's revolution. Occasionally it even led to open protests against official work norms, as in Berlin in 1953 and the Polish city of Poznan in 1956.

Partial Reforms

Following Stalin's death and the end of the Korean War, Moscow lessened its emphasis on heavy industry. It insisted less rigidly on the pursuit of Soviet-style planning. At the same time, the Sino-Soviet split gave authorities in Eastern Europe more room to maneuver. With the deceleration of growth in the mid-1950s following the initial investment-led surge, they began to tinker with the planning mechanism.

The first tentative reforms revised the planners' targets for output without altering the basic administrative structure. They lessened the emphasis on heavy industry, paid more attention to the supply of consumer goods, and substituted more labor- and knowledge-intensive methods for energy- and raw-material-intensive modes of production. They allocated a smaller share of investment to heavy industry and more to agriculture and housing while converting part of the capacity of the armaments industry to the production of consumer durables.

More ambitious reforms, which came later, sought to streamline the planning mechanism, strengthen incentives, decentralize some decisions, and create a limited role for the market. The powers of the industrial ministries were concentrated in the state planning commission, as in East Germany. Or enterprises were formed into associations with "colleges of directors" to make collective planning decisions and provide conduits for information flowing to and from the ministries, as in Poland. Or piece rates were replaced by wage and salary scales with bonuses keyed to enterprise performance.

The most ambitious reforms sought to give enterprise managers more freedom to carry out their tasks. Managers were offered rewards for economizing on the use of resources. Prices were used to guide enterprise decisions, albeit prices set by the planning office rather than by the forces of supply and demand. In some cases, enterprises were given a say about the magnitude of the wage bill or the composition of investment.

The extent of these reforms varied across countries. Bulgaria and Albania engaged in essentially no reform; East Germany, Poland, and Romania pursued modest reforms; and Hungary and Yugoslavia undertook more ambitious reforms. But almost everywhere entrenched interests resisted change, whether in the direction of "market socialism," as the use of price, tax, and credit policies to guide decentralized decision making was called in Hungary, or creating a link between bonuses and financial results, as recommended by the Polish Economic Council in 1956. Inevitably, partial reform lacked coherence. For example, when decentralizing decision making, the authorities simultaneously insisted on increasing industrial concentration, since this simplified the task of monitoring the decisions of individual enterprises.[27] Greater scale and concentration made enterprises even slower on their feet and neutralized—or worse—any tendency toward competition.

One of the first of these reform efforts was in Poland. In 1956, the Council of Ministers appointed an Economic Council under the chairmanship of the economist Oskar Lange. Lange's council recommended placing less weight on targets and more on incentives embodied in contracts between suppliers and purchasers. Enterprises were to be given more control of their day-to-day operations and more say over investment decisions. The central authorities would then be less preoccupied by detail and could concentrate on long-term planning.

---

[27] See Swain and Swain (1993), chapter 5.

The number of centrally allocated commodities was consequently cut, and enterprises were granted autonomy over selected investment decisions. But absent other reforms, investment had essentially no cost for managers, who displayed an insatiable appetite for capital. Socialist theorists, aware of this problem, referred to the tendency toward "limitless investment" in this system of soft budget constraints. Resources were dissipated in massive construction and capacity-building projects with little payoff or even realistic prospect of completion. When growth slowed, planners and enterprise managers responded with more of the same: they sought to boost investment still further. This only aggravated shortages and intensified inflationary pressure. Ultimately, administrators reacted by reimposing restrictions on the financial autonomy of firms and by recentralizing investment. Partial reform thus ran aground over its own contradictions. Poland's early experiment, for example, was aborted by the end of the 1950s.[28]

In East Germany, the targets of the first five-year plan were largely met. Prewar consumption standards were restored by the middle of the 1950s despite the fact that the Soviet Union had carried off much of the surviving industrial capacity as reparations and despite the continuing burden of supporting Soviet troops on East German soil. Basking in this success, such as it was, in 1957 the government of Walter Ulbricht issued a blanket condemnation of "revisionist market tendencies," disregarding signs of unrest among the populace. To be sure, this disregard was not complete: in an effort to stem emigration, the government abolished food rationing and adjusted the output targets of the plan from producer durables to consumer durables, offering refrigerators and televisions for sale in state shops in significant numbers for the first time.

But these Band-Aids did nothing to resolve the contradictions inherent in the system. Additional difficulties were then created by West Germany's cancellation of its bilateral trade pact in 1960, which forced East German enterprise to shift to domestic or Soviet

[28] The only permanent achievement of the reformers and protestors was the cancellation of agricultural collectivization and reestablishment of peasant farms. See also the next note.

sources of supply, often at considerable cost, and by the exodus of additional rural workers in response to agricultural collectivization. The regime was led, reluctantly, to contemplate more fundamental reform. But the party hesitated to cede power, and Khrushchev's tolerance for experimentation was uncertain. These factors constrained the extent of feasible reform. In 1964, the Council of Ministers announced its intention of creating a more balanced economy emphasizing not just heavy industry but also chemicals and machine tools. (If this was balance, it was a very restrictive use of the concept.) Ministers agreed to the creation of a "New Economic System" in which tax rates were varied to encourage certain activities and prices were more closely related to the costs of production. Enterprises were given more leeway to formulate production plans. Enterprises that showed profits in excess of their targets were allowed to retain 60 percent of the surplus and to use it for bonuses and for investment in fixed and working capital.

Predictably, piecemeal reform had many of the same unintended consequences in East Germany as in Poland. Managers facing soft budget constraints engaged in limitless investment. Although profit-related incentives held out the promise of increased efficiency, they also threatened to interfere with execution of the state output plan, which still specified production norms for each sector. Incentives keyed to enterprise profits and prices were allowed to operate only to the extent that they did not threaten plan fulfillment. When conflicts arose, profit-based incentives were overridden by directives.

Once more the planners sought to close the productivity gap vis-à-vis the West by channeling resources toward industry. They introduced automated machinery into the metalworking industries, sectors long seen as "leading links" in the industrialization process. Doing so required cuts in other investment projects and, more difficult for the populace, in consumption standards, again fueling popular discontent. In response, the group around Erich Honecker strengthened its hold on the party and halted reform. By the early 1970s, enterprise-level targets had been restored, autonomy in pricing had been abolished, and bonuses related to productivity had been eliminated.

In Hungary, ambitious reform efforts got under way in the early 1960s. As part of the "New Course" reforms of the 1950s, Nagy had sought to decentralize investment and restore a better balance between industry and agriculture, but he was ousted by hard-liners in 1955, and his reforms were rolled back following the Soviet military intervention that put down popular protests in November 1956.[29] In the wake of these events, Nagy's successors were reluctant to contemplate any reform that might be perceived as relaxing economic and political control. Eventually, however, failure to meet the targets of the second five-year plan forced Nagy's successor, János Kádár, to initiate new reforms under the cover of continuous proclamations of loyalty to the Soviet Union. Foreign trade was increased starting in 1964, and the worst price distortions were eliminated. Free-market prices were introduced for half of all consumer goods. Modest capital charges were imposed to offset the tendency toward limitless investment. Enterprises were given more autonomy.

But more autonomy meant, among other things, more autonomy for waste and self-aggrandizement. The planners responded in 1968 with the more ambitious "New Economic Mechanism." Plan disaggregation now stopped at the branch level; detailed instructions were no longer passed down from there to the enterprise. Enterprise managers could decide the volume of production and the mix of products; they could choose the methods used to produce them and invest in the development and acquisition of new technology. They had only to agree to a very general five-year plan and did not even have to conform to the amendments proposed by the relevant supervising ministry. Increasingly, the authorities relied on the price mechanism to guide managerial decisions, fixing some prices at levels very different from those prevailing in the rest of the world, while allowing others to move but subject to control, and leaving still

---

[29] Nagy returned to power at the height of the protests but was tried and executed by the new government following Soviet military intervention. As in Poland, the only enduring legacy of the first round of reforms was in the agricultural sector, where peasants were released from the compulsory sowing plan and compulsory delivery system. In Hungary, as in Poland, relations between the peasants and the state were mediated by the price system, although the planners, not the market, still set prices. Unlike Poland, however, Hungary resumed its march in the direction of agricultural collectivization, albeit with mixed success.

others entirely free. Approximately 30 percent of prices were fixed, 30 percent were free, and 40 percent were controlled in some way. In addition, the planners used taxes and credit allocation to steer production and investment decisions. Because enterprises' own funds were inadequate to fund investment and the authorities still controlled banking and credit, they retained considerable influence over the composition of capital formation. Two areas where the state's influence was particularly strong were defense-related industries (a criterion that was interpreted broadly) and large-scale investment projects.

The New Economic Mechanism eliminated some of the worst inefficiencies associated with the illusion that technocrats in Budapest could control the production and allocation decisions of thousands of enterprises. It gave managers and workers an opportunity to respond in more rational, efficiency-enhancing ways. But if they now had the opportunity, their incentive was weak. Even where profits rose as a result of initiative, most of these ended up being garnished by the state. As a result, successful managers received only modest rewards.[30] Although retained earnings supposedly were earmarked for investment and wages, the portion earmarked for investment was taxed at marginal rates up to 85 percent.

Thus, although the Hungarian reform removed some of the worst distortions associated with central planning, it provided little incentive to increase efficiency. The problem of overinvestment that plagued efforts at decentralization in Poland and elsewhere also reared its head following the introduction of the New Economic Mechanism, as enterprises borrowed heavily from the state banks to finance speculative increases in capacity. Enterprises competed for workers, driving up wages and wreaking havoc with the planners' vision of labor allocation. Since managers knew that their enterprises were too important to be allowed to go bankrupt, they responded to the relaxation of controls by investing in additional ca-

---

[30] Initially, the 1968 reforms foresaw performance-linked bonuses of up to 80 percent of basic compensation for top management, but this scheme elicited an angry response from rank-and-file employees and was scaled back. In practice, bonuses for top management were limited to one-third of basic salaries.

pacity, betting that a big increase in output would produce equally big increases in profits and therefore bonuses.

Observing these problems, the Hungarian authorities slowed the relaxation of controls and limited the types of investment that could be determined by the enterprise. In 1973, they returned fifty key enterprises to the control of the Council of Ministers and created a new State Plan Committee to "reinvigorate" the role of central planning. Once more, reform was rolled back in response to its unexpected consequences and contradictions. Although reform went further in Hungary than in most other East-bloc countries, it clearly had not gone far enough.

The other notable approach to reform was that of the Yugoslav labor-managed firm. Its establishment in the second half of the 1960s had been preceded by other reforms, reflecting Tito's desire to distance himself from all aspects of the Soviet system. Many prices had been freed, and enterprises were permitted to engage in foreign trade, although the state still made extensive use of tariffs, multiple exchange rates, and import and export licenses to limit their access to world markets and influence the prices that they faced. Councils chosen by the workers, which were to figure so importantly in subsequent Yugoslav reforms, were established in the early 1950s. They gained increasing influence over the conditions of work, the composition of the wage bill, and the production and marketing decisions of the enterprise.

But even after the abolition of directives to guide the physical allocation of resources in the early 1950s, the state continued to appropriate the largest share of enterprise revenues and controlled the banking system. It still made many investment decisions. Hence Yugoslavia experienced many of the same problems as Hungary and other planned economies that went partway down the road of reform.

By the first half of the 1960s, mounting problems of inflation, unemployment, and external deficit made clear that the authorities were going to have to choose between moving forward in the direction of further reform and backtracking toward a more controlled economy. In 1965, they responded by decentralizing investment, commercializing banking, and abolishing the taxes on enterprise revenues that had been used to finance the state investment funds. Their most distinctive reforms empowered the workers' councils to elect the management board and appoint the director in chief in conjunction with the local government in an effort to strengthen management accountability. Net revenues were distributed between a business fund earmarked for investment and a wage fund distributed to the workers. Considerable variation in earnings was permitted in the effort to encourage labor effort. Discretion over the business fund meant that, in contrast to Hungary, decentralization extended even to the planning of long-term investment decisions. The hope was that more rational investment would be encouraged by the prospect of it generating a large wage fund later.

But while the Yugoslav system avoided some of the worst inefficiencies of central planning, especially after moving further in the direction of price liberalization in the second half of the 1960s, the results were disappointing. If the Yugoslav system really was a variant of market socialism, as advertised, then there was reason for workers to fear that inefficient enterprises, unable to cover their costs, might go out of business. This created an incentive for workers to pay themselves as much as possible as quickly as possible, transferring to themselves not only their share of the enterprise's capital stock but also that portion belonging to society.[31] In turn this created the danger that the government might reverse course and recentralize along more traditional lines. Although this did not happen, the authorities did respond with administrative intervention designed to limit the payment by workers of wages to themselves. But this only encouraged the workers' councils to take as many resources as possible out of the firm in advance of any further tightening of administrative measures, exacerbating the problem of underinvestment.

To be sure, workers now had more control over their destinies. Enterprises seeking to maximize the wage fund had an incentive to produce goods better tailored to the market, making consumers' lives more pleasant. Overall, however, the economy did not perform

---

[31] A point first made by Furubotn and Pejović (1970).

much better than its more traditionally planned Eastern European rivals. Although there was much fascination with the Yugoslav model, it was not clear that it provided a path to feasible and sustainable socialism.

Planning Innovation

Aside from Yugoslavia, experiments with decentralization did not extend to planning innovation, the greatest weakness of the socialist economies. Even where markets were allowed to exert more influence over current production, the state was still responsible for planning the future. And state socialism provided only weak incentives for innovation. The Schumpeterian pressure that forced capitalist firms to innovate or die was not present in the planned economy.[32] There was no exit in the centrally planned system. For their part, workers figuring out ways of speeding up production might only find their piece rates cut. Managers discovering ways of boosting output might only find their production targets raised the following year. Innovation is a source of economic and technological uncertainty, and for socialist managers uncertainty jeopardized bonuses that hinged on meeting current production targets, not on increasing efficiency. Both the development and the diffusion of product and process innovations were slower in centrally planned economies.[33] What some commentators referred to as the "drowsiness" of the socialist enterprise was simply an extreme manifestation of a problem that eventually also became evident in Western Europe, albeit to a lesser extent—that a set of institutions tailored to the imperatives of extensive growth was less suited to radical innovation.

Since enterprises had little incentive to invest in new technologies, this task was assigned to the industrial ministries. Each ministry had its own research institute receiving finance from the central authorities. Unfortunately, these R&D institutes had little

---

[32] Schumpeter (1942).

[33] For example, on the Soviet case see Amann, Cooper, and Davies (1977) and Bergson (1983).

regular contact with enterprises and little familiarity with the practicalities of production. And there was no mechanism by which one industrial institute could be encouraged to take into account the implications for other industries of the new products and processes that it sought to develop.

The authorities sought to solve this problem through even greater centralization, contrary to the trend in other economic spheres. The East German government reorganized R&D as an integrated complex, establishing large-scale research centers within each of its *Kombinate* (industrial holding companies). In Czechoslovakia, where resources for R&D had been allotted to small as well as large enterprises, these were now concentrated in the large ones in the hope that this would lead to the development of innovations of wide applicability. In Hungary the National Office for Technological Development allowed R&D to remain decentralized but sought to coordinate the tasks of the various research institutes. In the early 1970s, the problem of integrating research with production was acknowledged with the establishment of so-called research-production units, but these were of no real significance.

Regional Integration

Since the prices set by the planners were different from those prevailing in the rest of the world, planning at home was incompatible with trading abroad. Yet many Central and Eastern European economies were too small to emulate the model of self-sufficiency pursued by the Soviet Union. They lacked the scale necessary to produce the entire range of goods and services required by a modern industrial economy.

Solutions to this dilemma included placing trade in the hands of specialist foreign trade enterprises, which were the only entities facing world prices, and using tariffs, quotas, and licenses to equalize domestic and international prices. Another solution was to privilege trade with other East-bloc countries, where prices were similar. A first step in this direction was the establishment of the Council on

Mutual Economic Assistance (CMEA) in January 1949.[34] When Moscow barred Czechoslovakia, Hungary, and Poland from participating in the Marshall Plan, it had to offer an alternative; hence the CMEA. The CMEA was also a device for heading off plans for a customs union among the Eastern European economies that, by freeing cross-border trade, would have enhanced the role for market forces and thus could not have included the Soviet Union. Finally, the CMEA was seen by the Soviets as a mechanism for coordinating national plans among the countries of the Eastern bloc.

The CMEA's founding members, Bulgaria, Czechoslovakia, Hungary, Poland, and Romania, together with the USSR, were joined by East Germany and Albania later in 1949.[35] From the start, the new entity displayed little life. Not only were the Eastern European economies heavily controlled, leaving little scope for trade, but each sought to develop along similar lines. In each country the planners sought to import coal, iron ore, and staple foodstuffs while exporting iron, steel, and machinery. Although the USSR had significant reserves of raw materials, these were often located in Siberia, from where they could be transported only at considerable cost. In the event, the Soviet Union, like its potential partners, preferred to develop its own capacity to produce machinery and other industrial goods rather than importing them—although the higher quality of some Eastern European products allowed it to overcome this preference.

Notwithstanding these obstacles, the collapse of trade with the West necessarily meant that the countries of Central and Eastern Europe conducted the majority of their trade with the USSR. With the escalation of the Cold War, the United States embargoed Western exports of strategic and high-technology products and required all recipients of Marshall aid to follow suit. The outbreak of the Korean War then led Stalin to encourage the expansion of iron and steel capacity throughout Eastern Europe. This required importing raw materials from the Soviet Union. As a result, the share of intra-

---

[34] See van Brabant (1980) for discussion of the event and its proper dating.
[35] In 1962, Albania left and Mongolia entered. Cuba then joined in 1972.

CMEA trade in the total trade of the region rose to more than 50 percent in the first half of the 1950s.

Inadvertently, a pattern of trade began to emerge resembling specialization along lines of comparative advantage, albeit subject to a strong element of bilateral balancing. The USSR imported machinery, equipment, and other engineering and steel products from more advanced East-bloc economies such as Czechoslovakia, Hungary, Poland, and the GDR in return for petroleum and petroleum products, coal, iron ore, ferrous and nonferrous metals, and cotton. It exported machinery, equipment, engineering products, and steel to Bulgaria and Romania in exchange for agricultural products and raw materials. This was the so-called radial pattern of intra-CMEA trade in which Eastern European countries traded mainly with the Soviet Union rather than one another.

This pattern dovetailed with Moscow's ambition to forge the Eastern bloc into an integrated planned economy subservient to the Soviet Union. For countries such as Czechoslovakia, it held out hope that industry might be permitted to specialize in the production of sophisticated capital equipment. It offered the possibility that the country might raise efficiency by exploiting economies of scale. But planners in Bulgaria and Romania saw the emerging pattern of specialization as undesirable. The idea that their economies should become mere suppliers of raw materials and food was incompatible with their socialist ideology and aspirations. In practice, each set of national planners, not least those in Southeastern Europe, sought to promote heavy industry and especially the production of machinery and equipment. They sought to occupy the industrial high ground and to maximize economic autonomy, not interdependence. They sought to create an economy in which industry accounted for half of output and agriculture accounted for less than one-quarter.

Thus, when Khrushchev sought to breathe new life into the CMEA following Stalin's death, creating a series of commissions to promote an "international socialist division of labor," their recommendations were resisted elsewhere, above all in Romania. When in the early 1960s, in response to the creation of the EEC, Khrushchev once more sought to promote greater specialization and division of labor along national lines, his entreaties were again resisted by the Romanians and others. From the early 1970s, there was limited cooperation in industries such as motor vehicle manufacturing where capital and component requirements were particularly demanding. Other East-bloc countries supplied parts for the Zhiguli (known outside the Soviet Union as the Lada), and the Soviet Union exported the cars thereby produced to the other countries of the East.[36] Hungary received a monopoly on the production of buses for the CMEA market, while Romania was awarded the right to produce diesel locomotives. It was far from clear that this allocation of export monopolies had an economic logic as opposed to simply being the outcome of a complex political process of intercountry bargaining. And even these limited examples of specialization were exceptions to the rule.

Trade among the non-Soviet East-bloc countries was therefore mainly intra-industry, as the constituent economies shipped their slightly different goods (different types of ball bearings, for example) back and forth. Each pair of countries negotiated operational trade agreements annually, setting prices and quantities so as to produce balanced bilateral trade with at most a small margin to be financed by short-term credits. They distinguished hard goods in short supply in the area, including any that might have a market in the West, from soft goods, namely, everything else. Increasingly, trade was balanced country by country, separately for hard goods and soft goods, with allowance for settling residual imbalances in hard currency earned by exporting hard goods to the West.[37]

Notwithstanding these obstacles to integration, Khrushchev sought to encourage intrabloc solidarity by canceling debts and

[36] This was the product of Italian–Soviet cooperation, as noted in chapter 7: the Lada was based on the Fiat Mirafiori. The Poles had their equivalent based on the Fiat 124.

[37] The Soviet Union allowed this practice from the later 1950s on. Trade with the West then expanded in the 1960s, especially on the part of countries such as Bulgaria and Romania, which produced primary commodities and relied increasingly on imports of Western equipment and machinery as a vehicle for technology transfer. The practice of settlement in hard currencies then expanded further in the 1970s, when the CMEA countries were able to obtain hard currency by borrowing in the West—and also desired payment in hard currency in order to service and repay their loans.

allowing Eastern European countries to buy back the Soviet shares of joint companies established after World War II to transfer resources to the USSR. He agreed to the use of something approximating world prices to value East-bloc countries' trade, reassuring those who had complained that the Soviet Union manipulated prices to its advantage. From 1958 on, prices in intra-CMEA trade were determined by the so-called Bucharest Formula, based on average world prices over a five-year period; those prices were then changed every five years.

But absent a market, deciding on appropriate valuations was not straightforward. As Smith described the resulting discussions, "Trade negotiators come armed with documentation to establish what the appropriate world market price for a commodity is, which involves problems of identifying which market is to be considered the 'world' market, the time at which the 'world price' is fixed and the most appropriate product for comparison. . . . Effectively, prices result from a process of bilateral negotiation between foreign trade ministries."[38] In practice, the relative prices of machinery and equipment tended to be higher in intra-CMEA trade than in the West, while the relative prices of raw materials tended to be lower.[39] This was the opposite of the price differential that would have flowed from the region's pattern of relative abundance and scarcity, since equipment and machinery were in ample supply, given policies of promoting heavy industry and the production of steel and engineering goods in particular, whereas much of the region was poorly endowed with industrial raw materials. Some suggested that this pattern reflected the supposedly greater difficulty in the case of manufactures of finding comparable goods on world markets for use in calculating prices. But it is not clear why this should have biased the relative prices of these products one way or the other.[40] More likely, this result reflected the planners' ideology, which valued machinery more

[38] Smith (1983), p. 165.
[39] This was the conclusion of Ausch and Bartha (1968).
[40] If trade negotiators were ignorant of quality problems and these were more prevalent in the case of machinery and equipment than other goods, this might explain a systematic bias. But it stretches credulity to think that the extent of the quality problem was unknown.

than raw materials. It also reflected the incentive for the Soviet Union to extend price concessions to advanced Eastern European countries in the effort to retain their allegiance. In effect, Moscow sold raw materials at concessionary prices in return for military bases, troop commitments, and defense production. Consistent with this strategy, the largest subsidies went to East Germany, which was on the front lines of the Cold War; Czechoslovakia, the other Warsaw Pact country bordering on the West; and Poland, the largest country in the region.[41] Evidently, the Soviet Union found it more economical to provide for its defense by buying the allegiance of the countries to its west than by devoting resources of comparable value to defense production. In doing so, it inadvertently provided an extra boost to growth in Eastern Europe.

Trade obviously contributed less to growth in Eastern than in Western Europe. Intraregional trade was far from free, since such freedom would have subverted the operation of the planning mechanism. It was not even clear whether that trade which occurred was efficiency-enhancing, since international transactions often reinforced and amplified other distortions—for example, encouraging Eastern European countries that concentrated excessively on heavy industry to expand that industry still further by giving them access to Soviet raw materials. The contrast with Western Europe is a reminder that trade is not always and everywhere an engine of growth and that regionalism is not always a desirable form of integration.

The End of Reform

By the end of the 1960s, most reform efforts had been halted and rolled back owing to their unintended consequences. The 1970s then saw few new initiatives along similar lines. Observing cases such as Czechoslovakia, where economic reform had produced demands for political reform, Eastern European leaders feared that moving further down the path of economic liberalization and decen-

---

[41] These are the conclusions of Marrese and Vanous (1983).

tralization could undermine political control. Despite censorship and prohibitions on travel, residents were not unaware that their economic system delivered low levels of productivity and consumption compared to the West. The party leadership was continually fearful of an eruption of political unrest like that of the Polish shipyard workers of Gdañsk and Szezecin in December 1970.

What socialism offered was job security and economic equality, values that were by no means alien to the ethos of the Christian Democrats but were even more integral to the ideology of communism. Reform socialism not only undermined the power of the Communist Party, but it also threatened these core values. It jeopardized the provision of the only social goods that central planning had the capacity reliably to deliver. Incentives for efficiency meant significantly higher pay for successful managers and ambitious workers, which sat uneasily with the ethos of equality. Industrial restructuring and decentralization had uncertain implications for job security, one of the few things credibly offered by the traditional socialist system. Resistance to reform consequently emanated not just from the political elite, who feared threats to their control, but also from rank-and-file workers, who feared the implications for security and equality. The Prague Spring of 1968 may have featured wide-ranging discussions of economic reform, but it was rank-and-file workers who were least willing to contemplate radical alternatives. When the Communist Party leader Wladislaw Gomulka proposed making take-home pay a function of the performance of individual enterprises, it was Polish textile workers who objected to the new ideas. In Hungary, it was factory workers who objected most strenuously to the inequalities and insecurity bred by the New Economic Mechanism. There was an element of rationality in their response insofar as they understood that partial reform might only make things worse. And radical reform was not on offer. If modestly strengthened incentives for management initiative and workforce cooperation failed to enhance enterprise efficiency, it was the workers who would bear the consequences in the form of lower pay or higher unemployment. Their fears flowed directly from the contradictions of the system.

161

Hence there was no one—neither leaders nor workers—to force the issue. For aspiring reformers there was also the threat to the political status quo, as became evident in Yugoslavia in the 1960s when decentralization accentuated economic inequalities, leading to worker unrest and feeding local nationalisms.[42] The immediate cause of these disruptions was the greater autonomy granted the banks, which led them to concentrate their investment in the most advanced parts of the Yugoslav federation, provoking complaints from other regions. Tito recognized the linkage to political unrest, and his crackdown on these national movements was accompanied by a measure of economic recentralization in 1971–1972. This was the kind of about-face that other regimes wished to avoid.

Not only had the scope for extensive growth been exhausted by the early 1970s, then, but early enthusiasm for economic reform had been lost as well. The limitations of the system were evident not just to the political elite but to the population at large. Indicative of this underperformance was the trend in adult male mortality, which had followed the Western Europe track until the mid-1960s but then began rising in Central and Eastern Europe while continuing to decline in the West.

For a time, the planned economies staggered on, with the help of cheap energy from the resource-rich Soviet Union. Compulsion sustained the production of petroleum and other industrial inputs, and cheap credit from Western banks seeking outlets for recycled petrodollars allowed technology and inputs to be sourced from abroad. These cheap inputs facilitated the expansion of "goulash communism," the essence of which was increasing the provision of consumer goods in order to buy popular support. By the end of the 1970s, however, most these facilitating conditions had disappeared. Stagnation set in, presaging the imminent collapse of the system.

---

[42] Denitch (1976) and Burg (1983) discuss economic and social differentiation as causes of this crisis.

- SIX -

THE INTEGRATION
OF WESTERN EUROPE

The formation of the European Economic Community (EEC) in
1958 and then the completion within a decade of a customs union
encompassing France, Germany, Italy, and the Benelux countries
were among the most important developments affecting Western
Europe in the third quarter of the twentieth century. Moving in
fifteen years from a devastating war to the creation of this unprecedented transnational entity surely ranks as one of the most extraordinary political and economic transformations the world has ever
seen. The achievement reflected special circumstances, specifically
a distinctive intellectual and structural inheritance, but also human
agency in the form of key decisions without which the consequences
of that inheritance might have been very different.

An important aspect of that inheritance, noted in chapter 2,
was a long-standing if inchoate tradition of integrationist thought.
Already in the 1920s and 1930s, some of those who rose to political
leadership after World War II, Konrad Adenauer and Georges Pompidou among them, saw the development of regional political institutions grounded a European political identity as the best way of
fostering reconciliation and preventing another war. The Congress
of Europe held in the Hague in 1948, the opening salvo of postwar
integrationist efforts, built on this tradition. That it counted among
its members the former British prime minister Winston Churchill
(a Conservative), the former French premier Léon Blum (an ex-

Socialist), the Italian premier Alcide De Gaspari (a Christian Democrat), and the future Belgian prime minister Paul-Henri Spaak (a Socialist) is indicative of how widely these ideas resonated among politicians. The same can be said of the European Movement that emerged from the Hague Congress and produced the Council of Europe and its Consultative Assembly, the forerunner to the European Parliament.[1]

Others saw the solution to Europe's political and security problems in strengthening the nation-state, but they too perceived pan-European institutions as a means to this end.[2] For France, the European Coal and Steel Community (ECSC) was intended to ensure a reliable supply of high-grade coal from the Ruhr and thus to enhance the efficiency of its armaments industry. Euratom, the atomic energy community, was a way of achieving energy security and political control of a European bomb. The French saw the atomic energy community as a logical successor to the ECSC, with similar links to national security.[3] For Charles de Gaulle, these initiatives held out hope that his country would never again be threatened by Germany and promised foreign policy independence from the United States. For Germany, the institutions of European integration were a vehicle for regaining international respectability. They were a way of "rebranding" Germany as a country of committed Europeanists. They offered a European cloak for the country's efforts to again acquire a foreign-policy role.

These motivations are sometimes portrayed as complementary. European integration lent legitimacy to the steps taken by national governments to rebuild their economies and strengthen their militaries, since it reassured their neighbors that these goals would not be pursued at the expense of other countries. By sharing power in

---

[1] On the origins of the Council of Europe, see Schuman (1951).

[2] This is a theme of Gillingham (1991), Milward (1992), and Milward et al. (1993).

[3] France supported Euratom only because it believed that it would dominate the production of basic nuclear materials, given subsidies extended to the French atomic energy industry under the government's early postwar development plans. By enhancing energy self-sufficiency, atomic energy also promised to free France from dependence on Middle Eastern oil (the value of which was underscored by the 1956 Suez crisis) and, not incidentally, to contribute to the solution of its balance-of-payments problems.

this limited way, European states could expand their room to maneuver. Yet at some level there was an intrinsic opposition between the idea of European integration, which entailed a pooling of sovereignty or at least a fundamental redefinition of the concept, and the strand of thought in which the institutions of the European Community (EC) were designed to reinforce the power of the nation-state. It is, therefore, not surprising that the political aspect of the process—how far political integration should go and in what manner it would proceed—was controversial from the start.

Superimposed on this political inheritance was the economic inheritance. As neighbors with complementary economic structures, Europe's economies were natural trading partners.[4] In the simplest terms, Germany supplied capital goods while France produced consumer goods and the Benelux countries provided food, finance, and transshipment services. But in the 1930s the gains from trade and specialization were squandered. Balkanized European economies unable to exploit economies of scale and scope had been slow to develop and adopt mass-production methods. In the absence of a stable global monetary framework, governments were unable to deploy monetary and fiscal policies to maintain high levels of investment. As a result, Europe's economies had fallen further behind the United States. The formation of an EEC was now seen as creating a regional market on a scale appropriate for the new technologies of the second half of the twentieth century. It was a way of facilitating stable policies. If not sufficient to solve all of Europe's problems, it was at least a step in the right direction.[5]

A third structural condition was the position of the United States. The extraordinary imbalance of economic, financial, and military power that developed in the wake of the war gave the United States unusual scope for shaping events. Although there was no single U.S. attitude toward European integration, the U.S. gov-

[4] Although this had always been true, the industrial development of the preceding century had made it even more the case.

[5] For an early statement of this view, which applies it not just to European integration but also to the development of the North Atlantic Treaty Organization (NATO), see Deutsch et al. (1957).

ernment was generally supportive on both political and economic grounds. The Americans saw European integration as anchoring the continent in an established democratic system. With the advent of the Cold War, they saw the creation of pan-European institutions as a way of forming a united front to beat back the Soviet threat. They saw stability and prosperity as the best guarantees that this united front would garner popular support. The Marshall Planners saw their own country's continental market in merchandise, capital, and labor as a source of economic strength that should be emulated in Europe. As Paul Hoffmann, the chief Marshall Plan administrator, put it in his famous October 1949 speech to the OEEC, prosperity required "the formation of a single large market within which quantitative restrictions on the movement of goods, monetary barriers to the flow of payments, and eventually, all tariffs are permanently swept away. The fact that we have in the United States a single market of 150 million customers has been indispensable to the strength and efficiency of our economy."[6] Together, these were powerful reasons for the United States to prefer European integration. And for a bit more than a decade after World War II, the United States possessed the leverage to make its preferences felt.

Although the first phase of the postwar integration process is often portrayed as a game with three players—France, Germany, and the United States—there was in fact at least one more consequential party, the United Kingdom, even if it was prominent mainly by its absence. Britain's position was ambiguous, given continuing strong commercial and financial ties to the Commonwealth and Empire that rendered it reluctant to reorient its economic relations toward Europe. Politicians and the public were skeptical about political integration (understandably, given Britain's status as an island). But at the same time they were unwilling to turn their backs on Europe, which was within swimming distance of Dover. Britain's history as a great power and as the last Western European redoubt from Nazi domination gave it the stature or at least the aspiration to help shape the integrationist project. All this left France, which saw Europe as

[6] Cited in Killick (1997), p. 138.

a platform for its own great-power ambitions, reluctant to accept Britain as an equal partner. Ultimately, this meant that European integration would proceed as a project of the six continental countries that founded the ECSC (Belgium, France, Italy, Luxembourg, the Netherlands, and West Germany). It also bequeathed a legacy of uncertainty about how quickly and in what manner the founding members would embrace additional members.

But not even this unique structural constellation guaranteed the creation of the EC, completion of its customs union, and the subsequent progress of the integrationist project. There was also an important role for human agency and historical happenstance. Without Konrad Adenauer and the Korean War at the beginning of the 1950s or Georges Pompidou and U.S. balance-of-payments policy at the end of the 1960s, for example, things might have turned out differently.[7] National interests and bargaining power mattered for the outcome, but so did individual attitudes and actions.

Initial Steps

All of these factors were at play in the first successful effort to integrate Europe, the ECSC. At one level, the ECSC was an economic initiative: it was designed to facilitate the recovery and rationalization of Europe's steel industry by coordinating national production and investment plans. But there was also a political aspect. The Schuman Plan for the ECSC, named for the Alsatian-born French foreign minister Robert Schuman, who had fought for Germany in World War I and dedicated his political career to Franco-German reconciliation, was in fact drafted by Jean Monnet, who saw it as a first step down the path of political integration. As Monnet's draft put it with remarkable forthrightness, "The pooling of coal and steel production will immediately provide for the establishment of common bases for economic development as the first step in the federa-

---

[7] For more on this way of thinking about the evolution of the EC, see Parsons (2003).

tion of Europe."[8] Monnet and Schuman sought to place the French and German coal and steel industries under a common *political* authority and to foster *political* rapprochement between the countries. The ECSC would be governed by a supranational High Authority, whose powers would be checked by a Special Council of Ministers, a Common Assembly of seventy-eight advisers from the six participating countries, and a High Court of seven jurists, at least one from each member state. These arrangements were needed to lend legitimacy to the new economic entity by imposing checks and balances and strengthening the political accountability of those responsible for managing it. But the result was to impart further momentum to the political dimension of the integrationist project. This was all to the good from the standpoint of Schuman and Monnet, the second of whom, not coincidentally, became founding president of the new High Authority.

But this does not mean that there existed an elite consensus for political integration, much less broad-based popular support. Planning for the ECSC was conducted in secret, presented to the French Cabinet as a commitment to be honored, and announced to the French Assembly as a fait accompli. In the subsequent negotiations with other countries, Monnet consulted with his government only once, presenting the draft agreement as a done deal. The French prime minister Georges Bidault and the justice minister René Mayer harbored deep reservations about the EC's supranational aspect. Bidault and the secretary of state for economic affairs Robert Buron criticized the proposal for excluding the British.[9] The main employers federation, the Confédération nationale du patronat français, opposed the scheme, reflecting the iron and steel industry's hostility to government intervention. Criticism came from nearly every quarter. Only the outbreak of the Korean War, which led the Americans to push for the removal of remaining restrictions on German industrial production, forced the opponents of Monnet's plan to acknowledge

[8] Cited in Urwin (1994), p. 46.
[9] Unlike West Germany and the United States, the United Kingdom had not even been consulted prior to Schuman's announcing the plan.

that renegotiation was not an option. With the need now to restrain a revitalized German steel industry, a flawed agreement was better than none at all. Thus, we see in this first step in building the EC the role of not just intellectual leadership and agenda-setting power but also of historical contingency in the form of the war in Korea and of the broader context in the form of American influence.

Eventually, the opponents of Monnet's vision of a politically integrated Europe had their day. In 1954 the French Assembly rejected a proposal, initiated by the country's defense minister René Pleven but again largely drafted by Monnet, for a European Defense Community (EDC) and a European Political Community to determine the foreign-policy ends to which Europe's new forces might be put. The EDC was intended to avoid the reconstitution of an independent German military force by integrating German troops and military capability into a European army. Although there would be no independent units of German troops under their own command, the other member states would maintain their own national forces and were obliged to assign only some of their troops to the European army. For acquiescing to this arrangement, Germany received assurances that the Allied occupation would end and that it would regain sovereignty over its foreign affairs.

But this vision of an EDC undergirded by a European Political Community was too much even for a French political class confident of its ability to shape Europe's institutions. The French government under Antoine Pinay signed the EDC agreement only with the understanding that no immediate steps would be taken to secure its ratification. Successive governments then fell whenever they showed any inclination to submit the treaty to the French Assembly. When his predecessors' inability to extract France from the quagmire in Vietnam brought the strong-willed Pierre Mendès-France to the premiership in 1954, the new premier made clear that he wished to clear the treaty from the agenda and that he would not resign if it was defeated.[10] On 30 August 1954, the EDC's doom was sealed

[10] Urwin (1994), p. 67. Once again we see here the role for historical contingency, in this case France's defeat at Dien Bien Phu, in shaping the progress of the integrationist project.

when the Assembly adopted a resolution opposing ratification by a vote of 319 to 264.

From that point, Europe organized its collective security as a group of sovereign states participating together in the U.S.-led North Atlantic Treaty Organization (NATO). Within Europe, what defense cooperation occurred was organized under the provisions of the 1948 Brussels Treaty, which provided the basis for a loose arrangement called the Western European Union. The United Kingdom committed to maintaining four divisions of troops and tactical air forces on the continent, reassuring other countries of its vigilance against German remilitarization. Adenauer agreed that the Bundeswehr (the West German armed forces) would have no separate general staff and be limited to five hundred thousand men. On this basis, Germany was permitted to join NATO. The French National Assembly accepted the arrangement reluctantly at the end of 1954. This was political accommodation without political integration.

The failure of the EDC was the first of several points at which governments signaled their reluctance to pursue the vision of a United States of Europe of committed federalists such as Monnet. The exceptional circumstances of the early postwar years that had allowed visionary leaders to push through ambitious political agreements receded with political and economic normalization. Coalition discipline could no longer be enforced by the fear that bringing down the government would inaugurate a period of political chaos and put the country at the mercy of foreign powers. This meant that functionaries such as Monnet and even elected officials had less agenda-setting power. U.S. leverage also diminished following the end of the Marshall Plan and as Cold War imperatives became less compelling with the end of the Korean conflict and Stalin's death.

For all these reasons, the opponents of political integration were able to reassert themselves. The advocates of deeper integration responded by focusing on Europe's bread and butter and specifically on the concrete task of creating a customs union. They attempted to capitalize on concerns about the competitiveness of the European economy and, in particular, the belief that the small size of national markets was a handicap in the competition with American producers. If integration required the development of political institutions to govern the new economic space and hold those responsible for its operation accountable for their actions, then all the better, in this view. The political agenda might then slip back into the European house through the back door. The opposing position was that a free trade zone was enough. It could be negotiated and implemented by national governments. There was thus no need for political institution building.

The stage for the customs-union initiative was set by the elimination of the dollar gap, Europe's structural deficit vis-à-vis the United States. The 1949 devaluations first strengthened Europe's competitiveness. As the continent then put the exceptional circumstances of postwar reconstruction behind it, savings and investment rates normalized, strengthening the balance of payments. By the end of 1958 Western Europe was ready for current-account convertibility (the freedom to buy and sell foreign exchange for trade-related purposes). In turn, current-account convertibility made feasible the creation of a European customs union.

But not all countries were equally enthusiastic about the prospect. Being in a strong competitive position, Germany had little to fear from trade. German leaders also saw the customs union as an important step toward the creation of European institutions guaranteeing the country continuing foreign-policy autonomy. Dutch competitiveness was similarly high. The economic interests of Germany and the Benelux countries were well aligned; they were natural trading partners, and the Benelux countries had already cut their tariffs in order to encourage German producers to use these countries as routes for transshipping their exports to the rest of the world. Although the Benelux countries were jealous of their sovereignty, they also saw the importance of restraining Germany and thus of the further progress of the European project. Italy was mainly concerned to guarantee access to other European markets for its excess labor, but it was anxious to maintain the opportunity, extended at the time the ECSC was created, of associating itself with a group of

171

economically advanced partners.[11] France, in contrast, harbored worries about the competitiveness of its exporters if exposed to the full force of German competition, since the country was burdened by high labor costs.

Not surprisingly, proposals for relaunching European integration on an economic basis following the defeat of the EDC came not from France or Germany but from the Benelux countries. These included a 1953 proposal by the Dutch foreign minister Jan Willem Beyen to create a customs union of the six members of the ECSC and a 1955 proposal by the Belgian foreign minister Paul-Henri Spaak to extend European integration into the fields of energy, transportation, and atomic energy.[12] In both cases France torpedoed the idea. France could not, however, afford to isolate itself from Europe. Rejecting the EDC had resulted in Germany joining NATO, not a happy outcome from the French point of view.

The French government now explored other options, notably economic union with the United Kingdom, which was proposed by Prime Minister Guy Mollet to his British counterpart, Anthony Eden, in 1956. There had been some wartime discussion of this idea, notably at the time of Winston Churchill's dramatic 1940 offer of political and economic fusion. The two economies now shared a number of common problems, notably disappointing growth and chronic balance-of-payments weakness. But it was not clear that economic union would solve them. Predictably, the British rebuffed Mollet's initiative. France was then left with no alternative to a customs union of the Six. Mollet's government had to satisfy itself with extracting as many concessions as possible. Thus, the Common Market agreement allowed the French to retain import taxes and subsidies for the time being and the newly created European Commission to authorize safeguards in response to persistent balance-of-payments problems.

[11] See Romero (1993).

[12] Spaak's initiative attracted the support of the Dutch foreign minister and Luxembourg's prime minister, both of whom had served with Spaak as ministers in exile in London during World War II and who had been instrumental in the creation of the Benelux customs union.

To be sure, some of the framers of the Treaty of Rome had loftier ambitions. These were heralded by the opening lines of the treaty referring to an "ever closer union." Chancellor Adenauer favored a joint Franco-German foreign policy, a context for which might be provided by an EC. The first president of the European Commission, Walter Hallstein, and the Commission's other founding members saw themselves as pursuing political as well as economic goals.[13] As Williams put it, "Monnet had been wise enough to declare in October 1958 that the prime necessity was to 'make the economic union effective.' But even then there was no doubt that the purpose of 'making economic union effective' was to promote the political union of tomorrow."[14]

Still, most governments remained skeptical of the merits of political integration. The Benelux countries worried about the threat to their independence. The French were willing to accept only as much political integration as might strengthen their ability to project military and diplomatic power abroad. Paris agreed to decision making by a qualified majority only on issues on which it was confident of forming a majority. The Treaty of Rome had foreseen that voting in the Council would move first to qualified majority rule and then to simple majority rule by the second half of the 1960s, but whether it would get there was open to doubt.[15]

In the United Kingdom the idea of political integration was received less enthusiastically still. Britain had its own nuclear program, and it had no interest in deeper political links as a way of advancing the Euratom Treaty. But, like Mollet before them, the Macmillan government realized that heading off a customs union of the Six required offering alternatives. The British therefore took the initiative of establishing a committee in the OEEC, headed by the Conservative member of Parliament Reginald Maudling, to study the possibility of a Europe-wide free trade area. A free trade area, which did not require negotiating a common external tariff, had less

[13] Von der Groeben (1987), p. 31.
[14] Williams (1993), p. 415.
[15] See "The Luxembourg Compromise" later in this chapter.

demanding political prerequisites than the customs union alternative. Britain's preference was to make this area as large as possible while infringing on national policy prerogatives only as much as absolutely necessary.[16]

Since German industry was highly competitive and German firms also exported to markets other than France, Italy, and the Benelux countries, that country's leaders were positively disposed toward the British proposal. The Benelux countries were prepared to go along with any free trade initiative that included their larger German neighbor. But a free trade area in which the country with the lowest tariffs set the pace for liberalization was not amenable to the French. Rules of origin being hard to enforce, tariffs would tend to be forced down toward the levels of the lowest-tariff member state. France preferred a customs union because this would permit it to control the common external tariff and liberalize more gradually. French officials consequently saw opening partially to the Six (or, more precisely, to the other Five) as safer than opening to Europe as a whole. Even French politicians who recognized the need for devaluation and structural adjustment believed that these reforms would be easier to implement in the context of the phased introduction of a customs union of the Six.[17] And France was unlikely to obtain the Euratom Treaty unless it gave its partners the Common Market in return.[18]

Germany could have swung either way. Industry was inclined toward the British proposal, which promised a large free trade area and a low external tariff. Politicians and opinion leaders who believed strongly in market liberalization, the economics minister Ludwig Erhard and the economist Wilhelm Röpke among them, worried that a small economic community tilted toward France would discriminate against nonmembers and protect inefficient producers. On

---

[16] When the Six made clear that they preferred to proceed with a common market, Britain then proposed the creation of a free trade area in nonagricultural products in which the EEC would participate as a unit.

[17] Lynch (1997), p. 176.

[18] French negotiators had unsuccessfully sought to delink the two treaties. See Lynch (1997).

the other hand, Germany's commitment to the European project and need to cultivate its image as a country of committed Europeanists led politicians such as Adenauer to favor a Europe of the Six, which promised to be more than a free trade area.

The Macmillan government then tipped by balance by insisting on the maintenance of imperial preference and the exclusion of agricultural goods from the free trade area. It drove Germany into France's arms by proposing an arrangement in which British manufacturers would have free access to European markets but European farmers would have no market in Britain, insofar as that country could continue importing foodstuffs from the Commonwealth and the Empire under preferential arrangements dating to the 1930s.[19] As at many points in the second half of the twentieth century, Britain had one foot in Europe and one foot out. Its historical ties to the Commonwealth and the Empire prevented it from committing to the European project.

Predictably, France and Germany insisted on equal access for their farmers, albeit with price supports and protection from extra-European supplies for their less competitive producers.[20] Once de Gaulle returned as prime minister in June 1958 and a new French constitution strengthening his powers was adopted in the autumn, the writing was on the wall. In November, on the occasion of a meeting of the Maudling Committee, de Gaulle had his minister of information announce, in a manner designed to embarrass the British, that discussions of the free trade option were at an end.

Proceeding now was straightforward. Institutions could be modeled on the ECSC. Like the ECSC, the new communities would be governed by a Commission, a Parliament, and a Court of Justice (plural "communities," since there would be three: Euratom, the

[19] The United Kingdom hoped that the Commonwealth and the Empire would use the revenues earned from exporting agricultural goods to the British market to purchase British manufactures (Commonwealth and colonial markets still taking more than half of all British exports in this period).

[20] Of course, France had colonies too, to which it sought to extend foreign aid and European market access. But the French colonies produced mainly tropical products, which, in contrast with the goods of the British Commonwealth, did not compete with European farm products.

EEC, and the ECSC, the last of which was wound up only by the Merger Treaty of 1967). The Commission, the Court, and the Parliament all had an uncomfortable supranational aspect, but if similar arrangements had been acceptable for the ECSC, why should they be unacceptable now? "To avoid isolation in foreign policy and to guarantee France's economic security by tying the Federal Republic to western Europe," as Frances Lynch put it, the French Assembly voted by a large majority for the EEC and Euratom treaties.[21] In the other five countries, ratification was cut-and-dried.

Thus, already in the negotiations over the European Communities' founding treaty one sees two conflicting visions, one in which the EC was essentially a glorified free trade area, and another in which it was a stepping-stone to political integration. One sees the tension between those preferring open regionalism, in which any country willing to meet minimal conditions could participate, and those preferring a more exclusive club with loftier ambitions. One sees disagreements among countries more and less well positioned to capitalize on the removal of barriers to competition. These same divisions would define the fault lines within Western Europe for the balance of the century and beyond.

EFTA and the British Dilemma

Notwithstanding these disagreements, the attractions of the Common Market were strong. Europe's own market was growing faster than those of its former colonies. Even the United Kingdom, with its historic links to the Commonwealth and the Empire, was forced to acknowledge that its future lay with Europe.

Responding to these pressures, Britain and six smaller European countries—Austria, Denmark, Norway, Portugal, Sweden, and Switzerland—agreed in 1960 to establish the European Free Trade Association (EFTA), an entity whose limited aspirations, not encompassing

---

[21] Lynch (1997), p. 182.

political integration, were evident in its name.[22] Unfortunately, all but one of the EFTA countries, Portugal, traded more extensively with the Common Market than with their fellow members. Reflecting the dynamism of the continent's large countries, even Britain's exports to the Six grew faster than its exports to EFTA in the first half of the 1960s. As a rival free trade area, EFTA made little sense.

Nor did EFTA solve the problem that the outsiders had no say in the development of the EC. Britain opposed an ambitious Common Agricultural Policy (CAP). It worried that stronger intra-European economic ties would come at the expense of its colonial dependencies and extra-European allies. It opposed an EC foreign policy, fearing the revival of German power. But lacking a seat at the table, it could not directly influence these decisions. And the longer it waited to join, the more aspects of the EC it would have to take as a fait accompli.

Inevitably, then, Britain was led to apply for EEC membership in 1961. The French president Charles de Gaulle feared that the accession of another large member state would frustrate his efforts to control the EC's agenda. British membership would make it more difficult for France to use the EC as a platform for securing and maintaining great-power status. It would make it harder for de Gaulle to achieve his goal of a tripartite directorate for the West composed of the United States, Britain, and a French-led EC. As he told one of his ministers, "Europe is the chance for France to become what she has ceased to be since Waterloo: the first in the world."[23] American brinkmanship during the Cuban Missile Crisis of October 1962 underscored for de Gaulle the importance of establishing an independent foreign and defense policy through the EC. Accepting for membership a Britain skeptical of French ambitions was inconsistent with this goal.

Macmillan invited de Gaulle to his home at Birch Grove. The French president invited Macmillan to the Château de Champs and

---

[22] Hansen (2001) calls the EEC "a customs union with dressing" and EFTA "a free trade area without dressing." Another country, Finland, became associated with EFTA in 1961.

[23] Cited in Jackson (2003), p. 99.

then to the Château de Rambouillet outside Paris. But there was no reconciling the problems of the Commonwealth with France's global aspirations. De Gaulle delivered his definitive *non* at a press conference on 14 January 1963. Another decade would have to pass, with a change in French political leadership, before Britain would finally be allowed to join.[24] But already the lure of the EC was clear.

Economic Effects

It took until 1969 for the six founding members of the EC to remove all their tariffs vis-à-vis one another. Even then, nontariff barriers of various kinds remained, and their elimination had to wait for the 1992 Program discussed in chapter 11. Similarly, although the Treaty of Rome had proclaimed the right of residents of the EC to live and work throughout the economic zone, the creation of something vaguely resembling a single labor market would have to wait for several decades. But even the gradual reduction of tariff barriers allowed the member states to specialize more in the production of goods in which they had a comparative advantage and to better exploit economies of scale and scope. It weakened the market power of monopolies and cartels, forcing previously cosseted producers to shape up or lose market share.

The impact of the customs union was most dramatic in France, where producers had been heavily sheltered from foreign competition. The share of French consumption accounted for by imports now doubled from 8 percent in 1959 to 16 percent in 1969.[25] The share of French trade conducted with other EC countries nearly doubled from 30 to 57 percent.[26] For Italy the increase was from 30 to

---

[24] More fundamentally, there had to be a shift in the balance of power between France and Germany. By 1970, Germany had emerged as the stronger power financially (see chapter 8) and was increasingly assertive in its *Ostpolitik*. Georges Pompidou, de Gaulle's successor, judged—wrongly, in the event—that British entry might provide an effective counterweight to Germany's power in Europe and thereby shore up France's position. Berstein and Rioux (2000), pp. 25–26.

[25] Adams (1989), pp. 156–157.

[26] These are figures for 1958 and 1970.

TABLE 6.1

Intraregional exports as a percentage of total exports, 1955–1970

From	To	1955	1960	1965	1970
EEC-6	EEC-6	32	35	44	49
	Western Europe	59	60	68	69
Western Europe	EEC-6	28	31	37	41
	Western Europe	55	56	64	66

Source: International Monetary Fund, *Direction of Trade Statistics, Historical Summary,* 1948–1980.

Note: Western Europe includes Austria, Belgium, Denmark, Finland, France, Greece, Ireland, Italy, Luxembourg, the Netherlands, Norway, Portugal, Spain, Sweden, Switzerland, the United Kingdom, and West Germany. The EEC-6 are the six founding members of the European Economic Community: Belgium, France, Italy, Luxembourg, the Netherlands, and West Germany.

50 percent. For Germany it was from 37 to 52 percent. Overall, the share of Western Europe's trade that stayed within the region rose by ten percentage points, from 56 to 66 percent (table 6.1).

Admittedly, some of this increase in intra-European trade would have occurred even in the absence of the Common Market. Given the recovery and growth of the European economies, there would have been a tendency in any case for Europe's now-richer residents to consume a wider variety of goods, including goods produced by their European neighbors. But evidence for twenty-one industrial countries, EC and non-EC alike, obtained after controlling for the impact on trade of changes in national incomes, populations, and real exchange rates, suggests that intra-EC trade grew 3.2 percent per year faster over the two decades from 1953 through 1973 than would have been the case in the absence of the Common Market.[27] The boost to trade among the Six began immediately following the formation of the EC and continued through the 1960s, peaking in 1965–1967. The same timing, albeit with somewhat smaller trade-creating effects, is also evident in the case of EFTA.

There is some evidence that this additional trade within the EC and EFTA came partially at the expense of their trade with other

[27] Bayoumi and Eichengreen (1997), p. 150. An earlier study by Aitken (1973), although using a slightly different country sample and specification, yields similar results. So too does a subsequent study by Eichengreen and Vasquez (2000) using an entirely different methodology.

industrial economies. The same study points to a decline in EC trade with non-EC and non-EFTA countries following the creation of the Common Market. However, this effect had largely died out by 1962.[28] In 1975, Bela Balassa conducted a comprehensive study of empirical evidence on the trade-creating and trade-diverting effects of the Common Market. He concluded that the magnitude of trade creation was several times the magnitude of any associated trade diversion.[29]

One explanation for these relatively benign effects may have been the EC's desire to avoid antagonizing the United States, which supported the Common Market and tolerated the CAP.[30] When implementing the first round of tariff cuts in 1959, the Council of Ministers agreed that internal reductions should also be extended to nonmember countries such as the United States whenever the Common Tariff was lower than existing national tariffs. Another explanation is that the removal of barriers on intra-European trade took place in the context of the Kennedy Round of GATT negotiations.[31] (See table 6.2.) The Kennedy Round reduced tariffs by more than one-third on products accounting for almost 75 percent of world trade. With Europe lowering its tariffs on imports from the rest of the world at the same time it was eliminating intra-European trade barriers, freer intra-European trade complemented rather than substituting for freer trade with the rest of the world. Improvements in competitiveness, such as those of French industry, encouraged European governments to welcome multilateral liberalization within the GATT. Finally, the possibility that the EEC might develop into a rival trade bloc encouraged the United States to negotiate across-

[28] Evidence of trade diversion away from nonmember countries is even weaker in the case of EFTA, although it is not entirely absent. The estimates in Bayoumi and Eichengreen (1997) suggest that EFTA's trade with non-EFTA and non-EC countries grew more slowly, by 0.8 percent per year, as a result of the regional arrangement than would have been the case otherwise. However, this point estimate is not significantly different from zero at standard confidence levels. Again, estimates in Aitken (1973) are strikingly similar.

[29] Balassa (1975). The only exception was the CAP (see the next section), which was a source of severe trade diversion and had significant welfare costs.

[30] See the next section.

[31] The round was initiated by the U.S. president John F. Kennedy, but was negotiated only after his death, between 1964 and 1967.

TABLE 6.2
Average tariff rates in the European Community before and after
integration (Percent)

	1958	External tariff in 1968	External tariff after the Kennedy Round
Benelux	9.7	10.4	6.6
France	17.0	10.4	6.6
Germany	6.4	10.4	6.6
Italy	18.7	10.4	6.6
Simple average	13.0	10.4	6.6
Change from previous level	—	−20%	−40%

Source: Sapir (1992), table 6.

the-board tariff cuts of up to 50 percent in the context of the Kennedy Round. Without the existence of a strong and equal European counterpart capable of credibly offering reciprocal concessions, this offer would not have been made.

By how much did the stimulus to trade from the creation of the Common Market boost Europe's growth? Assuming that intra-European trade grew by an additional 3.2 percent per year as a result of the Common Market, Eichengreen and Vasquez (2000) estimate that one-third of a percentage point was added to the annual average rate of growth of GDP. This captures not just the gains from trade narrowly defined (the reallocation of resources to sectors in which productivity was higher) but also the incentive effects of more intense competition. Applied to the period 1959–1969, it suggests that incomes in the Six would have been about 4 percent lower in the absence of the Common Market. A less conservative estimate, following Frankel and Romer (1999), suggests that the increase in European incomes due to the growth of intra-European trade in the 1960s may have been closer to 8 percent.

In addition to creating trade, the Common Market had a variety of subtler effects. Its advent was accompanied by a substantial net increase in both intra- and extra-European foreign direct investment (FDI) flows as the creation of what began to resemble a unified internal market provided an incentive for European firms to branch abroad in order to better exploit economies of scale and scope and for non-European firms to establish European operations

181

as a way of securing market access and producing close to the consumer. The largest increase in FDI, in fact, came from countries outside the Common Market, notably the United States, suggesting the presence of complementarities between intra-EC trade and extra-EC FDI.[32] In a period when the task for Europe was to assimilate the remaining backlog of technology and when FDI was an effective conduit for technology transfer, these complementarities were important.

The Common Agricultural Policy

Not all of the effects of the EEC can be cast in this favorable light. The CAP is a case in point. Each member state already operated its own agricultural policy, involving in most cases price supports and subsidies. The priority placed on agriculture reflected not just the political leverage of farmers but also memories of wartime food shortages. As in the case of coal and steel, this association of food with security was anachronistic but powerful.

These programs varied in their particulars, not surprisingly, insofar as farmers operated at different levels of efficiency. These variations complicated the task of formulating a common policy. However, a customs union without free trade in agriculture was unattractive to France, Italy, and the Netherlands as exporters of fruit, vegetables, wine, and other agricultural goods. At the same time, Germany and France had many high-cost farmers who regarded free trade in agricultural products as tolerable only if married to price supports.

The Treaty of Rome had obliged the Commission to present proposals for a CAP.[33] The scheme to which the Commission gave birth, to no one's surprise, was for an integrated market with temporary levies to smooth the harmonization of domestic policies and

---

[32] See Dunning (1997a, 1997b).

[33] Already in the 1950s, before the Treaty of Rome, there had been discussions of a Franco-Dutch initiative for a European agricultural policy (the "Green Plan").

permanent price supports. The alternative of allowing prices to be determined in world markets and extending deficiency payments to farmers if prices were lower than costs of production (as in the United Kingdom) was deemed infeasible given the EC's limited budget. Instead the EC would support prices by purchasing surplus production, while the cost of its operations would be limited by restricting imports of cheap agricultural goods from outside—the solution the British had feared when they proposed that the Commonwealth and the Empire be incorporated into the European free trade area—and by temporarily assigning customs revenues to the EC's budget. This would require developing a system of variable import levies that rose as world prices fell. With European agricultural markets thereby insulated from supplies from outside, farm products could ultimately be traded within the Community at a single EEC-wide price.

The CAP was phased in from 1964 to 1968. Setting support prices for the entire range of agricultural products was challenging, to say the least. If prices for feed and other inputs used by animal producers were set too high, there would be shortages of beef, pork, and poultry. If the prices for dairy products and viniculture were set too high, the EC would have to make massive expenditures and accumulate mountains of butter and lakes of wine. In effect, the administrators of the CAP faced the same nightmare as Eastern European planners but on a sectoral scale.

The decision to harmonize agricultural price supports at high levels rather than abolishing them in favor of lump-sum transfers was an opportunity missed. To be sure, the CAP provided impetus for further integration insofar as it occasioned the growth of an extensive bureaucracy in Brussels. It also encouraged the pursuit of monetary integration, since its operation was incompatible with fluctuations in intra-European exchange rates. Currency movements disturbed the alignment of domestic-currency support prices and created the danger of massive cross-border flows of agricultural goods. In August 1969, when the French franc was devalued, and later that year, when the deutschmark was revalued, the EC was forced to devise a convoluted system of "green exchange rates" (artificial rates for agricultural products) and "monetary compensatory amounts" (levies on exports of agricultural products from the devaluing countries and subsidies on exports from their revaluing partners to make green rates differ from market rates). This encouraged additional subsidization, since it was harder to eliminate bonuses for farmers in the revaluing countries than to abolish taxes on exports from their devaluing partners. It also increased the drain on the EC's budget. The system of green exchange rates had to be adjusted repeatedly as prices and production costs responded to the exchange rate change. An apocryphal story had the German chancellor emerging from a meeting of the Council complaining that he had only one official who understood the system of green exchange rates but could not explain it, and one official who could explain it but did not understand it.

Despite itself, the CAP had some positive effects. For example, the opportunity to expand exports and the threat of import competition encouraged rationalization and productivity advance in French and Italian agriculture. But its subsidies and support prices were another matter. Initially these were a priority mainly for high-cost farmers in southern Germany and Alpine France.[34] With time, however, other farmers grew accustomed to suckling at the nipple of the EC. What had once been a small if vocal minority became a formidable lobby. Scaling back those subsidies, much less abolishing them, was rendered politically infeasible. Moreover, no one anticipated how quickly agricultural production would expand, heightening the cost of supporting prices. Expenditures on the CAP quickly came to account for 90 percent of the EC budget, constraining the EC's ambitions to expand into other areas. More than two decades would pass before Europe began to move toward a more economical system of lump-sum subsidies.[35]

[34] This, together with the belief that granting other countries access to the German market for foodstuffs was necessary for other countries to agree to establish the Common Market, something from which German industry stood to benefit, explains the German government's willingness to go along with the other countries' proposals for a unified agricultural market.

[35] This refers to the MacSherry reforms of the early 1990s, discussed in chapter 11.

The Luxembourg Compromise

On the political front, the most significant event was the battle over majority voting. De Gaulle had always attached great importance to his government's freedom of action. Taking decisions by majority vote in the Council, as foreseen in the Treaty of Rome, promised to streamline decision making but created the danger that other member states would band together to override French wishes. Augmenting the resources of the Commission and giving the Parliament say over the EC's budget similarly threatened to limit French room to maneuver. Among other things, these measures might strengthen the hand of others less supportive of a generous agricultural policy.

This problem broke open on 1 July 1965, with the expiry of the temporary arrangement assigning to the EC revenue from customs duties and variable import levies. The Commission proposed that this arrangement be made permanent, providing France with reassurance that the CAP would be adequately funded. At the same time, it proposed giving to the European Parliament and itself greater power over the use of those funds. This package was intended to offer something for everyone. For France it guaranteed CAP funding. For the Netherlands and Germany, which were less enamored of agricultural subsidies, it opened up the possibility of reform.

Not for the first time, de Gaulle insisted on having his cake and eating it too. He countered by suggesting that a permanent decision be put off for four years, ensuring continuing financing for the CAP without any concessions on his part. Not surprisingly, this counterproposal was coolly received in the Council. France, finding itself isolated, then withdrew from negotiations. This led in June 1965 to the crisis of "the empty chair," in which the French government, whose turn it was to chair the Council of Ministers, boycotted meetings, preventing the Council from doing business for seven months.

For de Gaulle, the sticking point was the federalist aspects of the Commission's package, which looked like the EDC and the European Political Community all over again. But skepticism about the desirability of further steps toward political integration was not limited to France. In fact, the view was widely shared. The

185

problem was de Gaulle's refusal to offer concessions. His strategy was predicated on the assumption that the EC was even more important to other countries than to France. If so, the threat to the EC posed by his empty-chair policy could be used to force concessions from other members.

But de Gaulle had not figured on the importance of the EC to his own constituents. It is revealing of how deeply the Common Market and the EC had begun reshaping the European economy that the French government's high-stakes gamble provoked opposition at home. French farmers, fearing that their government was jeopardizing the CAP, wrote a letter critical of the strategy to Premier Georges Pompidou. Industrialists complained that de Gaulle's brinkmanship was placing the Common Market at risk. These and other groups manifested their dissatisfaction at the polls. Although de Gaulle was reelected at the end of 1965, he had to fight a second ballot and obtained only a slim majority.

This political reaction explains de Gaulle's subsequent readiness to compromise. Face, always at a premium when the general was involved, was saved by holding an extraordinary meeting of the Council in Luxembourg rather than Brussels without the attendance of the Commission. It was agreed to give the EC a permanent source of income, ensuring continuing financing for the CAP, although the powers of the Commission and the Parliament were not enhanced to the extent foreseen in Hallstein's original package. In return, the extension of majority voting was accepted in principle, although a reservation was attached stating that matters would not be taken to a vote unless all members were prepared to abide by the result. Governments were entitled to block this step when they felt that their vital interests were at stake.

Ultimately, the compromise reaffirmed the power of national governments. The latter had all but total freedom to decide when their vital interests were involved and thus prevent the other member states' forcing through a decision by qualified majority. Although a number of the Commission's proposals were adopted, the process by which these decisions were reached, and in particular the strong resistance of the French government to delegating agenda-setting powers, weakened the hand of the Brussels bureaucracy. The agreement to replace the committed federalist Walter Hallstein with a more pliable chairman, at de Gaulle's initiative, was a further indication of this fact.

Thus, the EC would remain an intergovernmental institution rather than a protofederation, frustrating the agenda-setting ambitions of the Commission. Laborious negotiations would be needed to reach unanimity on decisions of any consequence. Negotiations among six sovereign nations were likely to be messy, and if the EC was enlarged they would grow messier still. Thus, there was an incentive for the two large countries, France and Germany, whose concurrence with any agreement was essential, to negotiate bilaterally and present their conclusions to the Council as a fait accompli, as they did from the early 1970s on.[36] Governments recognized that they were most likely to enjoy popular support if they focused on deepening and broadening the Common Market rather than on a political agenda. The progress of the European project exhibiting cycles, there would be further pushes for political integration, but not for several decades.

Inklings of Monetary Integration

This was not a propitious backdrop for discussions of monetary integration. A single currency for the members of the customs union required a single central bank to regulate its issuance. More problematically, it required a more powerful European Parliament capable of holding Europe's monetary policy makers accountable for their actions. In the debate over the EDC and again in the Luxembourg Compromise, governments had indicated that they viewed such efforts to further develop the political aspect of the European project as premature.

At the same time, the issue of monetary integration never entirely disappeared from the scene. Having been raised by the

[36] See the discussion in Simonian (1985).

Marshall Planners, it was kept alive by Paul-Henri Spaak in discussions of the Treaty of Rome, by Robert Marjolin and Pierre Uri in the agencies of the EEC, and by Jean Monnet through his Action Committee for the United States of Europe. Taking up the mandate given it at the Hague Summit in December 1969, the Council of Ministers authorized the formation of an expert committee on monetary integration chaired by Pierre Werner, the prime minister of Luxembourg. Werner sought to skirt the issue of whether the creation of a single European currency would require the creation of a new supranational central bank, much less the ceding of more power to the European Parliament.[37] But, in the end, these questions could not be finessed.

The fact that European governments were willing to contemplate this issue when their customs union had just been completed and the debate over how to finance the CAP was still raging testifies to their worries about monetary instability. The devaluation of the franc and revaluation of the deutschmark, which led to the imbroglio over green exchange rates in 1969, were a reminder that currency instability might destroy their laborious investment in a unified agricultural market. Contemporary fears may have been exaggerated—Le Monde concluded, prematurely, that the franc's devaluation had "buried the common agricultural market"—but the corrosive effects were there.[38] More fundamentally, exchange-rate instability was associated with macroeconomic instability in both the writings of specialists and the minds of officials. The belief that exchange-rate instability had fanned international tensions in the 1930s was conventional wisdom. In contrast, the stability of exchange rates following the general realignment of 1949 was seen as facilitating the export-led growth of the golden age. Since, in this low-inflation environment, keeping exchange rates stable was tantamount to keeping wages and labor costs stable, exchange-rate stability facilitated not just export growth but also the other elements of the postwar bargain, in particular, agreement to trade wage modera-

[37] For more on the Werner Report, see the discussion later in this section.
[38] The quotation is cited in Giavazzi and Giovannini (1989), p. 11.

tion for high investment. And without stable exchange rates, there would have been less restraint on the growth of public spending and more pressure on central banks for inflationary finance.[39]

Then there was the fear that exchange rate instability would disrupt the integrationist project. Shifts in intra-European exchange rates enhanced the competitiveness of some countries at the expense of others. Although retaliatory tariffs were no longer feasible, governments could still resort to nontariff measures such as subsidies and concessionary loans in response to pleas for help from their constituents. But doing so would undermine the spirit of their customs union agreement, calling into question the viability of the project.

The urgency of this problem was growing. Capital mobility was on the rise as financial markets recovered from the disruptions of the 1930s and the devastation of World War II. Capital flows limited the scope for countries to peg their exchange rates and yet go their own macroeconomic way. The 1967 sterling crisis, which had highlighted the power of capital flight to undermine a currency peg, was a harbinger of things to come.[40] The growth of the Eurodollar market was yet another indication of the limited ability of European countries to maintain a level of interest rates significantly different from that in the United States and, by implication, to run independent monetary policies.[41]

And with inflation accelerating in the United States under pressure from public spending on social programs and the Vietnam War, the notion that currency stability could be grounded in a global system appeared less plausible. There were warnings from the Belgian economist Robert Triffin and others that the Bretton Woods System would not last much longer.[42] As the world economy ex-

[39] For evidence, see Alogoskoufis and Smith (1991).

[40] On this, see chapter 7.

[41] Eurodollars were dollars acquired by banks outside the United States and used for lending to nonbank customers. Originally the market arose when European exporters earned dollars that they wished to keep in banks not resident in the United States ("Eurobanks"). The Eurobanks would then lend these dollars, creating an international market in these liabilities. The volume of Euro-currencies rose from about seven billion dollars in September 1963 to fifty-seven billion dollars by the end of 1970.

[42] See, for example, Triffin (1960). Triffin's warnings were much commented on in the 1960s. The Bellagio Group of academics and officials, convened by the U.S.-based but Eu-

panded, central banks and governments needed more international reserves to smooth the balance of payments. But only two forms of reserves were available, gold and dollars, which were pegged to one another at a fixed price of thirty-five dollars an ounce.[43] With gold in inelastic supply, the demand for additional reserves inevitably took the form of dollars. Reflecting the operation of these forces, external dollar holdings exceeded U.S. gold reserves as early as 1960. As this disproportion grew, doubts developed about the ability of the United States to convert dollars into gold on demand. When one country (many anticipated that it would be France) began converting its dollars into gold, others would rush in behind in order not be left in the queue when the United States slammed shut the gold window, as it ultimately did in 1971.

Triffin and others repeatedly invoked these arguments in support of their view that Europe needed to secure its monetary and financial future.[44] Already in 1955, European countries took a first step by negotiating the European Monetary Agreement (EMA), which committed countries participating in the EPU to provide one another with expanded amounts of emergency balance-of-payments assistance. In practice, short-term pressures were dealt with through the IMF—whose resources the United States proposed to increase partly in response to the specter of a competitive, Europe-based institution—and by a series of ad hoc agreements among the industrial countries (the so-called General Arrangements to Borrow). At the same time, the members of the EEC sought to tailor global monetary agreements to their regional needs. For example, Bretton Woods rules allowed other currencies to fluctuate against the dollar by as much as plus or minus 1 percent. This implied that intra-European exchange rates could move by as much as 4 percent if one European currency rose by the full 2 percent against the dollar while another

---

rope-oriented economists Fritz Machlup and Robert Mundell, made this issue the focus of a series of consciousness-raising meetings.

[43] The U.S. Treasury stood ready to make gold available to official foreign creditors for dollars at this rate of exchange.

[44] Triffin had described this flaw in the Bretton Woods System as early as 1947 (Triffin 1947).

fell by the same amount. Regarding such flexibility as dangerous, European governments agreed to limit such fluctuations to 3 percent.[45] They also began developing mechanisms for regional surveillance of national policies. The Treaty of Rome had recognized exchange-rate and macroeconomic policies as matters of "common concern."[46] Soon thereafter the member states established a Monetary Committee of officials of each country's central bank and finance ministry, together with representatives of the Commission, where information about national economic policies could be exchanged and frank discussion could take place. They then established a committee of central bankers ("the Committee of Governors of the central banks of the Member Countries of the European Community") to discuss problems of monetary policy at monthly meetings on the premises of the Bank for International Settlements.

At the outset there were few problems to address. The 1961 revaluations of the deutschmark and the Dutch guilder were not disruptive because intra-European trade had only recently begun to grow and the CAP did not yet exist. The repercussions of the 1967 devaluation of sterling were limited because the United Kingdom was not a member of the EC and had only begun to reorient its trade toward the Six.

The 1969 currency realignments were a different matter.[47] The crisis dragged on for more than a year from the hot summer of 1968 owing to the inability of France and Germany to agree on an acceptable set of exchange-rate changes. Germany's refusal to revalue the deutschmark and its insistence that the burden of adjustment should be borne by the franc were embarrassing to a proud French government. They did much to convince Gaullist skeptics of the need for a European arrangement guaranteeing a better balance of monetary power. Then, in the second half of 1969, when German officials reluctantly acknowledged that restoring balance-of-payments equi-

---

[45] In this respect, their decision anticipated the Snake of the 1970s and the European Monetary System of the 1980s, discussed in chapters 8 and 9.

[46] In paragraphs 103–107.

[47] For more details of this episode, see "The French Crisis and the German Response" in chapter 8.

librium required both a devaluation of the franc and a revaluation of the mark, their decision to revalue by 9 percent was condemned by German exporters and farmers who felt the effects in the form of lower prices and complained that they should not have to bear the consequences of French profligacy. Against the backdrop of worries about the stability of the dollar—the newly elected U.S. president, Richard Nixon, having even less sympathy for the foreign repercussions of U.S. policy than his predecessor, Lyndon Johnson—these events made clear that the time was ripe for discussion of a European alternative to Bretton Woods.[48]

On the political front, de Gaulle's replacement by Pompidou in 1969 helped to dispel the atmosphere of distrust that had been created by the policy of the empty chair. In Germany, the new government of Willy Brandt was anxious to launch a policy of *Ostpolitik*, or engagement with East Germany, cover for which could be provided by a revitalized EC. At the Hague Summit in 1969 it was therefore agreed to explore prospects for monetary unification, leading to the formation of the Werner Committee. Its report sketched a compromise between the hopeful view that monetary union could foster economic convergence, and the more cautious "coronation theory" that economic convergence and the harmonization of policies had to come first.[49] The Committee developed a plan for a three-stage transition to economic and monetary union (EMU) over ten years in which economic and monetary convergence would proceed simultaneously. Monetary union meant "the total and irreversible convertibility of currencies, the elimination of margins of fluctuation in exchange rates, the irrevocable fixing of parity rates and the complete liberalization of movements of capital."[50] While acknowledging that monetary union could entail the creation of a single currency, the report held out the possibility that national currencies

[48] On the contrasting attitudes of the Johnson and Nixon administrations toward international monetary cooperation, and Europe in particular, see Gavin (2004).

[49] The two views are sometimes referred to those of the "monetarists" and the "economists," who thought that the driver should be, respectively, monetary and economic convergence.

[50] Werner (1970), p. 10.

would continue to circulate side by side in the same way that dollar bills issued by different U.S. Federal Reserve banks circulated alongside one another. This was designed to reassure the opponents of political integration by avoiding the implication that the national currency—along with the flag the most potent symbol of political sovereignty—would vanish with EMU.

However much proceeding in this way reassured those preoccupied by symbols, it did not finesse the substance of the matter. It would still be necessary to create a supranational entity with the power to determine the supply of each national currency, given that these currencies would have to trade at fixed prices. Unable to avoid this difficult fact, the Werner Report proposed the creation of a European System of Central Banks. But it did not specify how that system would operate, again in order to avoid raising political hackles. While arguing that monetary union required a mechanism for ensuring adequate coordination of the fiscal policies of the participating member states and for those operating that mechanism to be accountable to the European Parliament, here too it was vague, referring only to the need for a "centre of decision for economic policy."[51]

Predictably, the French reacted negatively to a scheme that smacked of political integration.[52] Brandt was less hostile to the political implications of the monetary project; at the Hague he had proposed strengthening the role of the European Parliament, which would have represented a further step in the direction of political integration and provided a political counterpart to the new monetary institution. Given the stability of German monetary policy, Brandt's willingness to embrace the radical alternative of giving over control to a European System of Central Banks can be understood only as part of this broader political agenda.[53]

But, like Siamese twins, neither France nor Germany could proceed without the other. The recommendations of the Werner Com-

---

[51] Werner (1970), p. 12.
[52] Parsons (2003), pp. 162–163.
[53] Simonian (1985), p. 92.

mittee were therefore toned down. A safeguard clause permitted a country dissatisfied with progress to withdraw from the agreement after three years. The resulting compromise was adopted by the ECOFIN Council (the EC's council of economics and finance ministers) and then by the heads of state and government of the Six and of the three new members of the EC (Denmark, Ireland, and the United Kingdom) in October 1972.

Compromise or not, it was striking that this diverse group of countries was prepared to endorse an agreement with such far-reaching implications. As at a number of earlier points in the development of the EC, the historical context was key. It is hard to imagine this outcome, in other words, without the intervention of some very specific events. In May 1971, pressure on the Bretton Woods System and flight from the dollar to the deutschmark led Germany to unilaterally float its currency, again wreaking havoc with the CAP. This prompted a crisis meeting of Europe's farm ministers and the reimposition of border taxes by Germany, threatening the fabric of the CAP. In 1972, when the heads of state and government of the Six considered the revised Werner plan, the Smithsonian Agreement reached at the end of 1971 (which had sought to preserve the Bretton Woods System of fixed exchange rates) was already showing signs of breaking down. If Europe truly valued currency stability, these events implied, a regional response was required.

But none of this meant that Europe's political leaders were actually prepared to go ahead with a scheme that implied significant political integration. The Werner plan required few institutional compromises before the third stage of the proposed transition. This was still a long way off, and opting out was still possible along the way.

Revealingly, the Council, where governments spoke their minds, never reconciled itself to the need for new transnational institutions. It rejected the proposal for a new "center of decision for economic policy." As a result, the Werner Committee's ambitious plans for monetary integration were stillborn. It would be nearly two decades before the EC was prepared to revisit the issue.

The Common Market as an Established Fact

By the early 1970s, the EC had emerged as a defining feature of the European landscape. Already the Common Market had done much to stimulate trade among the Six. It encouraged previously cloistered countries such as France and Italy to open to their EC partners. By forcing them to accept a greater export orientation, it required the member states to restructure their economies. The CAP, by offering export markets and threatening import competition, similarly encouraged farmers in France and Italy to rationalize, consolidate, and increase efficiency, although a system that had made more room for the operation of the price mechanism and trade with the rest of the world would have done so even more effectively. In other issue areas advances were slower, but there too signs of progress were undeniable. In the area of macroeconomic-policy coordination there was the Committee of Governors of the central banks. There were regular consultations among policy makers. Although the discussions of the Werner Committee did not lead directly to monetary union, they signaled the enduring concern of the member states with this set of issues.

The impact on growth and productivity is hard to quantify, but the sharp negative reaction of French firms and farmers to de Gaulle's policy of the empty chair was a visible sign that the benefits were real. The same can be said of the decision by Britain and other EFTA countries to apply for EC membership: after only a few years, it had become evident that the EC was too powerful an engine of growth for them to stay outside even if they had reservations about political aspects of the project. The EC was too powerful a motor for change to leave decisions about its future shape to others. Similarly, willingness to contemplate an initiative as far-reaching as monetary unification because the volatility of exchange rates between separate national currencies posed a danger to the operation of the Common Market and the CAP again suggests that the member states attached considerable value to these achievements.

The political dimension of the project was more controversial. Some desired the development of a federation of states that would help to foster a European identity and make wars of national aggression inconceivable. Others sought a set of institutional arrangements that would leave all significant political powers in the hands of national governments. The first vision invigorated important elements of the intellectual and political elite, but the second clearly dominated society at large.

The difficult question was whether economic integration and political integration were really separable. Would it be possible to cement the Common Market and move from there to an even more efficiently integrated European economy with free mobility of labor and capital and the removal of barriers behind the border without deeper political integration? Would it be necessary to vest more power in the Commission (the EC's protoexecutive branch), the Parliament, and the Court of Justice in order to effectively govern such a deeply integrated economic unit and hold policy makers accountable for their actions? Or was it feasible to proceed on the basis of a set of simple rules? Countries could agree, for example, to extend recognition of one another's product standards and technical credentials—they could agree that if a regulation applied in one member state then it automatically applied in the others.[54] There would then be only limited need for the ongoing coordination of these regulatory and licensing policies and hence no rationale for more powerful transnational institutions.

These dilemmas were more immediate for some economic policies than others. A customs union needed relatively little management, and what management it required could be provided by the member states in intergovernmental negotiations. But a single currency required a single central bank, which was a transnational entity whose existence, by its nature, created demands for a political counterweight such as a strengthened European Parliament to hold those responsible for its policies accountable for their actions. For the skeptics of political integration, this created an obvious dividing line between desirable and undesirable forms of economic integration.

---

[54] This policy of "mutual recognition" was something to which they did eventually agree in the 1980s. See chapter 11.

The problem was that the various elements—it is tempting to use the word *stages*—of the process of economic integration were not so easily separated. If the Common Market could not survive wide fluctuations between the currencies of the member states, for example, and if the only way of preventing such fluctuations was by moving forward to monetary unification, then drawing the line on political integration might not be that simple either.

A final complication was that different countries had different priorities, their governments different objectives. Germany saw the EC as an umbrella under which it could regain legitimacy and assume a foreign-policy role. The Brandt government had little appetite for monetary integration per se, since by the end of the 1960s the deutschmark had emerged as Europe's strongest and most stable currency. But it was willing to contemplate moves in that direction in return for agreement on steps toward political integration that promised it scope for a more assertive foreign policy. France, in contrast, saw advantages in monetary integration that would free it from having to beg at Germany's monetary door. The Pompidou government was reluctant to pursue political integration but willing to consider relaunching the European project if this was the price to be paid for the creation of a monetary framework at the EC level. Again, the implication was that the economic and political strands of the integrationist project were not so easily untwined.

At the beginning of the 1970s the EC was delicately poised. It was not clear whether its economic achievements, notably the Common Market, could stand alone or whether they would have to be supplemented by some kind of monetary agreement. It was not clear whether the EC could remain primarily an economic entity, or whether securing its economic achievements would require further steps in the direction of political integration. Rising capital mobility, unstable U.S. policies, and a more difficult environment for growth would help to determine the answers.

197

- SEVEN -

THE APEX OF THE GOLDEN AGE

Growth accelerated again in the 1960s. Output per employed person rose at more than 4 percent per year in Western Europe, up from 3.6 percent in the 1950s. The growth of exports was sustained by the advent of the Common Market and the Kennedy Round of GATT negotiations. Investment rates also rose further. Although Europe's investment was more than fully financed by its own savings, the continent was also on the receiving end of foreign direct investment (FDI) from the United States.[1] This FDI was a conduit for the transfer of advanced technology to sectors such as chemicals, computers, and transportation equipment. It was attracted by the establishment of the EEC, since the creation of the Common Market made Europe an attractive production platform for American firms.[2] All the while, growth was sustained by the movement of workers to the continent's industrial heartland, more than five million in number, from Mediterranean Europe, North Africa, and the Middle East. This was truly a golden age of growth, fostered by institutions and policies supporting the expansion of trade, the maintenance of high investment, and elastic labor supplies.

By the end of the 1960s, questions inevitably arose of whether growth built on these foundations could last. The more rapid Eu-

---

[1] This FDI was offset in the balance-of-payments accounts (more than offset, actually, since the current account was in surplus) by Europe's accumulation of liquid financial claims on the United States, which it used to augment its international reserves. See chapter 8 for additional discussion.

[2] See Dunning (1997a).

rope's growth and the longer it was sustained, the lower the levels to which unemployment sank. Guest workers from Southeastern Europe, North Africa, and Turkey could augment supplies of unskilled labor, but they did not discipline the wage demands of skilled workers or subdue union militancy. They also provoked a political reaction that led European countries to progressively tighten their immigration policies.

Toward the end of the decade, the labor market erupted in a wave of strikes. Mounting inflation and declining profitability signaled that the golden age was drawing to a close.

The Heyday of Extensive Growth

Only in Austria and West Germany, where growth had soared to exceptional heights in the period of postwar reconstruction, were there signs of slowing in the 1960s. But even these countries' slower rates of growth remained impressive. Although the average annual rate of German GDP growth fell by more than one-third from the high levels scaled in the 1950s, at nearly 5 percent it still exceeded the Western European average. Germany reassumed its traditional role as supplier of machine tools and other producer goods to the rest of Europe. Investment goods now accounted for more than half of all German exports. That Germany specialized in producer durables in a period when capital formation was booming also helps to explain how the country was in such a strong balance-of-payments position. At home, meanwhile, buoyant export markets together with wage moderation encouraged investment. The German investment–GDP ratio rose again, from 22 percent in the 1950s to 24 percent in the 1960s.

Other countries now raised their growth rates by applying this same formula of investment and exports. The restoration of current-account convertibility and the formation of the EEC and EFTA enhanced the attractiveness of this strategy. The Netherlands raised its already high growth rates by boosting its exports to the EEC. Foreign capital augmented domestic savings as foreign multinationals acquired

199

Dutch companies, injecting additional funds. The country moved increasingly into capital-intensive industries such as food processing, chemicals, and oil refining in response to demands by Dutch workers for higher wages as a reward for more than a decade of restraint.

In France, reconstruction and capacity expansion in six key sectors, encouraged by the government's indicative plan, created the conditions for a growth rate of nearly 6 percent. An economy no longer saddled by controls and cartels responded energetically to the reforms of the Rueff Plan and the export opportunities of the Treaty of Rome. On 1 January 1960, when the Rueff Plan came into effect, 90 percent of all trade with European markets and 50 percent of trade with the dollar zone were freed. The plan tackled the country's chronic fiscal deficits by limiting public-sector pay increases to 4 percent, cutting subsidies for nationalized companies, and eliminating pensions for able-bodied ex-servicemen. It addressed inflation inertia by abolishing index linking, except in the case of the minimum wage. Capital formation was encouraged by tax provisions allowing for the accelerated depreciation of fixed investment. Although sensitive to the power of the farm lobby, de Gaulle nonetheless enacted a series of measures scaling back the protection afforded small farmers. The results were out-migration from agriculture, rising farm productivity, and elastic supplies of labor to industry.

French companies consolidated and reorganized to take advantage of new opportunities in the export sector. The government encouraged this consolidation, arguing that economies of scale were required in order for firms to be able to compete internationally. Here the hand of indicative planning was evident; the government used the FDES (Fonds de développement économique et social) to provide financial support for the process. Gross fixed investment as a share of GDP rose from 17 percent in 1952–1959 to 22 percent in 1959–1969.[3] Much of this additional investment was concentrated in the export sector, attracted there by France's ready access to European markets and by the 1958 devaluation of the franc, which re-

[3] Still, inward FDI never accounted for the same share of total investment as in smaller European countries (notwithstanding the complaints of popular books such as Servan-Schrieber 1967).

duced labor costs in dollar terms. Exports rose from 12 percent of GDP in 1958 to 16 percent in 1970. Eventually, balance-of-payments problems reemerged, but not on the same scale as in countries such as the United Kingdom.[4] Not until the end of the decade, in 1968–1969, was the government again forced to apply restrictive macroeconomic policies to reduce a balance-of-payments deficit. With France now imbibing the standard European formula of investment and exports, industry raced ahead, led by motor vehicle manufacturing, whose rate of expansion nearly matched Japanese automobile production.

Italy, similarly, had spent the 1950s modernizing its industrial sector and now opened to Europe and the world. Export growth accelerated to 12 percent per year, while the investment–GDP ratio rose to 25 percent. With this impetus, the overall rate of growth accelerated to 6 percent. Italy graduated to exporting industrial technology: in 1966 the Soviet Union turned to Fiat to build one of its first modern automobile factories, and Italian chemical producers such as Montecatini and Edison built production facilities in the Eastern bloc.

Even the laggards now joined the high-growth club. Belgium, Denmark, and Norway, which had all done relatively poorly in the 1950s, experienced a marked acceleration. Opening to trade and joining EFTA held out to Norway's engineering industry, which accounted for roughly one-third of manufacturing employment, the carrot of foreign markets but also the stick of foreign competition. Engineering firms that traditionally concentrated on the home market became committed exporters, developing optical-control flame cutting and numerically guided drawing techniques originally for shipbuilding but eventually for a range of industrial applications. In Denmark, where firms once sheltered from import competition had found it difficult to cope with trade liberalization, producers rationalized in order to compete. In parallel with the process in France, inefficient producers of engineering products and electrical equipment were either wound up or absorbed by their more efficient rivals, enabling the survivors to benefit from economies of scale.

[4] See chapter 8.

Growth in Belgium also accelerated, there too reflecting the belated adoption of policies encouraging exports and investment. Exports were fostered by the development of the Common Market, of which Belgium was a founding member, allowing sectors exposed to international competition to outperform sheltered sectors. The Expansion Laws of 1959 extended loan guarantees, interest subsidies, and tax benefits to fully one-third of gross fixed capital formation. Liberalization of the financial system allowed Belgian banks, previously required to keep the majority of their assets in government securities, to direct a larger share of their credits toward private investment. As in other small European countries, additional investment was contributed by foreign multinationals, U.S. multinationals in particular.[5]

Even Ireland, which previously had performed poorly, now showed new signs of life. Already in the late 1950s, policy had shifted in the direction of attempting to attract foreign investment in manufacturing. Joining EFTA and concluding a free-trade agreement with the United Kingdom were important next steps. So was educational reform, which was strongly recommended by a mission from the OECD, though in fact the ongoing reorientation in the direction of greater openness had already convinced many Irish leaders of its importance. Responding to complaints of a shortage of skilled workers, the opposition of the clergy and agrarian interests to technical education was overcome. Vocational training was expanded, and two new National Institutes for Higher Education were created, boosting enrollment in practical subjects such as accounting and business organization.[6] Reform culminated in 1968 with the adoption of free secondary education.

The gestation period between educational reform and economic performance being long, these reforms had only a modest impact on Irish growth in the 1960s (although emigration slowed relative to

[5] A study by the National Bank of Belgium suggested that more than half of net investment in the manufacturing sector between 1960 and 1972 was undertaken by foreign firms. See van Ruckeghem (1982), pp. 592–593.

[6] The two new National Institutes subsequently became the University of Limerick and Dublin City University. The expansion of vocational education in the 1960s and early 1970s was then reinforced by an emphasis on scientific and technical skill formation financed in part by EU Structural Funds from the late 1980s (Bradley 2004).

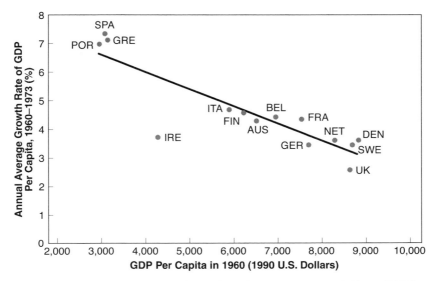

Figure 7.1. The starting point and growth in the 1960s. *Source*: Maddison (2001). *Note*: Gross domestic product per capita is expressed in 1990 U.S. dollars.

the rate of natural increase, reflecting expectations of better times to come). A further problem was that Irish labor markets remained fragmented, frustrating efforts to control wages. This was in contrast with Spain and Portugal, two countries whose per capita incomes and therefore scope for catch-up were comparable but where strong government oversight of negotiations prevented excessive wage push.[7] The capacity of the Irish state was more limited, and trade unions were segmented along craft lines. In the absence of a coordination mechanism, wage pressure was intense.[8] The resulting pressure on costs limited the growth of exports and investment. Relative to the expectations created by its starting point, Ireland continued to underperform.[9] (See figure 7.1).

[7] See the next section.

[8] While Portuguese and Spanish wages rose by 60 and 81 percent, respectively, between 1960 and 1973, Irish real wages rose by 90 percent (Barry 2003, p. 902). To be sure, Irish growth accelerated in the 1960s with the removal of the most distortionary subsidies and opening to foreign trade. See "The Laggards" in chapter 4. But in contrast with Spain and Portugal, where growth proceeded even more rapidly than in the rest of Europe, this was not yet true for Ireland.

[9] The gap was finally closed following more thoroughgoing reform and the negotiation of a series of corporatist compacts in the 1980s and 1990s; see chapter 12.

Thus, the 1960s were the heyday of extensive growth, driven by the creation of the EEC and EFTA and supported by policies that sustained investment in the face of pressure on profits. Growth at twice the historical norm became commonplace. Growth in Austria and Germany declined marginally from the high levels of the 1950s, but other European countries picked up the pace. Countries now clustered even more tightly around the average relationship linking initial per capita incomes with subsequent growth.[10]

The Incorporation of the European Periphery

Growth accelerated most dramatically in Southern Europe, as Greece, Portugal, and Spain liberalized and opened. In Spain the key turning points were the 1959 Stabilization Program, which unified the exchange rate and eliminated structural distortions, and the 1960 trade reform, which removed approximately half of all barriers to imports from OECD countries. For Portugal the pivotal event was joining EFTA. For Greece it was negotiating an association agreement liberalizing trade with the EEC. In each case, rather than transforming the economy into an agricultural backwater as some had feared it would, the process of opening stimulated the growth of labor-intensive manufactures.

The Portuguese case is illustrative. The country had considerable scope for catch-up and convergence if it put in place the basic prerequisites for growth. Growth in the 1950s, at 3.5 percent per year in per capita terms, had just matched that of France, a more advanced economy with less scope for catching up. This put Portugal squarely at the middle of the European growth leagues but behind more dynamic Southern European economies such as Italy that more effectively exploited opportunities for convergence.[11]

Given this starting point, even limited restructuring delivered impressive results. Growth accelerated from a rapid 6.2 percent per

[10] Compare figure 7.1 with figure 4.1, which depicts the same relationship in the 1950s.

[11] This is evident in figure 4.1, where Portugal lies significantly below the norm relating initial per capita incomes to subsequent growth.

year in 1959–1965 to an even more impressive 7.5 percent per year in 1966–1973. Now, in contrast to the 1950s, Portuguese growth was every bit as fast as predicted by the Europe-wide relationship between initial per capita income and growth. This acceleration was more remarkable to the extent that the economy still labored under a range of structural and policy handicaps. The country had a low level of educational attainment by European standards; as late as 1970, illiteracy among persons at least ten years old was more than 25 percent.[12] It was engaged in an ultimately futile war to hold onto its African colonies that weakened the budget, diverted resources from investment, and alienated the younger generation.

All this makes it seem as if Portugal had few advantages other than the fact that it started out behind the Central and Northern European core. And, of course, starting out behind explains little by itself. Other non-European countries started out even farther behind without coming close to matching Portugal's growth performance in the 1960s. As Abramovitz (1986) reminds us, catch-up and convergence require not just a lower level of productivity and technical attainment than the technological leader but also the capacity to close the gap.

In the present case this capacity emanated from two sources: the government's control of industrial relations and its commitment to integrating with Europe. The longtime authoritarian prime minister, António Salazar, had incorporated unions and employers confederations into the state structure in the 1930s, and these arrangements persisted into the postwar years. Limits on political and economic freedom left these organizations little autonomy prior to the 1974 revolution, giving the state the power to set wages at levels consistent with its policy objectives. One product of this state corporatist system was wage moderation. The release of labor from agriculture further limited the growth of industrial wages. Low inflation meant a favorable real exchange rate.[13] Competitive labor costs supported

---

[12] To be sure, the third quarter of the twentieth century saw improvements in this realm (the adult illiteracy rate had been twice as high at the end of World War II), and after the 1974 revolution, access to higher education was further enhanced. See Neves (1994).

[13] Indeed, competitive real wages and a competitive real exchange rate are two sides of the same coin, as noted in chapter 2.

the growth of light industry, mainly textiles, from which the country gradually moved into the production of more technologically sophisticated goods. Among the corollaries were additional resources for capacity expansion and high gross investment rates, which rose from a not atypical 21 percent of GDP in 1958 to 26 percent in 1965. In an economy with a relatively low capital–labor ratio, a little bit of additional investment made a big difference.

Small country size made exporting essential. Even Salazar, who jealously guarded his control of the economy, recognized that Portuguese firms lacked minimum efficient scale and acknowledged the need to participate in the general European movement toward opening and integration. Politicians and producers abroad who might have resisted incorporating a low-wage country into an integrated Europe, for their part, were willing to make an exception for Portugal owing again to the small size of the economy.

Thus, Portugal was a founding member of EFTA. It conducted a significant share of its trade with other EFTA countries, mainly Britain, which suggests that it benefited more than the other participants from the formation of this grouping. In 1962 it subscribed to the GATT, taking on additional obligations to liberalize.[14] With impetus from these reforms, the share of exports in GNP rose from 15 percent in the 1950s to 20 percent in 1965 and 26 percent in 1973.[15] Opening encouraged exports of agricultural products such as wine, cork, olive oil, and wool. It stimulated the development of the country's industrial structure, as first textile producers and then firms in other light industries began penetrating European markets. The share of Portuguese exports accounted for by agriculture, foodstuffs, and primary products fell steadily after 1960, while the share accounted for by textiles, apparel, and footwear rose from 16 percent in 1958 to 30 percent in 1973. Exports of chemicals, machinery, and even certain forms of transportation equipment followed.

These results were more striking for the fact that a handful of large conglomerates still dominated the industrial landscape, re-

[14] As a poor European country, Portugal did, however, receive limited exemptions from the obligations of membership in both GATT and EFTA.
[15] Neves (1996), p. 338.

flecting the legacy of state corporatism and the planners' preoccupation with scale. Those same conglomerates owned the banks that dominated the financial sector, guaranteeing their favorable access to finance. They faced only limited import competition, being protected by a Law of Control of Industry that prohibited the creation of new factories or even the expansion of existing enterprises without government approval. This was not exactly an environment charged by the chill winds of competition.

Yet the existence of these conglomerates posed few obvious problems in the 1960s; to the contrary, they may have played a positive role. The influence of conglomerates in Portugal was not unlike that of state holding companies in Italy or, to cite a more recent example, of industrial groups in South Korea and Indonesia, two still poorer countries that entered their high-growth periods later. They were able to undertake substantial investments in machinery, transportation equipment, and other manufactures, none of which would have been profitable in the absence of the others. They thus addressed coordination problems whose solution would have otherwise eluded decentralized markets. Given the existence of an extensive technological backlog, it was not hard for the heads of these conglomerates, together with their counterparts in government and finance, to identify the appropriate sectors to favor. They could simply emulate other European countries that had gone down the same road in earlier years. To be sure, this model became problematic as the economy prepared to exit extensive growth for an era of technological uncertainty that placed a greater premium on innovation and new firm formation. The 1974 revolution, however, overthrew Portugal's old system before it could become an insurmountable obstacle to growth.

The situation in Spain was if anything even more extreme. The 1940s had been a dark decade of industrial regression. The economy was closed to the world by prohibitions on foreign ownership and by import quotas, licenses, and controls.[16] Francisco Franco's nation-

---

[16] Foreign investors were prohibited from holding more than 2.5 percent of the capital of a Spanish company except with special permission from the Council of Ministers.

alist economic policies were an elaboration of policies pursued in the 1920s by the Primo de Rivera dictatorship, which had similarly promoted national self-sufficiency and industrial development, controlled agricultural prices, and engaged in a series of protocorporatist experiments.[17] Government officials were almost Soviet-like in their zeal for self-sufficiency. As a result, capital equipment, raw materials, energy, fertilizer, high-quality seed, and even food were in chronic short supply. Spanish living standards in 1950 were estimated by the World Bank to be below even the depressed levels of 1935.[18]

An implication of these policies was a low level of foreign trade. Exports were barely 5 percent of GDP following World War II, earlier policies having discouraged the allocation of resources to export-linked uses. Virtually all imports and exports were subject to license, and through 1953 the country was subject to a U.N. boycott. At home, the prices of both consumer and producer goods were controlled. Agricultural prices were set at low levels to foster industrialization and ensure cheap grain supplies to the cities.[19] All industrial investment required authorization by the Ministry of Industry. In turn this created entry barriers that allowed many Spanish industries to be effectively monopolized.

Historians of Spain betray some uncertainty about the appropriate characterization of the 1950s. Lieberman, for example, describes the decade as one of stagnation but then almost immediately observes that real GNP rose at an average annual rate of 7.9 percent between 1951 and 1958.[20] Spain's performance is less impressive, of course, when one observes that its population and labor force also grew rapidly. In per capita terms, Spain's growth rate was exactly the

[17] The army officers and military engineers responsible for managing the economy had also taken inspiration from the autarkic policies and nationalist ideology of Fascist Italy. Dirigisme and autarky were presented as necessary for the maintenance of their "imperial military state." Carr and Fusi (1979), p. 51.

[18] World Bank (1963), p. 46.

[19] In practice, these price ceilings had the effect of discouraging farmers from expanding production and induced them to shift out of cereals, whose prices were strictly controlled, thereby creating shortages of essential foodstuffs. Between 1950 and 1959, the price of industrial goods relative to agricultural goods rose by nearly one-third (after having already risen by some 50 percent in the 1940s). Tortella (2000), p. 322.

[20] Lieberman (1995), pp. 1, 44.

same as that of France, squarely in the middle of the 1950s growth leagues and considerably behind that of more dynamic Southern European economies such as Italy. One would have expected faster growth, Italian-style, from an economy starting out so far behind the European norm.[21]

The best way of characterizing the 1950s is probably as a decade of transition between the "lost years" of the 1940s and the more economically dynamic 1960s.[22] A general strike in Barcelona in 1951 induced Franco to change the composition of his government, adding new men more favorably inclined toward reform to the Falangist inner circle. The new leaders pushed to simplify the system of multiple exchange rates. They sought to expand imports of capital goods, which required rebuilding links with the rest of the world, and to move cautiously toward a free-market economy. Even if growth in the 1950s disappointed expectations, the limited reforms of that decade were still important as prerequisites for the more fundamental reforms and faster growth that followed.

Also supporting growth in this period were policies promoting investment, together with balanced budgets and low labor costs that freed up resources for capital formation. Between 1949 and 1959, investment rose from 11 to 18 percent of GDP. Wage stability supported profits and encouraged capital formation. The country's system of state corporatism had its genesis in the Basic Labor Law adopted immediately after Franco assumed power. Workers were required to affiliate with sectoral unions (*sindicatos*) that were in turn affiliated with a national trade union organization whose role was to facilitate implementation of the government's economic policy. Strikes were outlawed, dismissals were restricted, and wages were fixed by decree. Though there was pressure in the 1950s to adjust the salary schedule, especially for skilled workers in short supply, labor costs remained stable.[23] Tortella, in reviewing this period, re-

---

[21] As figure 4.1 showed, Spanish growth in the 1950s was disappointing, given the scope for convergence provided by its comparatively backward postwar starting point.

[22] A leading exponent of this view is García Delgado (1987). The views of this school are surveyed in Harrison and Corkill (2004), p. 73.

[23] The main exception was in 1955, when the Franco regime granted generous wage increases to buy labor peace; the predictable result was growing balance-of-payments difficulties

fers to "the iron discipline the state imposed on the labor market" and comments on how this led entrepreneurs to invest "as they had not done since 1930."[24]

With the outbreak of the Korean War, the fervently anticommunist Franco regime received financial assistance from the United States.[25] U.S. assistance rose as the Cold War intensified; by the 1960s, Spain had become the second largest recipient, after Japan, of U.S. loans and grants.[26] Much of this aid was tied to purchases of commodities in the United States, but some could be used to import capital goods and embodied technology. And there was a growing amount of private investment from the United States once restrictions on this were relaxed in 1953. As in Portugal, a little bit of investment went a long way in a capital-scarce economy.

The balance-of-payments constraint was relaxed by these official transfers and tourism receipts. In addition, there were remittances from immigrants to Latin America and Spanish guest workers in France. Eventually, many of these guest workers returned home, bringing with them technical skills and work habits needed for the expansion of the capital goods sector. But industrial specialization was not really possible given the low level of trade. Nor could firms rely on imported capital goods for the expansion of productive capacity. Already in the 1940s producers had complained of the debilitating effects of shortages of basic metals, building materials, energy, transportation, and equipment, but there was little incentive to expand capacity in any of these sectors absent increases in capacity in the others. Rather, it was necessary to get a range of industries up and running simultaneously in order for any of them to flourish.

The Instituto Nacional de Industria, or INI, created in 1941 with inspiration from Italy's IRI, now helped to relax these bottle-

---

in the second half of the 1950s, which led indirectly to the Stabilization Plan of 1959 and to a 20 percent effective devaluation (see the discussion later in this chapter).

[24] Tortella (2000), p. 323.

[25] Recall that Spain had not been a recipient of Marshall Plan aid. Franco, ever appreciative of the value of symbolism, sent Spanish troops to fight alongside the United States in Korea. In return for its financial assistance, the United States received airbases in Morón de la Frontera, Zaragosa, and the environs of Madrid, together with a naval base at Rota, near Cádiz.

[26] Harrison (1978), p. 154.

necks and coordinate complementary investments.[27] INI invested in two large electric companies, ENDESA and ENHER, and in the National Enterprise for Aluminum, which was a voracious consumer of electricity. Neither of these initiatives would have been viable without the other. INI invested in the production of iron and coal and then metallurgical refining, shipbuilding, and variety of other basic sectors, none of which could have flourished alone. It invested in petroleum refining and motor vehicles (neither of which would have been viable in the absence of the other, given the regime's policies of autarky), establishing the Sociedad Española de Automóviles de Turismo (SEAT) using technology licensed from Fiat. Between 1943 and 1960, INI accounted for perhaps 15 percent of all investment in Spanish industry.[28] By 1960 two of these INI-created firms, E.N. Calvo Sotelo, engaged in petroleum distilling and refining, and E.N. Bazán, in shipbuilding, were the fourth and eighth largest firms in the country.[29]

This emphasis on INI's role in coordinating complementary investments is consistent with the view of Spanish economists and historians that the limited reforms of the 1950s set the stage for sustained industrial growth. As in other European countries, these interventions were particularly favorable in this period of extensive growth based on known technologies, when bureaucrats could identify attractive investment opportunities as easily as entrepreneurs. To be sure, the clientelism that arose in the course of INI's operations came in for much criticism. INI was also criticized for empire building—for entering industries where private enterprise was already well established. This led to an attempt starting in 1959, in conjunction with the stabilization crisis discussed later in this section, to discipline its managers by shifting from a regime in which INI firms could finance their expansion by direct recourse to the public budget to

---

[27] The legislation establishing INI referred to the case for public investment in industries essential to national defense, but it also stated that INI should enter fields where the size of the requisite investments or first-mover problems limiting profitability precluded relying exclusively on the private sector.

[28] Anderson (1970), p. 40.

[29] Carreras and Tafunell (1997), p. 284.

one in which they had to compete for capital in the market. These reforms had the not undesirable effect of slowing the rate of growth of INI enterprises relative to the economy as a whole.

The doubling of industrial production in the 1950s and growth at the average Western European rate were visible successes by Spanish standards. Nonetheless, by the end of the decade doubts had developed among businessmen and officials, notably in the Ministry of Commerce and the Bank of Spain, about whether progress could continue in this cloistered, regulated environment. Imported inputs were expensive. The capital stock was still antiquated, reflecting the high price of imported capital goods. In 1958, the United Nations Educational, Scientific, and Cultural Organization (UNESCO) noted that 45 percent of Spanish industry was still using pre-1920 equipment, two-thirds of the Spanish merchant fleet was of pre-1939 construction, and some ships still in active use had even been built before 1898.[30] Not only did export industries lack competitiveness, but firms producing for the domestic market operated on too small a scale to justify the adoption of mass-production methods. To encourage domestic absorption of consumer goods produced by Spanish firms, the government had authorized a pair of public sector wage increases in 1954 and 1956, but these only aggravated the problem of inadequate competitiveness and worsened shortages of imported raw materials.

Evidently, the regime's policies of self-sufficiency and import substitution had reached the point of diminishing returns. But even after Franco reshuffled his cabinet to include a group of neoliberal ministers in 1957, he remained reluctant to contemplate reform. His hand was forced by devaluation in neighboring France, as a result of which the competitiveness of Spanish exports declined further. This precipitated a balance-of-payments crisis that threatened to exhaust the country's foreign reserves.

The only options available to the government to cope with the crisis were to further restrict imports, ration gasoline, and curtail supplies of consumer goods, which would have aggravated the ex-

---

[30] Cited in Lieberman (1995), p. 44.

isting difficulties of Spanish industry and antagonized the workers (who were already growing restive), or alternatively to encourage exports. After some hesitation, Franco opted for the second course. He announced that Spain would join the IMF, the World Bank, and the OEEC. In June 1959, he received the IMF's managing director, Per Jacobsson, who recommended—no surprise—the relaxation of import controls and devaluation of the peseta and was given extraordinary access to Spanish television to make his case.[31] Jacques Rueff, the architect of France's recent stabilization, was invited and also made the case for comprehensive liberalization. Clearly, this was a case that Franco now wanted to have made. "The time has come," as he put it in a presentation to the IMF and the OEEC, "to redirect economic policy in order to place the Spanish economy in line with countries of the Western world, and to free it from interventions inherited from the past, which do not correspond to the needs of the present situation."[32]

Following a month of preparation, with technical assistance from the IMF and the OEEC, Spain's system of multiple exchange rates was dismantled in favor of a unified rate of sixty pesetas to the dollar, constituting an effective devaluation of 20 percent. The state monopoly of imports was relaxed. Quota restrictions on private imports were replaced by ad valorem tariffs, permitting greater flexibility to import up-to-date equipment.[33] The retention of export taxes was limited to a transitional period, and bilateral agreements inherited from the early postwar years were abolished. Regulations on FDI from Western Europe were relaxed in an acknowledgment that restrictions designed to encourage foreign firms to license their technologies à la Japan had been less than successful. Restrictions on freedom to emigrate to France and Germany for purposes of temporary employment were loosened. Here Spain looked not to France but to Italy, which had previously adopted similar measures. Public

---

[31] James (1996), p. 109.

[32] Cited in World Bank (1963), p. 46.

[33] Where imports remained subject to quota, those quotas were unified, allowing consumers and producers to substitute more freely between products.

spending was cut, taxes were raised, and the discount rate was hiked to contain inflation and restore external balance.

This orthodox package of expenditure switching and reducing measures quickly resolved the balance-of-payments crisis. The drain of reserves was halted. Within twelve months, the trade deficit had fallen by half. Nor was the incipient gain in competitiveness eroded by price increases. To the contrary, inflation fell from 12 percent in 1956–1958 to 2 percent in 1959–1961 despite the devaluation.

In the short run, exposing sheltered Spanish firms to foreign competition and limiting domestic demand had chilling effects; GDP fell by 0.5 percent in 1960 despite the receipt of loans from the OEEC, the IMF, and the U.S. Export-Import Bank. Growth then resumed in 1961, supported by improved competitiveness and a more favorable external environment. The impact of the 1959 devaluation was sustained by the state corporatist regime that guaranteed the stability of wages and allowed the improvement in labor cost competitiveness to endure.[34]

But Spain did not have the stimulus for opening and the commitment against backsliding conferred by EFTA membership, the continuity of the Franco regime barring its participation. Notwithstanding the rhetoric of trade liberalization, it maintained higher import tariffs than any other European country.[35] Even when concluding a preferential arrangement, the Luxembourg Accord, with the European Community in 1970, the Spanish government only agreed to phase in tariff cuts over seven years. Liberalization of the trade regime may have been accompanied by the selective relaxation of restrictions on domestic economic activity, but many such restrictions remained. Monopolies were still favored, and the government offered a variety of inducements for mergers and acquisitions in the hope that scale might compensate for Spanish industry's other deficiencies. It intervened heavily in the financial system with the goal of channeling funds toward infrastructure and industry. It ex-

[34] See Prados and Sanz (1996). Note, however, that these authors also argue that the other side of the state corporatist coin, restrictive labor-market regulations limiting layoffs and part-time employment, was a source of inflexibility that posed a growing burden for the economy.
[35] For details, see Balassa (1965).

tended tax credits and credit facilities to favored companies in exchange for their agreement to maintain specified levels of investment. The system's rigidities and propensity for rent-seeking (that is, seeking profits through manipulation of the economic environment rather than through trade or wealth creation) did not bode well for the future.[36]

If the openness of the Spanish economy remained limited, the modest increase in outward orientation initiated in 1959 still had discernible effects. The share of exports in GDP rose from 5.8 percent in 1959 to 10.7 percent in 1974, while the share of agriculture in exports fell by half, to 30 percent. From the late 1960s, traditional agricultural exports were increasingly superseded by footwear, leather goods, and other labor-intensive manufactures. Ultimately, they were replaced by machinery, motor vehicles, and other transportation equipment, foreign sales of which rose from negligible levels in 1960 to 10 percent of exports in 1974. Although exports did not grow as quickly as in other European countries, their expansion far surpassed Spain's own past performance.

Gross fixed investment as a share of GDP similarly expanded from 16 percent in the second half of the 1950s to 22 percent in the 1960s.[37] However, the retention of tariffs on imported capital goods continued to artificially raise the cost of machinery and equipment. Nor was FDI as important as in other Western European countries, although it too expanded in the wake of the 1959–1960 reforms, transferring technological and organizational knowledge and augmenting domestic savings.[38]

---

[36] The system went into crisis at the end of the 1960s, when the MATESA scandal (involving a manufacturer of textile looms that had fraudulently sold its products to its branches abroad in order to obtain export credits) revealed the scope for corruption and raised questions about the competence of government technocrats. This episode encouraged tentative efforts at reform and liberalization, but these proceeded at a very slow pace until the second half of the 1970s—that is, until a fundamental change in political regime had taken place.

[37] Merigó (1982), p. 556.

[38] Foreign capital accounted for 7 percent of investment in the 1960s; see Donges (1976). The Franco regime also sought to shift from the Italian approach of coordinating investment by relying on INI to the French model of indicative planning, adopting a First Development Plan in 1964.

As in the other Mediterranean economies, there was now considerable migration from rural to urban regions and extensive reallocation of labor from agriculture to industry. Between 1960 and 1975 the share of employment in agriculture fell from 41 to 23 percent, the labor released moving to industry, construction, and services. Industry grew half again as fast as the economy as a whole. With average incomes in agriculture in 1960 still only 65 percent of the national average, sectoral shift contributed significantly to the aggregate rate of growth.

Having unperformed in the 1950s, the economy now more effectively exploited its scope for catching up to the European norm.[39] The average annual rate of GDP growth accelerated by 1½ percent per year between the 1950s and the 1960s. Through the miracle of compound interest, growth at these rates had a revolutionary effect on living standards. In 1960, only 4 percent of Spanish households had refrigerators; by 1973, this share had risen to 82 percent.

Thus, Spain now moved in the same direction as countries such as Italy and France that had been quicker to apply the postwar formula of investment and export growth. But its reforms were less complete. In addition, the government now attempted to put in place the mechanisms of indicative planning precisely when other countries saw the wisdom moving away. By the early 1970s, the scope for further growth in this still heavily cosseted economy was essentially played out. This then set the stage for the more fundamental reforms that followed with Franco's death, the revolution, and Spain's accession to the European Community.

Wage Explosion and Labor Conflict

In all these countries, economic growth was predicated on investment. And investment in turn depended on the postwar bargain of wage restraint in return for the retention of profits. Any intensification of wage inflation consequently threatened the entire process. It

[39] Compare figure 7.1 with figure 4.1.

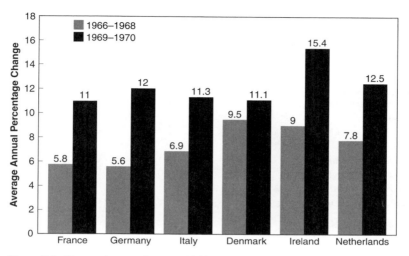

Figure 7.2. Nominal wage changes, 1966–1970. *Source:* Boltho (1982). *Note:* Figure shows average annual percentage changes of wages and salaries per employee. For France, figures are based on statistics for 1965–1967 and 1968–1969.

was therefore alarming when, in 1968–1969, after two decades in which observers had contemplated the "withering away of the strike," work stoppages erupted over much of Europe.

The most dramatic such episode, in May 1968 in France, started as a series of protests by students against the inefficiency of the university system but quickly spread to the labor market. To subdue the wave of strikes and demonstrations, the government upped the minimum wage by 35 percent; in sympathy, other wages rose by more than 10 percent. Strikes broke out the next year in other European countries and evoked a similar response. Between 1966 and 1969, nominal wages rose by 11 percent in Italy and Denmark, 13 percent in the Netherlands, and 15 percent in Ireland. (See figure 7.2.) Although real wages rose by only half that amount, the other half being dissipated by increases in consumer prices, labor productivity failed to keep up. The resulting increase in unit labor costs was substantial. Days lost in strikes also rose. Evidently, the long postwar period of labor peace was drawing to a close.

Several factors contributed to these developments. Employment in agriculture having fallen to less than 15 percent of employment

TABLE 7.1

Contribution of different supply sources to dependent nonagricultural employment growth
in the European Economic Community (Percent)

	1955–1960	1960–1965	1965–1970	1970–1975
Growth in dependent non-agricultural employment	1.7	1.7	0.8	0.4
Contribution of:				
Urban labor force	0.20	0.01	−0.16	0.19
Unemployed	0.57	−0.04	−0.07	−0.48
Immigrant labor force	0.33	0.52	0.29	0.20
Migration from agriculture	0.64	1.02	0.72	0.41
Self-employed and family workers outside agriculture	−0.04	0.12	0.02	0.08

Source: Boltho (1982).

continent-wide, elastic supplies of rural labor were no longer available to industry. Unemployment, which had been substantial over much of Europe in the 1950s, now fell to low levels. In the 1950s, fully one-third of the growth of the labor force had come from putting the unemployed to work; the scope for additional reductions in unemployment was exhausted by the second half of the 1960s. (See table 7.1.) In the first half of the decade, migration from agriculture, supplemented by immigration from abroad, continued to support the growth of the nonagricultural labor force at the customary rate. But by the second half of the 1960s, the reallocation of labor from agriculture to industry was largely complete. Meanwhile, the rise in immigration from North Africa, the Middle East, and the Caribbean incited a political reaction, leading governments to tighten immigration policies. Between 1960–1965 and 1965–1970, these developments halved the rate of growth of dependent nonagricultural employment. They halved it again between 1965–1970 and 1970–1975.

Whereas unemployment had exceeded vacancies in the 1950s across much of Europe, the relationship between these variables was now reversed. In Germany in the mid-1950s, the number of persons unemployed had exceeded the number of vacancies by a factor of ten. By 1960, the number unemployed had fallen to barely half of vacancies, and the ratio continued falling from there. (See figure

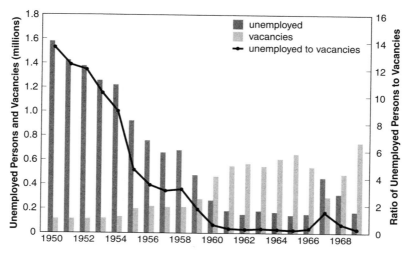

Figure 7.3. Unemployment and vacancies in West Germany, 1950–1969. *Source:* Giersch, Paque, and Schmieding (1992).

7.3.) The risk of long-term unemployment was perceived as minimal. As Johansen characterizes the situation in Denmark, "In the mid-1960s the registered unemployed were either workers who were in the process of changing from one job to another and had a few idle days in between, or older people staying in isolated municipalities in Northern Jutland or the smaller islands from where they did not want to move."[40]

Thus unemployment—both actual and potential—no longer disciplined wage demands to the same extent. Memories of high unemployment in the 1930s faded as the older generation aged and retired.[41] Readiness to sacrifice in the interest of postwar reconstruction gave way to demands for immediate gratification, and concessions to such demands could not be put off indefinitely. The push for higher wages and consumption standards was especially intense in the same places where wage restraint had been most impressive in the 1950s. Dutch workers, for example, who had been so dedicated to their country's low-wage, export-oriented growth strategy

[40] Johansen (1987), pp. 148–149.
[41] This factor is emphasized by Newell and Symons (1990).

in earlier decades, were now in the vanguard of those demanding higher incomes.[42]

Then, with the weakening of the Bretton Woods System, inflationary expectations lost their anchor. So long as countries were committed to defending their currency pegs, there was no possibility that they would succumb to sustained inflation; keeping the exchange rate stable required keeping inflation at the same low levels as in other countries. Since the expectation was that bursts of inflation were temporary, workers had only a mild incentive to demand compensatory wage increases. The Bretton Woods System of pegged but adjustable rates thereby moderated the impact of inflation on wages. But once the Bretton Woods anchor began to drag, unions began worrying that inflation would persist. Keynesian demand stimulus provoked increased wage demands, not additional output and employment.[43] As Giersch, Paque, and Schmieding describe union psychology in Germany, "the persistently inflationary character of the late Bretton Woods System may also have contributed to the drastic change of wage policy: with accelerating price inflation becoming a lasting feature of the economy's performance, inflationary expectations began to play a particularly important part in wage bargaining and may at times have led to full or even super-indexation of nominal wage demands."[44]

Thus, each element that had contributed to the earlier climate of wage restraint weakened in the second half of the 1960s before breaking down in the 1970s. Wage increases won by strikers in 1968–1969 were about twice those of the preceding three years.[45] Money wages rose faster in 1969–1973 than in 1962–1969 in each

---

[42] In retrospect, this is not surprising. Wage moderation and export-led growth had brought unemployment rates to well below 1 percent in the period 1960–1968. Wage restraint therefore began to break down: double-digit increases in nominal wages were already evident in the Netherlands in 1963–1964, well before other European countries. The precocious timing of these events explains why Dutch unemployment began to rise in advance of unemployment throughout the rest of Europe. These facts also help to explain why the country was a leader in the development of the welfare state, passing laws on child allowances in 1963, general assistance in 1965, and paid sick leave in 1967. See Hartog and Theeuwes (1993).

[43] Evidence of the persistence of inflation and its impact on the economy is provided by Alogoskoufis and Smith (1991).

[44] Giersch, Paque, and Schmieding (1992), pp. 157–158.

[45] Allsopp (1983), table 3.4.

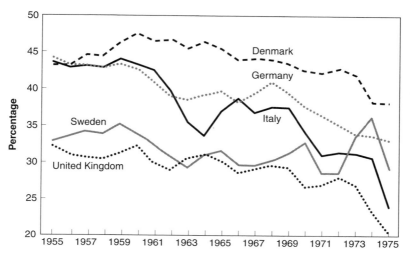

Figure 7.4. Profit shares in selected Western European countries, 1955–1975 (Percentage of national income). *Source*: Hill (1979).

of the nine European countries considered by Flanagan, Soskice, and Ulman (1983). Real wages also rose faster.[46] And, coincident with the wage explosion, productivity growth slowed. The result was a sharp fall between 1965–1969 and 1970–1973 in the share of profits in national income. (See figure 7.4.) By the early 1970s, the share of profits in European national incomes was one-fifth lower than it had been fifteen years earlier.[47]

Governments did what they could to contain these pressures. The French government sought to draw the unions into a voluntary incomes policy. The Fifth Plan, covering 1965–1969, expressed its targets not in terms of the volume of production but in millions of francs, challenging workers to decide in what proportions the increase in nominal income would be divided between higher inflation and higher output.[48] Other governments attempted to encourage neocorporatist cooperation. Denmark established an Economic

[46] Except in Norway, where their rate of growth declined marginally. See Nordhaus (1972) for a comparative analysis of these trends.

[47] The profit share began falling, in other words, even before Europe was hit by the 1973–1974 oil-price shock. See also Flanagan, Soskice, and Ulman (1983) and Marglin (1990).

[48] This was an unusual episode in what economists refer to as nominal income targeting. Unfortunately, there was nothing to bind the government and the Banque de France to the stated target, which robbed the approach of its force.

221

Council made up of twenty representatives of unions, employers, the civil service, and farmers to negotiate voluntary ceilings on increases in nominal incomes. The Council recommended that negotiations over industrial wages, public sector salaries, and agricultural subsidies be more closely coordinated to prevent leapfrogging. Belgium developed a system of "social programming" to limit wage increases and reconcile them with the profitability needed to sustain investment. The Irish government sought union agreement on a national wage recommendation in 1964–1966. In the United Kingdom a statutory freeze on wages and prices was in effect from July 1966 through June 1967, a period of weakness in the British balance of payments.[49] The Netherlands operated legal price controls from 1961 through 1966, after which employers agreed to a voluntary extension of the program.

These policies were "not very successful," in the measured words of the authors of the definitive postmortem on the subject.[50] Where tripartism (cooperation among labor, employers, and government) was underdeveloped, it was impossible to quickly install effective arrangements for wage restraint. In France, for example, the government's efforts to negotiate a social pact went nowhere. In Belgium, social programming did not prevent spontaneous strikes against what dissident workers dismissed as "agreements of poverty."[51] In Ireland, the attempt at a centralized agreement heightened "trade union suspicion of incomes policy, and decentralized bargaining followed until 1969."[52]

Price controls might restrain inflation for a time, but these too were bound to break down. Producers sought exemptions on grounds of exceptional increases in costs. They lobbied for abandoning controls when unions refused to freeze wages. Similarly, efforts to enlist union federations in the anti-inflationary campaign met with only

---

[49] Following the 1967 devaluation, the "nil norm" was maintained but increases up to a ceiling of 3½ percent were authorized to offset a portion of the devaluation-induced increase in the cost of living. See chapter 8.

[50] Ulman and Flanagan (1971).

[51] Molitor (1978), p. 37.

[52] Ó Gráda and O'Rourke (1996), p. 416.

limited success. An agreement to restrain wages on the part of the central labor federation might not extend to nonunion workers. Or negotiations at the plant level violated caps set in economy-wide bargaining in the phenomenon known as wage drift. Fearing that they alone would bear the burden of restraint, rank-and-file members of the central federation went out on wildcat strikes.

The End of the Golden Age

By the end of the 1960s, the special circumstances creating a social consensus that prioritized growth had receded. In France, economic growth was no longer seen as synonymous with national security, and in Germany it was no longer a necessary alternative to discredited activity in the political sphere. The passage of time made it more difficult to suppress the demand for higher living standards, especially in countries such as the Netherlands where workers had allowed real wages to lag productivity as their contribution to growth and accumulation. The very speed of postwar growth caused European unemployment to fall to low levels. And by the end of the 1960s, the special conditions that had made ample supplies of labor available to the modern industrial sector—unemployed labor in European agriculture, the influx of refugees and repatriates from Europe's East and from its overseas dependencies—were largely spent.

The tighter the labor market became, the less discipline it imposed on wage demands. Wage restraint diminished further as memories of high unemployment in the 1930s receded, workers with first-hand experience in that environment retired, and the first members of the postwar baby boom generation who identified with the student protests of 1968 entered the labor force.

With wages now rising faster than productivity, profits were squeezed, reducing the availability of retained earnings for capital formation. So long as growth was maintained at high rates, funding remained adequate, as did the incentive to invest. But the special technological circumstances that had supported rapid growth for

223

more than two decades, notably a backlog of standardized mass-production technologies ready to be imported from the United States, was now all but exhausted. Sustaining growth increasingly required indigenous innovation, and it was not clear that the institutions developed to support technology transfer in the age of extensive growth, from indicative planning in France to state holding companies in Italy and Spain and industrial conglomerates in Portugal and Sweden, were well suited to this task. And if a major disturbance came along, slowing growth and depressing profitability further, investment, one of the two foundation stones of the postwar golden age, would suffer.

For the time being, the other foundation stone, the rapid expansion of trade, remained in place. The Common Market was completed, and already there was talk of enlarging it to include the countries in EFTA. With the completion of the Kennedy Round of GATT negotiations in 1967, tariffs on manufactured goods were cut by a further 50 percent. Again, however, the question was whether comparable successes could be expected going forward. Slower growth might make it more difficult for workers in industries experiencing consolidation to find employment in expanding sectors. More adjustment difficulties might mean greater resistance to trade liberalization and increasing resort to nontariff protection.

Finally, the instability of currencies, although still more a fear than a fact, potentially threatened the cohesion of the European Community and the dynamism of global trade. The expansion of trade was predicated on the stability of the international monetary framework. And by the end of the 1960s, that framework was suffering from mounting strains. Increasingly, questions were raised about whether the golden age of export-led growth and even the European Community itself could survive its demise.

- EIGHT -

MOUNTING PAYMENTS PROBLEMS

In the first half of the 1960s, Western Europe's current account moved further into surplus.[1] Rising savings meant that the availability of foreign finance no longer constrained domestic investment. The deutschmark in particular remained highly competitive despite its 5 percent revaluation against the dollar in 1961.

In a few European countries, pressure on wages and rising consumption demands led to a deterioration of the external accounts, and the balance of payments reemerged as a constraint. Two places where the pressure on wages boiled over, creating problems of external balance, were Italy at the beginning of the 1960s and France at the end of the decade. In Italy the government avoided devaluing the lira but at the cost of precipitating a recession. In France there were political constraints on the use of fiscal and monetary austerity to defend the currency, and devaluation could not be avoided.

Payments problems were chronic in Britain, where the 1960s were effectively one long balance-of-payments crisis. When devaluation finally came in 1967, it relieved these pressures only temporarily. Sterling's devaluation signaled the impending end of the Bretton Woods System of pegged but adjustable exchange rates. If the second most important reserve currency, sterling, could be devalued, then the same fate might ultimately befall the dollar. The implication was that the prospects for the Bretton Woods System, one of the

---

[1] The annual average surplus rose from $0.5 billion in 1958–1958 to $1.7 billion in 1959–1965, doubling as a share of GNP.

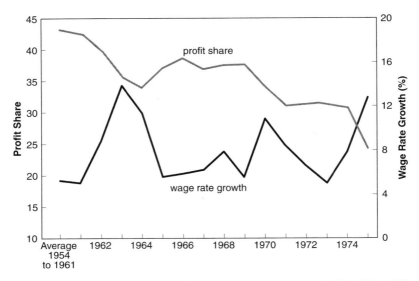

Figure 8.1. Profit share and growth of money wage rates in Italy, 1954–1975. *Sources*: Hill (1979); European Commission, AMECO database.

foundation stones of the postwar golden age, were uncertain. And that uncertainty gave Europe all the more reason to contemplate reorganizing its financial relations on a regional basis.

Italy's Crisis

Italy was the first place where serious payments problems developed. Wages shot up by 10 percent in 1962 and 15 percent in 1963, far in excess of their customary 4 percent annual rate of increase. (See figure 8.1.) More than a decade of growth had tightened labor markets in the north, and migrants from the Mezzogiorno region of southern Italy lacked the skills and training that were in high demand. Contemporaries thus referred to islands of shortage amidst a sea of labor. Inhabitants of those islands were able to secure significant increases in earnings, and the impact of their agreements spilled over to other parts of the economy since Italy lacked centralized mechanisms for internalizing the broader macroeconomic implications of wage increases at the plant or enterprise level. The large

226

state sector had little incentive to resist demands for wage increases, given its preferential access to credit.

The result was a sharp rise in unit labor costs, by 5 percent in 1962 and nearly 15 percent in 1963. The share of profits in national income fell from 42 percent in 1961 to 39 percent in 1962 and 35 percent in 1963.[2] (Again, see figure 8.1.) After growing strongly through 1962, investment slowed in 1963 and turned negative in 1964. Growth fell to less than 3 percent in 1964, half the economy's 6 percent norm, in what observers referred to as the first significant recession in more than a decade.

Room to maneuver was limited by the balance of payments. When investment slowed in 1963 and slumped in 1964, savings declined even more sharply as households continued their buying spree. Consumer expenditure adjusted for inflation rose nearly twice as fast as in preceding years. The result was that in 1963, imports of goods and services rose by nearly one-quarter in real terms—three times as fast as exports.[3] The current account swung from modest surplus, the norm since the mid-1950s, to substantial deficit. (See table 8.1.) Capital began flowing out.

The government borrowed from the U.S. Treasury and the IMF, buying time, but this delay only fueled capital outflows. The Bank of Italy, under pressure from the government, waited until September 1963 to raise interest rates. It followed this in 1964 with another round of restrictive monetary measures. To further buttress the balance of payments, the government then raised taxes on automobiles and gasoline and imposed a generalized increase in turnover taxes. This was not what the economy needed, given the weakness of demand, but the priority attached to the stability of the currency left no alternative. Macroeconomic measures thus reinforced the slowdown.

By 1965 the deterioration in the current account had been stemmed by these restrictive measures, and domestic demand began

[2] Profits are defined here as value added minus employee compensation as a share of value added.

[3] In addition to the wage increases emphasized here, a poor harvest contributed to the trend.

TABLE 8.1
Italian current account, 1959–1965, selected years (Millions of U.S. dollars)

	1959	1961	1963	1965
Visible exports	2,856	4,101	4,973	7,104
Visible imports	2,994	4,679	6,877	6,458
Balance of visible trade	−139	−573	−1,903	+646
Freight and insurance (balance)	−99	−186	−284	−343
Other transport (balance)	+35	+62	+112	+142
Tourism (balance)	+448	+647	+749	+1,062
Income from capital (balance)	−5	−51	−114	−88
Services and government transactions (balance)	+93	+49	+27	+46
Other services (balance)	+167	+199	+319	+403
Total goods and services (balance)	+501	+141	−1,904	+1,867
Private transfers (balance)	+251	+339	+355	+408
Public transfers (balance)	−7	−7	−6	−65
Total current-account balance	+759	+474	−745	+2,209
Capital-account balance	+199	−170	−485	−455
Basic balance	+850	+574	−1,252	+1,594

Source: Allen and Stevenson (1974), pp. 76–77.

to recover, reflecting the buoyancy of the European economy. The authorities used this breathing space to raise public-works spending and public-enterprise investment, and the central bank relaxed its credit restraint. Thus, in both the downturn and the upswing, monetary and fiscal policies were procyclical: at both stages they worked to amplify the economic cycle.

Podbielski observes that the use of demand-management policies in Italy "was not dissimilar to that of many other countries. . . . Action was hesitant and belated; measures were applied piecemeal and ad hoc."[4] This she attributes to the authorities' unfamiliarity with the use of stabilization policy. The comparison with other countries suggests otherwise, as does the fact that Italian policy makers had pursued an explicitly countercyclical fiscal policy during the previous slowdown in 1958.[5] An alternative explanation is the balance-of-payments constraint. In 1958 the current account had been

---

[4] Podbielski (1974), p. 35.
[5] For an analysis of this episode, see Fuà (1964).

in surplus; in 1963 it was in deficit. This left the authorities no choice but to tighten, given their reluctance to devalue. Then, with the return of external balance in 1964, the capacity to apply an expansionary impulse was restored, and the government took advantage of the opportunity to increase public spending.

International capital flows, for their part, did little to relieve the pressure on the balance of payments. Domestic conditions were unsettled: not only was there the labor militancy discussed in chapter 7, but there was an extended political deadlock prior to the formation of the new center-left coalition. Italy's IMF quota was inadequate: as in the case of other countries whose trade had grown rapidly in the 1950s, the quota had not been adjusted to reflect this reality. To be sure, the U.S. Treasury and a consortium of commercial and central banks contributed nearly four times the finance committed by the IMF, and the combined total was just enough to offset the loss of reserves in 1963. But without restrictive macroeconomic measures, not even these substantial loans would have sufficed to stem the loss of dollars and gold.

The wage explosion of 1962–1963 was not repeated until the end of the decade. Comparably severe balance-of-payments problems did not recur, given that Italy still had considerable scope for rapid productivity growth, which made for the maintenance of international competitiveness and relaxed the balance-of-payments constraint. But the Italian crisis set the pattern for the problems that countries such as France and Britain would encounter later in the decade. The main difference in these later episodes was that, by the time they occurred, international capital mobility had recovered further and the pressure on currencies was even more intense.

Britain's Problems

If 1962–1963 was a period of intense balance-of-payments pressure in Italy, for the United Kingdom the 1960s was one continuous payments crisis. Cairncross, in his review of the decade, calls the balance of payments "the central problem" of the British economy.[6] Sterling had come under pressure in 1951, 1955, 1956, and 1957. The years 1961 through 1968 then comprised an extended period in which "balance of payments difficulties were serious enough to threaten the exhaustion of . . . reserves and gold and foreign currencies. . . . The government was at intervals faced with crisis situations, which were resolved partly by improvised measures designed to make the external balance less unfavorable, partly by hastily negotiated rescue operations to supplement the reserves."[7]

A common feature of these crises was the tendency for British governments to run the economy under high pressure of demand that spilled over to the balance of payments. The context was a disappointingly slow per capita growth rate of 2 percent.[8] Only Ireland did worse, and the median per capita growth rate across European countries was nearly twice as high. The period that opened with Britain's withdrawal from Greece and retreat from India and the Middle East was also marked by a diminishing capacity to project military power abroad, reflecting the slow growth of the economy, which in turn heightened unease about the security situation.

The solution, politicians from both ends of the political spectrum agreed, was faster growth. Keynesian economics in its distinctively British incarnation taught that the main way in which government could contribute to growth was by stimulating demand. Strong demand ensured healthy profits and investment, enabling producers to use the new technologies embodied in the latest capital equipment. High levels of capacity utilization led to increasing returns and faster productivity growth.[9] Strong demand was "a necessary, and almost sufficient, condition for rapid growth," in the unvarnished language of the National Institute.[10] And fiscal policy was

[6] Cairncross (1996), p. 18.

[7] Tew (1978), p. 304.

[8] As described in more detail in chapter 4.

[9] The idea that manufacturing is subject to increasing returns so that policies to promote its expansion might result in sharply improved competitiveness was a theme of the writing of Nicholas Kaldor, a Cambridge don and adviser to the Treasury. See Kaldor (1966). Kaldor was subsequently to argue in favor of floating the pound as a way of stimulating the demand for British goods and producing the hoped-for increase in productive efficiency.

[10] National Institute of Economic and Social Research (1962), pp. 55–56.

the main instrument with which the government could sustain a high level of demand, Keynes having taught, or his disciples in any case having learned, that monetary policy was ineffectual or at best useful only for restraining demand.[11] The resulting argument for fiscal stimulus to promote growth dovetailed with political pressure for spending on social programs, delivering a consistently expansionary budgetary stance.

Say's Law, the idea that supply creates its own demand, may have been discredited by the slump of the 1930s, but its inversion, the idea that demand creates its own supply, still had political appeal, if not economic logic. Britain's fundamental problem was on the supply side, a fact of which the slow rate of total factor productivity growth was symptomatic.[12] The fragmentation of the union movement and the confrontational attitudes of labor, management, and government made it difficult to coordinate wages, investment, and public spending. The country lacked institutions for imparting vocational training, making it difficult to adopt Fordist mass-production technologies. Labor resisted the introduction of new technologies, fearing that the result would be redundancies rather than more employment in export-linked industries.[13] That Britain was slow to reorient its economy from the slowly growing markets of the Commonwealth and the Empire to the more rapidly growing markets of Europe further validated these fears. In addition, first having chosen and then having been forced to stay out of the European Economic Community, the United Kingdom was less attractive as a platform for foreign multinationals seeking to produce for the European market. Hence it was the recipient of less technology transfer and for-

---

[11] The definitive contemporary statement of this view was the report of the Radcliffe Committee (see Committee on the Working of the Monetary System 1959).

[12] See table 2.4.

[13] Management, for its part, was reluctant to invest in new projects for fear that unionized workers would seek immediately to capture the return in the form of higher wages. In addition, management feared that craft-oriented trade unions would resist the changes in work practices required in order for the new capital to be operated efficiently. This was particularly a problem where workers were split among a number of separate unions, none of which was prepared to sacrifice its prerogatives in order to increase efficiency for all. For evidence, see Denny and Nickell (1992).

eign finance. Foreign multinationals such as Ford that did set up shop in the United Kingdom found that their facilities were significantly less productive and profitable than in, say, Germany.[14]

As a result, when unemployment was pushed down to 1 percent, the pressure of demand spilled out into the balance of payments. Even strong demand did not produce high inflation because sterling was pegged to the dollar and thereby to the currencies of other European countries. Import prices being given, the entire structure of prices was loosely tied down. Excess demand did, nonetheless, place some pressure on prices. It produced an increasingly overvalued real exchange rate, a trade deficit, and, reflecting fragile confidence in sterling, capital outflows.[15] Each time outflows accelerated, the government was forced to raise taxes or cut spending, and the Bank of England was forced to apply the monetary brakes. The resulting slowdown depressed the return on investment, while the risk premium incorporated into interest rates as a result of the deterioration of confidence and the specter of devaluation elevated funding costs. Thus, policies intended to stimulate investment more often than not ended up having the opposite effect. The result is nicely described by Surrey: "As Britain's relatively slow rate of growth became apparent, [it was argued] that this too was partly attributable to government policy in that the alternation of periods of rapid expansion and stagnation reduced entrepreneurs' confidence in the likelihood of sustained and steady expansion of demand and so reduced the rate of investment in new plant, machinery and buildings, hence further lowering the underlying rate of growth of technical progress and of output per head."[16]

To be sure, neither Conservative nor Labour governments neglected the supply side entirely. The Conservatives agreed in 1962 to establish a National Economic Development Council (NEDC,

[14] The famous study is Pratten (1976).

[15] These last symptoms were aggravated by the problem of the sterling balances, described in more detail later.

[16] Surrey (1982), p. 536. Surrey goes on to observe, somewhat implausibly, that one can also argue that policy was confidence-inspiring insofar as investors cared more about the government's intentions than the actual effects of its policies.

or "Neddy") charged with identifying strategies to support a faster rate of growth. Neddy's main achievement was to announce a target rate of growth in the hope that companies would draw up their investment plans accordingly and that the target would thereby be attained. In 1964 Neddy was joined by a National Economic Development Office, which was responsible for drafting a national investment plan more or less along French lines. But Britain lacked the large firms and cohesive employers associations that facilitated coordination in pursuit of such schemes in the smaller countries of the continent. The Trades Union Congress (TUC) insisted that Neddy be organized around a tightly knit body of powerful union leaders and industrialists, but these leaders were unable to mobilize a fragmented rank and file. Reflecting a different tradition from, say, France's, the civil service opposed policies that would have favored some firms over others. And even if the authorities had wished to do so, they lacked levers like those used by the French to direct the flow of credit.

Thus, chronic balance-of-payments problems requiring fiscal consolidation and the absence of mechanisms to facilitate implementation prevented these tentative steps in the direction of national investment planning from bearing fruit. They led the Labour government that took office in 1964 to consider other approaches. It sought to expand vocational training and extended tax subsidies for research and development. Many of its structural policies were targeted at export industries and at sectors that produced substitutes for imports. These measures included special investment allowances, accelerated depreciation, a variety of related financial subsidies and, starting in 1966, a tax on employment in nontraded goods sectors (the so-called Selective Employment Tax).[17] Some observers saw no reason why, with these policies, Britain could not enjoy the same rapid output and productivity growth as continental Europe.

But even under this optimistic scenario, time would have to pass before the effects of productivity-enhancing policies were felt. Meanwhile, the government would be forced to devalue, deflate, or

---

[17] This last scheme was another proposal by Nicholas Kaldor.

borrow. Devaluation had not been contemplated since the first half of the 1950s, when the Conservative government toyed with a scheme called "Operation Robot" for floating the pound. Now political considerations militated against any change in the parity. The Labour government might have devalued upon taking office in 1964 and blamed the need for the action on its predecessor. But the prime minister, Harold Wilson, worried that Labour, having overseen the devaluations of 1931 and 1949, would be tarred as the party that always devalued. Some of the government's economic advisers warned that devaluation, by rekindling memories of similar measures in 1931 and 1949, would damage sterling's status as a reserve currency and undermine the status of London as one of the world's foremost financial centers.

Then there were the sterling balances, a legacy of the pound's reserve currency status and of Britain's history as a colonial power. Holdings by foreign central banks exceeded three billion pounds at the end of 1964. Their existence meant that a devaluation that again shook confidence in the stability of the currency might lead foreign holders to liquidate those balances, creating more problems than it solved. Devaluing might also antagonize Britain's allies, including the Americans, who had reason to worry about the stability of the dollar. It might make it harder to secure General de Gaulle's support for British membership in the Common Market.[18] And, as always, there was the unconscious tendency to regard the exchange rate as a matter of national pride. Each of these considerations constituted another entry on the side of the intellectual ledger headed "arguments against devaluation."

The prime minister and his chancellor of the exchequer, James Callaghan, were skeptical that devaluation offered a durable solution to Britain's ills. Devaluation would not solve the problem of slow productivity growth, and any beneficial effect on competitiveness would likely be dissipated in a wage–price spiral. Their fears were borne out when the pound was finally devalued in 1967. Com-

---

[18] In early 1967, the prime minister and the foreign secretary made a tour of the six member states of the EEC to lobby for admission.

petitiveness was enhanced for a period, but inflation accelerated and within three years the payments problem was back.

Those arguing for fiscal consolidation, such as the economist Frank Paish, were voices in the wilderness. Paish's argument, which hardly seems radical in retrospect, was that the authorities should not use demand management to push unemployment below 2 percent, the level around which it had hovered in the 1950s.[19] His recommendations were politically unattractive, given the low levels to which unemployment had fallen in other European countries. They were unpalatable to a Labour government for which full employment was a paramount policy goal. Deflation and devaluation being ruled out, the only remaining option was a temporary import surcharge and borrowing abroad in the hope that improvements in competitiveness and productivity would turn up. Officials again hoped that subjecting the economy to strong pressure of demand—engaging in a "dash for growth"—might encourage the necessary improvements.

In the meantime, the government borrowed from the IMF.[20] It obtained an additional three billion dollars' credit from a consortium of foreign central banks.[21] Foreign support was forthcoming because of sterling's importance for the operation of the international system. With doubts already developing about the stability of the dollar, a devaluation of sterling, the second most important currency, could bring the entire Bretton Woods structure crashing down. The industrial countries had tasted the consequences in 1960, when uncertainty surrounding the U.S. presidential election precipitated flight from the dollar, and in 1961, when revaluation of the deutschmark and guilder had prompted movement out of sterling. They had no appetite for another course.

[19] See Paish (1962).

[20] It had already done so in 1961; now in 1965 it did so again.

[21] Foreign support had been extended in 1961 in anticipation of an IMF agreement and in 1965 to supplement one. Then, in addition to normal balance-of-payment support to bridge the current-account gap, starting in June 1966 the country received exceptional support from nine central banks and the Bank for International Settlements to counter sales of sterling balances.

But with the recovery of international capital flows, even exten-sive foreign financing could not bottle up the pressure. The gov-ernment therefore taxed foreign investment income to discourage outward investment, tightened exchange controls on capital trans-actions, and discouraged portfolio investment outside the sterling area. But investors seeking to sell sterling found ways around these measures. The temporary surcharge of 15 percent on imports of most manufactured and semi-manufactured goods imposed in October 1964 was less subject to evasion but breached Britain's obligations to EFTA and the GATT. The government was forced to relax the measure and then to remove it in November 1966. In any case, the tariff was only a temporary palliative. Even had it remained in place, it would not have provided a permanent solution to the country's structural problems, any more than a one-off devaluation.

The other expedient was incomes policy. The Conservatives had experimented with a "pay pause" during the 1961 sterling crisis in an effort to reconcile rising costs with lagging productivity. That initiative had not been backed by legislation; the government had simply sought to use its leverage as employer in the public sector to set norms for other employers and their union counterparts. But the proliferation of unions even within the civil service prevented con-certed action. The establishment of a National Income Commission to marshal a consensus in favor of the government's wage norms had little effect. As it became clear that an election was approaching, union leaders grew restive. In any case, it is hard to imagine how voluntary measures could have worked given the absence of slack in the labor market and the fragmented nature of British industrial relations. There was no social consensus for cutting costs, boosting investment, and encouraging the adoption of new technologies in return for employment guarantees like those that worked to resolve potential payments problems and to support faster growth rates in the Continent's neocorporatist economies.

Even once Labour replaced the Conservatives in Downing Street, efforts to implement voluntary incomes policies had little effect. Initially, the Labour government convinced trade unionists and employers' representatives to sign a joint statement on wages, prices, and productivity. The TUC General Council agreed to a 3–3½ percent norm for wage increases. But labor leaders had limited influence over the union rank and file, which continued to push for increases. Wages thus rose at double-digit rates between mid-1964 and mid-1966.

Next the government resorted to a statutory incomes policy backed by the Prices and Incomes Act of 1966. Facing a worrisome deterioration of the balance of payments and sharp upward movement in money wages, it imposed a six-month wage and price freeze, to be followed by six months of severe restraint during which only exceptional increases were permitted. These measures were more effective than their predecessors by virtue of their legal status, but there was limited willingness on the part of the unions to countenance their retention. Employers, for their part, saw that exceptions would have to be made to retain valued workers. Thus, following the initial twelve-month experiment, controls were relaxed in favor of normative guidance in the manner of previous voluntary policies. Wages rose sharply, making up the ground that had been lost.

The end of the period of severe restraint in June 1967 predictably coincided with strong pressure on sterling. Foreign financial assistance could put off the day of reckoning, but the overhang of sterling balances and the porousness of capital and exchange controls brought about by financial innovations such as the Eurodollar market meant that even large amounts of foreign assistance could not delay it indefinitely.

In June, closure of the Suez Canal disrupted international trade and raised the price of imported oil, and then a series of dock strikes held up exports. Although these events influenced the timing of developments, it was the fundamental incompatibility of the government's internal and external objectives that made devaluation inevitable. By November, the IMF had concluded that the exchange rate was unsustainable and had rejected the request for another three-billion-dollar U.S.-led rescue package. A panic-driven run on the Bank of England then forced the issue. The government responded by devaluing the exchange rate against the dollar from $2.80 to $2.40 on 18 November.[22]

This time, unlike 1949, only a handful of countries followed. Even the domestic effects were mixed. The government was reluctant to supplement devaluation with fiscal retrenchment, causing the volume of imports to rise rather than falling. Helped by strengthening world demand, the change in the exchange rate finally produced an improvement in the current account of the balance of payments in 1969. But the policy package delivered little in terms of an increase in the underlying rate of productivity growth. By 1972, costs had adjusted upward to match the fall in the exchange rate, and the current account began deteriorating again.

The French Crisis and the German Response

The interaction of politics and labor markets was again prominent in the French crisis of 1968–1969. The crisis occurred against a rising trend, French exports having expanded and the balance of payments having strengthened since the 1958 devaluation, the adoption of the Rueff Plan, and the creation of the Common Market. As the country accumulated reserves, General de Gaulle entertained hopes that the franc might eventually supplant the dollar as the leading reserve currency. The events of 1968, starting with student unrest but soon spreading to mass demonstrations and sympathetic strikes, put an end to these ambitions. Suddenly, social and political prospects, and the intentions of the French electorate, were fundamentally unclear. In particular, the spring protests, by making evident the depth of popular discontent with the status quo, raised questions about the prospects for maintaining investment- and export-friendly policies, which in turn precipitated capital flight. Solomon (1977) describes the difficulty of getting money out of the country when the banks were closed by a general strike and the authorities imposed exchange controls. Some Frenchmen drove

---

[22] The IMF then agreed to provide a standby arrangement to support the new parity.

across the border to Belgium or Switzerland with trunks full of cash, which they used to purchase gasoline and groceries as well as to convert into foreign currency. With the majority of workers out, enterprises shut, and protestors blockading the streets, tourism fell off, dealing another blow to the balance of payments.

The Bank of France bought time by tapping its swap line with the Federal Reserve, a facility that was expanded from one hundred million to seven hundred million dollars as part of an international support package. It drew 745 million dollars from the IMF and sold some of the gold acquired in previous years. The government and employers then settled the strike, raising hopes that the period of turbulence might be drawing to a close. But the terms of the settlement, which conceded wage increases of 10 to 35 percent, increased labor costs, which heightened doubts about the competitiveness of French exports and the sustainability of the deficit. Although higher wages meant more consumption demand, the disruptions of May and June reduced the supply of goods and services.[23] The trade deficit widened in response, and French reserves fell from seven billion dollars in April to barely four billion dollars at the end of the year.

Addressing these problems required more fundamental measures. The Bank of France raised its discount rate from 5 to 6 percent in November. The government announced four hundred million dollars of budget cuts. Again the authorities tightened exchange controls; now in addition they imposed measures requiring French banks and residents to repatriate balances held abroad. They solicited two billion dollars of foreign credits.

But there was no effort to roll back the wage increases of the summer, the government now being worried about provoking a near-revolutionary mass mobilization. If anything, labor-market developments evolved in the opposite direction, as workers receiving the least generous increases pushed to close the gap vis-à-vis their more fortunate comrades. And there was little appetite for additional budgetary economies to hold the parity through 1969. Although tighter exchange controls and additional foreign borrowing put off

[23] In calendar year 1968, these fell by roughly 3 percent.

239

the need for an exchange-rate adjustment to restore international competitiveness, they did not eliminate it.

For de Gaulle, never one comfortable with economic matters, devaluation was subversive to his lifelong campaign to restore French *grandeur*. At a minimum, the president and his advisers hoped that devaluation of the franc could be preceded or accompanied by a revaluation of the deutschmark, thereby dressing up the French adjustment as a general realignment of currencies. The Bundesbank, unable to fully sterilize the inflationary effects of capital inflows, had some sympathy for the French position.[24] In the corridors of the Bundesbank, revaluation came to be seen as the only effective way of combating inflationary pressure.

But German exporters opposed revaluation and had the ear of the finance minister, Franz Josef Strauss. A government committed to export-led growth was understandably reluctant to tamper with a tried-and-true model. And it was the government, not the central bank, that controlled the decision of whether to change the parity. This encouraged the conviction that a solution to the problem should be found in France. At a meeting of the G-10 in Bonn in November 1968, Karl Schiller, the German economics minister, lectured the French finance minister, François-Xavier Ortoli, on the need for stable policies. Ortoli's request to revalue the mark was rejected. To avoid being forced into a humiliating unilateral devaluation, de Gaulle again tightened exchange and credit controls. This would not be the last time when monetary adjustment in Europe would require Franco-German cooperation or when the stability of the franc would hinge on Germany's readiness to compromise its domestic objectives in order to stabilize the system.[25]

---

[24] Not even a 100 percent reserve requirement on the increase in external bank liabilities and a licensing requirement on nonresident deposits could neutralize the effects of capital inflows, with the markets finding a variety of new ways of circumventing the banking system. Here the growth of Eurocurrency markets demonstrated their importance. In addition, the Bundesbank tried to encourage German banks to reexport the capital inflow by offering profitable swap rates and allowing such investments to be deducted from the deposits on which reserves were calculated. See Emminger (1977) and Herring and Marston (1977).

[25] Germany had already come under pressure to revalue the deutschmark in 1957–1958, the previous period when the French franc had come under attack. Another prominent instance would be in 1992–1993; see chapter 11.

In April 1969, de Gaulle resigned following the defeat of his reform proposals in a referendum, and in May he was succeeded by Georges Pompidou. Strauss, alarmed that pressure to devalue might turn the French government in a less integration-friendly direction, signaled that he was now prepared to revalue as part of a general realignment. This was a turnaround for a minister who had previously been a staunch opponent of revaluation. His shift was indicative of the importance that the German political class now attached to European integration.

It was clear that France would have to accept a change in parity because it lacked the stomach for the further cuts in spending needed to sustain the peg. In early August the government announced an 11.1 percent devaluation backed by an IMF program. Germany waited until after its general election on 28 September to float the deutschmark and then to revalue by 9.3 percent.

After a difficult first year, France's trade balance moved into surplus, and the economy surged ahead with stimulus from the improvement in international competitiveness. Fast growth fed back into investment; by the mid-1970s, France had the highest investment rate in the OECD, a sharp turnaround from the 1950s. Output rose rapidly in sectors producing industrial machinery and chemicals. Investment in consumer durables and infrastructure were not neglected; this was the period when telephones and the private ownership of motor vehicles became widespread.

Thus, devaluation may have been embarrassing from the perspective of French *grandeur*, but in narrowly economic terms the effects were strongly positive. It restored the economy's international competitiveness. This unleashed a growth spurt that stimulated investment, in turn setting in motion a virtuous cycle. This was not unlike 1958–1959, when a previous devaluation had also had strongly positive growth effects. When serious balance-of-payments problems reemerged in the early 1980s (it seemed as though France had serious balance-of-payments problems on a more or less regular ten-year cycle), devaluation was seen as the remedy de jure.[26]

[26] See "The EMS Initiative" in chapter 9.

It was not always understood that the measure would work only if accompanied by supportive domestic policies.

The Collapse of Bretton Woods

We thus see in the British, French, and Italian cases how political events undermining wage discipline, together with the underdevelopment of institutions for coordinating a response, could erode competitiveness and precipitate a loss of reserves. As counterexamples these national cases similarly show how the same neocorporatist institutions that helped to sustain low inflation, high investment, and rapid growth in other European countries also underpinned exchange-rate and balance-of-payments stability. Where those institutions were underdeveloped, the economic and financial system had the least capacity to accommodate disturbances. Thus, when shocks hit these countries, their currencies were destabilized. Once the casualties included the issuer of the world's second leading reserve currency, the United Kingdom, and one of the leading holders of monetary gold, France, it was clear that the days of Bretton Woods were numbered.

The other factor corrosive of currency stability was rising capital mobility. The Bretton Woods System of pegged but adjustable exchange rates was predicated on the maintenance of capital controls. But markets had an irrepressible tendency to find ways around them. Officials had been alarmed in 1961 by the magnitude of capital flows set afoot by the German and Dutch revaluations. This problem only grew more acute with the continued development of markets and arbitrage techniques in the course of the subsequent decade.

There was a tendency toward stiffening controls to bottle up these pressures: Britain and France tightened capital-account restrictions at various points in the 1960s, as we have seen. Germany tightened controls on inflows in 1970, 1972, and 1973. But against the backdrop of growing trade and financial innovation, half measures did not suffice. Speculation that governments were considering exchange-rate adjustments could still set off massive, destabilizing capital flows. The authorities responded by putting off adjustments and denying that they were contemplating changes in their Bretton Woods parities. After 1964, for example, the Wilson government treated the idea of a sterling devaluation as "the unmentionable." Unavoidably, the prospects for regional and global monetary cooperation were diminished.

It is thus not surprising that exchange-rate adjustments were few and far between. Aside from the cases just mentioned, the only other European devaluations were those of Denmark, Finland, Ireland, and Spain in 1967, when those countries took the occasion of sterling's devaluation to adjust their currencies to more competitive levels.[27] In the end, the conflict between pegged-but-adjustable exchange rates and rising capital mobility could not be finessed.

This was not just a European story, of course. Behind the scenes was the United States, Europe's most important export market, the origin of its foreign direct investment, and the source of its international reserves. U.S. contributions to the reintegration of Europe following World War II had gone beyond the generosity of the Marshall Plan. Successive U.S. administrations had supported the European Payments Union, the European Coal and Steel Community, the Common Market, and even the Common Agricultural Policy (CAP), recognizing that regional cooperation was essential for trade, investment, and ultimately Europe's security. America's motives were strategic as well as economic, but the economic effects were no less powerful for that fact.

Now the United States played a less constructive role. It was less willing to sacrifice its national objectives to support the international system that it had done so much to create. Its new attitude was epitomized by Treasury Secretary John Connolly's notorious ob-

---

[27] Recall that Denmark and Ireland, along with the United Kingdom, were members of EFTA (Finland and Spain would have been as well but for their special political circumstances), which created additional pressure for them to move together with sterling. In addition, Ireland maintained a one-for-one link with sterling, so devaluing against the dollar was a mechanical consequence of the status quo. Breaking the sterling link, which would have required a conscious shift in policy, would have resulted in a sharp loss of competitiveness, given that more than 60 percent of Ireland's trade was with the United Kingdom.

servation, "The dollar may be our currency, but it's your problem."[28] Inflation and gold losses may have been necessary corollaries of America's social- and foreign-policy ambitions, but they did not inspire confidence in the Bretton Woods System. Fears for the stability of the dollar and the future of the system made life harder for European governments and central banks seeking to stabilize their currencies. If the dollar could be devalued in response, then there were new reasons to question whether the 14 percent devaluation of sterling in 1967 would be enough to restore British competitiveness. And the collapse of the Gold Pool and creation of a two-tier gold market in 1968 suggested that a change in the value of the dollar might not be long in coming.

Some have asked whether a more disciplined U.S. policy might have permitted Bretton Woods to survive.[29] Less deficit spending and higher Federal Reserve interest rates might have slowed U.S. gold losses, but a stronger U.S. balance of payments would have meant a weaker European payments position. European governments and central banks then would have had to adopt more restrictive policies. With the United States pumping out fewer dollars, the supply of international reserves lubricating the growth of world trade would have expanded more slowly.[30] Higher interest rates would have meant less investment, while the slower expansion of international reserves would have meant less export growth. In turn Europe's growth would have been less dynamic.

In the end, such speculations are hypothetical. The United States was unwilling to modify its monetary and fiscal policies to

---

[28] He was also reported to have put the point less prosaically: "Foreigners are out to screw us, and it is our job to screw them first." Both quotations are cited in James (1996), p. 210. Connolly became the U.S. treasury secretary only in March 1971, but his stance of unilateralism set the tone for U.S. negotiators at the Smithsonian Institution later that same year.

[29] See, for example, Meltzer (1991).

[30] As Robert Triffin had observed as early at 1947, there was no avoiding some expansion of global reserves, given the expansion of the world economy. And with the United Kingdom, Germany, and France maintaining—in some cases even tightening—their capital controls, the only form that such reserves could take was U.S. dollars. Thus, the growth of U.S. official foreign liabilities would have continued to outstrip the growth of U.S. gold reserves, albeit at a somewhat slower pace in this counterfactual. On this, see chapter 6.

support the dollar against Europe's currencies and sustain the Bretton Woods System. As this reality became clear, capital fled the dollar for the deutschmark on a scale that dwarfed flight from the franc in 1968–1969. In the spring of 1971, fearing the inflationary consequences of continuing to buy dollars for marks, Germany halted its intervention and, unable to make a decision about a new rate, allowed its currency to float upward. Schiller, Germany's economics minister, attempted to negotiate a joint float against the dollar by all EEC countries, but in the end only the Netherlands participated. In August there were reports that France and Britain, seeing the writing on the wall, were preparing to convert dollars into gold. Over the weekend of 13 August, President Richard Nixon preemptively shut the gold window, effectively ending the U.S. commitment to pay out dollars for gold to foreign central banks and governments at thirty-five dollars an ounce.

European countries still pegging to the dollar responded by halting intervention in the foreign-exchange market. Like Germany and the Netherlands before them, they allowed their currencies to float upward. Together with Nixon's 10 percent surcharge on U.S. merchandise imports, this forced the leading players into negotiations for reform of the system. Following discussions at the Smithsonian Institution in Washington, D.C., the dollar was devalued by 8 percent, while the deutschmark, the currencies of the Benelux countries, the Swiss franc, and the Japanese yen were revalued. Fluctuation bands were widened from 1 to 2¼ percent. Nixon famously characterized the result as "the most significant monetary agreement in the history of the world," but the reality was that it changed nothing. With a presidential election approaching in 1972, U.S. policy remained strongly expansionary. And the Smithsonian Agreement's modestly widened bands still offered precious little room to maneuver. The United Kingdom was first to be forced to abandon its Smithsonian Agreement band, in 1972. The United States then followed in 1973. The Bretton Woods System was no more.

The European Response

The stability of exchange rates, which contemporaries saw as conducive to the growth of trade, and the low level of inflation, which provided support for policies of wage moderation and high investment, had been foundation stones of the postwar golden age. As Bretton Woods crumbled and collapsed, fears mounted that the period of high growth might follow it down.

The Europeans were understandably more reluctant than the Americans to see Bretton Woods go. They worried that volatile exchange rates would interfere with the expansion of intra-European trade. They feared the consequences for the CAP. They worried that cutting the exchange-rate anchor line would fan inflation, undermining the wage moderation that had supported profitability, investment, and growth. All this rendered them reluctant to accept the demise of a monetary framework perceived as integral to the golden age.

Two responses to this dilemma then came together in distinctively European fashion. The first was to acknowledge that the rise of capital mobility had undermined the viability of Bretton Woods–style pegged but adjustable rates. But floating rates were not feasible, given the importance of intra-European trade and the development of the CAP. This left only the option of eliminating exchange-rate variability through a forced march to monetary union. For France, discussions of monetary union also offered the promise of more symmetrical management of European monetary affairs after the embarrassing episode when the stability of the franc had depended on German support that was not forthcoming. For Germany they suggested a route to deeper political integration. This was the same confluence of interests that would shape and sustain discussions of monetary union all the way up through the advent of the euro in 1999.

The other response was to deny the conflict between pegged rates and capital mobility and blame the collapse of the Bretton Woods System on the United States. In this view, the problem was the unwillingness of the United States to subordinate its domestic policies to the imperatives of exchange-rate stability and to invest in the survival of the system. Things were different in Europe. Given the continent's history, there was a deeper appreciation of the importance of currency stability. The creation in the 1960s of a Monetary Committee of EC finance ministry and central bank officials offered greater scope for policy coordination. Rather than pursuing ambitious plans for monetary union, a more practical approach was thus to recreate the Bretton Woods System on a regional basis.

This was the strategy that culminated in the creation of the Snake in the Tunnel, credit for which ironically belonged to John Connolly, the U.S. treasury secretary. By widening bilateral exchange-rate bands to 2¼ percent, the Smithsonian Agreement would have permitted each pair of European currencies to fluctuate by as much as 9 percent in the event that one European currency appreciated against the dollar by the full 4½ percent now permitted while another depreciated by the same amount. Not only would such a high degree of flexibility have disrupted the operation of the CAP, but it promised to artificially enhance the dollar's status as a reserve and vehicle currency, since the greenback would vary by only half as much against each European currency as each pair of European currencies varied against each other. European leaders therefore determined to limit their bilateral fluctuation bands to half the permissible width. The metaphor was that of a European snake slithering through the Smithsonian tunnel. When the Smithsonian Agreement collapsed in 1973 and the dollar began floating, mention of the tunnel was dropped and pundits referred, only half in jest, to the snake floating in a lake.

The six EC member states established the Snake in April 1972. Within a week, they were joined by the three states that had been accepted for EC membership but had not yet entered: Denmark, the United Kingdom, and Ireland (the last of which was already in a currency union with the United Kingdom).[31] Arrangements were patterned after Bretton Woods in that countries were authorized

---

[31] Denmark, the United Kingdom, and Ireland then joined the EC on schedule on 1 January 1973. Sweden became associated with the Snake (but not the EC) in March 1973.

to retain controls on capital movements although not on current-account transactions, consistent with their obligations to the IMF and the OECD. Short- and Very-Short-Term Financial Facilities were established to extend financial support to weak-currency countries, mimicking the role of the IMF under Bretton Woods, although on German insistence their extent was strictly limited. A board of central bank governors was created to oversee the operation of these credit facilities, monitor monetary policies, and authorize realignments. It was as if European officials believed that none of the structural changes contributing to the demise of Bretton Woods had come to pass.

Predictably, the Snake quickly began exhibiting many of the same deficiencies as Bretton Woods. Financial supports were limited, and governments did not have the stomach for the austerity measures needed to defend their parities. None of the mechanisms for encouraging the coordination of national economic policies had teeth. In the United Kingdom, the new chancellor, Anthony Barber, applied expansionary policies in yet another "dash for growth." After barely two months in the Snake, Britain was again experiencing chronic balance-of-payments weakness, the boost to competitiveness from the 1967 devaluation having worn off. The weakness of the dollar led currency traders to shift into deutschmarks, driving the mark up and sterling down and forcing the Bank of England and other European central banks to intervene.[32] A statement by the shadow chancellor, Denis Healy, that the pound might have to be devalued then led to a renewed flurry of speculative sales. On 23 June sterling was floated out of the Snake, accompanied by the Irish pound and, temporarily, the Danish krone. The Italian lira followed in February 1973. With the collapse of the Smithsonian Agreement the next month, capital fleeing the dollar sought refuge in German financial markets, pushing up the deutschmark against other European currencies. To relieve the pressure, the deutschmark was revalued, immediately by 3 percent and then, three months later, by an

[32] For further discussion of this pattern, see "From the Delors Report to the Maastricht Treaty" in chapter 11.

additional 5.5 percent.[33] With the oil shock and consequent large wage increases, the French government decided that it attached higher priority to expansionary policies than exchange-rate stability and withdrew from the Snake in January 1974. For Pompidou, who valued his country's freedom of action, this outcome was not entirely unwelcome; he rejected German finance minister Helmut Schmidt's offer of a three-billion-dollar loan to help keep the franc in the Snake.[34] Two months later, Pompidou died of a secret illness, and Valéry Giscard d'Estaing was elected president. With inflation threatening to run out of control, the new president initiated an economic "cooldown," allowing the franc to return to the Snake at the previous parity in July 1975 (on the occasion of the twenty-fifth anniversary of the Schuman Plan). But Giscard's anti-inflationary policies intensified recessionary pressures, leading his premier, the Gaullist Jacques Chirac, to initiate a major fiscal expansion. (Giscard had meanwhile grown concerned that the recession was propelling the left's rise in the polls.) The *relance Chirac* predictably weakened the trade balance, reignited inflation, and forced the country to withdrawn from the Snake again in March 1976.

Germany was forced to intervene in increasing amounts in support of the remaining participants, fanning worries in the Bundesbank over inflation. The following October the members attempted to relieve the tensions within the system by undertaking a general realignment: the Benelux countries and the Scandinavian participants all devalued against Germany. As a quid pro quo for agreeing to this realignment, the German authorities demanded more frequent adjustments by their partners so that their own intervention obligations would be limited. Although adjustments in rates did in fact become more frequent, these did little to enhance the stability of the system. After Sweden, Denmark, and Norway devalued in 1977, Sweden was forced to withdraw from the Snake. After the Netherlands and Belgium revalued in 1978, Norway then withdrew.

On one level, these trials and tribulations were not surprising. The oil shock in 1973 was disruptive, and its effects varied across

---

[33] The Netherlands and Norway followed.
[34] Hellmann (1979), p. 44; Parsons (2003), p. 164.

countries. As commodity prices began rising, countries experienced not just explosive wage growth but also rising unemployment. Governments then attempted to counter the rise in unemployment with fiscal stimulus, which fanned inflation. To the extent that the impact of the initial shock, the unemployment response, and tolerance for inflation varied across countries, different currencies were affected differently. Superimposed on this was the decline of the dollar in 1973 and once more toward the end of the decade, undermining European competitiveness but to different extents in different countries and perturbing cross rates between European currencies. It is hard to imagine that any system of pegged exchange rates would have been capable of withstanding these strains.

In addition, there was a reluctance to consistently subordinate domestic policies to the requirements of exchange-rate stability. The swings in French economic policy are the most vivid example, but the tendency was general. It was difficult for governments to resist domestic pressure for policy responses when unemployment rose unexpectedly from the low levels to which the citizenry had grown accustomed, and for them not to respond aggressively even when doing so put exchange-rate stability at risk.

Finally, the instability of the Snake reflected the fact that the 1970s was a low point for European cooperation. Strong-currency countries were prepared to extend only limited support to their weak-currency partners, and there was little willingness to subordinate domestic policies to the imperatives of the system. There was no analog to the customs union of the 1960s or the Single Market Program of the 1980s to which governments might point as the reward for agreeing to monetary sacrifices. Opportunities for cross-issue tradeoffs were few. Participants in the Snake were a diverse lot, including even countries such as Sweden and Norway with no immediate aspirations of joining the EC.

Hard lessons were drawn from this experience. Officials learned that the deutschmark had emerged as Europe's strong currency. They now understood that, like it or not, any regional monetary arrangement would have to revolve around Germany. They learned that any new monetary project would have to be sponsored and organized by the EC, which was the only way of building solid institutional foundations. This meant that a new regional monetary arrangement would succeed only as part of a reinvigorated process of European integration. And since it had to be a project of the EC, any such system would have to include not just Germany but also France. Establishing the new arrangement—what eventually became known as the European Monetary System—therefore required the initiative of both the German chancellor Helmut Schmidt and the French president Valéry Giscard d'Estaing.

- NINE -

Declining Growth, Rising Rigidities

By the 1970s, the opportunities for rapid growth through repair of wartime damage had long since vanished. Extensive growth had run its course. The backlog of high-return investments had been exhausted, and the underemployed rural labor that had supported the expansion of urban manufacturing was all but fully utilized. Institutions designed to encourage wage moderation and high investment came under strain as a result of these changes. All this raised questions about Europe's capacity to maintain its customary rates of growth.

Further complicating the transition was the collapse of the Smithsonian Agreement and the demise of the Bretton Woods System. Exchange rates began to fluctuate, disturbing competitiveness and fueling a backlash against international trade. Then there was the OPEC oil-price rise following the outbreak of the 1973 Yom Kippur war and its echo in 1979. These were major disturbances to a European economy dependent on imports for the bulk of its energy supplies.

Above all there was the slowdown in productivity growth affecting the entire industrial world. Between 1962–1973 and 1973–1982, the average rate of growth of output per worker fell by 50 percent in France and Germany, 60 percent in Britain, and 75 percent in Italy.[1] This sharp slowdown was not a propitious backdrop for the transition to intensive, innovation-based growth.

[1] Helliwell, Sturm, and Salou (1985), table 1, column 2.

The Productivity Slowdown

A flood of studies soon appeared analyzing the slowdown in growth of output per employed person. Some authors, anxious to indict their presumed culprit, attributed the entire slowdown to a single factor rather than analyzing the phenomenon in an encompassing way. Subsequent studies were more satisfactory, although many of these were better at analyzing proximate sources than at identifying the root causes of the problem. Helliwell, Sturm, and Salou (1985) laid out what came to be regarded as the canonical model of the determinants of productivity growth, one that incorporated roles for both supply and demand. They model the long-term productive potential of the national economy as depending on a bundle of capital and energy inputs combined with efficiency units of labor. This is the point at which the long-run rate of technical progress enters the story by determining the efficiency of labor.[2] In addition, actual productivity fluctuates around normal levels as a function of unexpected changes in final demand, abnormal movements in profitability, and undesired inventory changes.

This framework can be used to identify roles for both the supply and the demand sides of the productivity equation. On the demand side, falling profitability, rising inventories, and unexpectedly low final sales led to declines in factor utilization. Thus, the return of the business cycle, which led to unexpected declines in sales and rises in inventories, precipitating a fall in capacity utilization, helps to explain why productivity grew more slowly in a period that included the relatively severe post-1973 and post-1979 recessions. The oil shock, by reducing consumer confidence, could have been part of this, as could tightening by central banks in response to the acceleration of inflation. Helliwell, Sturm, and Salou concluded that 80 percent of the slowdown between 1962–1973 and 1973–1982 was due to these demand-side factors.[3] This is not to deny a role for

[2] Or, more precisely in the Helliwell, Sturm, and Salou (1985) study, man-hours needed to provide an efficiency unit of labor.

[3] Bruno (1982), writing earlier on the basis of more limited data, concluded that about 50 percent of the slowdown in private-sector productivity was due to the weakness of demand. The contrast makes sense: the second OPEC oil-price hike, on the impact of which Bruno had less information, presumably had less disruptive supply-side effects, both because it was

the oil shocks in creating problems on the supply side; one-fifth of an important phenomenon is still important. Nor should one underestimate the role of the oil shocks in undermining consumer confidence and squeezing profitability, thereby producing the weakness in demand.[4] Be this as it may, these results suggested that the productivity slowdown, at least in its early phases, was more than just a supply-side story.

But even if the severity of the post-1973 and post-1979 recessions was part of the explanation for the initial decline in productivity, this cannot explain why growth failed to recover subsequently. The annual rate of growth of GDP per worker fell by half between 1960–1975 and 1975–2000.[5] That fall was a pan-European phenomenon: it was evident in every European country in table 9.1 with the sole exception of Ireland, which had underperformed in the 1950s and 1960s and now surged ahead as a result of structural reform and inward foreign direct investment.[6]

Here is where studies of this sort shed less light. At an immediate level it was clear that higher oil prices caused producers to economize on their use of petroleum, reducing the amount of energy in the composite capital-energy bundle. Capital and labor, having less energy with which to work, would have been rendered less productive. Unfortunately for this thesis, subsequent studies found that the quantitative impact of the effect was slight. The share of energy in the composite capital-energy bundle was only about 5 percent. Nor was there much evidence that reducing the share of energy in the bundle reduced the efficiency of capital. If capital had been rendered

shorter lived and because it was not the first, so European firms had some experience in managing oil-price disruptions. The somewhat later analysis in Bruno and Sachs (1985, chapter 8) attributes the majority of the slowdown to demand-side factors.

[4] In addition, some authors (for example, Hamilton 1988) argued that the oil shocks caused consumers to substitute away from energy-using products such as motor vehicles, requiring costly reallocation of labor from the automotive industry toward other sectors, costs that in turn reduced value added.

[5] Calculated as an unweighted average of the figures in table 9.1.

[6] See "Reducing Unemployment" in chapter 12. Nor is the same deceleration evident in the United States, which as the technological leader had grown relatively slowly in the earlier period and whose subsequent growth performance was boosted by the productivity "miracle" of the second half of the 1990s (also analyzed in chapter 12).

TABLE 9.1

Average annual rate of growth of output per worker and its determinants, 1960–2000, various subperiods (Percent per year)

Country	1960–1975				1975–2000			
	y	k	h	tfp	y	k	h	tfp
Austria	4.65	7.03	0.50	1.99	2.00	2.58	0.98	0.49
Belgium	3.88	4.55	0.79	1.85	1.79	1.97	0.72	0.66
Denmark	2.07	3.21	0.36	0.77	1.74	1.39	0.33	1.06
Finland	3.70	5.68	1.11	1.08	2.14	2.21	0.98	0.75
France	3.87	6.09	0.96	1.22	1.67	2.27	0.80	0.39
Germany	3.45	6.19	1.06	0.69	1.21	0.83	0.72	0.45
Greece	6.47	9.33	0.71	2.92	1.06	1.03	1.02	0.03
Ireland	3.68	3.30	0.54	2.23	4.23	3.96	0.86	2.35
Italy	4.40	5.15	0.78	2.18	2.05	2.01	1.02	0.70
Netherlands	2.78	4.54	0.83	0.73	1.11	0.99	0.90	0.19
Norway	2.62	3.00	0.41	1.36	2.21	2.12	0.52	1.16
Portugal	4.64	5.46	0.61	2.43	2.69	3.63	0.79	0.96
Spain	6.47	6.30	0.37	4.14	1.28	1.99	1.17	−0.16
Sweden	2.56	4.43	0.69	0.63	1.15	1.31	0.88	0.13
United Kingdom	1.96	5.14	0.58	−0.13	1.86	2.05	0.73	0.69
Memo item: United States	1.81	1.61	0.80	0.74	1.94	2.62	0.53	0.72

Source: See appendix.

Notes: y = output per worker; k = physical capital per worker; h = human capital per worker; tfp = total factor productivity per worker.

obsolete, the price of used equipment should have fallen. In fact, such price falls were minor, and in some cases the price of energy-intensive equipment actually rose.[7] Nor was there clear evidence of larger falls in output, employment, and productivity in more energy-intensive industries.[8]

Finally, studies written in the early 1980s assumed—incorrectly, as it turned out—that high energy prices were now a fact of economic life. In fact, the real price of energy and related commodities was not significantly higher after 1985 than before 1973, reflecting the difficulty of holding together the cartel of oil-producing countries. (See figure 9.1.) Thus, if changes in the energy/labor mix really explained the supply-side deterioration of the 1970s, then it was not

[7] See, for example, Hulten, Robertson, and Wykoff (1989).
[8] See Bohi (1991).

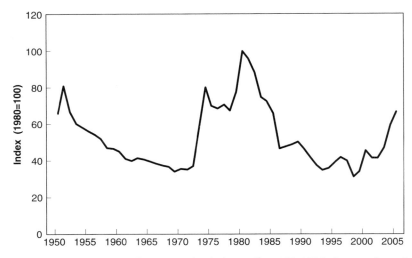

Figure 9.1. Real commodity prices (including oil), 1950–2005. *Sources*: Layard, Nickell, and Jackman (1991); International Monetary Fund, *Primary Commodity Prices* (various years).

clear why producers did not now simply move back to the more efficient factor mix of the 1960s. Some invoked uncertainty about energy prices in explaining permanent shifts in the factor mix in a direction that reduced the growth of labor productivity. But there was a sense that economists, by turning from something they could see (the increase in energy prices) to something they could not (an increase in perceived uncertainty) were grasping at straws.

The slowdown in the rate of technical progress was greatest, by these calculations, in countries such as Italy that had started out behind and were still attempting to close the gap vis-à-vis the technological leaders. Not just Italy but also Japan, another country that the started the postwar period with relatively low levels of labor productivity but quickly narrowed the gap, now experienced a particularly sharp deceleration in the rate of productivity growth. This suggests that the slowdown was a function not just of the OPEC shock and the collapse of Bretton Woods but also of the adjustment to a more intensive, innovation-based model of growth following the end of the catch-up process.

Innovation

Continuing to raise technical efficiency at the customary pace now became more difficult. As they moved through the postwar period, European economies depleted the technological backlog inherited from World War II. By the end of the 1960s they found it hard to sustain growth through the sheer multiplication of capital and labor inputs. The Fordist model of using assembly-line methods to divide, conquer, and scale up the labor process gave way to flexible production and decentralized work organization. The challenge now was to develop new products and processes and reorganize production accordingly.

Judged by the aggregate statistics, the United States had a leg up. America devoted 3 to 4 percent of its GDP to research and development. Of the major European countries, only in the United Kingdom was the R&D share of national income even half as high. (See table 9.2.) In smaller European countries, where returns on investments in technology were harder to capture at the national level, R&D spending ratios were lower still. In the computer industry alone, the United States spent five times as much on R&D as all of Western Europe combined. Whereas the United States devoted nearly 8 percent of government expenditure to R&D, in no European country was the comparable ratio even half as high.[9] To be sure, a substantial fraction of this public-sector R&D was on defense- and space-exploration-related projects with uncertain commercial potential. On the one hand, much U.S. defense spending was on hydrogen bombs and nuclear submarines; on the other hand, the U.S. space program led to the development of microlasers, advanced welding torches, and high-pressure waterstripping, among other industrial spin-offs, and funding from the Defense Advanced Research Projects Agency (DARPA) contributed to the development of the Internet.

[9] Some two-thirds of U.S. research expenditure in the 1960s was financed by the government, a much higher share than in any Western European country except France.

257

TABLE 9.2

Gross expenditures on research and development by principal sources of funds as a percentage of gross national product, 1963–1971, selected years

	Business enterprises and abroad			Government and other national resources		
	1963	1969	1971	1963	1969	1971
France	0.68	0.71	0.70	1.02	1.20	1.08
Ireland	0.15	0.26	0.31	0.31	0.37	0.39
Italy	0.37	0.45	0.53	0.26	0.38	0.37
Netherlands	1.12	1.25	1.18	0.78	0.76	0.83
Norway	0.33	0.40	0.42	0.42	0.58	0.56
Sweden	0.67	0.78	0.90	0.61	0.56	0.68
United Kingdom	1.00	1.07	0.98[a]	1.31	1.24	1.28[a]
West Germany	0.79	1.04	1.15	0.58	0.68	0.91
Memo item: United States	0.85	1.07	1.01	1.86	1.72	1.54

Source: van der Wee (1986).
Note: [a] 1972 statistics.

European governments, for their part, perceived that the United States had a head start in both pure and applied research. They therefore took steps to close the gap. Smaller European states concentrated on applied research relevant to the existing industrial base. (Recall the example of Norway and optical-control flame cutting mentioned in chapter 7.) Larger countries, where R&D spending tended to be government- rather than business-linked, concentrated on science-based sectors. With the notable but not surprising exception of the United Kingdom, all Western European countries succeeded in expanding their shares of total world exports of research-intensive goods between the mid-1950s and mid-1960s.

Still, there was no way that Europe could match the United States in the development of science-based technologies. The United States invested more in general education, especially at the postgraduate level. Its universities had closer links to industry. Its securities markets allowed investors to take bets on competing technologies. All this made the United States a motor for radical innovation.

Europe's advantage, in contrast, lay in incremental innovation. Where the United States devoted a disproportionate amount of its

R&D to aerospace and electronics, the radical new technologies of the era, European R&D focused more on microinventions and incremental improvements in chemicals, textiles, and electrical and mechanical machinery. Rather than replacing old textile looms with entirely new technologies, for example, firms in Emilia-Romagna in the Third Italy modified their machines to do new tricks, adding numerical control to automatic looms.[10] This allowed producers who had guessed wrong about the latest fashion trends to reprogram their machinery and offer their services as subcontractors to luckier competitors with an excess of orders. The region as a whole was thereby able to provide final products on the scale demanded by large retailers despite the fact that individual suppliers were relatively small. This technological orientation was compatible with the fact that small and medium-sized firms lacked the research departments, R&D budgets, and above all the scale needed to pursue a portfolio of ambitious research projects, one of which might pay off handsomely but whose prospects were uncertain and required a lengthy gestation period. Smaller firms concentrated on more modest and predictable innovations in line with their inability to pursue a variety of research projects simultaneously.

Elsewhere, interfirm relations were vertical rather than horizontal, but there too innovation was incremental and ongoing. German producers of cutting lathes, confronted with Japanese competition, developed modular-design systems that allowed them to better tailor their machines to their customers' needs.[11] In the coal mining industry of the Ruhr, machine-building firms improved their products through an ongoing process of interaction with their customers.[12] When large firms produced significant innovations, the smaller members of their networks developed them further. In other regions, such as Baden-Württemberg, innovation took the form of learning

---

[10] Piore and Sabel (1984), p. 215. This was the book that popularized the notion that European regions had a comparative advantage in "flexible specialization," or what German specialists refer to as "diversified quality production" (Streeck 1991). Emilia-Romagna and the surrounding region were referred to as the Third Italy to distinguish it from the First (the old industrial northwest) and the Second (the underdeveloped south).

[11] See Herrigel (1989).

[12] See Grabher (1991).

to retool quickly in response to changes in demand and thereby reducing the cost gap between standardized (U.S.-style) components and custom-tailored European equivalents.

None of this implies that European R&D was inferior, only that it was organized differently. Firms developing and applying these incremental innovations tended to form communities of loosely cooperating competitors and suppliers. This clustering led observers to speak of "industrial districts." It allowed suppliers to specialize without becoming vulnerable to hold-up problems, since there existed alternative downstream producers. It allowed those downstream producers to outsource the production of components, since there similarly existed alternative suppliers.[13] The existence of these industrial districts encouraged the development of support services such as marketing syndicates (like those of the textile firms of Emilia-Romagna), specialized finance (like that provided by the regional *Sparkassen* and *Volksbanken* in Baden-Württemberg), and joint research projects (like those coordinated by the German trade associations).

This comparative advantage in incremental innovation was no coincidence. The Third Italy, where one such network of small and medium-sized enterprises took root, was a region of low in- and out-migration, certainty in comparison with the United States and even compared with other parts of Italy. Social stability was conducive to the development of ongoing relations between the firms comprising the district, encouraging information sharing, limiting opportunistic behavior, and reducing transactions costs. In the Ruhr, it was the turnover of firms that was unusually low, making for stable interfirm relations. Europe's regional banks were ideally suited to assembling information about the credit needs of this network of local producers, and their patient finance contributed to the low turnover of firms. The continent's system of vocational education and apprenticeship training produced workers with the specialized knowledge to identify the technological challenges facing their employers and

---

[13] In addition, the dependence of firms on the acquisition of new technological knowledge from other members of the community and the cohesiveness of the network enabled them to deny new knowledge to producers who attempted to act opportunistically.

260

the skills needed to devise solutions. Firms that might have been reluctant to invest in on-the-job training for fear of losing workers to their competitors were reassured by the existence of cohesive employers associations that discouraged poaching.

These institutions reflected Europe's history. Lacking the middle-class living standards and extensive market of the United States, product standardization and assembly-line methods had never taken root to the same extent. Efforts to transplant them after World War II, although encouraged by the large unexploited backlog of mass-production technologies, never eliminated craft-based production. Now, with advances in computation and their application to production, the advantages of scale and standardization were no longer so dominant. Where coordinating activities and input supplies had once suggested integrating them into a large multidivisional corporation, these problems could now be solved by networking the smaller, more nimble firms that still figured prominently on the European scene.[14]

Increasingly, then, Europe's strength lay in small and middle-size companies using "medium-tech" methods and in skilled labor with long-term attachments to a particular employer. These companies specialized in developing not so much new and better mousetraps as better ways of building familiar mousetraps. There still being a rapidly growing market for mousetraps, as it were, there was scope for raising productivity by concentrating on high-quality products tailored to the market. Moreover, the demand for high-quality consumer and producer goods was not as sensitive to business cycle fluctuations as the demand for mass-produced family sedans or cold-rolled steel, which was advantageous in a period when business cycle fluctuations returned with a vengeance. This flexibility also gave firms the capacity to move into industrial subsectors sheltered from weakening demand.

Thus, it is not surprising that between 1973 and 1979, a period of pronounced volatility, the annual rate of increase of GNP per

---

[14] These issues of strategic interaction are central to the reformulation of the Piore-Sabel hypothesis by Hall and Soskice (2001).

261

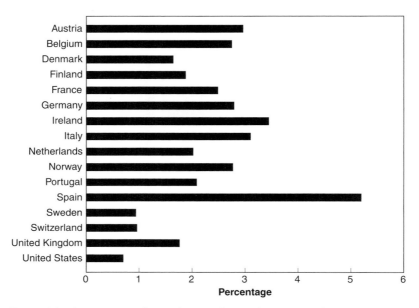

Figure 9.2. Average annual growth rate of gross domestic product per employed worker, 1973–1979. *Source*: Groningen Growth and Development Center, Total Economy Database.

employed worker was higher in France, Germany, Denmark, and Sweden than in the United States. (See figure 9.2.) If one takes the longer period from 1973 through 1990, the result is the same: output per employee rose by 1.8 percent in Europe versus 1.1 percent in the United States, while output per hour worked rose by 2.5 percent versus 1.3 percent per year.

Of course, it can be argued that the payoff to radical innovation lay in the future. Maybe Europe seemed to be doing well because the United States was investing heavily in radical new technologies that would not bear fruit commercially for a decade or more. It was still possible that a set of institutions well attuned to the needs of factor accumulation and incremental innovation would be more of a hindrance than a help once the payoff to these radical innovations materialized. Compared with other European countries, the United Kingdom and Ireland, institutional outliers both, took relatively quickly to the computer. They had market-based financial systems, and their greater emphasis on general education may have had

262

something to do with the special aptitude of the labor force for the more freewheeling work environment that comes with information technology. This is a reminder that the same institutions that were well suited to the golden age of extensive growth may have been less conducive to innovation and productivity growth subsequently, but also that Europe had always been characterized by a good deal of institutional diversity.

Unemployment

The greater part of Europe had been a full-employment economy for nearly two decades. Unemployment had fallen to below American levels, reaching 2 percent and less. (See table 9.3.) Now, after 1973, those rates began rising. From 2½ percent in 1973, unemployment moved up to more than 5 percent in 1979, where it showed signs of leveling off. But it then doubled again, to more than 10 percent by the middle of the 1980s. And unlike U.S. unemployment, which seemed to fluctuate around an unchanging mean (thus encouraging references to the "natural rate"), European unemployment ratcheted up in steps and showed no sign of returning to previous levels. (See figure 9.3.)

The sources of this increase in unemployment are no mystery.[15] The rise in oil prices was a shock to consumer and investor confidence, and weak demand clearly created problems for the labor market. Higher input prices that squeezed profitability depressed the demand for labor further.[16] And with wage inflation showing little tendency to subside, labor became more expensive. Grubb, Layard, and Symons (1984) estimate a set of wage and price equations, showing how the rise in import prices can explain a good deal of the adverse shift in the inflation-unemployment relationship shown in figure 9.4.

---

[15] Why unemployment remained so high for so long will be addressed later in this chapter. Here we ask why it rose in the first place.

[16] There is little evidence of labor–energy substitution of the sort that would have limited the rise in unemployment. If anything, substitution of capital for energy was probably more important.

TABLE 9.3

Unemployment rates, 1960–2004

	1960–1964	1965–1972	1973–1980	1980–1987	1988–1995	1996–1999	2000–2004
Austria	1.6	1.4	1.4	3.1	3.6	4.3	4.1
Belgium	2.3	2.3	5.8	11.2	8.4	9.2	7.3
Denmark	2.2	1.7	4.1	7.0	8.1	5.3	4.9
Finland	1.4	2.4	4.1	5.1	9.9	12.2	9.2
France	1.5	2.3	4.3	8.9	10.5	11.9	9.1
Ireland	5.1	5.3	7.3	13.8	14.7	8.9	4.3
Italy	3.5	4.2	4.5	6.7	8.1	9.9	8.8
Netherlands	0.9	1.7	4.7	10.0	7.2	4.7	3.2
Norway	2.2	1.7	1.8	2.4	5.2	3.9	4.0
Portugal	2.3	2.5	5.5	7.8	5.4	5.9	5.2
Spain	2.4	2.7	4.9	17.6	19.6	19.4	11.1
Sweden	1.2	1.6	1.6	2.3	5.1	8.7	5.5
Switzerland	0.2	0.0	0.8	1.8	2.8	3.7	3.4
United Kingdom	2.6	3.1	4.8	10.5	8.8	6.9	5.0
West Germany	0.8	0.8	2.9	6.1	5.6	7.1	8.3
Memo item: United States	5.5	4.3	6.4	7.6	6.1	4.8	5.2

Sources: Nickell (2003b); Organisation for Economic Co-operation and Development (2005).

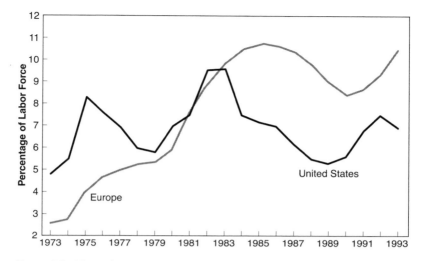

Figure 9.3. Unemployment rates in Europe and the United States, 1973–1993. *Sources*: International Labor Organization, Labor Statistics Database; European Commission (1995). *Note*: The Europe line is the average of the EU-12 countries: France, Germany, Belgium, Luxembourg, Netherlands, Italy, the United Kingdom, Ireland, Denmark, Greece, Portugal, and Spain.

A similar story can be told about the second increase in the 1980s. Inflation having accelerated beyond acceptable levels, the chairman of the Board of Governors of the Federal Reserve, Paul Volcker, and the British prime minister, Margaret Thatcher, resorted to higher interest rates to bring it down.[17] Higher interest rates depressed demand, investment demand in particular. (Note that these were higher real interest rates, with nominal interest rates going up and actual and expected inflation coming down.) Higher interest rates were also a supply shock of sorts, making it more costly for firms to carry inventories and finance other operations. By increasing the user cost of capital, they discouraged capital formation and slowed the accumulation of cooperating factors that would have raised productivity and labor demand.

---

[17] Given the integration of international capital markets, those higher interest rates were then transmitted across Europe. The abrupt curtailment of foreign lending by the advanced industrial countries, not least to the centrally planned economies, reflected these same phenomena. See chapter 10.

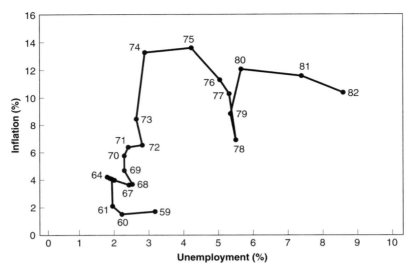

Figure 9.4. Inflation and unemployment in Europe, 1959–1982. *Source*: Eurostat. *Note*: Figure shows aggregate statistics for nine European countries: Belgium, Denmark, West Germany, France, Ireland, Italy, Luxembourg, Netherlands, and the United Kingdom.

The rise in unemployment following the first OPEC shock is evident in table 9.3. The highest levels were reached in Belgium and Ireland, while the largest change was in Denmark. Evidently, small open economies with limited production of energy were particularly vulnerable to the shock. But not all small open economies reacted similarly. Unemployment remained at a strikingly low 1.5 percent in Austria and Sweden, neither of which possessed abundant energy. In Germany, a larger economy but still one dependent on imported energy, unemployment averaged only half of Belgian and Irish levels.[18] The United Kingdom and Italy were intermediate cases with unemployment rates of 4.8 percent and 4.5 percent, respectively.

An explanation for these differences can be found in the ability of neocorporatist institutions to restrain wage increases. Expectations had built up over the course of decades about the warranted

[18] Partly as a result of the export of the unemployed to Greece, Yugoslavia, Turkey, and, to a lesser extent, Spain and Portugal.

rate of increase of real earnings.[19] In countries where workers had accepted lower wages in order to make profits available for modernization, they now expected to make up lost ground.[20] With the onset of the productivity slowdown, the rate of real wage growth consistent with full employment shifted down. But expectations and actual wage demands adapted more slowly. It was not yet clear whether productivity had really slowed or employers were only claiming, as they are wont to do, that they needed lower wages to sustain profitability. This difficulty of interpreting the shock left the unions reluctant to grant concessions.[21] And once prices started rising, there was a tendency to demand higher wages in compensation for the now higher cost of living. Inflation having already accelerated in the late 1960s, sometimes this tendency had been formalized by the addition of escalator clauses to wage contracts. In the Netherlands, for example, indexation provisions had been added to virtually all collective agreements by the early 1970s, making real wage adjustment more difficult.

If the rate of increase of wages did not moderate, firms would mark up their prices further, reflecting their now higher costs. Central banks would pursue more expansionary policies to ensure that purchasers had the money to buy these now more expensive goods. The cost of living having risen, workers would insist on another round of wage increases, provoking more price increases and more monetary accommodation. This was the genesis of the wage-price spiral of the second half of 1970s.

Ultimately, nothing was gained by this leapfrogging behavior. Higher wages leading to higher prices left real labor costs and labor demand unchanged. The only enduring legacy was inflation, as central banks accommodated higher wages and prices in order to stabilize demand. Better would have been agreement by all concerned to

---

[19] Thus, Bruno and Sachs (1985) frame their analysis in terms of real wage targets, and explain the rise in unemployment in terms of the incompatibility of inflexible targets with the new, lower trend rate of productivity growth.

[20] Flanagan, Soskice, and Ulman (1983), chapter 3 and especially pp. 135–141, discuss experience in the Netherlands, a classic case in point.

[21] Grossman and Hart (1981) model this phenomenon and show how this could have slowed the adaptation of real wage demands.

limit the rise in wages and prices, minimizing inflation. Similarly, real wages above market-clearing levels only generated unemployment. Better would have been agreement among unions to moderate their growth.

More neocorporatist economies had greater success in achieving such agreement—not surprisingly, since stabilizing wages was precisely what the post–World War II period's neocorporatist institutions had been elaborated to do. Where, as in Germany, labor participated in the supervisory boards of joint stock companies as a result of the operation of the co-determination law, they could verify management claims of a profitability squeeze. Where, as in Sweden, wage negotiations were highly centralized, employers and unions could work together to maintain prevailing norms, and the government could offer increases in public employment to relieve workers of the risk of unemployment. Where, as in Austria, negotiations were tightly coordinated, unions and employers could more effectively engineer restraint among their members.[22] Thus, when the oil shock unexpectedly reduced the rate of growth of national income, Austrian unions quickly agreed to correct the discrepancy in the following year's negotiating round, this despite the fact that the shortfall in nominal income growth reflected not less inflation (to the contrary) but less growth.[23] Labor's share of national income fell after 1975, and the squeeze on profits was moderated.[24] This solved the supply-side problem, but higher oil prices still threatened to depress demand by diverting spending away from domestic consumption. The government countered this by raising public investment and adding tax incentives for private consumption, having been reassured by the social partners that doing so would not simply fuel inflation.

[22] That this was the period when the Austrian system of co-determination was extended from nationalized firms to the rest of the economy is not coincidental from this point of view. Austria also possessed an Advisory Board (the Beirat für Wirtschafts- und Sozialfragen), composed of representatives of the social partners and government as well as academic experts, which verified the existence of the threat to profits and helped to build social consensus.

[23] Scharpf (1991), p. 56.

[24] Katzenstein (1984), p. 39; Hemerijck, Unger, and Visser (2000), p. 184.

TABLE 9.4
Coordination indexes, 1960–1995

	1960–1964	1965–1972	1973–1979	1980–1987	1988–1995
Austria	3.00	3.00	3.00	3.00	3.00
West Germany	3.00	3.00	3.00	3.00	3.00
Denmark	2.50	2.50	2.50	2.40	2.26
Norway	2.50	2.50	2.50	2.50	2.50
Sweden	2.50	2.50	2.50	2.40	2.15
Finland	2.25	2.25	2.25	2.25	2.25
Switzerland	2.25	2.25	2.25	2.25	2.25
Belgium	2.00	2.00	2.00	2.00	2.00
Ireland	2.00	2.00	2.00	2.00	3.00
Netherlands	2.00	2.00	2.00	2.00	2.00
Spain	2.00	2.00	2.00	2.00	2.00
France	1.75	1.75	1.75	1.84	1.98
Italy	1.50	1.50	1.50	1.50	1.40
United Kingdom	1.50	1.50	1.50	1.40	1.15
Memo item: United States	1.00	1.00	1.00	1.00	1.00

Source: Nickell (2003b).

Notes: Countries are arrayed by value of the index in the period 1973–1979. The index ranges from 1 to 3, where 1 denotes loosely coordinated and 3 closely coordinated.

1 = Fragmented company/plant bargaining, little or no coordination by upper-level associations.

1.5 = Fragmented industry and company-level bargaining, with little or no pattern setting.

2 = Industry-level bargaining with irregular pattern setting and moderate coordination among major bargaining actors.

2.5 = Informal coordination of industry and firm-level bargaining by (multiple) peak associations; coordinated bargaining by peak confederations, including government-sponsored negotiations (tripartite agreements, social pacts), or government imposition of wage schedules; regular pattern setting coupled with high union concentration and/or bargaining coordination by large firms; government wage arbitration.

3 = Informal coordination of industry-level bargaining by an encompassing union confederation; coordinated bargaining by peak associations or government imposition of a wage schedule/freeze, with a peace obligation.

Table 9.4 shows a measure of the coordination of bargaining in the second half of the 1970s and compares it with the preceding and subsequent periods. The index ranges from 1 (when bargaining is fragmented and takes place at the plant or enterprise level with little coordination) to 3 (when bargaining is formally or informally coordinated by the peak associations). By this measure, the most coordinated economies were Austria and Germany, two of the countries where the rise in unemployment was least. The pairing of Austria and Germany is a reminder that coordination could occur in different ways, either by centralizing wage bargaining under the supervision of the state (as in Austria) or by developing institutional arrangements such as union and employers federations to help bargainers to act in concert even when that bargaining ostensibly occurred at the firm or industry level (as in Germany).

In less coordinated economies such as the United Kingdom and Italy, the rise in unemployment was greater. In 1971–1972, the British prime minister Edward Heath attempted to use industrial-relations legislation to bring coherence to wage bargaining and then to negotiate an incomes policy, but his efforts broke down in the face of a miners' strike—and with it support for the government. In the February 1974 electoral campaign, the Labour Party offered significant improvements in social benefits in return for the TUC's agreement to voluntary wage restraint, but following Labour's narrow victory the TUC was unable to deliver on its promise, given its hundred-plus constituent unions.[25] The failure of these initiatives is indicative of the difficulties facing countries whose corporatist institutions were underdeveloped.[26] From a longer-run perspective, the success of the more corporatist economies in restraining the growth of wages and rise in unemployment, incomplete as it was, was one reason why countries were slow to move away from these arrangements in the 1980s in the face of growing evidence that the sharp wage compression and the barriers to firm entry and exit that they created constituted obstacles to innovation.

The Labour Party's strategy was followed more generally. Faced with accelerating inflation and declining profitability, governments also sought to extend the system of bonds, sanctions, and rewards

---

[25] When inflation soared to 24 percent in 1975, TUC leaders and the government agreed to limit wage increases to seven pounds a week. This attempt at voluntary restraint worked for a year, after which it broke down. See Scharpf (2000), p. 40.

[26] The ability of countries to enforce wage restraint was also a function of the depth of the central bank's hard-currency commitment. Where that commitment was strong, as in Germany, it was clear that if the unions' wage demands overshot, the central bank would not accommodate the increase in costs in order to prevent unemployment from rising. In countries such as the United Kingdom and Italy, where that commitment was less, unions were encouraged to err in the direction of additional increases in order to compensate them for past inflation and to keep up with their rivals, because they knew that if their demands proved excessive, the central bank would accommodate the increases, damping any adverse consequences for employment.

TABLE 9.5
Unemployment benefit replacement rates, 1960–2001 (Percent)

	1960–1964	1965–1972	1973–1979	1980–1987	1988–1995	1996–2001
Austria	19	19	24	28	30	32
Belgium	40	36	47	43	41	39
Denmark	20	25	42	53	55	58
Finland	5	5	27	30	37	33
France	25	25	24	33	37	39
Germany[a]	30	30	29	29	28	27
Ireland	17	17	23	30	28	29
Italy	4	2	1	0	10	29
Netherlands	13	48	48	51	53	52
Norway	4	4	14	34	39	41
Spain	9	17	19	31	33	31
Sweden	4	6	20	28	28	25
Switzerland	2	1	6	17	26	36
United Kingdom	25	26	24	21	18	17
Memo item: United States	9	10	13	14	12	14

Source: Organisation for Economic Co-ordination and Development (2004).
Note: [a] West Germany before 1990.

with which they had previously helped to maintain wage stability and investment. In return for promising wage restraint, workers were offered more generous health benefits and social security stipends. These programs did not come cheap: public expenditure rose from 38 percent of Europe's gross domestic product in 1967–1969 to 46 percent in 1974–1976.[27] The growth of spending was particularly rapid in Germany, the Netherlands, Denmark, and Sweden, where it was tied to the expansion of transfer payments and social programs.

With falling employment security, workers also demanded and received increases in employment protection and unemployment compensation. Portugal introduced its first unemployment benefit scheme in 1975. Luxembourg and Switzerland replaced schemes offering very limited coverage with compulsory national insurance systems. Table 9.5 shows changes in the level of benefits, constructed as the share of previous earnings replaced in the first year of an unemployment spell. Virtually everywhere in Europe we see an in-

---

[27] This is an unweighted average for nine countries, calculated from data in table 1-6 of Flanagan, Soskice, and Ulman (1983).

crease in the replacement rate between 1965–1972 and 1973–1979.[28] Table 9.6 shows contemporaneous changes in employment protection legislation. France, Germany, Ireland, Portugal, and Sweden all significantly increased the stringency of employment protection in this period. Finally, table 9.7 presents a measure of taxes on labor, which raise the cost to firms of offering jobs and reduce the benefits to workers of taking them. It shows that these rose most dramatically in 1973–1979 in Spain and the Scandinavian countries.

Specialists dispute the role of these welfare-state policies in the rise in unemployment and in its stasis subsequently at high levels. Some attach considerable weight to increases in levels of employment protection and unemployment compensation that already were generous by North American standards.[29] They argue that the rise in benefits reduced the willingness to work of the unemployed. Others are more skeptical. Europe had already possessed a relatively generous welfare state, they object, even before the post-1973 slowdown. As Blanchard puts it, "It is [simply] not true, as some claim, that current European labor-market institutions emerged in the 1970s: Stories which blame the increase in unemployment on the rise of the welfare state simply rewrite history."[30] Or, as another well-known economist has put it, "While there has been a rise in the tax burden in Europe since 1970, especially in social insurance contributions, European welfare states were already notably generous in the low-unemployment era of the early 1970s. Most analysts have there-

---

[28] The principal exceptions are France, Germany, and the United Kingdom, where the ratio falls very slightly. The replacement rate also fell in Italy, but from levels that were relatively low; Italy still had no effective benefit system for the vast majority of the unemployed. At least as important from the point of view of household incentives was the increase in the duration of unemployment benefits, calculated as a weighted average of the replacement rate in each of the first five years of an unemployment spell. Here changes between the periods 1965–1972 and 1973–1979 were more heterogeneous. Benefit duration rose in the Netherlands and Scandinavia, fell in Belgium and Ireland, and remained unchanged in a number of other European countries. Increases in the duration of benefits become somewhat more prevalent in the 1980s. They are therefore part of the explanation for chronic unemployment in chapter 12.

[29] See, for example, Nickell (2003b).

[30] Blanchard (2000), chapter 1, p. 3.

TABLE 9.6
Employment protection, 1960–1999 and 2003 (Index, 0–2)

	1960–1964	1965–1972	1973–1979	1980–1987	1988–1995	1996–1999	2003
Austria	0.65	0.65	0.84	1.27	1.30	1.10	0.90
Belgium	0.72	1.24	1.55	1.55	1.35	1.00	1.00
Denmark	0.90	0.98	1.10	1.10	0.90	0.70	0.70
Finland	1.20	1.20	1.20	1.20	1.13	1.00	1.00
France	0.37	0.68	1.21	1.30	1.41	1.40	1.50
Germany[a]	0.45	1.05	1.65	1.65	1.52	1.30	1.30
Ireland	0.02	0.19	0.45	0.50	0.52	0.50	0.50
Italy	1.92	1.99	2.00	2.00	1.89	1.50	1.50
Netherlands	1.35	1.35	1.35	1.35	1.28	1.10	1.10
Norway	1.55	1.55	1.55	1.55	1.46	1.30	1.30
Portugal	0.00	0.43	1.59	1.94	1.93	1.70	1.70
Spain	2.00	2.00	1.99	1.91	1.74	1.40	1.40
Sweden	0.00	0.23	1.46	1.80	1.53	1.10	1.10
Switzerland	0.55	0.55	0.55	0.55	0.55	0.55	0.55
United Kingdom	0.16	0.21	0.33	0.35	0.35	0.35	0.41
Memo item: United States	0.10	0.10	0.10	0.10	0.10	0.10	0.10

Sources: 1960–1995 data are from Nickell et al. (2002), table 6. 1998 data are from Nickell, Nunziata, and Ochel (2005), figures that are in turn derived from table A3.11 in Nicoletti, Scarpeta, and Boyland (2000). Subsequent figures from Organisation for Economic Co-operation and Development (2004) are rescaled to render them consistent with the metric used in previous columns by comparing the values for 1998 in Nickell, Nunziata, and Ochel (2005) with those for the "late 1990s" in Organisation for Economic Co-operation and Development (2004).

Notes: Value of index ranges from 0 to 2, with higher values indicating more extensive protections.

[a] West Germany before 1990.

273

TABLE 9.7
Total tax rate on labor, 1960–2000 (Percent)

	1960–1964	1965–1972	1973–1979	1980–1987	1988–1995	1996–2000
Austria	47	52	55	58	59	66
Belgium	38	43	44	46	50	51
Denmark	32	46	53	59	60	61
Finland	38	46	55	58	64	62
France	55	57	60	64	67	68
Germany[a]	42	44	48	50	52	50
Ireland	23	30	30	37	41	33
Italy	57	56	54	56	67	64
Netherlands	45	54	57	55	47	43
Norway	—	52	61	65	61	60
Portugal	20	25	26	33	40	39
Spain	19	23	29	40	46	45
Sweden	41	54	68	77	78	77
Switzerland	30	31	35	36	35	36
United Kingdom	34	43	45	51	47	44
Memo item: United States	34	37	42	44	45	45

Sources: Nickell et al. (2002); Nickell, Nunziata, and Ochel (2005), table 8.
Notes: Total tax rate on labor is the sum of payroll, income, and consumption tax rates.
[a] West Germany before 1990.

fore looked for the explanation of the upward trend not in changed policies but in a changed environment."[31]

Two aspects of the environment that may be relevant here are social norms and economic volatility. Although governments had long provided generous unemployment and disability benefits, workers may have been loath to use them in the period of full employment.[32] When jobs were easy to find, those drawing unemployment and disability compensation for an extended period were suspected of gaming the system. But when unemployment rose due to the oil and disinflation shocks, the stigma of the dole was removed. When someone remained out of work for an extended period, it was no

[31] Krugman (1994), p. 31. Others (for example, Nickell 2003a and Saint-Paul 2004) would object that this dismissal of institutional developments goes too far. As we have seen, a number of measures show increases in the generosity of unemployment benefits, employment protection legislation, and labor taxes across a range of European countries. The question is whether these limited institutional changes suffice, by themselves, to explain the dramatic rise in unemployment rates.

[32] This is the thesis of Blanchard and Wolfers (2000).

longer presumed that he was exploiting the generosity of the system. It could well be that he was suffering from lack of job opportunities for reasons not of his own making. Thus, a system of relatively generous unemployment benefits did more to encourage extended spells of unemployment once joblessness became widespread.[33] It was not just the institutions of the labor market or the severity of post-1973 shocks but their interaction that transformed Europe from a low-unemployment to a high-unemployment economy.

In an accounting sense, the interaction of shocks and institutions can explain a considerable fraction of the variation in unemployment rates across countries and over time.[34] But at another level the evidence is less compelling. Norms are unobservable. There is no direct evidence, in other words, that changes in socially acceptable behavior produced the change in labor-market outcomes.

A variation on this theme emphasizes not the interaction of shocks and institutions but the interaction of institutions and volatility.[35] In the golden age, when growth was fast but structural change was slow, workers who happened to lose a high-paying job could be confident of quickly finding another in the same industry. The fact that they could have half of their earnings replaced by unemployment benefits consequently provided little incentive for remaining out of work. But as economic turbulence and structural change rose, the next offer that came along was more likely to be in a new industry where accumulated skills and training had little applicability, leaving only the option of an unskilled, low-paid position. Now an unemployed individual had more reason to turn down a job offer in the hope that a better one would come along. And the greater the generosity of the unemployment insurance system, the greater the incentive to exercise patience. Once more the implication is that institutions that had been largely irrelevant now mattered importantly for unemployment.

---

[33] This interpretation is supported by microeconomic studies showing that flows into unemployment are less sensitive to the unemployment insurance replacement ratio than are flows from unemployment back into employment.

[34] That is to say, Blanchard and Wolfers' panel regressions have relatively high R^2's.

[35] This is the hypothesis of Ljungqvist and Sargent (1998).

Again the intuition is appealing but the evidence is less than compelling. There was an increase in the variance of earnings in the 1970s, consistent with the notion of faster structural change. But this increase could have many explanations.[36] Similarly, there was a tendency for a larger fraction of unemployment to be long-term and for that long-term unemployment to be concentrated among former manufacturing workers with industry-specific skills.[37] But this fact too is open to alternative interpretations. There may be good reason to think that, with the transition from extensive to intensive growth, there was a rise in the pace of structural change. But without knowing by how much, it is hard to know to what extent this explains the rise in European unemployment.[38]

It is important not to conclude that we are ignorant about the origins of Europe's high unemployment. In fact, there is little disagreement about the causes of the initial rise. The productivity slowdown, together with the oil-price and real-interest-rate shocks go a long way in explaining this. Nor is there disagreement about whether more corporatist economies succeeded in restraining wage growth and limiting the initial rise in unemployment. The difficult question is why unemployment then remained so high for so long. Here the competing explanations, some emphasizing changes in the broader macroeconomic environment and social norms and others emphasizing the institutions of the welfare state, are not really incompatible. Even scholars who point out that many of Europe's labor-market institutions predate the 1970s acknowledge that policies and programs offering employment protection and unemployment support "were extended in the 1970s and the 1980s when times turned bad, and governments tried to temper the effects of adverse

---

[36] The 1970s also saw a rise in the dispersion of unemployment rates across industries, which might be taken as an indication of faster structural change, but this was less a secular trend than a consequence of increased business cycle volatility—that is, some industries are more cyclically sensitive than others and see their unemployment rates rise more dramatically in recessions.

[37] As discussed in, among other sources, Organisation for Economic Co-operation and Development (1992).

[38] As Nickell (2003a, p. 17) observes, "these facts hardly add up to a full empirical test of the theory."

shocks on unemployment."[39] Even in the absence of increases in volatility and changes in norms, the expansion of those programs would have resulted in some increase in the level and persistence of unemployment. But it is a stretch to attribute the entirety of Europe's transformation from a low- to a high-unemployment economy to these limited changes in policy and legislation. This is where changes in norms and macroeconomic volatility in altering individual incentives must be added to the story.

Stabilization in Britain

Initially, central banks responded to the rise of wages and prices by expanding money supplies. Failing to do so would have only compounded the weakness of demand. But doing so meant accommodating the inflationary shock. The average rate of inflation in Western Europe doubled between 1960–1973 and 1973–1979, from 5 to 10 percent. It rose to 6 percent in Austria, 7 percent in the Netherlands, 11 percent in France, 15 percent in Ireland, and 16 percent in the United Kingdom. It even accelerated to 5 percent in Germany, although the Bundesbank was predictably reluctant to accommodate the shock.

The explosion of inflation meant that when Europe was disturbed by the second increase in oil prices in 1979, it was more difficult to respond again with monetary stimulus. Since expectations had adapted, it was no longer feasible to bring down real wages and unemployment with a monetary surprise. Constraints had also tightened on the fiscal side. Public employment had been boosted in response to the previous recession, by 3.4 percent per year in twelve European countries between 1974 and 1978. Fiscal burdens had risen, as noted earlier, leaving less room for invoking this same strategy again. Moreover, inflation having broached double-digit levels, delay in addressing the problem became increasingly costly.

[39] Blanchard (2000), chapter 1, p. 3.

Rapidly rising prices threatened to demoralize investors and cause social-democratic cooperation to break down.

For all these reasons, central banks and governments were unwilling to accommodate the second oil shock as they had the first. Whereas governments had applied an additional 2 percent of GDP in fiscal stimulus between 1973 and 1975, they now tightened fiscal policy. Whereas real interest rates had fallen by two and a half percentage points between 1973 and 1975, they rose now by four percentage points between 1979 and 1981.[40]

The inflation problem was addressed head on, in characteristic fashion, by the United Kingdom's new prime minister, Margaret Thatcher. Thatcher's government announced a four-year declining path for the growth of the broad money supply (sterling M3), backed by a supporting path for government borrowing (the so-called public-sector borrowing requirement, or PSBR).[41] The fight against inflation was thus linked to Prime Minister Thatcher's goal of reducing the role of the government in the economy. In contrast to the Labour government, from which the Conservatives inherited the practice of targeting monetary aggregates, no recourse was made to incomes policy. More generally, Thatcher moved to eliminate labor involvement in the design of macroeconomic and industrial policies and limit government intervention in the labor market. She abolished the Pay Comparability Commission that had been established in an effort to coordinate public-sector pay settlements. Her government scaled back the legal immunities enjoyed by the unions. It abolished legal restrictions on the hiring and firing of temporary workers. Earnings-related supplements to the basic unemployment benefit were eliminated in 1982, and benefits were made subject to taxation. The government reaffirmed its dedication to financial deregulation, removing the regulations known as "the corset" that had limited the growth of interest-bearing deposits.

[40] These figures are for long-term interest rates adjusted for the change in consumer prices in eight European countries.

[41] The Bank of England had begun to consider the use of monetary targets after discussions of bringing sterling into the Snake collapsed in 1972. It began publishing its targets in 1976. Britain's agreement with the IMF, concluded at the end of that same year, focused further attention on the behavior of the money stock.

With a credible monetary stabilization in place and market forces free to operate, pressure in the labor market was supposed to moderate. The target for sterling M3 was overshot despite the Bank of England's high interest rates, creating doubts about the credibility of the new regime. This overshooting reflected both the removal of the corset and pressure for public spending, notably on unemployment relief. Nor did wage inflation come down as rapidly as anticipated by Thatcher's advisers. Average earnings continued to rise by 20 percent in 1980, and the rate of increase fell only to 15 percent in the first half of 1981.[42] Britain still lacked a mechanism for coordinating the wage demands of its fragmented unions, much less an effective structure for tripartite negotiations. Eventually, Thatcher's attack on the union movement and the collapse of major steel and coal strikes moved the country further in the direction of atomistic, U.S.-style labor markets, in which decentralization and competitive pressure facilitate rapid adjustment. But that was the future. For the moment, adjustment remained painfully slow.

With wage and sterling M3 growth slow to moderate, price increases slowed only modestly. Inflation came down only to 11 percent in the first half of 1981. The main effect of higher interest rates was a dramatic appreciation of sterling, since financial markets did not display the same inertia as labor markets.[43] On a trade-weighted basis, the nominal effective exchange rate appreciated by more than 25 percent between the end of 1978 and the end of 1980. The real effective exchange rate (the nominal rate adjusted for inflation at home and abroad) appreciated nearly as fast, in yet more confirmation that wages and retail prices were slower to adjust than asset markets.

This sharp loss of competitiveness made recession unavoidable. The deactivation of the country's automatic fiscal stabilizers as a result of partially successful efforts to adhere to the preannounced

[42] Basic rates for manual workers, who bore the brunt of unemployment, rose more slowly but followed a similar trajectory. Buiter and Miller (1981), p. 328.

[43] The idea that monetary contraction would lead to a sharp appreciation of the currency—even sharper on impact than in the new steady state—was the central prediction of the Dornbusch (1976) overshooting model, which gained renown as a result of this British experience.

PSBR path did not help. GDP fell by 5 percent between the fourth quarter of 1979 and the fourth quarter of 1980. All components of aggregate demand declined, excepting only government consumption, and the rate of unemployment doubled to 10.4 percent between the third quarter of 1979 and the second quarter of 1981. This stress on the labor market was not entirely unwelcome to the Thatcher government, which favored anything that might weaken the hand of a union movement that had exercised an effective veto on economic reform.[44] The government also saw more flexible labor markets as key to the creation of a more flexible economy. But a severe recession threatened to alienate Thatcher's supporters in the board rooms of industry. Bowing to political realities, the government shifted in 1981 toward a looser monetary policy and a tighter fiscal policy in the effort to continue disinflating without placing additional upward pressure on sterling. This was an early acknowledgment that there was no simple monetarist equation capable of magically solving all problems of macroeconomic management.

Backing away from the monetarist formula and tinkering with the policy mix did not enhance credibility. And allowing taxes to rise in 1981 in the teeth of a global recession—for that was what the shift toward a looser monetary and tighter fiscal-policy mix entailed—only reinforced the collapse of demand.[45] For all these reasons, the output and employment costs of disinflation did not fall as anticipated.[46] Against the backdrop of falling petroleum prices, which were unhelpful now that North Sea oil was flowing, competitiveness was slow to return even as the exchange rate slid from a high of $1.91 against the dollar, reached at the end of 1981, to $1.50 in mid-1983 and $1.10 at the beginning of 1985.

[44] See Holmes (1985). The trade unions had also torpedoed the incomes policy of the previous Conservative government, causing it to be voted out of office, and Thatcher wished to avoid something similar happening again.

[45] The increase in tax revenues was effected by eliminating the indexation of tax brackets for inflation. Relying on this device rather than overtly raising rates allowed Thatcher to claim that she remained true to her core belief in downsizing the state.

[46] If anything, the opposite was true. Thus, Crafts (1992) shows that in the first nine years of the Thatcher government, the United Kingdom had the fourth highest Misery Index (the sum of inflation and standardized unemployment) in Europe (exceeded only by high-unemployment Ireland, Italy, and Spain).

Thatcher was then faced with the embarrassing prospect of being the first British prime minister to preside over a one-dollar pound. Interest rates were therefore ratcheted up to 14 percent, their highest level since 1981. Sterling's decline was halted, but British industry suffered another blow. Discomfort with these developments caused some, such as Nigel Lawson, now Thatcher's chancellor of the exchequer, to advocate entering the Exchange-Rate Mechanism (ERM) of the European Monetary System (EMS). In the event, another five years would pass before that fateful decision was made.

What of the broader agenda of deregulation and economic restructuring? Reducing the top marginal income tax rate to 40 percent; privatizing British Aerospace, British Petroleum, British Airways, British Telecom, British Gas, and the British Airports Authority; selling off council houses (public housing); and outlawing the closed shop certainly constituted a radical break with the past. The idea that mass privatization would create a constituency for market capitalism and render reform irreversible may not have worked subsequently in Russia (see chapter 10), but it gained some purchase in the United Kingdom, where it created a sizeable shareholder class. The 1979 Banking Act and the 1988 Financial Services Act, which deregulated British capital markets, further broadened the constituency for reform. They made it harder for future governments to reverse Thatcher's measures by making the politicians hostage to the markets.

As for results, Thatcher's supporters could point to the rise of labor productivity in manufacturing by 18 percent between the end of 1980 and the beginning of 1983. This, they reminded everyone, was the fastest rate of productivity growth since 1973. The question was whether it reflected mainly the closing down of Britain's least efficient plants in response to the recession or a permanent acceleration.[47] And to the extent that the efficiency gains of the early 1980s resulted from one-time reductions in manning levels, reflecting the weakened bargaining power of the unions, there was further reason to question whether they would last.

Longer-term comparisons do in fact provide some evidence of a sustained improvement in labor productivity growth, although at

---

[47] Mendis and Muelbauer (1983), in an early assessment, attributed the rise in productivity mainly to production being discontinued at the least efficient plants.

more modest rates than in Thatcher's first three years. Output per worker in manufacturing rose by 50 percent between 1979 and 1988. The rate of growth of labor productivity in the business sector, a broader measure, rose from 1.5 percent per year in 1973–1979 to 2.6 percent per year in 1979–1988.[48] A Britain that had brought up the rear of the European labor productivity leagues, together with Norway and Switzerland, in the first period leapt to their head in the second.[49] O'Mahony and Wagner (1994) conclude that about half of the increase in productivity between these two periods was due to job shedding and plant closures, and the other half represented a sustained improvement due to the creation of a more flexible and efficient economy.

Thatcherism, whatever its strengths and weaknesses, was not transplantable to other countries. The British electorate was willing to vote into office an economic radical, for that was what the prime minister was, because of three decades of disappointing economic performance. Previous governments pursuing policies of moderation and compromise had failed to deliver the goods. Thatcher now sought to tear out the old system root and branch. Reflecting the same dissatisfaction with old ways, the Labour Party now moved further to the left; its abandonment of the center gave Thatcher more room to maneuver and helped keep her in power. Similar tendencies were evident elsewhere in Europe, but nowhere else was there such intense dissatisfaction with conventional politics. No other European democracy produced a national leader as radical as Prime Minister Thatcher.

The EMS Initiative

By the 1970s the European Community had essentially bifurcated into two groups of countries. The first group, made up of Germany, the Benelux countries, and Denmark, had succeeded in limiting in-

---

[48] See Kendrick (1990).
[49] Along with Finland and Spain.

flation to the mid to high single digits and in keeping their exchange rates stable by adhering to the margins of the Snake.[50] In practice, this was a deutschmark-based arrangement, since Germany was the lowest-inflation country and accounted for more than two-thirds of the collective GDP of the group.

The second set of countries—France, Italy, the United Kingdom, and Ireland—had more difficulty restraining inflation and were therefore unable to keep their currencies within the margins of the Snake. As inflation accelerated and the contrast with the deutschmark-centered group became more glaring, they feared being relegated to second-class status within the Community. A report on the future of Europe drafted by a committee under the chairmanship of Leo Tindemans, the Belgian prime minister, and submitted in 1976 to the European Council meeting in the Hague recommended accepting the reality of a two-tier Community.[51]

For France, being relegated to second-tier status was embarrassing and unacceptable. Remaking Europe's monetary system so that it operated more symmetrically was the obvious way out of this box. If doing so also provided a solution to the problem of French inflation, all the better in the view of French leaders.[52] More generally, negotiating a monetary agreement offered an opportunity to reinvigorate an integration process that had slowed in the 1970s. It was a way for Paris to reassert its leadership at the European level—and globally insofar as the European Community could serve as a platform for projecting French *grandeur*.

All this appealed to the government of Valéry Giscard d'Estaing and Raymond Barre, which was as Europe-minded as any that France had possessed for three decades. The only question was how far France would have to bend to accommodate itself to the strength of the deutschmark and the strict policies of the Bundesbank and how far it could get Germany to bend in its direction. Giscard and

---

[50] Norway was effectively an associate member of this group for a time; see chapter 8 for details.

[51] Dyson (1994), p. 94. Not incidentally, Belgium was a member of the emerging deutschmark bloc and hence of the first tier.

[52] Simonian (1985), pp. 278–279.

Barre were prepared to bend. Indeed, they did not regard accommodating France to the rigors of German policy as uncongenial. But they could not commit their successors to doing so, as the early 1980s would reveal.

The German chancellor Helmut Schmidt similarly believed that a reinvigorated Community could provide a platform for his country to help fill the international economic vacuum created by the collapse of the Bretton Woods System. Schmidt was also a long-standing advocate of monetary union. But as soon as discussions moved to particulars, he was reminded that his German colleagues felt differently. They saw the deutschmark's dominance of European currency markets as a natural consequence of Germany's commitment to price stability and of the inability of other countries to display adequate discipline. Bundesbank officials were instinctually opposed to any initiative that challenged this state of affairs. They worried that a more symmetric European monetary system might be less a mechanism for France to import German monetary discipline than a vehicle for France to export inflation to its neighbors. Thus, although Schmidt and his circle may have favored deeper monetary integration, they had to overcome the opposition of the Bundesbank and bring along the German polity.

Schmidt and Giscard sought to preempt this debate by proceeding in secret, echoing the tactics used by Monnet to push through the European Coal and Steel Community three decades before. At first the two leaders did not even inform their respective finance ministers of their bilateral discussions. The EMS initiative that they sprang on the European Council in Copenhagen in April 1978 sought to reconcile France's desire for a more symmetrical system with Germany's insistence on discipline. In the new system, as Schmidt and Giscard envisioned it, the need for discipline would be addressed by 2½-percent bands like those of the Snake.[53] France's insistence on symmetry would be satisfied by creating a

---

[53] Italy, which continued to suffer from stubborn inflation, would be permitted to maintain a wider 6 percent band for an interim period.

"trigger mechanism" based on an agreed set of indicators that would force strong-currency countries to relax monetary conditions and weak-currency countries to tighten when stability was at risk. This would be supplemented by binding intervention obligations and, after a two-year transitional period, by the pooling of foreign-exchange reserves.

This last measure, in particular, would have been a significant step in the direction of transnationalism. In proposing it Schmidt and Giscard sought to breathe new life into a political integration process that had been largely moribund for two decades. They also sought a European alternative to American policies that were increasingly seen as an engine of instability. The dollar's sharp decline in 1977–1978, which precipitated financial flows into Germany that pushed up the deutschmark, was an important influence here. It encouraged Schmidt to overcome his reservations about Giscard's ambitious monetary plans. Like Richard Nixon before him, Jimmy Carter now did much to encourage the Europeans to forge ahead with their monetary project.

But the head of the Bundesbank, Otmar Emminger, and other German officials objected to a trigger mechanism that might force Germany to expand, fanning inflation, if reckless policies in other European countries fed the weakness of their currencies. Emminger attempted to veto provisions that might allow his country's hard-earned reserves to be used to support the currencies of profligate foreign governments. Schmidt countered with an impassioned speech to the Bundesbank Council invoking World War II and characterizing the new monetary agreement as a capstone of the effort to achieve postwar reconciliation.[54] His intervention carried the day; though its status as the guardian of price stability made it hard to cross, the Bundesbank could not allow itself to be cast as an opponent of Franco-German fellowship.

---

[54] His language even led some members to wonder whether he was prepared to propose amending the Bundesbank law to reduce the central bank's independence if it did not drop its objections to his proposal. Kennedy (1991), p. 81.

But as its price for acceding, the Bundesbank was able to insist on elimination of the trigger mechanism and the pooling of reserves. At the same time, it bowed to the insistence of other central banks that the amount of credit that might be drawn from the Short-Term and Very-Short-Term Facilities should be increased. Strong-currency central banks were still obliged to intervene in support of their weak-currency counterparts without limit, at least on paper. But Emminger obtained a statement of reassurance from his government, the so-called Emminger letter, authorizing the Bundesbank to opt out in the event that its commitment to price stability was threatened.[55] As Otto Graf Lambsdorff, the German economics minister, made clear in a speech to the Bundestag at the end of 1978, the commitment to unlimited intervention would always be subordinate to the Bundesbank Act of 1957 giving the German central bank a mandate to pursue price stability.

The EMS in Operation

On this basis the EMS got underway with the participation of all EC member states except the United Kingdom.[56] With other European currencies now anchored to the deutschmark, inflation came down, albeit gradually, from more than 10 percent in 1980 to 8 percent in 1982, 6 percent in 1984, and 2 percent in 1986.[57] But unemployment showed no tendency to fall; to the contrary, it continued rising through the period of disinflation. The EMS clearly was no painless fix.[58]

Inflation was actually a bit slower to fall in the EMS countries than in the rest of the OECD through the middle of the decade.

[55] Dyson (1994), p. 109. This precedent figures importantly in the 1992 EMS crisis discussed in chapter 11.

[56] A general election was approaching in the United Kingdom and Prime Minister Callaghan wished to avoid dividing his party over the issue.

[57] These are averages for the EMS countries.

[58] Thus, there is little robust evidence that sacrifice ratios (the amount of additional unemployment incurred in the course of eliminating a percentage point of inflation) were any lower in EMS than in non-EMS countries (Gros and Thygesen 1992, pp. 128–131).

This is not surprisingly when one recalls that the non-EMS group included not just the United Kingdom but also the United States. It is also a reminder that the deutschmark anchor line was not always taut. EMS countries retained capital controls that gave them scope to run higher inflation rates than Germany without suffering an immediate balance-of-payments crisis. Indeed, controls were tightened further during the turbulent early years of the new system. And in the longer run there was always the opportunity to restore competitiveness through realignment.[59]

That said, policy autonomy was still limited. Controls were never watertight, and if imbalances grew large the markets would find ways around such statutory restrictions. This was what France's socialist government learned to its chagrin in 1981–1982. As the head of the first left government to take power since the establishment of the Fifth Republic in 1958, the aloof, cerebral François Mitterrand did not enjoy a favorable inheritance. Inflation in 1980, the year preceding the election, was stubbornly high at 12 percent. Unemployment had risen to more than 6 percent, reflecting slow growth at the end of the 1970s and the absence of corporatist cooperation. Mitterrand's predecessor, Giscard, had been openly hostile to the unions, precluding systematic collaboration. The Socialists now vowed to do better. But not having held power for a quarter of a century, they had little sense of the feasible and little appreciation for the constraints imposed by the country's integration into Europe and the world.

The Socialists immediately tromped on the fiscal accelerator, anticipating that stronger growth would spur investment and productivity. The first budget submitted by Laurent Fabius, Mitterrand's activist, modernization-oriented budget minister, increased the deficit by one-quarter. Echoing the policies of Léon Blum's Socialist government of a half century earlier, the new government also raised minimum wages and legislated a shorter workweek.

---

[59] For evidence, see Fratianni and von Hagen (1990). Of course, all this would change following the adoption of the Single European Act in 1986. Creating a true single market entailed the removal of capital controls, requiring the closer harmonization of monetary policies and making periodic realignments problematic (see chapter 10). Thus, inflation in the EMS countries fell to even lower levels than in the rest of the OECD from this point.

With stimulus from Mitterrand's *program commun*, the GDP growth rate rose from 1.2 percent in 1981 to 2.6 percent in 1982. But, like the *relance Chirac* before it, the new policies were put in place against the backdrop of a global recession that limited their effects and weakened the external position. The franc was quickly devalued, but this failed to solve the problem. The deterioration in the trade balance brought the currency under pressure and threatened the country's participation in the EMS. Interest rates on French francs in London rose to more than 20 percent, indicating that the markets saw a great likelihood of further devaluation.

Interest rates in Paris rose less, since capital controls continued to bite. Their presence helps to explain how the Mitterrand government managed to hold on for two years before abandoning its expansionary policies. But that interest rates did rise in Paris, and significantly, suggests that the day of reckoning could not be put off forever. Inevitably, the franc was devalued a second time, in June 1982. Capital formation was slowed by the high interest rates associated with this turmoil. Investors were unsettled, not just by the high interest rates but by the new government's nationalizations and the appointment of four Communist ministers, a first since 1947.

In principle, Mitterrand and his colleagues could have responded by tightening controls still further and continuing with the policy of serial devaluations. They might have abandoned the ERM entirely in order to maintain the government's expansionary posture. Previous French governments had withdrawn from the Snake whenever exchange-rate stability and domestic policy were at odds. Some of Mitterrand's advisers, including Fabius, the minister for industry and research Jean-Pierre Chevènement, and even the normally cautious minister of social affairs Pierre Bérégovoy, recommended withdrawing from the ERM and imposing a surcharge on imports, à la Nixon in 1971. There was even some support among French business leaders for abandoning the ERM if this would permit the maintenance of expansionary policies.[60]

[60] Parsons (2003), p. 173.

Here Mitterrand hesitated. It had been a government of the left that had abandoned the gold standard in 1936. Like Harold Wilson two decades earlier, Mitterrand feared the consequences of allowing the left to be tarred with the devaluationist brush. More immediately, withdrawing from the ERM and imposing a unilateral tax on imports would have jeopardized France's status as a founding member of the European Community—and perhaps even jeopardized the Community itself.[61]

But by the early 1980s, France's links with Europe were too deep for this to be an option. French exporters feared the damage to their trade. Farmers feared the risk to the Common Agricultural Policy. Politically, withdrawing would have damaged France's aspiration to build a European counterweight (*contrepoids*) to the United States. It would have prevented Paris from influencing the evolution of the European construction. It would have closed the door on French ambitions to become an equal partner with Germany in shaping the monetary and financial future of the Community.

Finally, given the extent of the imbalances afflicting the French economy, confidence in the franc might have been undermined further by withdrawing from the ERM. Faith in the government's ability to steer the economy was, shall one say, less than complete. The Socialists had lost much of the country's foreign reserves and had accumulated additional debt since taking office two years earlier. If the currency now collapsed, stabilization might require even more severe policies of *rigueur*. For the first time, there was a realization that freedom of action might be even more limited outside the ERM.

Faced with this these difficult realities, Fabius switched sides. Mitterrand concluded that leaving the ERM constituted a bridge too far. Like other French leaders before him, he now sought to save face by dressing up the inevitable devaluation as a general realignment that included a revaluation of the mark.

On being approached, the German chancellor's office was unreceptive. Germany was only beginning to emerge from recession, and

---

[61] Indeed the Communist Party, on whose support Mitterrand relied, advocated sticking with expansionary policies precisely because it favored withdrawing from the EEC.

revaluation would have been unhelpful from this point of view. Mitterrand, through his finance minister Jacques Delors, continued to threaten French withdrawal from the ERM.[62] In the end, Germany was frightened into agreeing to revalue by 5.5 percent and France's devaluation was limited to 2.5 percent. Mitterrand was able to negotiate a sizeable stabilization package with the EU, although the German government conditioned this on France adopting austerity measures. Mitterrand obligingly cut public spending and raised taxes. He abandoned the strategy of expansionary fiscal policies.

With fiscal consolidation, France's external accounts quickly righted themselves. Within two years the current account was back in balance and the franc was no longer under attack. Growth and full employment were slower to be restored. Unemployment rose to 10 percent in 1985, half again as high as when Mitterrand took office in 1981.

This was a turning point for France and for Europe. The Socialists had learned that unilateral expansionism was not possible. To avoid being tarred as incompetent managers, they now stayed closer to the middle of the economic road. If growth-friendly macroeconomic policies were to be put in place, this would now have to occur at the EU level so as not to destabilize the EMS, which had become emblematic of macroeconomic prudence. Mitterrand began repositioning himself as a European statesman in order to be able to better advance this agenda. His reorientation and that of his government would have profound implications for the European project.

The Legacy

The stage was set for Europe's subsequent difficulties by the efforts undertaken in this period to address the problems of rising unemployment, declining productivity growth, and accelerating inflation.

---

[62] As a compromise, Delors also suggested a substantial widening of ERM bands, which would have permitted the franc to depreciate against the mark without the embarrassment of an overt realignment. Note that this was the same response taken to the crisis in the EMS in the summer of 1993 (see "The EMS Crisis" in chapter 11).

The extension of job-security provisions left firms reluctant to take on additional workers, since management knew that it would be forced to continue paying them even if the need for their services disappeared. Nonwage labor costs shot up as governments sought to provide additional support for the unemployed. The generosity of unemployment benefits was increased. The policies and mindset that allowed workers to claim disability benefits indefinitely and draw after-tax compensation of 90 percent of their previous incomes were products of this decade. To limit the rise in unemployment, governments, unions, and employers agreed to shorter hours, subsidized the early retirement of older workers, and discouraged the labor force participation of women. Lower participation rates meant that higher taxes had to be levied on active workers in order to support the now customary level of social benefits for the population as a whole.

All this rendered European labor more expensive. It left labor markets less flexible. And the recipients of governments' largess became formidable opponents of reform.

The desire for a more elaborate welfare state reflected deeply held social values—the sway of communitarianism in contrast with the individualistic attitudes of the United States. After several decades of rapid growth, European societies could better afford to indulge their appetite for equality and redistribution.[63] In addition, European economies had grown significantly more open over the course of the 1950s and 1960s. There is a natural tendency for residents of more open economies to demand more elaborate social insurance against externally generated sources of insecurity.[64]

These observations do not change the fact that the more elaborate welfare state of the 1980s reflected the expedients to which governments resorted in the late 1960s and 1970s to contain inflation and avert the breakdown of the postwar social compact. The growth of government revenues did not keep up with the growth of

---

[63] Higher incomes are among the key factors emphasized by Lindert (2004) as determinants of variations across countries and over time in welfare spending.

[64] This is the argument of Rodrik (1997).

government spending, resulting in the accumulation of worrisomely large public debts. At the end of the 1970s it was still possible for officials to claim that they had no way of anticipating the extent of the productivity slowdown that had caused revenues to lag earlier trends. By the mid-1980s, however, ignorance of structural change was no longer an excuse for fiscal imbalances. At this point, mounting debt problems brought countries such as Denmark and Ireland to the verge of financial crisis, to which they responded with fiscal retrenchment and radical public-sector reform. Elsewhere it led to a protracted fiscal crisis, with the consequences of which governments were still attempting to cope two decades later.

In addition to the fiscal consequences of these efforts to reinforce the postwar social compact, there was the fact that a set of institutions adapted to the imperatives of extensive growth was not well suited to the challenges of a more innovation-intensive process. A heavy state presence was less suitable to sustaining growth when there no longer existed an extensive technological backlog and it was not possible to extrapolate the future simply by observing the experience of the United States. Growth now depended more on the operation of markets, something that sat uneasily with the institutional inheritance. Innovation-based growth is risky, uncomfortably so for security-oriented European societies. It responds to financial incentives, which is difficult to reconcile with the value Europeans assign to earnings equality. It requires continuous reallocation of labor resources, which is at odds with the importance they attach to job security.

Thus, a number of European economies that had performed well in previous periods now experienced mounting difficulties. Sweden, having seen per capita incomes grow at the OECD average for thirty years, fell increasingly behind from the second half of the 1970s. Corporatist institutions designed to preserve wage restraint and a large government sector that used public spending to sustain demand succeeded in inducing recovery for a time, but growth was disappointing, contributing to problems of inflation and inadequate international competitiveness. In the Netherlands, the problems caused by accelerating inflation were compounded by the growing production of natural gas after 1973, aggravating the deterioration of competitiveness, and by a decline in corporatist cooperation. By the early 1980s, unemployment had reached double digits.[65]

The question now was how European societies would respond to these difficulties. Would they attempt radical reforms in order to meet the imperatives of the new era of intensive growth, or would the institutional inheritance prove resistant to rapid change? Would such adjustments as took place reflect decisions at the national level or occur in response to pressure from the European Community and the wider process of globalization? In both cases, the answer turned out to be more complicated than suggested by the either/or form of these questions.

[65] As described in more detail in chapter 12.

- TEN -

THE COLLAPSE OF CENTRAL PLANNING

The collapse of the Eastern bloc was the most momentous event affecting Europe in the final decade of the twentieth century. An economic and political system under which more than one-third of Europe's residents had lived disintegrated abruptly. The eastern half of the continent moved to put in place democratic political systems and the elements of a market economy. The downfall of the old regime in the Soviet Union and then the collapse of the USSR itself followed in short order.

Certainly, the shortcomings of central planning had long been apparent. These included the impossibility of formulating a plan that took into account the complex internal wiring of a modern economy and the difficulty of eliciting effort in a system that offered few positive incentives. The growth of net material product had decelerated between the 1950s and 1960s, as the extensive-growth strategy began encountering diminishing returns. In the 1970s the return on investment fell further.

Although the contradictions of planning were not new, the limitations of the system grew more prominent as the economies of the West turned from manufacturing to services and from the hierarchically controlled corporate form and Fordist mass production to the decentralized organization and flexible specialization made possible by digitally controlled machine tools, just-in-time inventory man-

agement, and new information technologies. The planned economies might be capable of producing simple goods using familiar technologies, steel being the classic example, but they were less well
suited for producing the more complex products of the postindustrial
era, much less for developing such products themselves. Hierarchical
control was all that the planners knew how to do. And the diffusion
of technologies facilitating the free flow of information was the last
thing that the authoritarian regimes of Central and Eastern Europe
sought to encourage. Concerned to maintain their grip on information, communist governments made access to these new technologies extraordinarily difficult. By the late 1980s, the Soviet Union
had at most three hundred thousand computers, whereas Western
experience suggested that a country of its size and wealth should
have had more than twenty million. Bringing along a personal computer for "scientific purposes" and selling it on the black market
became the standard way for Western graduate students studying the
economics of central planning (and, increasingly, the contradictions
of central planning) to fund their research trips.

For all these reasons, the gap widened between East and West.
The planned economies then experienced a debt crisis, an inflation
crisis, and a growth crisis, until the system broke down completely
at the end of the 1980s. With the economy unable to deliver the
goods, political apathy gave way to unrest and then to open revolt,
culminating in the collapse of the Eastern bloc, political democrati-
zation, and transition to the market economy.

At the time, of course, few Western observers—few if any of the
economic analysts employed by the Central Intelligence Agency,
for example—recognized the gravity of the problem. But even with
benefit of hindsight, there is a mystery. Why, when the problems
of central planning had already surfaced in the 1950s and become
increasingly pervasive in the 1960s, did they culminate in a crisis
only twenty years later? How was stability maintained through the
1970s and into the 1980s, given that the scope for extensive growth
had long since run its course?

The Survival of Central Planning

In practice, the socialist system survived by doing more of the same—by concentrating ever more heavily on the production of basic industrial goods. Although Central and Eastern Europe was already heavily industrialized by the end of the 1960s, industrial output doubled again between 1970 and 1988 in Czechoslovakia, Hungary, Poland, and Yugoslavia. It rose by a factor of three in Bulgaria and a factor of five in Romania.[1]

But the system showed a disturbing tendency to consume its own seed corn. It neglected the railways, sewage and water systems, and telephone networks developed in earlier years, whose quality and reliability deteriorated as a result. It depleted its endowment of nonrenewable resources, including both the physical environment and the health of its residents. Eastern Europe's industrial plants polluted the environment to an extent that would have been unthinkable in the West, where leaders were democratically accountable. Eastern European enterprises were not required to install smokestack scrubbers or to pay for the safe disposal of industrial wastes. By the late 1980s, wide swathes of Eastern Europe and the Soviet Union had become toxic wastelands. The heavy use of cheap brown coal bred emphysema and lung cancer. In the short run, free disposal of by-products and the absence of abatement requirements were advantageous for industries such as chemicals and steel, in which the Eastern European economies specialized. But in the long run they dissipated valuable resources, including the health and goodwill of the population.

For a time, the system was sustained by throwing ever more capital at the growth problem. The Gierek government in Poland, responding to what it perceived as an impending crisis of growth, programmed a doubling of investment in the first half of the 1970s. Most of that additional investment was devoted to heavy industries and traditional technologies that were being abandoned by the more adaptive economies of the West. The economic viability of these

---

[1] According to U.N. estimates cited in Berend (1996), p. 191.

investment projects then became even more dubious with the rise in energy prices in 1973.

Not surprisingly, the results in terms of growth were disappointing. Between 1971–1975 and 1976–1980, the incremental capital–output ratio (the additional capital needed to produce an additional percentage point of growth, a convenient measure of the return on investment) rose throughout Eastern Europe.[2] In the 1980s it rose again. Marshaling resources for investment became more difficult as living standards lagged relative to the West and relative to expectations. Maintaining social stability required shifting resources to the production of consumer goods, a trend in which even the Soviet Union participated from the 1970s on. It dictated making available televisions, refrigerators, and washing machines. These reforms were obviously inconsistent with the desire to devote a larger share of national income to the fabrication of producer goods.

In the 1970s this circle was squared by Western lending. With the lifting of prohibitions on the export of machinery and equipment to Eastern Europe in 1969, the U.S. Export-Import Bank provided Eastern European countries with credits for purchasing American merchandise. U.S. and Western European banks on the receiving end of the recycled dollars earned by the oil-exporting countries then sought outlets for these funds. They found them in, among other unlikely places, Poland, Hungary, and the GDR. By the end of the 1970s, Central and Eastern Europe's cumulative borrowing had risen to nearly fifty billion dollars, roughly 250 percent of annual hard-currency export receipts.[3] And once the borrowers began experiencing difficulties in servicing and repaying these loans,

---

[2] United Nations (1980), p. 109. To be sure, this was also a period of declining returns on investment in the West (as we saw in chapter 9). This observation suggests that not merely the contradictions of central planning but also the more problematic global environment (reflecting the difficult transition from extensive to intensive growth) contributed to the declining payoff to investment in Eastern Europe. But, of course, it is precisely the greater difficulty that the planned economies had in grappling with the challenges of intensive growth that is at the center of the present story.

[3] Loans outstanding (not including the Soviet Union) came to forty-seven billion dollars in 1979, compared with the value of exports to Western countries, which was twenty billion dollars.

they received IMF and World Bank assistance. Without this foreign lending, consumption would have been squeezed more severely, making it necessary to cut back on investment to quell unrest.

With benefit of hindsight, the enthusiasm of the money center banks for lending to Eastern Europe resembles nothing so much as a fit of collective insanity. To be sure, loan officers and their bosses may had been misled by the same overly optimistic assessment of the region's economic prospects that infected the CIA and the U.S. State Department. They may have believed that authoritarian regimes could suppress popular discontent, enabling them to mobilize resources for debt service in a crunch. Although this may have been true in extreme cases such as Romania, where the Ceauşescu regime made freeing the country of debt a priority and the populace endured no end of hardship in order to make this possible, it was not true generally. Elsewhere the decision to raise fuel taxes or cut the provision of consumer goods in order to meet debt service obligations provoked protests that challenged the legitimacy of the regime. Alternatively, some bankers may have believed that the Eastern European countries enjoyed a collective financial guarantee from Moscow not unlike the collective security guarantee extended by a supposedly stronger Soviet Union. Finally, having come under pressure to lend from their own governments, European banks may have anticipated that if things went wrong they would be bailed out by their domestic authorities either directly or working through the multilateral financial institutions.[4] Here too their hopes ultimately were disappointed.

So long as it lasted, foreign lending was a boon. For Eastern Europe it had the advantage of relaxing the balance-of-payments constraint and providing access to Western equipment and technology. With the decline of East–West tensions, the U.S. government placed fewer restrictions on the transfer of advanced technologies. Imports of machinery, equipment, and technology licenses were directly proportional to the volume of foreign loans. Western tech-

[4] West German loans to East Germany were a special case, since Bonn guaranteed them in an effort to bring the GDR closer into its sphere. See Jeffries (1993).

nologies were licensed for the production of steel and chemicals, and Western companies were permitted to participate in the development of production facilities. Machinery imports from the West as a share of total Eastern European imports rose from less than 30 percent in the mid-1960s to nearly 40 percent in the second half of the 1970s.[5] Where electricity-generation capacity lagged, countries imported equipment to modernize this key sector. Where the production of chemicals for fertilizer was a priority, they purchased turnkey plants. Where textiles, apparel, and leather manufacturing were important, they imported production machinery.

The acquisition of foreign technology helped to sustain the Eastern European system not only through the second half of the 1970s, when foreign capital was flowing, but into the 1980s, when the imported machinery was operational and reverse engineering allowed it to be duplicated and further applied. But the larger hopes engendered by this influx of foreign technology were disappointed. In some cases, the investment projects designed to capitalize on its availability were never completed. Even where they were, the assembly plants in question then required an ongoing flow of imported components, sourcing of which turned out to be impossible. Still other enterprises using foreign technology were plagued by poor quality and low productivity. A telling case was the Zastava motor vehicle factory in Kragujevac, Yugoslavia. Despite heavy investments in imported technology, its efforts to produce an internationally competitive economy car, the Yugo, and break into the U.S. market in the 1980s was to be a signal failure owing to problems of quality and reliability.

The situation in Eastern Europe looked better insofar as the 1970s, the decade of the productivity slowdown and the OPEC shock, and the first half 1980s, the years of disinflation, were difficult times in the West. In fact, Eastern Europe was even more energy-dependent than the West, reflecting its concentration on heavy industry and its dearth of indigenous resources. But unlike the West,

[5] Data for the Council for Mutual Economic Assistance (CMEA) six, from Köves (1985), p. 84, cited in Aldcroft and Morewood (1995), p. 162.

which was vulnerable to a Middle East oil embargo, Eastern Europe could at least count on reliable supplies from the USSR. Initially, it imported Soviet oil at submarket prices, since trade within the CMEA valued merchandise and commodities, including oil, at the average world market prices prevailing over the previous quinquennium and modified those prices only every five years to conform to the horizon of the five-year plan.[6] This gave the planners an even greater incentive to pursue energy-intensive growth and production strategies.

Modest subsidies were one thing, but the Soviets were not prepared to give oil to their Eastern European neighbors for half of what it might command on the world market, especially once the Soviet Union gained the opportunity in the 1970s to purchase Western technology using the proceeds of commodity sales. The pricing formula was therefore modified to reflect average prices over the last three years and updated annually. Not only did this raise prices toward world levels, but it meant that the cost of oil imported from the Soviet Union stayed above world market prices when the latter fell back following the OPEC shock.

Finally, the resumption of piecemeal reform addressed some of the planned economies' most glaring deficiencies. Where earlier reforms had been designed mainly to increase the efficiency of the planning mechanism, a number of Eastern European countries now grafted onto the command economy elements of a market system. Prices, notably in the farm sector, were allowed to respond to the balance of supply and demand. More individuals were permitted to leave agricultural cooperatives and farm on their own. Enterprises were permitted to keep a portion of their receipts in foreign currency and use them to finance imports of intermediate inputs and capital goods. Even in East Germany, where the commitment to Stalinist planning was even stricter than in the Soviet Union, the *Kombinate* (state-owned conglomerates) were given limited autonomy to make production decisions.[7] In Hungary, the central bank's monopoly on

---

[6] See "Regional Integration" in chapter 5.

[7] The reforms of the Honecker regime were admittedly grudging; enterprises in the GDR still had less autonomy than at the height of the New Economic System in the 1960s.

credit was eliminated. Enterprises were permitted to issue bonds, reducing their dependence on the government-controlled banking system.[8] Bankruptcy procedures were reformed in an effort to harden budget constraints.

These reforms did not eliminate the contradictions of central planning. As emphasized by Kornai (1990), the concept of "market socialism" underlying these reform efforts was flawed. It did not define ownership. It provided only limited incentives for responding to price signals. It did not prevent managers from devoting their efforts not to enhancing the efficiency of the enterprise but rather to obtaining subsidies from the authorities. Still, in the short run it attenuated some of the worst inefficiencies of the planned economies by allowing more flexibility in production and procurement and more scope for the operation of the price mechanism. Despite some unanticipated negative consequences, it allowed "actually existing socialism" to stagger on.

The Collapse of Communism

Although the old regime collapsed first in Eastern Europe and only subsequently in the Soviet Union, the destabilizing impulse came from Moscow. The Soviets had become skeptical about the value of their cordon sanitaire. And they had grown worried about their ability to finance it, given the economic problems and mounting defense expenditures provoked by Ronald Reagan's defense buildup and their war in Afghanistan. Increasingly, they demanded that other CMEA countries pay world market prices for Soviet energy and that they receive discounts on their imports of manufactures from Eastern Europe commensurate with the quality differential vis-à-vis Western goods. This turned the terms of trade against Eastern Europe.

Mikhail Gorbachev was the first of a new generation of Soviet bloc leaders, most Eastern European countries still being controlled by Cold War ideologues and their inheritors. His policies seemed

---

[8] This, however, favored large enterprises and led to further industrial concentration.

like a breath of fresh air even if they were intended to maintain communism rather than undermining it. What they lacked in coherence they made up for in appearance. They resonated with the ambitions and resentments of people throughout Eastern Europe. As such they undermined whatever little legitimacy was still possessed by the old regime.

With declining respect for the organs of the state, intimidation as a mechanism for eliciting compliance became increasingly ineffectual. In Hungary and Poland, where the state police moderated their methods, spontaneous protests developed into mass movements. Without Soviet backing, the regimes saw resorting to martial law, as Poland had done in response to agitation by Solidarity in 1981, as doing more to jeopardize their control than to protect it.

The consequences were nothing less than the collapse of the planned economies. As long as the secret police were a force to be reckoned with, workers could be intimidated into exerting effort. With political liberalization, intimidation as a motivating factor was removed, and the absence of positive incentives became a fatal liability. There was nothing now to stop workers from walking off with equipment and tools. The economists' antiseptic label for this behavior, *spontaneous privatization*, hardly captures the disorderly, delegitimating nature of the phenomenon. With political liberalization, the central contradiction of state socialism came clear: property that officially belonged to everyone effectively belonged to no one. No one had an incentive to protect it.

The result was the further deterioration of economic performance. In East Germany, where the government had long relied on secret-police intimidation, 1987 was a poor year for growth, but 1988 was worse, and 1989 was the worst year in nearly three decades. An extreme case was Romania, where output fell by 8 percent in 1989, partly reflecting the policies of austerity associated with Nicolae Ceauşescu's megalomaniacal fixation on paying down the national debt. But throughout the region, annual average growth rates fell to less than 1 percent in the second half of the 1980s. Governments sought to quell popular unrest by granting wage increases, but with more money chasing an ever-diminishing supply of goods, this only produced explosive inflation, which rose to 20 percent in Hungary and more than 200 percent in Poland in 1989.

The disintegration of the economic system further undermined whatever vestiges of legitimacy the political regime still possessed. In Poland there existed a rival for power in the form of the Solidarity trade union movement. The Communist leadership was forced to meet with Solidarity and agree to parliamentary elections that resulted in a stunning defeat for the government and the formation of a new coalition led by the dissident trade unionists. In Hungary a relatively liberal Communist Party had allowed an opposition movement to develop; now the two factions agreed to free parliamentary elections to be held in March 1990. In the GDR, the ruling party was less accommodating. There political change required a popular uprising, catalyzed by Hungary's opening its border with Austria, which provided an escape route and precipitated the mass exodus of East Germans to the West, creating a crisis and forcing concessions on the Communist government.[9] In Czechoslovakia, mass demonstrations by opposition groups united in the Civic Forum, led by Vaclav Hável, forced the resignation of the Communist president and the formation of a new government with a majority of Civic Forum members.

Recession and Adjustment

The new governments did not have an easy economic ride. Output was already falling prior to their assumption of power. Now that decline accelerated. The cumulative fall in GDP after 1990 varied from a "low" of 12 percent in the Czech Republic to 18 percent in Hungary, 24 percent in Slovakia, and 38 percent in the Baltic States. (See table 10.1.) This was not the measured adjustment anticipated by the apostles of the market economy.

To be sure, since much of the earlier output of Central and Eastern European industry had contributed nothing to living standards,

---

[9] See "German Reunification" later in this chapter.

TABLE 10.1

Transition economies: Output performance, 1989–2004

	Year the transition started (T)	GNP (PPP) per capita in 1989	Year in which output was lowest	Maximum output decline since T − 1	Cumulative output growth, lowest to 2004	Average output growth since lowest level until 2004
Central and Eastern Europe	1990–1991	5,760	1991–1997	24.7	52.2	3.56
Czech Republic	1991	9,000	1992	12.1	38.8	2.98
Hungary	1990	6,810	1993	18.1	46.7	3.48
Poland	1990	5,150	1991	13.7	84.5	4.71
Slovak Republic	1991	8,000	1993	24.4	61.2	4.34
Baltic States	1992	7,973	1993–1994	38.1	74.2	5.75

Source: Fischer and Sahay (2004).

Note: PPP = purchasing power parity, a conversion factor used to equalize the purchasing power of currencies.

its disappearance now did nothing to reduce them. No one missed the capital goods that had been produced to support the production of low-quality steel that went into the production of capital goods used to support the production of low-quality steel. In addition, that the decline in electricity consumption was milder than the decline in measured GDP suggests that the fall in production as recorded by the official statistics may have been overstated. Many enterprises simply stopped reporting to government ministries, and the tax systems used to gauge production by statistical agencies in market economies were not yet fully functioning. In particular, the output of new private enterprises tended not to be captured in the statistical net.[10]

Thus, despite the double-digit decline in recorded GDP, the number of Central and Eastern European households possessing refrigerators, televisions, and automobiles rose from the outset of the transition. Households obviously appreciated the reallocation of capacity from the production of capital goods of little intrinsic value to consumer goods for which there was actual demand. And even if firms simply concentrated on intermediate goods, high-quality steel for example, for which there was a market in the West, exporting these goods meant acquiring foreign exchange that could be used to import high-quality consumer durables. All these are reasons for thinking that welfare rose even as output was falling.[11]

[10] This also created problems for cross-country comparisons and evaluations of alternative reform strategies, for the more quickly a country restructured its economy and shifted resources into the private sector, the greater the likely understatement of output. Associated with these structural shifts were index number problems for statistical agencies seeking to estimate GDP. Should they use 1989 or 1993 relative prices and sector weights, for example, when comparing levels of output in those two years? There were no easy answers to these questions, which casts further doubt on the accuracy of estimates of the extent of the output fall in the early years of the transition.

[11] Moreover, except in the Baltic States and Russia, there was no rise in mortality rates, an obvious indicator of the welfare of the population. In the more advanced transition economies, Poland, Hungary, and the Czech Republic, for example, mortality of adult males between the ages of forty and fifty-nine immediately improved starting in 1990. Eventually, there was also some improvement in Bulgaria and Romania, but only after 1996, reflecting the botched transition strategies of the former Communist Parties then in office. European Bank for Reconstruction and Development (1999), p. 15.

But some contraction was unavoidable.[12] Shifting from central planning to the market entailed reallocating capacity from the production of capital goods to the production of consumer goods and shifting resources from manufacturing to services. But it was easier to curtail production by heavy industry by removing subsidies and final demand than it was to conjure up new production of consumer goods and services. Old state-owned enterprises used to producing for a captive market could not adapt overnight to the disciplines of competition and immediately start producing goods that would appeal to households that now enjoyed freedom of choice. With time, new firms might spring up to fill this void, but the investors to fund them, managers to direct them, and workers to staff them did not materialize overnight. There were limits to how quickly new private enterprise could ramp up production.

Some observers pointed to Western Europe after World War II, which had similarly had to redeploy resources from military to civilian uses and from heavy industry to consumer goods but succeeded in doing so without precipitating a major recession, as evidence that Eastern Europe might now have avoided a recession had it followed different policies. But Western Europe then enjoyed major advantages not shared by Eastern Europe now. A well-developed private sector and a large cohort of private-sector managers had survived the war. Western Europe had bankers to provide financial-intermediation services. It had court systems to adjudicate disputes and enforce contracts. It had political institutions with the power to modify and adapt the relevant institutional arrangements and the capacity to hold those undertaking these actions accountable for their decisions. In Central and Eastern Europe, where this experience and institutional inheritance were lacking, adjustment to the market was unavoidably more difficult.

Like Western Europe after World War II, the countries of Central and Eastern Europe now sought to provide the institutional template for a market economy by putting back in place earlier ar-

---

[12] This point is made rigorously by Atkeson and Kehoe (1997) and Roland and Verdier (1997).

rangements. Faced with the challenge of restoring political democracy, Eastern European countries restored the political systems developed in their own most recent period of democratic rule, namely, the 1920s. Unfortunately, there were no established party systems, and political movements that had cut their teeth by fighting the earlier authoritarian regime now found it hard to make the transition to peacetime politics. In addition, those earlier political institutions had exhibited serious weaknesses; for example, strongly proportional electoral systems had led to political fragmentation that resulted in unstable coalition governments and ultimately the collapse of democracy in the 1930s. Now once again the combination of proportional representation with political flux made for a proliferation of narrow-based parties and unstable parliamentary coalitions.

What was true of politics was equally true of economics. Poland could restore its pre-1939 commercial code, but there were few enterprise managers or bank loan officers experienced in its application. There were few experienced investors to hold those managers accountable for their decisions. There were few jurists with reputations for impartiality to adjudicate disputes and enforce contracts.

Nor was there a Marshall Plan for the East, only dribs and drabs of aid from the EU and multilateral financial institutions.[13] After World War II, Marshall aid, conditioned on policies of macroeconomic stabilization and trade liberalization, had strengthened the hand of market-friendly governments. Now, in contrast, reformist governments could not point to substantial amounts of foreign aid as a reward for enduring the short-term pain of stabilization and adjustment. The Marshall Plan had encouraged European govern-

---

[13] To be sure, the EU did provide limited amounts of technical and financial support for the reform process through the PHARE Programme created in 1989. (PHARE was shorthand for Poland, Hungary, Assistance for Reconstruction of the Economy. The program was quickly expanded from Poland and Hungary to include eleven Central and Eastern European economies.) Member states also provided financial assistance bilaterally and through the European Investment Bank. They established the European Bank for Reconstruction and Development to mobilize private capital for investment in the transition economies (of the Commonwealth of Independent States as well as Eastern Europe). There were also large-scale transfers to the former GDR via the Federal Republic, which proved a mixed blessing for reasons explained later.

ments to stabilize their exchange rates and liberalize their trade. It had provided credits for countries experiencing balance-of-payments difficulties in the course of readjusting their trade. Now there were fewer credits. Eastern Europe's trade collapsed with the disintegration of the CMEA and the Soviet Union, removing the one remaining source of demand for the military hardware and producer goods churned out by the region's heavy industry.

Dilemmas of Transition

Obviously, governments faced enormous difficulties, not just in the institutional but also in the macroeconomic sphere. The collapse of output and the old administrative apparatus meant the collapse of public-sector revenues. Governments had already been running substantial deficits, reflecting the explosion of wages, massive expenditures on food subsidies and pensions to quell social unrest, and the growing losses of state enterprises. Those deficits now widened further. Putting new tax systems in place took time, and yields were contingent on the recovery of production.

At the same time, the collapse of output and employment provoked urgent calls for income maintenance for the unemployed, the elderly, and the indigent. Subsidies for firms in distress similarly absorbed fiscal resources. There being no functioning financial markets, there was no scope for borrowing to finance deficits, leaving no alternative to monetization. As a result of this increase in the money supply, inflation soared, ranging from 26 percent in Hungary to 46 percent in the Czech Republic, 245 percent in Bulgaria, 314 percent in Romania, and 1,096 percent in Poland.[14]

These pressures encouraged the retention of controls on the prices of essential commodities. Controlling prices meant a reluctance to produce for the market and pervasive shortages. Decontrolling some prices but not others meant that enterprises producing

[14] These figures are for the twelve months prior to the month of implementation of each country's stabilization program. Measured over shorter periods—one month, for example—the peak in inflation was often much greater.

goods whose prices were artificially depressed could not afford inputs from the rest of the economy, intensifying the pressure for subsidies. Curtailing public spending threatened to depress demand still further, aggravating the collapse of employment and arousing opposition among workers who had already begun to feel that the transition had fewer benefits than costs. But maintaining public spending meant fueling inflation, diluting the information content of prices, and discouraging saving and investment. Subsidizing heavy industry only encouraged the production of goods whose cost was higher than the value of the resources consumed.

The most difficult task was enterprise privatization. Corner stores and back-street workshops could be privatized by just giving them to their operators, who in any case knew more than anyone else about running them. But handing over large state enterprises to their managers would have had arbitrary and illegitimating distributional consequences.[15] The same was true of transferring ownership of an enterprise to its workers, given that only some firms were viable and different companies had different market values. But giving every citizen a share, or the right to bid for a share, was unlikely to be efficient, since potential bidders lacked the information needed to make sound decisions. The resulting holdings were often so scattered that no investor had a stake sufficient to make it worthwhile to object to self-serving decision making by managers. And selling off enterprises to foreigners was either politically unacceptable or met with many of the same practical difficulties.

Governments therefore waited, keeping state enterprises in public hands until financial markets developed, corporate governance was strengthened, and other solutions were found to these problems. Or else they privatized anyway, and control ended up in the hands of those with privileged information and access to credit, be they former managers or financial operators.

Ultimately, none of these problems could be solved without simultaneously solving the others. Liberalizing prices without balanc-

---

[15] In any case, it was far from clear that former managers were the best people to run newly corporatized firms.

ing the budget meant inflation, not the creation of an efficient price mechanism. Liberalizing and stabilizing without privatizing meant that managers lacked the incentive to make efficient production and investment decisions. But privatizing without first developing financial markets and legal protections for shareholders meant that there was nothing to prevent managers from pursuing their personal interests at investor expense. Without comprehensive reform, what the Polish economist Leszek Balcerowicz (1995) referred to as a "critical mass," the new market-oriented system could not achieve coherence.

Unfortunately, solving these problems in one fell swoop was not feasible either. In practice, no country actually applied the "shock treatment" of rapid liberalization, privatization, and stabilization. There were just too many political constraints.

Economic Response

That said, there was considerable variation in the pace of stabilization, liberalization, and reform. Poland and the Czech Republic, for example, moved relatively quickly, reflecting the ideology of the leadership. Slovakia, which had depended on the production of armaments for the Soviet Union and where popular resistance to closing down heavy industry was strong, adjusted more slowly. Through the first half of the 1990s, Bulgaria and Romania, where members of the old Communist establishment maintained power, reformed hardly at all.

In Poland, where prices were liberalized quickly and state subsidies were abruptly withdrawn in an effort to consolidate the budget and bring down inflation, output declined sharply. Production fell by 12 percent in 1990, the year that central planning was abolished, and by a further 7 percent in 1991. In countries such as Hungary, where liberalization was more gradual, the initial drop in output in 1990 was only one-third as severe. In Slovakia it was only one-quarter as severe as in Poland.

But the decline in output in the more gradual reformers then picked up speed, whereas in Poland production stabilized and growth resumed in 1992. In the Czech Republic output stabilized in 1993, in Slovakia and Hungary in 1994. Elsewhere, however, output continued to fall. Thus, countries undertaking relatively radical reforms suffered sharper contractions in the early years of the transition but enjoyed earlier recoveries.

The advocates of radical reform had a ready interpretation of this pattern. Restoring budget balance and halting inflation strengthened the price mechanism and improved the allocation of resources, as did curtailing subsidies for state enterprises, removing relative price distortions, and eliminating barriers to the establishment of new enterprises. Structural reform depressed output in the state sector as hard budget constraints forced state enterprises to shed workers, but boosted it in the private sector. The private sector started out small, which explains short-run association of structural reform with recession, but it then gained ground as new private enterprises emerged as the engines of productivity growth.

Where reform was phased in more gradually, in contrast, the contraction persisted. The gradual reformers succeeded in limiting the initial fall in output by running substantial budget deficits and supporting the old state sector, but they were less successful at growing the private sector. And unviable state enterprises could not be supported indefinitely, given their low levels of productivity and the fact that in many cases their products could not compete on world markets at any price. Consequently, output declines in these countries continued for longer, and the cumulative contraction was more severe. In Bulgaria, an extreme case, output fell by a cumulative 33 percent and the trough was reached only in 1997. In Latvia, initially another slow reformer, the trough was reached a bit earlier, in 1996, but the cumulative fall in output was even greater.

In the long run, what mattered for growth was the amount of cumulative restructuring: how much state enterprise was transferred to the private sector, how effectively labor markets were reformed, how comprehensively budget deficits were reduced. Once five years had passed, it was clear that those countries that had done the most extensive structural reform were enjoying the fastest rates of growth.[16] Some still worried that the cold bath of reform might undermine political support. Gradualism might enable the public to learn about the merits of a market economy with less discomfort. Starting with popular reforms would help to build constituencies and political support for other, initially less popular measures.[17] Larger deficits and lower interest rates would permit governments to more effectively support living standards, limiting the danger of a political backlash.[18]

The disadvantage of this approach, its critics warned, was that phasing in reform would slow the growth of the private sector. It would allow the managers of state enterprises faced with soft budget constraints to continue arbitraging between controlled and market prices and stripping enterprises of their remaining assets. It would allow special interests to capture the policy making process. Rapid reform, in contrast, confronted managers with hard budget constraints. It maximized residents' exposure to the market, heightening their awareness of the need for market-supporting institutions. This made it important to capitalize on the period of "extraordinary politics" immediately following the collapse of the old system, when old vested interests had the least legitimacy, in order to push through as much reform as possible. Mass privatization, it was argued, would create a political constituency for private property and market-oriented reform. Although this strategy was most prominently adopted by the architects of Russia's privatization program, it figured in the thinking of reformers in other countries as well.

The problem was that privatization undertaken before there existed courts and institutional investors to protect the rights of outsiders allowed the privatized resources to end up in the hands of insiders. In 1995, at the end of Russia's voucher-led mass privatization

---

[16] Åslund (2002), p. 144.

[17] Models of the conditions under which this might be the case were provided by Dewatripont and Roland (1995, 1997).

[18] For this view see, for example, Portes (1993).

program, two-thirds of shares in the average privatized firm were in the hands of its managers and workers. The second wave of privatization was less transparent still and led to even more concentrated ownership. Insiders stripped the newly privatized enterprise of its assets. By transferring important enterprises to the politically well connected, this approach encouraged the retention of subsidies and weakened the incentive for restructuring. These results diminished the legitimacy of the market system. Nor did mass privatization create a constituency for the rule of law. Where there was the most uncertainty about property rights, the new owners preferred to minimize their risks by continuing to strip assets, which gave them an interest in prolonging the absence of the rule of law. Powerful insiders opposed reforms of corporate governance designed to give small stakeholders a more effective say in decision making.

Other countries such as the Czech Republic that also proceeded with mass privatization experienced similar problems. There every citizen was given a booklet of vouchers and a pen with which he or she could bid for shares of state enterprises. Using this approach, the bulk of state enterprises, large and small, were quickly privatized. But not only were large numbers of small shareholders unable to effectively rein in management, they were unable to even monitor the firm's financial affairs. Investors might have sold their shares in firms with which they were disenchanted, but stock markets were illiquid, reflecting weak regulation and those same information asymmetries. There was therefore little market discipline on managers. Investors deposited their holdings with investment funds that were in principle better able to execute these functions. But these funds were state-influenced, weakly managed, and poorly regulated; they were no better than the firms they oversaw at representing shareholder interests.[19]

The more gradual approach began with small-scale privatization and proceeded only thereafter to the privatization of large enter-

---

[19] They were also reluctant to pull the plug on the firms in which they held controlling stakes for fear of the financial consequences. See Ellerman (1998).

313

prises, through initial public offerings on the stock market or direct sales to outsiders.[20] In the case of a corner store, the owner, manager, and principal employees were one and the same, removing the incentive for asset stripping. It was easier to impose hard budget constraints on small enterprises, which strengthened the incentive for restructuring. Starting with the privatization of small enterprises, which operated in a relatively intense competitive environment, also avoided putting the newly privatized firm in the position of a monopolist where it could charge exorbitant prices and deter entry.[21] Countries that concentrated on small-scale privatization also did better in developing competition policies, reforming corporate governance, strengthening banking systems, building securities markets, and enhancing the effectiveness of their legal systems, since these were all things that owners of small enterprises valued and advocated. But they paid a price in the form of allowing the politically connected managers of large enterprises still in state hands to strip resources by, inter alia, transferring them to private companies under their control. Again, there was no easy solution to the privatization problem.

Backlashes against reform occurred in countries that proceeded rapidly and in countries that moved slowly. Probably the most concerted resistance was in Bulgaria and Romania, which did relatively little early reform. But in no Central or Eastern European country, whether it proceeded rapidly or slowly, did market-oriented reform suffer a fatal setback. More important for these outcomes than the pace of reform was the political system. One would expect informed citizens to vote for parties advocating policies that had succeeded in other countries. And, not surprisingly, more democratic transition economies—those with relatively high Freedom House scores for

[20] Poland is widely cited as an example of this approach, although Åslund (2002) objects that the pace of privatization was actually no slower than in Russia, and that insofar as the results were superior this reflected not so much the privatization strategy as the fact that Poland had already put in place complementary reforms.

[21] This was particularly a problem in the smaller economies of the region prior to the development of effective competition policies (see the discussion later in this chapter).

political and social liberties—did the most reform in the 1990s.[22] Similarly, in countries with competitive political systems, as measured by the frequency of turnover of government (here the Czech Republic, Hungary, and Poland rated much higher than Bulgaria and Romania), voters were better able to discipline leaders who did not pursue productive policies, and reform proceeded more rapidly. In addition, countries with encompassing coalition governments that gave representation and voice to diverse interest groups gave even those disproportionately burdened by the costs of reform some say in their determination. Such encompassing coalitions facilitated side payments that prevented potential losers from holding up reform. (See figure 10.1.)

This brings us to the role of institutions in the transition. It is fair to say that few early observers fully appreciated the difficulty of building market-supporting institutions. Eventually, the observation that transition economies located at a greater distance from Western Europe and with more years under communism had more difficulty in navigating the transition engendered an appreciation for how history shaped the prospects for institutional reform. That much of Eastern Europe had not operated a market economy for the better part of forty years meant that putting in place market-supporting institutions was more difficult than in Western Europe after World War II. The further east one traveled, it seemed, the fewer of the relevant institutional preconditions were in place.

The idea that market-supporting institutions could be imported lock, stock, and barrel from the West ignored the need to tailor arrangements to the special circumstances of the transition economies, as the transplantation of West German institutions to the eastern *Länder* (states) that had once comprised the GDR illustrated so graphically. It ignored the need to cultivate a sense of ownership by

---

[22] Åslund, Boone, and Johnson (2001), p. 93. In particular, Romania rated lower than other Eastern European countries on the Freedom House scale, and the former Communist Party held on to power, with a brief interruption between 1997 and 1999, for the better part of a decade. Not surprisingly, the government's commitment to reform was exceptionally weak.

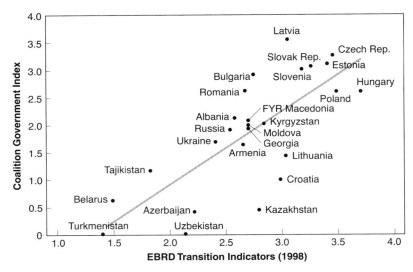

Figure 10.1. Political coalitions and economic reform. *Source*: European Bank for Reconstruction and Development (1999). *Notes*: Key to coalition government index scale: 0 = noncompetitive political system, 1 = one-party governments or presidential systems with majority support in parliament, 2 = two-party governments or presidential systems without majority support in parliament, 3 = three or more party coalitions, and 4 = minority governments. Key to European Bank for Reconstruction and Development (EBRD) transition indicators: range from 1.0 (little progress) to 4.0 (substantial progress).

giving citizens and their elected representatives voice in their design and above all the difficulty of supplementing this "hardware" with the relevant "software" (jurists, bank inspectors, and the like).

Some suggested that it was necessary to slow the pace of reform until more of the institutional preconditions for an efficient market economy were put in place. But this assumed that governments had the capacity to run the state sector at the same reasonable levels of efficiency that they imagined it had been run in the 1980s. Both the greater complexity of the late twentieth-century economy and political liberalization rendered this assumption problematic. In addition, those who advocated slowing the pace of reform until the relevant market-supporting institutions had developed assumed that their development was independent of the pace and extent of

316

reform, whereas in fact there was a danger that slowing reform might slow institutional development. Slow reform meant more influence for bureaucrats who saw institutional development leading to the creation of a market economy as putting them out of a job. It meant limiting the growth of private enterprise, which was the main interest group calling for the creation of market-supporting institutions.

Some critics pointed to China, which was adjusting without a serious recession, as evidence that gradual reform could work.[23] But China's state sector was smaller. Only one-fifth of the labor force was employed by the state, in contrast to upwards of 90 percent in Eastern Europe. The Chinese economy was heavily agricultural, which meant that it could be marketized simply by giving farmers rights to their land and deregulating agricultural prices. In Eastern Europe, the importance of state enterprise reflected forty years of Soviet-style industrialization. Since many of these industries were value subtracting, raising living standards required closing them down. The protoprivate sector, including agriculture, had long been starved of resources. This meant that a gradual transition during which state enterprises continued to operate and private agriculture took up the slack was not an option. Eastern Europe's transition necessarily involved a more abrupt adjustment and, unavoidably, more unemployment. It entailed government budget deficits and a more difficult stabilization problem.

The transition in Eastern Europe also took place in different political circumstances. In China the old guard retained its legitimacy and control. In Eastern Europe, in contrast, there was an all but universal wish to jettison the old system. It was not only foreign advisers who preferred a rapid shift to the market. It was Eastern Europe's own citizens as well. Rapid liberalization and privatization were an economic and political strategy. But, more than that, they were a cry of freedom.

---

[23] A representative example of this view is Stiglitz (1999).

CHAPTER 10

German Reunification

In East Germany, there was no discussion of the optimal design of economic, political, and legal institutions. The former German Democratic Republic (GDR) simply imported the institutions of the Federal Republic of Germany (FRG) in one fell swoop. With the relaxation of authoritarian control elsewhere in the region, the residents of the GDR began using neighboring countries as escape routes to the West. When the Honecker government responded by tightening visa restrictions, thousands of East Germans crowded into the FRG's embassies in Prague and Warsaw. This provoked mass demonstrations in Leipzig and Berlin that culminated in November 1989 with the opening of the Berlin wall.

The East German government had hoped that lifting restrictions on short-term visits to the West would stem the flight of refugees. Apparently they intended to open border crossings in an orderly fashion and still require stamped visas for travelers. But the announcement to this effect by the minister of propaganda Günter Schabowski at the end of a rambling 9 November news conference was ambiguous. (Schabowski had been on vacation and evidently did not know the party line on who would be permitted to cross the border and under what conditions.) Residents of East Berlin, hearing what they wished, concluded that they were free to travel to the West and began queuing up at the divided city's border crossings. With encouragement from Western observers, including television crews, their assemblies were quickly transformed into spontaneous demonstrations. Late the same evening, the ranking East German border guards at four crossing points in the center of the city took matters into their own hands and opened the gates.

With the creation of this exit, intimidation as a disciplining device lost its remaining force. Workers stopped showing up at the office and factory, and output collapsed. The East German government sought to delay the inevitable, first by creating a new administration, the Treuhandanstalt, to maintain, reorganize, and privatize state enterprises, and then by holding free parliamentary elections. But the citizenry rejected anything less than a market economy and

318

immediate fusion with the FRG. They voted with their feet, moving west in unprecedented numbers.

The West German chancellor Helmut Kohl seized the moment, presenting a unification plan to the Bundestag and then to the four post–World War II occupying powers (the United States, the United Kingdom, France, and the USSR). He then announced, to the horrified surprise of the president of the Bundesbank, Karl Otto Pöhl, a plan to transfer the deutschmark to East Germany. Monetary unification had both symbolic and practical value; East Germans in their street demonstrations had chanted *"Kommt die D-Mark, bleiben wir. Kommt sie nicht, gehen wir zu ihr"* ("If the D-Mark comes, we stay here. If it doesn't, we go to the D-Mark").

In May 1990, Kohl and his new East German counterpart, Lothar de Maizière, signed a state treaty agreeing to economic and monetary unification. The treaty came into force on 1 July. It was at this point that the telescoped process of transferring West German institutions, including West German money, took place. The currency conversion occurred on 2 July. The FRG's legal system was transferred at a stroke. A modern financial system was installed as West German banks set up branches in the east, first in trailers and then in permanent structures. The unification treaty was finalized by the end of August, and the four occupying powers signed the "2 + 4 Treaty" in Moscow in September. On 3 October 1990, when the treaty took effect, the GDR was permanently erased from Europe's map.

It had been widely argued that installing Western institutions was the key to initiating rapid economic revival. As an extreme case, where West German institutions were transferred to the former GDR all at once, what followed proved difficult to reconcile with this view. The severity of the recession was striking even by Eastern European standards. Real GDP in the former GDR fell by 30 percent over the course of 1990 and 1991, while industrial production fell by a staggering 50 percent.[24] Unemployment rose to one-third of the

---

[24] Recall, for comparison, that Polish GDP fell by 14 percent and Hungarian output fell by 18 percent between the year preceding the collapse of central planning and the trough.

CHAPTER 10

Table 10.2

East Germany–West Germany comparison of basic labor market indicators, 1991–2000, selected years (East as percentage of West)

	1991	1992	1993	1994	1995	2000
Gross nominal wages	50.8	61.8	68.9	72.5	74.9	76.8
Labor productivity	34.4	48.3	59.5	64.3	65.1	68.5
Unit labor costs	146.8	127.9	115.8	112.8	115.0	112.2
Unemployment rates	205.8	300.2	251.0	213.8	196.6	254.8

Source: von Hagen, Strauch, and Wolff (2002).

labor force. It was possible that West German institutions were not particularly well suited to the particularities of East Germany's transition. One could object that the Bundesbank's monetary policy was too tight for a transition economy desperate for credit or that the FRG's bankruptcy procedures were too clumsy to resolve problems of widespread insolvency. But with one exception, that of labor-market institutions, these factors turned out to be of secondary importance. They had little to do with why output fell so dramatically in the five new eastern states of the FRG.

Admittedly, some of the contraction took place in the first half of 1990 prior to the installation of West German institutions, but it showed no tendency to diminish thereafter. Signs of stability began surfacing at the end of 1991, and green shoots of recovery sprouted in 1992. Thus, as an example of "big-bang" reform, even more than, say, Poland, the German case reinforces the observation that the more drastic the stabilization and liberalization, the more severe the output collapse but the earlier the trough.

From 1992 through 1994, the eastern *Länder* grew at an average annual rate of 9 percent, encouraging comparisons with the post–World War II *Wirtschaftswunder*. The reorganization of production, supplemented by new investment, raised gross value added per employee from barely 40 percent of West German levels at the beginning of the transition to nearly 70 percent by mid-decade. (See table 10.2.) But growth declined to 5 percent in 1995, 4 percent in 1996, and 2 percent in 1997. Growth in the eastern *Länder* then averaged just 1.4 percent between 1996 and 2003, below the 2.3 percent of Germany's West.

Problems of adaptation to a market economy there obviously were for people who had spent their entire lives in a planned system, but these were no greater than in, say, neighboring Poland. Problems of inadequate infrastructure—an antiquated telephone system, for example—also existed, but these too were no more severe than elsewhere in Eastern Europe.[25] Rather, the key factor in the disappointing recovery was the evolution of labor costs. Even prior to unification, the West German union confederations had pushed for the creation of new industrial trade unions in East Germany. The unification treaty extended to the East the right of free association and free wage bargaining that existed in the FRG. The new unions immediately opened negotiations with the German employers associations, which similarly lost no time in opening branches in the East. The Treuhand, in its wisdom, decided not to participate in these negotiations, despite now being the de facto owner of the enterprises whose wage contracts were being negotiated. In effect, West German unions and employers were allowed to set East German wages. Seeking to defend western jobs against low-wage competition from foreign firms interested in setting up in the ruins of the East, they advocated a policy of rapid wage adjustment toward western levels.

Although the federal government could have intervened, it was reluctant to take a stand. Many Germans feared that a significant East–West wage differential might set off large-scale internal migration. The good burghers of the West then might have to live with "*ossies*" camped out in their parks, something for which the Kohl government did not wish to be blamed. And although the government was not dependent on the support of the unions, neither could it afford to provoke their hostility. The unions for their part saw the convergence of wages between East and West as symbolic of social solidarity. More pragmatically, they feared that the emergence of a low-wage region might undermine their own bargaining position. The most that labor would concede in the metal-industry negotiations, which set the tone for wage negotiations economy-wide, was

---

[25] To the contrary, actually, since in eastern Germany the old infrastructure was more rapidly updated and replaced courtesy of massive expenditures by the federal government.

that wages in the East should converge with those in the West no later than the first half of 1994.

The problem was that labor productivity in the East was barely one-third of West German levels. Plant and equipment were antiquated. There was little demand for what was produced, given the now free access of consumers to the products of the West. At the one-to-one conversion between östmarks and deutschmarks applied to wage payments, 1989 wages would have similarly been one-third of West German levels.[26] But wages were rising before the currency conversion took place. Contracts negotiated in the first half of 1990 secured increases of 17 percent.[27] Those negotiated in the second half of 1990, following the conversion, provided for increases of 25 to 60 percent. The unions insisted that wages in the East should rise to 60 percent of West German levels immediately, and there was no one to resist them, with the West German employers associations on the other side of the table happy to see the East rendered unattractive to foreign firms seeking a low-cost production platform. The doubling of labor costs rendered even previously viable state enterprises unprofitable. Already in October 1990 these wage increases in conjunction with the one-to-one conversion rate left the vast majority of the *Kombinate* unable to cover their variable costs.[28]

Wage increases at an average annual rate of 32 percent between 1991 and 1992 and 19 percent between 1992 and 1993 further compounded the problem. (See table 10.3.) By the third quarter of 1994, gross wages had been pushed up to nearly 80 percent of West German levels, but output per worker, including the self-employed, was still only 46 percent that in the West (most of the increase having been accomplished by laying off the least productive workers).[29] In the

---

[26] Following the precedent of the 1948 West German monetary reform, a sliding scale was applied to financial assets. Money was converted at one to one for small amounts and two to one for the balance; other financial claims were converted at two to one. Most money acquired in the year of unification was converted at three to one. The average conversion rate was 1.6 to one.

[27] Sinn and Sinn (1992), p. 64.

[28] Akerlof et al. (1991). The authors estimated that only 8.2 percent of industrial employees would have kept their jobs, given these wage increases, in the absence of subsidies.

[29] Siebert (1995), p. 6.

Table 10.3
Productivity trends in East Germany, 1992–2000 (Gross value added per employee, 1991 = 100)

	1992	1994	1996	1998	2000
All Sectors	125	156	168	175	183
Manufacturing	143	229	285	313	353
Construction	117	133	130	126	125
Trade, tourism, traffic	126	152	156	160	166
Finance, rent, and corporate services	100	112	122	127	130
Public and private services	108	120	122	122	122
Public administration, army, social security	119	130	135	142	NA
Education, health, others	104	116	117	115	NA

Source: von Hagen, Strauch, and Wolff (2002).

short run, loans from the Treuhand could keep loss-making enterprises running. But in the long run, unemployment was inevitable.

The decision to convert wages into deutschmarks at a parity of one to one was widely blamed for the collapse of output. The Bundesbank, for example, had advised in favor of converting wages at a ratio of two to one in order to limit the rise in labor costs and ensure the viability of firms in the East, and it was critical of the rate actually chosen. But its argument assumed that a different conversion rate would have made a difference for the subsequent evolution of labor costs. In fact, had wages started on 1 July 1990 at, say, 20 percent of West German levels instead of 40 percent, the unions presumably would have insisted on their immediate tripling, rather than a more "modest" increase of one-half, to bring them to the stated goal of 60 percent of West German levels. Given this goal, there is no reason to think that a different conversion rate would have produced a different outcome. The argument for the one-to-one conversion was simplicity and transparency. It introduced real money into the former East German economy. The argument against, that a different conversion rate could have somehow altered the evolution of real wages, held little water under the circumstances.[30]

[30] There was also some discussion of whether the very idea of monetary unification was a mistake—whether it might better have been put off for some time, perhaps for years. The

The danger that widespread unemployment might cause the residents of the East to move west in large numbers was headed off by social transfers and unemployment benefits. The West German insurance system was immediately extended to the East. Until 1994, when rates were scaled back modestly, the share of wages replaced by unemployment benefits was 68 percent for persons with children and 63 percent for persons without. In this situation, the fear that high costs might precipitate unemployment did little to discourage aggressive wage demands. As wages rose, unemployment benefits rose right along with them. And the bill was picked up by the federal government, which transferred resources to the new *Länder* to finance unemployment benefits and pensions for early retirees.[31]

These transfers were politically supportable because of the relative economic size of the two Germanys. The population of the pre-reunification GDR was less than one-third that of the FRG. Output per worker was similarly one-third. In economic terms, the GDR was thus less than one-tenth the size of the FRG. The FRG could raise living standards in the East by more than half by transferring a "mere" 5 percent of its national income to its new citizens in the form of unemployment relief, job-creation schemes, and other programs.[32] In addition, residents in the East had cheaper housing. They were reluctant to leave friends and family. Raising living standards by half was more than enough to avert the large-scale migration feared in the West. Net migration from the East to the West (including between the two parts of Berlin) fell from 169,000 in 1991 to 88,000 in 1992 and then to a low of 10,000 in 1997.[33]

---

exchange rate between the two German currencies could then have been allowed to float, and labor costs in eastern Germany could thus have floated down to competitive levels. But this was a purely hypothetical possibility, given the political circumstances of the time. The demand of East Germans for "real money" and more generally for first-class economic status could not be denied.

[31] From 1995, the new *Länder* were then integrated into the FRG's existing system of fiscal equalization, which regularly transferred resources from states with large tax bases to those with small ones.

[32] More than a decade later, in 2004, transfers from West to East Germany of eighty-three billion euros still accounted for 22 percent of East German consumption while costing "only" 4 percent of German GDP.

[33] Immigration then picked up again, reflecting the slowdown of growth in eastern Germany. By this time, it was in any case no longer the same kind of explosive social problem as in the immediate postunification years.

If this problem of higher labor costs was not enough, private investment was further discouraged by uncertainty about property rights. Many state enterprises had simply dumped their toxic wastes, and it was uncertain whether, when buying a site, an investor would also be acquiring the cleanup costs. Then there was uncertainty about whether properties in the East would eventually be returned to their earlier owners. The unification treaty made all property nationalized since the establishment of the GDR and still in government hands eligible for restitution. There was then pressure to extend coverage to property seized by the Nazis between 1933 and 1945. Only property expropriated by Soviet forces between 1945 and 1949 was free from uncertainty about the possibility of restitution, although it was still subject to the uncertain intentions of the Treuhand.

A clean solution would have been to give the former owners cash payments in lieu of property.[34] These could have been financed out of the FRG's revenues from sales of the properties themselves. Cash might not have satisfied those emotionally attached to particular properties, but by reducing uncertainty over property rights it would have helped to jump-start investment. In the event, uncertainty about restitution rendered potential buyers reluctant to undertake improvements, since the restitution law assigned to the original owner not just the real estate but also all capital improvements made subsequently. It left banks, uncertain of collateral value, reluctant to lend. Some old companies had been merged into *Kombinate*, creating multiple claimants to assets. Others had been transferred several times, first by the Nazis, then by the Soviet Union, and finally by the GDR. Land registers and title records were incomplete. Following reunification, more than 40,000 ownership claims on 17,000 enterprises were filed, and by mid-1992 only 4,700 were settled. Not surprisingly, nearly 40 percent of members surveyed by the Deutscher Industrie- und Handelskammertag, the leading industrial association, cited legal uncertainty as a deterrent to investing in the new *Länder*.[35]

[34] This was in fact proposed by the first freely elected GDR government in the spring of 1990.

[35] Dornbusch and Wolf (1994), p. 170. A law to remove impediments to privatization passed in March 1991 specified that the original owner could take physical possession only if he could guarantee continuation of the enterprise and adequate investment; otherwise he

The problem was exceptionally difficult because property had been nationalized more extensively in East Germany than elsewhere. There had been less reform in the 1980s, including less privatization, given the "more Stalinist than thou" attitude of the Honecker regime. The Treuhand thus owned roughly eight thousand firms and more than 40 percent of the land area of the GDR. All this complicated the task of the privatization authorities. But the Treuhand aggravated the problem through its reluctance to break up conglomerates, hesitancy to sell enterprises to foreigners, and insistence on employment guarantees.[36] It worsened the situation by injecting its own funds into enterprises that would have been better downsized or disbanded. In these and other ways it interfered in restructuring that was better done after privatization than before. It chose between potential buyers not according to price but on the basis of which bidder promised to maintain the enterprise and its original business. It insisted on selling enterprises for cash, not attempting to arrange joint ventures that would have made share issues a possibility. And, as noted earlier, it perversely refused to participate in wage negotiations even where it was the employer. Privatization may have been the hardest nut to crack, but collective efforts to crack it were especially inept in Germany.

All this would lead one to expect disappointing investment rates. But, in fact, by the middle of the 1990s aggregate investment rates had risen to an astounding 50 percent of the eastern states' GDP. Although some of this investment was stimulated by extensive subsidies and tax concessions, most of it reflected investment by the public sector. Governments, including those of the new *Länder*, accounted for two-thirds and more of the total. In virtually every city, antiquated water, sewer, and telephone systems were replaced. Airports and railway stations were renovated. In some places every road was repaved.

would receive financial compensation. This provided some reassurance to potential new investors, although it did not remove uncertainty about the identity of the original owner where this still existed.

[36] West German firms were invited to send members of their management teams to work with the Treuhand in formulating privatization plans, which goes a long way toward explaining why there were few if any sales to foreign buyers.

So long as it continued, all this investment lent considerable stimulus to activity, employment, and growth. But high-return public investment projects, such as replacing the telephone network, could be undertaken only once. And, in the course of undertaking them, the new *Länder* incurred heavy debts. Inevitably, public investment rates had to fall, as they began doing in 1997. And as the stimulus from public investment tailed off, growth tailed off as well.

Aware that public investment was winding down, the authorities now sought to encourage private investment by offering even more extensive investment subsidies, which in some cases actually turned the cost of capital negative. Sinn (2000) argues that this may have encouraged uneconomical investment decisions that saddled the eastern *Länder* with poorly allocated capital stocks that hindered the maintenance of rapid growth in subsequent years. Von Hagen, Strauch, and Wolff (2002) similarly argue that eastern Germany would have been better off had skill-intensive production been allowed to flourish in lieu of the actual strategy of fostering capital intensity.

Growth not only slowed relative to the preceding years but now fell even below the modest levels of Germany's West. Growth rates of less than 2 percent became the norm. Incomes net of taxes leveled out at about 80 percent of western levels.[37] Unemployment stabilized at 18 percent, more than twice the already-high West German rate. The failure of living standards in what had been the GDR to converge toward those in the economies with which it was now integrated was the most troubling aspect of the German transition. The FRG itself had converged strongly toward the European norm from the 1950s. Ireland and other countries of the European periphery had converged strongly following their accession to the EU. Other more successful transition economies such as Poland now grew at two to three times the German rate, steadily closing the gap vis-à-vis Western Europe. But not the former GDR. The extension of restrictive labor legislation and burdensome social programs to the

---

[37] According to figures cited in Sinn (2000), p. 3. Other experts basing their calculations on different methodologies and sources offer slightly lower values for this ratio, but the basic implication remains the same.

new *Länder* and the high level of labor costs insisted on by Germany's powerful unions explain this underperformance. In terms of growth, the region that had once comprised the GDR now behaved more like a long-established German state than a transition economy. Indeed, income and productivity differentials of 20 percent, like that which now prevailed between the East and West of Germany, had not been uncommon among the long-established states of the FRG.[38] These similarities between the poorer parts of the former West Germany and the region that had once been the GDR suggest that the obstacles to faster growth in this region now had less to do with the legacies of communism than with the same handicaps—inflexible labor markets and high nonwage costs—from which the rest of the FRG also suffered.

Normalization and Integration

Geography made Western and Eastern Europe natural trading partners, as they had been before 1945. The result now was an immediate increase in trade between the two halves of the continent. Geography also made the transition economies natural destinations for investment by Western European multinationals seeking a low-cost production platform. The prospect of EU membership reinforced these effects by promising the Central and Eastern European economies access to the markets of the West. The residents of the former Soviet bloc, for their part, saw EU membership as signifying that they were once more citizens of Europe. They knew that the EU had operated as an engine of convergence in Ireland and the Iberian peninsula. By encouraging trade and foreign investment, membership had helped the European periphery to begin closing the per capita income gap. There was no reason to doubt that the gap could not be similarly closed by Eastern Europe. And Western European

---

[38] Or between Italy's North and South. Indeed, such differentials did not elicit intense dissatisfaction among residents in the East, since with the lower cost of housing and to a lesser extent other nontradables the difference in purchasing power was actually closer to 10 percent.

leaders saw EU accession as encouraging reform and guarding against backsliding.

But it was not yet clear which candidate countries shared the core values of the EU. Not all of them rated highly in terms of respect for civil and minority rights, media freedom, control of corruption, and property rights protection. In part their slow progress reflected the difficulty of quickly putting in place the institutions of constitutional liberalism after two generations of authoritarianism.

Tensions were heightened by the large labor-cost gap between prospective and incumbent members. At the time of the southern enlargement, wage costs in Greece, Portugal, and Spain had been about half the levels prevailing in the members of the EC. Now wages in the prospective accession economies were barely one-tenth of Western European levels. If efficiency and labor productivity picked up, substantial amounts of manufacturing might migrate east in search of lower labor costs. Or a sizable fraction of Poland's forty million citizens might move west in search of higher wages, creating political strains.[39] Large income differentials implied substantial transfers from West to East through the operation of the Structural and Regional Funds. In turn this might strain the EU budget and fuel resentment in Western European regions whose relative poverty no longer qualified them for transfers.

The EU responded constructively with trade concessions, which sped up the reorientation of Eastern Europe's production and trade, and with the Copenhagen criteria, which defined clear benchmarks for accession. Soon after establishing diplomatic relations, it removed import quotas on a number of products and extended the Generalized System of Preferences to the region. It signed commercial treaties with Czechoslovakia, Hungary, and Poland, leading to the Europe Agreements between these countries and the EC. The agreements with these three countries were signed in December 1991 and extended to the other Central and Eastern European coun-

---

[39] Geographic differences pointed in the same direction. Neither Greece nor Portugal shared a common border with the EC-9, unlike Poland, which is directly contiguous with Germany. Indeed, half of the Central and Eastern European countries share a common border with Austria, Germany, or Italy.

tries (CEECs) shortly thereafter.[40] They involved establishing a free trade area that excluded sensitive sectors. The EU abolished most quantitative restrictions on imports from the CEEC-10 excepting only coal, textiles, and agricultural products. It halved most tariffs on industrial imports from the CEEC-10 before eliminating them at the beginning of 1997.[41]

The volume of exports from the EU-15 to the CEEC-10 (the eight CEECs that ultimately gained EU membership in 2004 plus Bulgaria and Romania) quadrupled in the course of the 1990s. EU-15 imports from the CEEC-10 tripled over the same period, rising at an annual rate of more than 12 percent.[42] (See table 10.4.) By the end of the 1990s, trade with the EU represented more than half the foreign trade of the CEEC-10. This transformation was all the more remarkable given that the EU was slow to liberalize trade in the products of sensitive sectors (agriculture, chemicals, coal, iron and steel, textiles, footwear, furniture, and glass) that accounted for one-third to one-half of Eastern European exports to Western Europe. Its reluctance rendered some early observers pessimistic about the impact of the Europe Agreements.[43] Against this backdrop, the rapid rise of EU imports from Eastern Europe is striking.

The result was a considerable shift in the composition of Eastern Europe's exports. The initial pattern was characterized by horizontal specialization: the EU sold high-quality, technologically sophisticated products, including capital goods, to Eastern Europe, in return for steel, chemicals, and other intermediate products. With time, vertical integration increased. Western European companies ex-

[40] The Czech and Slovak Republics had to renegotiate their agreements following their split.

[41] The CEEC-10 agreed to do the same by 2002. The EU similarly cut import levies and tariffs on agricultural exports from Eastern Europe while still subjecting these goods to import quotas. For more on this, see the discussion later in this chapter.

[42] Again, expressed in volume terms. Predictably, agricultural exports lagged behind. Not only were these still governed by quotas, but there was often a mismatch between the preferences (favorable quotas) granted by the EU and the product mix that Eastern European farmers were able to provide. Thus, the EU granted Hungary larger quotas for cheese and Poland larger quotas for sausage than domestic producers could supply.

[43] See, for example, Wang and Winters (1991).

TABLE 10.4
Trade between CEEC-10 and EU-15

	1992	1993	1994	1995	1996	1997	1998	1999
I. CEEC-10 exports to EU-15 as a percentage of total exports								
Poland	—	—	63.0	70.0	66.3	64.2	68.3	70.5
Romania	—	—	48.0	54.1	56.5	56.6	64.5	65.5
CEEC-8	—	—	42.7	55.4	56.5	58.4	63.6	68.2
CEEC-10	—	—	48.0	58.8	58.9	59.7	64.8	68.6
II. CEEC-10 imports from EU-15 as a percentage of total imports								
Poland	—	—	58.0	64.6	63.9	63.8	65.9	64.9
Romania	—	—	46.0	50.5	52.3	52.5	57.7	60.4
CEEC-8	—	—	41.5	55.9	56.6	57.4	60.6	61.3
CEEC-10	—	—	46.1	57.6	58.3	59.0	62.0	62.3
III. EU-15 exports to CEEC-10 as a percentage of EU-15 exports to extra-EU-15								
Poland	1.9	2.1	2.0	2.7	3.2	3.5	3.8	3.8
Romania	0.4	0.5	0.5	0.7	0.7	0.7	0.9	0.8
CEEC-8	1.7	4.3	4.2	6.0	6.3	6.7	7.6	7.7
CEEC-10	4.0	6.9	6.7	9.3	10.2	10.9	12.3	12.3
IV. EU-15 imports from CEEC-10 as a percentage of EU-15 imports from extra-EU-15								
Poland	1.5	1.6	1.7	2.2	2.1	2.1	2.3	2.3
Romania	0.3	0.3	0.5	0.6	0.6	0.7	0.7	0.7
CEEC-8	1.6	3.6	3.7	5.3	5.4	5.7	6.6	6.8
CEEC-10	3.4	5.5	5.8	8.1	8.1	8.5	9.6	9.8

Source: European Commission (2001).

ported components for telecommunications equipment and motor vehicles to Eastern Europe, where they were assembled and shipped back to the West.

Associated with this transformation was extensive foreign direct investment (FDI), two-thirds of which originated in the EU. Between 1995 and 1999 the CEEC-10 received inflows averaging slightly more than 4 percent of their collective GDP. In 2000–2003 these inflows rose to 6 percent of GDP.[44] The leading FDI recipients

[44] Inflows into Central and Eastern Europe were $27.5 billion in 2000, $26.4 billion in 2001, $31.2 billion in 2002, and $21.0 billion in 2003.

in per capita terms were the Czech Republic, Estonia, Hungary, and, toward the end of the period, Slovakia. FDI flows were attracted by infrastructure privatization, for example the privatization of tele-communications. They were attracted by low labor costs in manu-facturing industries such as textiles, clothing, electrical machinery, and motor vehicles.

The criteria laid down in 1993 by the European Council in Copenhagen provided incentives for reform by specifying the conditions that had to be met in order to qualify for EU member-ship. Some of these were political (the existence of institutions guaranteeing democracy, the rule of law, human rights, and respect for and protection of minorities), while others were economic (the existence of a functioning market economy and the ability to cope with the competitive pressures and market forces that would be felt as a result of membership in the Union). By the end of 1995, ten CEECs had applied for membership.[45] Over the next two years the European Commission prepared and released opinions regarding their readiness and followed them with a series of annual evalua-tions. These reports provided a basis for the Council's assessment of the applicants' requests for membership. Countries were evaluated with respect to their implementation of the provisions of the major human rights conventions. They were graded with respect to the extent of price liberalization, the security of property rights, and macroeconomic stability. In addition, the Commission evaluated the extent to which they had adopted and were effectively applying the twenty-nine chapters of the *acquis communautaire* (the accumu-lated body of EU law).

This process, based on objective criteria and independent evalu-ations, gave the incumbents little opportunity to renege on the commitment to admit new members. By eliminating ambiguity about the steps needed to gain membership, it maximized the incentive for the applicants to undertake reforms. It created a "tran-sition tournament" in which CEEC governments competed with

---

[45] The eight CEECs that ultimately gained EU membership in 2004 plus Bulgaria and Romania.

one another in order to receive the highest rating from the European Commission.[46]

Eastern enlargement also could have been an opportunity for the EU to undertake its own reforms. The fifteen incumbent member states might have restructured their labor markets in preparation for low-wage competition. They might have reduced taxes on corporate income to provide corporations with positive incentives to continue producing in the West. They might have reformed the Common Agricultural Policy (CAP) in anticipation of millions of additional Eastern European farmers. They might have rationalized the Structural and Regional Funds to more efficiently address the problems of Europe's poorest regions.

There was some movement in these directions. The German chancellor Gerhard Schröder's Agenda 2010 of labor-market reforms was motivated, in part, by the specter of German manufacturing moving east if steps were not taken to reduce labor costs.[47] Austria reduced its corporate tax rates in response to the adoption of flat taxes in the countries immediately to its east. The EU agricultural commissioner Franz Fischler used the prospect of millions of additional farmers to push for CAP reform. But overall this was an opportunity missed. The EU addressed the threat of low-wage competition mainly by insisting on a transitional period of seven years during which freedom to migrate from the new to the incumbent member states was limited. In 2005, it rejected a services directive that would have made it easier for workers from Eastern Europe to be employed in service sectors in the West. It dealt with pressure on the EU budget from agricultural subsidies and price supports by limiting their extension to the new member states rather than by phasing them out in the old ones.[48]

[46] In the words of Roland (2001).

[47] On the 2010 Agenda, see chapter 12.

[48] Subsidies for farmers in the new member states were phased in over ten years, starting at 25 percent of the EU rate in 2004 and then rising to 30 percent in 2005 and 35 percent in 2006. Governments were permitted to top up these payments using their own resources. Discrimination was made easier by linking payments to farm incomes, which were lower in the East. Arguably, it would have been more difficult to apply this differential treatment to Eastern European farmers had payments still been based on the level of production, since a bushel of wheat is a bushel of wheat, regardless of where it is grown. In this sense, enlargement

The EU deserves enormous credit for how it brought the transition economies into Europe. The Europe Agreements, notwithstanding their limitations, offered access to Western European markets and helped to facilitate the reorientation of trade. The prize of EU membership reinforced the commitment to reform. By 2002, eight of what had formerly been called "transition economies" (Hungary, Poland, the Czech Republic, Slovakia, Slovenia, Estonia, Latvia, and Lithuania) had met the political, economic, and institutional criteria set down by the EU as conditions for membership. Joining the EU in 2004 symbolized their "return to Europe." It was proof that they were once more normal European countries.

---

played a role in the CAP reforms of 2003, which moved from payments based on the current level of production to direct income payments fixed on the basis of 2000–2002 production and outlays, conditional on farmers' efforts to upgrade their land's environmental condition. In addition, direct payments to the largest farms were reduced with the differential transferred to rural development programs.

- ELEVEN -

INTEGRATION AND ADJUSTMENT

The 1980s was not an obvious time for reinvigorating Europe's integrationist project. The continent was just beginning to emerge from its most serious recession in a half century, a downturn precipitated by intense inflationary pressures and the harsh measures taken to contain them. Even after recovery commenced, Western European unemployment showed little tendency to come down.[1] Countries such as Denmark and Ireland suffered not only chronic unemployment but also severe fiscal imbalances. France experienced an extended bout of fiscal and financial turmoil, and its new socialist government contemplated, however briefly, withdrawing from the European Community.[2] Europe stagnated while the United States and Japan surged ahead, the continent losing market share in automobiles, electronics, and a variety of other industries.[3] None of this obviously presaged a renewal of integrationist effort, much less the Single Market Program of 1986.

That deeper integration was seen as a tonic for these ills is less surprising when one notes how far the EC had come. The Commission, the Court of Justice, and the Parliament were firmly established. The customs union was complete. The Common Agricultural Policy was a fait accompli. The EC's first enlargement, incorporating Denmark, Ireland, and the United Kingdom, had been successfully completed, and the second enlargement—to in-

---

[1] In the first half of the 1980s, it averaged an alarming 8 percent.
[2] See "The EMS in Operation" in chapter 9.
[3] See Buigues and Goybet (1989) and Parsons (2003).

clude Greece, Portugal, and Spain—was in sight. The European Monetary System (EMS), established in 1979, was an accomplished fact. Although it had still been necessary to realign currencies (some more frequently than others), no country was forced to terminate its participation in the system in the first half of the 1980s, in contrast with experience with the Snake in the 1970s.

A consequence of these efforts was more extensive interdependence. As a result of the customs union, the Snake, and the EMS, the share of Western Europe's exports destined for other Western European countries rose from 56 percent at the end of the 1950s to 67 percent in 1980. For the first six countries to join the EC, the increase was from 35 to 56 percent, an even larger proportionate rise. Corporations such as Unilever and Philips maintained production facilities and sourced inputs in multiple European countries. Responding to these growing trade linkages, cross-border capital flows grew even more quickly, overwhelming the efforts of governments and central banks to contain them. All this made withdrawing from the EC a bridge too far for European governments of all stripes. It meant that when the status quo proved untenable, the dominant response was to push ahead with deeper integration.

Notwithstanding their differences, for governments such as those of France and Britain this suggested using the institutions of the EC to advance their national agendas. In some cases doing so meant delegating to the Commission and the Court of Justice responsibility for implementing painful economic reforms that governments were reluctant to assume on their own. In others it meant using the EC as the platform for a more activist approach to economic development—that is, for pursuing industrial policy at the European level. Neither of these conflicting visions carried the day. But they combined in the 1980s to lend new impetus to the process of European integration.

The Single Market

The founding document of the Single Market Program was a white paper authored by a transnational team of experts chaired by the British civil servant Arthur Cockfield and issued by the Commission

in 1985.[4] The Cockfield Report summarized both prevailing dissatisfaction with Europe's economy and the progress of the integrationist
project. Reinvigorating growth and accelerating the integration process were portrayed as synonymous. The solution to the prevailing
malaise thus lay in an initiative to create a single market free not
just of internal tariffs (that having been achieved by the Common
Market) but also of regulatory barriers to the movement of goods
and services. Unfortunately, economic and integrationist momentum had been lost as each member state "endeavored to protect what
was in its short term interests—not only against third countries but
against fellow member states as well."[5] The EC had become bogged
down in endless negotiations over contributions to its budget and
adjustments to the Common Agricultural Policy. The solution was
to streamline decision making within the EC so that priority could
be given to the collective rather than the national interest.

The white paper led to the convening of an intergovernmental
conference to contemplate changes in existing treaties. The result
was the Single European Act (SEA), agreed to in 1986, which came
into force in 1987. The SEA formalized the commitment to establish
a single market free of barriers to the movement of goods and factors
of production. The aspiration was less than revolutionary, these
same freedoms having been enumerated in the Treaty of Rome. The
difference now was that that the goal came with a deadline and, by
implication, a commitment by governments.

The SEA sought to reorganize EC institutions and procedures
to achieve these ends. It authorized greater use of qualified majority
voting in the Council, subject to a range of exceptions and qualifications in the tradition of the Luxembourg Compromise. It enhanced political accountability by establishing a so-called cooperation procedure empowering the Parliament, previously little more
than a listening institution, to reject regulations proposed by the
Council.[6]

---

[4] See European Commission (1985).

[5] European Commission (1985), p. 5.

[6] Proposed regulations then came into effect only if the Council adopted them unani-
mously. The Parliament was also empowered to offer amendments to the proposed legislation,
which, if approved by the Commission, were then referred back to the Council. These reforms
followed the first direct elections for the Parliament, which had occurred in 1979.

In addition, the SEA provided for expansion of the Structural Funds, the EC's program for funding of infrastructure investment in its poorer member states. Ireland, Spain, Portugal, and Greece feared for their ability to hold their own against stronger Northern European competitors in a single market. The expansion of Structural Fund transfers sought to enhance their competitiveness by improving their infrastructure. At a minimum it offered them side payments for agreeing to proceed with the Single Market Program.

Finally, the SEA emphasized the need for cooperation in the conduct of economic and monetary policies. Its preamble referred to the "progressive realization" of monetary union, rhetoric sufficiently ambiguous to satisfy both the advocates of monetary union and its opponents, notably the British prime minister Margaret Thatcher.

As a technical program the SEA was unremarkable. More striking was the development of the political will to push it through. This was facilitated by the presence of a powerful personality in Brussels, the new Commission president Jacques Delors. In addition there was the development of business support, notably among high-tech firms brought together by Viscount Etienne Davignon, the commissioner for the internal market.[7] There was also a fortuitous conjuncture of interests among the principal national participants. In particular, Germany, emerging finally from the shadows of World War II, aspired to a more prominent foreign-policy role. Chancellor Helmut Kohl and his foreign minister, Hans-Dietrich Genscher, recognized that their country could best acquire this in the context of a European foreign policy, since a unilateralist German policy, especially one advanced by a German army, was still precluded by the legacy of World War II. Kohl, Genscher, and others thus saw renewed integration as facilitating their pursuit of this larger goal.

German officials insisted that this relaunching of Europe include an economic component. German industry, being in a secure com-

---

[7] One of these CEOs, Wisse Dekker of Philips, proposed a "Europe 1990" program for reforming fiscal, commercial, technical, and government procurement policies, several aspects of which found their way into the 1985 white paper. Fligstein and Brantley (1995), p. 123.

petitive position (since, for the moment, the dollar was strong), was favorably inclined toward economic liberalization, aside from a few older industries such as coal mining and shipbuilding. The Kohl government had concerns about the efficiency effects of regulation in sectors such as transportation, telecommunications, and insurance and saw the SEA as a lever for liberalizing these markets. Thus, the German telecommunications reform commission could shift the onus for difficult measures onto EC officials, helping to overcome opposition to deregulation from the Bundespost and the unions.[8]

The French had some sympathy for these German ambitions. The French president François Mitterrand and Delors, mindful of France's unhappy recent experience with exchange-rate management, saw monetary integration as a potential solution to these problems. They recognized the need to ally with their German neighbors in order to acquire foreign-policy independence from the United States. The Socialists were supporters of political integration on the traditional grounds that this was a mechanism for locking Germany into Europe, which was increasingly important now that Germany threatened to leave France behind economically and had become more assertive in its *Ostpolitik*. Support for strong EC institutions also reflected French confidence, inherited from Monnet's time, that France would succeed in controlling the EC's bureaucracy.

In the United Kingdom, the private sector's export orientation allied with Margaret Thatcher's free-market beliefs to foster support for a European market free of regulatory barriers. In 1984, even before the group charged with drafting the white paper was convened by Lord Cockfield, Thatcher's government proposed an agenda for removing nontariff barriers to intra-EC trade. Britain's comparative advantage in the provision of financial services, reinforced by the positive effects of the deregulation of U.K. financial services underway since 1979, meant that the private sector was supportive of measures that might extend the removal of trade barriers from merchandise to banking and insurance. For a country that had seen industry contract rapidly in the first half of the 1980s, financial services held

---

[8] Moravcsik (1998), p. 330.

out hope for the future. For Thatcher and her followers, the Single Market Program offered U.K.-style liberalization on a European scale. It promised to put to rest once and for all the danger that the constraints of EC membership might force Britain to backtrack on liberalizing measures. Thatcher's government realized that some extension of qualified majority voting in the Council might be needed to push through significant liberalization and worried that this could also be used to advance a European social agenda and foreign-policy initiatives that it regarded as less congenial. In the end it accepted these risks as the price to be paid.

Britain was only the most obvious place where such attitudes were fostered by pressures for economic and financial liberalization. Markets had long since recovered from World War II. Securities markets in particular had grown more sophisticated and difficult to control. The end of extensive growth made tight financial regulation less appealing, while the uncertainties of an innovation-based economy made it more difficult for bureaucrats to efficiently guide the allocation of financial resources, leaving the market as the logical alternative. European integration, though mainly limited to trade in merchandise, had already begun to spill over to other areas, making attempts to segment national financial markets more difficult and distorting. It complicated efforts to pursue ambitious macroeconomic and regulatory initiatives in one country, as France had learned, since capital could now exit when confronted with low interest rates, high taxes, or excessive regulation.

All this made it more difficult for governments to resist the pressure for liberalization. In France, the Barre government had already acknowledged this in the second half of the 1970s when it offered tax incentives for the development of the stock market and authorized the creation of mutual funds. The Mitterrand experiment of 1981–1983 was then a graphic illustration of the futility of attempting to resist market forces. Not to liberalize financial services meant ceding this high ground to the United States and the United Kingdom. In 1983, Mitterrand's new minister of industry, Laurent Fabius, therefore relaxed regulations limiting the scope for firms to borrow on securities markets. When Fabius went on to form his own government, his finance minister, Pierre Bérégovoy, removed controls on bank interest rates, eliminated ceilings on bank lending, and authorized the creation of derivatives markets. If one factor was pivotal in the decision to proceed with the Single Market Program, it was the shift of the French Socialists from *régulation* (defined broadly as the interventionist approach to economic development) to market liberalization.

As in the case of German telecommunications reform, French governments saw pursuing domestic reforms in the context of EC liberalization as politically legitimating and also as a way of shifting responsibility for painful actions. To be sure, in some areas—specialty food products for example—there was no need for blame shifting; French exporters gained significantly from EC legislation. Other French producers remained committed to an industrial-policy agenda but saw government intervention in the allocation of resources as feasible only if policy was formulated at the EC level. Jacques Delors, the former finance minister who became president of the European Commission in 1985, was himself an advocate of a more extensive European technology policy, a European social policy, and—given his own unhappy experience with national exchange-rate management—a European monetary policy.

Thus, with the German, French, and British governments on board, reflecting their distinct if ultimately compatible objectives, the Single Market Program could proceed.

Integration in Practice

Creating a true single market required not simply abolishing border formalities but also removing or harmonizing a range of restrictive national regulations. A key tool was mutual recognition, which required member states to accept the regulations and standards of other EU countries as equivalent to their own and allowed activities lawful in one member state to be pursued throughout the EC. The European Court of Justice promulgated this principle in its *Cassis de Dijon* decision in 1979. A German firm had been denied permission to import Cassis de Dijon liquor, whose particular alcohol content violated certain provisions of German legislation. The Court now overturned the German regulation, determining that food products produced in one member state should be permitted to circulate throughout the EC.

In doing so, the jurists built on earlier discussions of the expediency of mutual recognition that stretched back to the Treaty of Rome.[9] The Commission then appealed to this body of case law, urging that the principle of mutual recognition be generalized to overcome resistance to regulatory harmonization. In 1985 it issued a communiqué titled "Completion of the Internal Market: Community Legislation on Foodstuffs," arguing that liberalization could be achieved by a series of framework directives issued by the Commission and accepted by the Council setting out Community-wide minima for national standards and legislation in essential areas such as additives, labeling, nutritional supplements, and hygiene—and through mutual recognition by the member states of the regulations and laws adopted by their partners in the EC.

Other directives specified rules for government procurement tenders with the goal of reducing bias toward domestic producers and mandated the mutual recognition of professional credentials. By the second half of the 1990s, governments were awarding 10 percent of the value of public contracts to bidders from other member states. That this number was not higher reflected the fact that much government procurement involved not just goods but also services. In some cases, those services were provided by bodies still under public ownership, notably public utilities. In others, efficiency arguments and tradition strengthened belief in the efficacy of natural monopoly and justified the maintenance of barriers to entry by competing suppliers, foreign as well as domestic. National associations continued to regulate the diplomas and professional qualifications of service providers in different ways. One can imagine good

[9] And on more recent proposals from Ralf Dahrendorf, a former member of the Commission, to elaborate this approach.

reasons why professional associations in some member states were reluctant to recognize the credentials of, say, doctors trained and licensed in others, but in other cases the rationale was less defensible. In 1995 the Commission issued an opinion that French unwillingness to recognize ski instructor diplomas issued in other member states violated EC law. Although the French government agreed to comply, French ski resorts continued to defy the directive by hiring only their own nationals.

The Commission approached this problem sector by sector, relying mainly on its authority to make competition policy—logically enough, since a single market can have only a single competition policy.[10] Starting in 1990 it issued regulations providing for the control of mergers under the authority of the commissioner for competition. It sought to restrain the tendency for member states to grant legal monopolies in telecommunications, transportation, postal services, gas, and electricity. It challenged the premise that legal monopoly was necessary to ensure the efficient provision of such services, leading to the relaxation of entry barriers and growing cross-border competition. Throughout, the Commission did not attempt to establish pan-European regulations but instead specified standards for national regulators, generally in the form of licensing and pricing policies.[11] And when governments extended state aid to national champions and large employers, the Commission claimed the power to force its reimbursement where such aid was corrosive of competition.[12]

Cross-border competition in services was the sticking point. In insurance and business services, member states continued to require foreign firms seeking to establish subsidiaries to undergo lengthy, complex, and sometimes discriminatory authorization procedures. In

[10] This power was embedded in Articles 85–94 of the Treaty of Rome, but enforcement was significantly tightened as a result of the Single Market Program.

[11] An exception was food safety, where the mad cow and dioxin crises—and the resulting public outcry—led to a white paper on food safety in 2000 and to establishment of the European Food Safety Authority.

[12] Although its decisions continued to be disputed and resisted by national governments and the recipients of their largess.

2005 the Commission tried again with a services directive that would have streamlined authorization procedures and, more controversially, granted companies the right to provide services in all member states so long as they followed the laws of their home states. Again its initiative was tabled in response to opposition from high-income countries.

Creating a single market in financial services of course entailed eliminating capital controls. This had been acknowledged in 1988 with the acceptance of an EC directive mandating the removal of controls on the cross-border transfer of financial assets by 1 June 1990. EU member states with shaky finances were authorized to proceed more slowly, and there was also the option of temporarily reimposing controls in the event of financial difficulties. Still, this aspect of the creation of the internal market proceeded rapidly.

The removal of capital controls increased the mobility of the tax base, applying pressure for reductions in rates of capital taxation. To limit the danger that high taxes would cause capital to migrate abroad, member states with large, proactive public sectors pushed for tax harmonization at the EU level. Countries such as the United Kingdom that saw the single market as a mechanism for forcing corporate and personal tax rates down to more reasonable levels predictably resisted this call.[13]

Starting in 1982 the EC initiated a number of programs to promote the development and adoption of new technologies, programs with evocative names such as *Esprit* and *Eureka*. It organized research programs under whose auspices the Commission cofinanced projects with multiple European partners. These were modest attempts to push forward the industrial-policy strand of the integrationist project. Overall, however, this aspect of the agenda languished. There existed general agreement, notwithstanding the diversity of ideological orientations, that the creation of a single

---

[13] They succeeded in blocking proposals for tax harmonization owing to the requirement of unanimity in the Council. The most that was achieved by the proponents of tax harmonization was agreement in the Council on a code of conduct for business taxation in 1997 and promulgation of a list of harmful tax practices, mostly related to state aid in violation of single market rules, in 1999.

market would enable producers to better exploit economies of scale and scope in the manner of their American competitors. More than 90 percent of leading European corporate executives saw the fragmentation of the European market as a barrier to efficiency, according to surveys conducted in the mid-1980s.[14] But there was no analogous consensus around government efforts to direct the allocation of resources, whether for research and development or more generally.

The creation a single market in financial services further frustrated governments' industrial-policy ambitions. Integrating the market in financial services meant removing regulatory barriers hindering the entry of foreign banks into domestic markets. It meant relaxing restrictive financial regulation generally. For nearly four decades, governments had used directed credit to advance their industrial-policy agendas. Not only was the financial sector now suddenly dominated by privatized banks operating at arm's length from the authorities, but also domestic intermediaries competed with foreign institutions, limiting the ability of officials to insist on anything that might undercut profitability. An unintended consequence of the SEA—unintended from the point of view of the advocates of industrial policy, at least—was thus to eliminate the planners' traditional levers.

Increasingly, then, European integration came to be identified with liberalization. This strand of the integrationist agenda was advanced by the Commission, which perceived itself as an agent of deregulation. The Commission had the advantage being able to issue directives, subject to checks and balances such as acceptance of its decisions by the Council. In contrast, industrial-policy initiatives required intergovernmental agreements in which member states committed to coordinate their policies. Sometimes they required unanimity. Often implementation necessitated changes in national law. This intergovernmental approach was necessarily more time-consuming and difficult to advance.

---

[14] Moravcsik (1998), p. 318.

From the Delors Report to the
Maastricht Treaty

The second half of the 1980s was a period of global expansion. This buoyancy was conducive to liberalization; adjustment was easier to accept when incomes and productivity were rising. The resulting progress allowed EC officials to declare on 1 January 1993 that their effort to establish a single market was complete. There had been significant price convergence within the EC. Although identical goods and services still did not command the same prices throughout the EC, price differentials had narrowed. The share of intra-EC imports in the apparent consumption of processed products by residents of the EC rose further from 22.6 percent in 1986 to 25.0 percent in 1992.[15] A more integrated European market led to the rationalization and consolidation of industries previously fragmented along national lines. It made it attractive for extra-European producers to seek a foothold in the European market. The EU attracted 21 percent of Japanese FDI outflows in the late 1980s, up from 17 percent in the middle of the decade. The proportion of U.S. FDI destined for Europe rose from 39 to 45 percent, while intra-EU FDI as a share of total EU FDI outflows rose from 31 to 51 percent.[16]

These efforts to complete the single market also lent momentum to the larger European project. Prominent among its aspects was monetary integration, which came to the fore in 1988. By this time already one-tenth of the legislation required for the single market was on the statute books. And there were a number of connections running from the single market to a single currency. Inevitably, price comparisons were complicated by the need to convert foreign prices into domestic currency, thereby diminishing the intensity of the competition that was one of the objectives of the program's architects. There was at least a vague awareness that removing capital controls implied the need to move on from the EMS of the 1980s to deeper monetary integration. A directive mandating the liberal-

[15] Sapir (1992), p. 1499.
[16] See Dunning (1997a, 1997b).

ization of capital movements was scheduled to enter into force on 1 July 1990, at which point capital controls would disappear.[17] Controls had given governments limited room to run different monetary policies. They had provided the insulation from market pressures necessary to arrange orderly realignments. Now, with the relaxation of controls, even discussing realignment was riskier. If investors got wind that such discussions were underway, they were free to buy or sell the currencies in question in advance of the fact. There were no limits on how much they could buy and sell, and the costs of such transactions were minimal. A 10 percent devaluation expected to occur within a month offered an annualized return on investment of more than 300 percent. Since it was clear which countries had problems of chronic inflation and inadequate competitiveness, speculating in currencies was a one-way bet.

As a result, it became risky even to contemplate realigning EMS parities. Whereas realignments had occurred on average every nine months in the first seven years of the EMS, there were no more realignments after early 1987.

In some circles the greater difficulty of organizing orderly realignments was dismissed as a nonproblem. In this self-congratulatory view, the convergence of economic conditions and greater flexibility resulting from the single market had rendered realignments superfluous. Alternatively, some observers saw the difficulty of realigning under these new circumstances as exaggerated. Still others saw the new system as dangerously rigid, fragile, and crisis-prone.[18] The implication—again, one that was not often clearly drawn—was that it was necessary to replace separate national currencies with a single European currency before the EMS fell apart, perhaps dragging down the single market in its wake.

As had been the case with the single market, agreement between France and Germany was necessary to lend momentum to this initiative. French dissatisfaction with the prevailing state of

[17] Subject to temporary derogations for certain member states with shaky finances, as explained earlier.

[18] For contemporary hints in this direction (this being the view that was ultimately proven correct), see Padoa-Schioppa et al. (1987) and Giavazzi and Spaventa (1990).

affairs was rife. Not only had there been the embarrassing devaluations of 1981, 1982, and 1983, but it was again necessary to lower the franc's central rate in April 1986 and January 1987. In each case, following the strategy employed in 1983, devaluation had been dressed up as a general realignment of EMS currencies; the Belgian franc, Danish krone, Irish pound, and Italian lira had also been adjusted downward. More specifically, they were adjusted downward against the German deutschmark, now the undisputed strong currency of the system.[19] This meant that the Bundesbank set the tone for monetary policy throughout Europe. Although academic studies differ in their conclusions of how freely Germany led and how strictly other EMS countries were required to follow, there is no question that the Bundesbank was less tightly constrained than its EMS partners. Inflation in Germany was low, and the deutschmark had a tendency to appreciate. In the absence of capital controls, other European central banks were forced to follow the Bundesbank's lead to prevent their exchange rates from depreciating excessively.[20]

To French officials, this meant that their country unfairly bore a disproportionate share of the adjustment burden. Thus, when the dollar depreciated following the Plaza Agreement of September 1985, all the pressure was felt by currencies such as the franc—this despite their having done nothing, at least recently, to attract this unwanted attention. In 1986, Jacques Chirac, the head of the newly formed center-right coalition (the Socialists having lost ground in the elections of the previous spring), attacked the Bundesbank for raising money market rates and failing to acknowledge its responsibility for the EMS. All the power resided with Germany, it seemed, while all the risks and embarrassment were felt by other countries.

This asymmetry grated against the cooperative spirit of the EMS. It was galling for those whose memories extended back to 1969, when France had been forced to accept an embarrassing deval-

[19] After 1983, the Dutch guilder moved together with the deutschmark.
[20] On this academic debate see, for example, Fratianni and von Hagen (1990).

uation after the German government had refused to revalue.[21] French officials now saw deeper integration as a device for restoring their government's room to maneuver. They had hoped that joining the single market and the EMS would create a collective policy space within which France's industrial- and monetary-policy goals might be pursued, if not unilaterally then jointly with the other members of the EC.

This hope, and especially the component involving a more expansionary thrust for macroeconomic policies, was now frustrated by German dominance of the EMS. The Basle-Nyborg Agreement of 1987, a modest reform of EMS arrangements, changed nothing.[22] As a frustrated Edouard Balladur, France's finance minister, put it in a memorandum to his ECOFIN Council colleagues in early 1988,

> ultimately it is the central bank whose currency is at the lower end of the permitted range which has to bear the cost. However, it is not necessarily the currency at the lower end of the range which is the source of the tension. The discipline imposed by the exchange-rate mechanism may, for its part, have good effects when it serves to put a constraint on economic and monetary policies which are insufficiently rigorous. [But] it produces an abnormal situation when its effect is to exempt any countries whose policies are too restrictive from the necessary adjustment. Thus the fact that some countries have piled up current account surpluses for several years equal to between 2 and 3 percent of their GDPs constitutes a grave anomaly. This asymmetry

---

[21] See "The French Crisis and the German Response" in chapter 8.

[22] Previously, the Very-Short-Term Financing Facility (VSTF) of the EMS could be drawn on only when a currency fell to its lower intervention margin. The French now argued that limiting intervention to the point when a currency fell to the limit of its fluctuation band did more to excite extrapolative expectations than restore confidence; by the time intervention commenced, the currency in question had already been identified as a weak sister. The Basle-Nyborg Agreement created a presumption that strong-currency central banks would allow borrowing of their currencies through the VSTF before this took place. This might introduce more uncertainty about exchange-rate movements and thereby deter one-way bets by speculators. The agreement also expanded the value of the short- and very-short-term credits available through the system, but only modestly. In the event, the limited amount of borrowing that strong-currency central banks were willing to put up with did little to alter the incentives facing investors (see the discussion later in this chapter).

is one of the reasons for the present tendency of European currencies to rise against the dollar and the currencies tied to it. This rise is contrary to the fundamental interest of Europe and of its constituent economies.[23]

Balladur did not mention Germany by name, but there was no question which country he meant. And although some of the particulars of his critique were disputed, many of his European colleagues, in Italy and elsewhere, shared his general view. The "rigorous" policies that were appropriate for Germany were not appropriate for its partners in the EC who placed a higher priority on growth. But so long as the Bundesbank set the tone for monetary policy throughout Europe, there was nothing they could do about the fact.[24]

The implication drawn by Balladur was that "we must thus find a new system." Making France a driving force for these changes was also a way for French leaders, from President Mitterrand on down, to advance French *grandeur* and, not incidentally, burnish their reputations as statesmen. More concretely, this strategy promised to give France a vote and a voice in European monetary policy, which, as things stood, Germany alone controlled.

This makes it straightforward to understand French support for the monetary unification initiative launched in 1988. A more difficult question is what made the project palatable to Germany. To be sure, the instability of the dollar–deutschmark exchange rate reinforced the priority that German officials attached to creating a wider zone of monetary stability. Whenever the deutschmark strengthened against the dollar, there was a tendency for other European currencies to weaken against Germany's, straining the EMS and provoking complaints about Bundesbank policy—whether or not the German central bank had been responsible for the swing in the dollar–deutschmark rate.[25] Monetary unification that entailed the irrevoca-

---

[23] Quoted in Gros and Thygesen (1992), p. 312.

[24] The implications would become starkly evident following German unification, when the Bundesbank hiked interest rates to rein in the inflationary consequences, to the discomfort of other, more slowly growing European economies. See "The EMS Crisis" later in this chapter.

[25] Exactly what accounted for this pattern, known as "dollar–deutschmark polarity," was never adequately understood. One theory was that deutschmarks were closer substitutes for

ble locking of intra-European exchange rates promised to free European monetary affairs from this disturbance and to insulate German policy makers from this source of criticism.[26]

Some officials also recognized that the elimination of capital controls created new uncertainty about the viability of the EMS. Although the German finance minister Gerhard Stoltenberg was a skeptic of monetary union, he was also a fervent advocate of the elimination of capital controls, and he saw acceding to French and Italian pressure for discussions of monetary integration as both a logical corollary and a quid pro quo. Chancellor Kohl saw monetary integration as a way of renewing the Franco-German partnership and furthering the cause of a politically integrated Europe. Foreign Minister Genscher, also a committed Europeanist, saw discussions of monetary union as a way of advancing the larger European project. He saw the status quo in which the Bundesbank was subjected to a drumbeat of foreign criticism as destructive of this goal. But he insisted that economic and monetary union (EMU) negotiations be linked to negotiations on deeper political integration and foreign-policy coordination.

Early in 1988, therefore, Genscher circulated a memo laying out the case for monetary union.[27] At a European Council meeting in Hanover in June, he proposed appointing a committee of independent experts to draft a statute for a European Central Bank (ECB) and to submit these to the governments of the member states. The Bundesbank, fearing that the new institution would not share its stability culture, and like any good bureaucracy seeking to protect its prerogatives, was quick to object. That Genscher's committee was nonetheless constituted under the chairmanship of the Commission president Jacques Delors reflected the strong complementarity of interests between the German and French governments. It was also

---

dollars than were other European currencies. Thus, when international investors grew anxious about the dollar's prospects, they shifted into marks, driving up the latter against other EMS currencies. For two contemporary discussions of this question see Frankel (1986) and Giavazzi and Giovannini (1989).

[26] For evidence that German officials such as Genscher were thinking along these lines, see Gros and Thygesen (1992), p. 313.

[27] Interestingly, he did so under his own name rather than that of his ministerial office.

an indication of the extent of business support—and of the depth of worries about the stability of the EMS. A coalition of leading companies formed the Association for Monetary Union in Europe and voiced its support for the project in broadsides and editorials. In Germany, the Deutscher Industrie- und Handelskammertag proposed a three-stage plan for the transition to monetary union. Corporations doing business in several European countries saw the fragility of exchange rates as a potential weak point in the single market and lent their principled support to the idea of monetary integration. European financial institutions saw a single market backed by a single currency as essential to their ability to exploit economies of scale and scope and face down U.S. competition. With this coalition of political and business leaders arrayed against it, the skeptical central bankers could only insist on the participation of their presidents on the newly formed committee. They were joined there by a second member of the Commission, together with Delors and three independent experts.

After eight meetings between September 1988 and April 1989, the Delors Report was submitted to the ECOFIN Council and published.[28] Like the Werner Report, the blueprint for monetary unification drafted two decades earlier, the new document emphasized the need for simultaneous economic and monetary convergence. But, in contrast with its predecessor, the Delors Report emphasized the importance of issuing the new currency quickly. It was explicit about the need to create an ECB and to pool the reserves of the participating countries. But it did not foresee the creation of a substantially larger EC budget, a unionwide system of fiscal federalism, or any other significant transfer of fiscal prerogatives from national governments, proposals for which had contributed to the demise of the Werner Report. Instead the Delors Committee emphasized the need for price flexibility and the operation of automatic fiscal stabilizers. Acknowledging the common interest in these national policies—and addressing German concerns—it included provisions strengthening the mutual surveillance of budgets. It recommended

---

[28] See Committee for the Study of Economic and Monetary Union (1989).

empowering the ECOFIN Council and the Parliament to impose binding ceilings on fiscal deficits. Finally, it proposed that a record of sound fiscal policies should be a precondition for joining the monetary union, over the objections of Delors, who feared that the wrong countries (read: France) might be excluded. Germany's proposals regarding the structure and mandate of the new ECB, which followed the Bundesbank model, went directly into the report.

In this way the Delors Committee staked out a middle ground, albeit one intellectually closer to Bonn and Frankfurt than to Paris. It offered a compromise between Germany's insistence on privileging price stability, central bank independence, and the operation of market forces, and the more politicized, top-down approach of the French. Its report was approved by heads of government in June 1989. The December 1989 European Council at Strasbourg then agreed to move to the treaty stage over the objections of the United Kingdom (and thus foreshadowing the opt-out that the country received in the subsequent negotiations).

The obvious change in circumstances between the appearance of the Delors Report and the intergovernmental conference convened in December 1990 was German reunification. Helmut Kohl's announcement in November 1989 of a ten-point plan for immediate reunification, issued without consulting other governments, did not reassure his partners.[29] The desire to lock a peaceful Germany into Europe—a traditional motive for European integration—came to be seen as more pressing now that the country's land area, population, and economic capacity had expanded overnight. In a March 1990 meeting with a delegation of historians, Margaret Thatcher reportedly sympathized with the view that a reunified Germany would be a belligerent Germany.[30] But by pointing to the Delors Report, she could at least reassure her constituents that one instrument of national power, the central bank printing press, would be removed

[29] See "German Reunification" in chapter 10.

[30] According to the account of the meeting by Charles Powell, Thatcher's private secretary, the consensus was that Germans were prone to "angst, aggressiveness, assertiveness, bullying, egotism, inferiority complex, sentimentality." The memorandum summarizing Powell's impressions was then leaked to two British newspapers. See Marsh (1994), p. 45.

from German hands. French politicians for their part could point to monetary union as a stepping-stone to political union and thus toward embedding Germany in a larger Europe.

Reunification required Germany to secure the assent of the four post–World War II occupying powers. To cultivate the support of Paris, Bonn approved France's scheme for a European Bank for Reconstruction and Development to facilitate restructuring in the former Soviet bloc and a French president for the new institution. In the event, Soviet assent to German reunification was quickly granted, and there was little that France could do to stand in the way. But the brief period of uncertainty was enough for Paris to secure an understanding that Bonn would not actively obstruct progress toward monetary and political integration. In the lead-up to reunification, Kohl and Genscher repeatedly voiced enthusiasm for EMU as a way of cultivating foreign support for their own integration project. Mitterrand was thus able to enlist Genscher and Kohl's support for an early date for the intergovernmental conference.

But by the time that conference finally convened, German reunification was a fait accompli. There being no possibility of again separating the two Germanys, there was nothing to prevent German negotiators from hardening their position, which French officials worried was already happening.[31] The Bundesbank hardened its position as well. It had been embarrassed by the German government's dismissal of its objections to converting ostmarks into deutschmarks at a rate of one to one. Bundesbank officials now saw their resistance to plans for European monetary unification as the institution's last stand. In any case, the monetary status quo was less objectionable to Germany than to France and Italy, since the Bundesbank set the tone for monetary conditions throughout Europe. Insofar as this gave Germany latitude for tailoring monetary conditions to local needs, an EMS centered on the deutschmark was acceptable to German business, which consequently supported monetary unification less enthusiastically than did business elsewhere in Europe. And

[31] Dyson (1994), p. 143.

other European countries could not go it alone, given the centrality of Germany to the European economy and the deutschmark to its monetary architecture.

For all these reasons, Germany could effectively veto any agreement unless it received reassurance on monetary matters and support for its broader agenda. For a country with a deeply ingrained stability culture, reassurance meant guarantees that the ECB would be committed to low inflation. In turn this meant that the new institution should be structured and organized along Bundesbank lines.[32] The ECB would be politically independent and have price stability as its primary objective. It would face strict limits on its ability to finance government budget deficits. It would be structured federally.

The need to balance national and EC interests would be addressed by including on the ECB board both representatives of the participating member states and representatives of the EC as a whole. The fact that this might imply an awkwardly large board was not an obstacle given the presumption that only a small subset of member states—those with impeccably strong and stable policies— would qualify for participation. To ensure this, the Maastricht Treaty (signed on 7 February 1992) included a set of institutional preconditions for participation, notably the requirement that national central banks be made politically independent of their governments. It also specified a set of macroeconomic preconditions, the so-called convergence criteria, laying down acceptable levels of inflation, interest rates, exchange-rate variability, budget deficits, and debt. Numerical ceilings for these variables were set out in a protocol to the treaty: an inflation rate within 1.5 percent of the rates of the three lowest-inflation countries, long-term interest rates within 2 percent of the three lowest, a national debt no more than 60 percent of GDP, a budget deficit of no more than 3 percent, and an exchange rate

[32] The one notable respect in which the draft statute for the ECB more closely resembled the U.S. Federal Reserve System in structure was in transparency and accountability; more requirements were laid down requiring the ECB to give accounts of its activities to the relevant EC bodies and the public, anticipating worries about the otherwise inadequate democratic accountability of this new transnational body.

that remained within the 2¼ percent bands of the Exchange-Rate Mechanism (ERM) for at least two years without exceptional difficulties. The actual language suggested some wiggle room in the application of these criteria, which was important as we shall see.

Finally, the Maastricht Treaty laid out a glide path to monetary union. It specified a three-stage transition during which there would be convergence of policies and institutions among countries committed to and capable of participating in the project, while countries with inadequate capability for and commitment to price and financial stability would be filtered out. In Stage I (1990–1993), countries would bring their national economic policies into line, remove remaining capital controls, and reinforce the independence of their central banks. Stage II, starting in 1994, would be marked by the further convergence of policies and the creation of a transitional entity, the European Monetary Institute, to shepherd the move to monetary union. Stage III, monetary union itself, would begin with a vote of the Council of Ministers but was in no case to be delayed beyond the beginning of 1999. No member state would be allowed to veto the decision to proceed with Stage III if others were prepared to go ahead. The fixed deadline and no-veto provision were the main achievements of French negotiators, who sought to make the transition inevitable.

A parallel set of negotiations advanced the political agenda. Given Germany's capacity to veto the monetary project, the results were again compatible with German objectives, although their actual content was modest. In a largely symbolic step, Paris and Bonn agreed to enlarge the Franco-German brigade. Governments agreed to deepen their efforts to coordinate foreign policies. They expanded the scope for majority voting and the co-decision procedure allowing the Parliament to negotiate directly with the Council over proposed amendments. And, with an opt-out for Britain, the other eleven members of the EC agreed to a Social Charter designed to facilitate the coordination of social policies.

Germany still could have vetoed the move to EMU, given that it had an acceptable monetary status quo on which to fall back. That it did not reflected the link between the monetary and political integration projects. But, as subsequent events would reveal, German leaders' willingness to extend monetary concessions in the interest of political solidarity could be pushed only so far.

The EMS Crisis

By the spring of 1992, with the Maastricht Treaty wrapped up and the task now to ratify it, a deceptive sense of calm had developed. Spain, with an eye toward impending negotiation of the monetary union treaty, had come into the ERM in June 1989. The United Kingdom entered in October 1990, removing one of the important remaining sources of volatility affecting European foreign-exchange markets.[33] Portugal joined in April 1992. Sweden, not yet a member of the EC, took to shadowing the EMS, suggesting that the zone of monetary stability was continuing to expand. French inflation fell to German levels and even below, providing reassurance that the two countries could cohabit within a monetary union.[34] Inflation in Italy, Spain, and Portugal remained higher, but interest rates were falling as investors confident of exchange-rate stability arbitraged away differentials. Currencies such as the peseta and the lira were thus pushed to the strong end of their ERM bands.

The recession that developed in 1991 was the main source of unease. Unemployment across Europe was already high, and recession only made it higher. Recession also made it more painful to contemplate the tax increases and expenditure cuts needed to

[33] Once it had vanquished high inflation at the beginning of the 1980s, the Thatcher government experimented with a number of alternative monetary policy operating strategies—targeting narrow money, targeting broad money, targeting the public-sector borrowing requirement, shadowing the deutschmark—none of which proved particularly satisfactory. Sharp depreciation in 1985 led Nigel Lawson, Thatcher's new chancellor of the exchequer and an aficionado of the nineteenth-century gold standard, to place growing weight on the exchange rate. Then, when sterling began falling again starting in 1989, threatening to rekindle inflation, a reluctant prime minister finally agreed to British membership in the ERM (first replacing Lawson with John Major, thereby limiting the embarrassment).

[34] German inflation had accelerated as a result of the financial management of reunification (see the discussion later in this chapter), leading French officials to suggest that the franc now rivaled the deutschmark as the anchor of the EMS system.

bring deficits down to the Maastricht Treaty's 3 percent reference value. The day of reckoning when the Commission and the Council would determine who qualified for participation did not leave governments much choice but to pursue restrictive fiscal measures. But given prevailing conditions, the macroeconomic implications were not happy.

The same was true of the high interest rates and strict monetary policies needed to keep inflation within 1½ percentage points of that in the three lowest-inflation countries. The difficulty was greater to the extent that Bundesbank policies were even more restrictive than usual. On the eve of reunification, Helmut Kohl had recklessly promised that "no one will have to give up anything for German unity."[35] This left him no choice but to finance transfer payments and infrastructure investment in the new *Länder* by running deficits. Deficits stimulated demand and inflation. When German inflation rose to 4 percent, not an exceptional level by European standards but one that horrified staid German central bankers, the Bundesbank responded by raising interest rates.[36] Immediately, those higher interest rates spread to other European countries, as investors shifted funds to now higher-yielding German markets. Higher interest rates, of course, were the last thing that Europe needed in an environment of widespread unemployment and anemic growth.

European leaders could at least reassure themselves that these difficulties were temporary. They could also point to the United States as the principal source of the recession.[37] Blaming the recession on the United States reassured them that the fundamental basis for growth remained strong. And by 1992, with recovery in North

---

[35] Marsh (1994), p. 31.

[36] Buiter, Corsetti, and Pesenti (1998), p. 41. As early as March 1990, Bundesbank officials had also mooted the idea of a revaluation of the mark, within the context of a general EMS realignment, to vent some of this demand pressure. See Dyson and Featherstone (1999), pp. 213, 391. In principle, this would have relieved the pressure on the EMS, at least for a time. But the proposal foundered on two obstacles. First, countries such as France did not see why they should have to realign downward—in other words, devalue—as part of this adjustment to the shock of German reunification. And second, any adjustment of ERM parities was immensely more difficult to negotiate and implement in the absence of capital controls.

[37] The fact that the United Kingdom, the European economy with the strongest ties to the United States, had been the first to feel its effects was consistent with this view.

America, they could look forward to better times. As adjustment to reunification proceeded (recall that growth of the Eastern *Länder* spurted by 9 percent in 1992), there were similarly grounds for hope that high interest rates and restrictive Bundesbank policies might soon be things of the past. There was little reason to anticipate the financial chaos to follow.

That chaos resulted, as financial chaos often does, from the interaction of politics with economics. The political scene was dominated by efforts to ratify the Maastricht Treaty. While most European countries did this by parliamentary vote, Denmark and France proceeded by referendum. Denmark, like the United Kingdom, was an EFTA graduate. It did not share the commitment to political integration of the EC's six founding member states and worried about the implications of monetary union for its political autonomy. Still, Danish voters' rejection of the treaty in their referendum on 2 June 1992 was an unexpected shock.

The implications were startling: if the Maastricht Treaty was not ratified by all twelve member states, there might be no monetary union. To be sure, there remained the possibility that Denmark would ratify the treaty in a second referendum.[38] And a majority of Europeans might in any case refuse to be held up by three million stubborn Danes. But another interpretation of Denmark's *nej* was that Europe's political elite was too far ahead of the public. The Danish referendum was a reminder of the value that the man in the street attached to national sovereignty. German leaders might see political integration as a way of acquiring a more assertive foreign-policy role, but, the population of the Federal Republic of Germany having just expanded by one-third, the French were less confident that their leaders would be able to direct and control any new political, defense, and foreign-policy entity. This excited memories of the European Defense Community torpedoed by France in 1954. Investors consequently began to question the inevitability of monetary unification.

[38] As it ultimately did.

In turn this created new uncertainty about whether there would be fiscal consolidation. If France followed the Danish precedent, rejecting the Maastricht Treaty in its own referendum, the process would be back to square one. Governments that had sucked in their budgetary guts in order to squeeze into Maastricht's tight fiscal trousers would be tempted to exhale. Central banks might similarly relax in response to the pressure of unemployment. Current sacrifices in the form of austerity at a time of high unemployment, extended in return for future rewards (above all, for permission to participate in the monetary union), might no longer look so attractive. This dilemma was understood by investment professionals such as George Soros, the U.S.-based hedge-fund manager, attuned as they were to political as well as financial affairs. As they began selling the lira, the pound, and the krona, the Bank of Italy, the Bank of England, and the Swedish Riksbank were forced to raise interest rates to stem their loss of reserves.

That the lira, the pound, and the krona were first to feel the heat was no coincidence. Italy had made some progress in moderating its inflation, but past inflation differentials had inevitably accumulated into overvaluation, given the absence of exchange-rate flexibility.[39] (See figure 11.1.) Over the preceding five years, unit labor costs had risen by 7 percent relative to those in the country's ERM partners. (See table 11.1.) In addition, the budget deficits fueling past inflation had cumulated into a public debt that now exceeded 100 percent of GDP. Although British debt and inflation problems were less pronounced, there were still complaints that the exchange rate at which the country had entered the ERM in October 1990 significantly overvalued the pound, aggravating the unemployment bequeathed by Thatcher's macroeconomic reforms.[40] Sweden, meanwhile, was saddled with banking problems as a result of the property

[39] Moreover, in January 1990 Italy had moved from the 6 percent band temporarily granted it (and subsequently granted to other new members of the EMS) to the 2¼ percent bands applicable to other members, further limiting the extent of exchange-rate flexibility.

[40] The dollar had weakened significantly in the second half of the 1980s, while the vigorous growth of the British economy had kept the pound strong (notwithstanding the difficulties of 1989). Now, as the British economy weakened, concerns that sterling was overvalued grew increasingly prevalent.

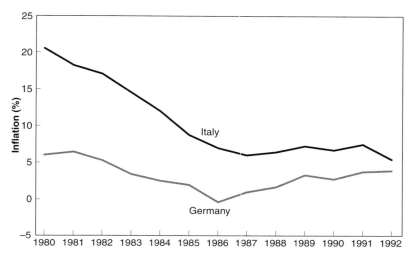

Figure 11.1. Inflation rates in Italy and Germany, 1980–1992. *Source*: De Grauwe (1994).

boom and bust through which it had passed in the late 1980s and the financial crisis in neighboring Finland.

What these countries had in common was inherited weaknesses. In these circumstances, raising interest rates in the effort to attract back flight capital and signal the authorities' resolve might create as many problems as it solved. In Italy, every 100 basis-point increase in the central bank's discount rate added 1 percent of GDP to the budget deficit. In Sweden, higher interest rates further weakened the banking system. In the United Kingdom, higher interest rates increased mortgage costs and threatened property prices, given the prevalence of variable-rate mortgages. Howls of protest followed as the "bailiffs began arriving in the leafy avenues of the Home Counties and in the chic new developments of London's Docklands to repossess the homes of Thatcher's children."[41] Politicians, for whom it was hard to think beyond the next election, were reluctant to incur these costs for the delayed gratification of membership in the monetary union. This was especially the case in Britain, where enthusiasm for the monetary union project was mixed, and in Sweden,

[41] Stephens (1996), p. 190.

TABLE 11.1

Indicators of cumulative competitiveness changes (Percent)

Country	Relative to other EC countries[a]		Relative to industrial countries		Relative to other EC countries[a]		Relative to industrial countries	
	Producer prices	Unit labor costs[b]	Producer prices	Unit labor costs[b]	Producer prices	Unit labor costs[b]	Producer prices	Unit labor costs[b]
	1987–August 1992				1987–December 1992[c]			
Belgium	4.0	5.6	1.3	2.7	0.9	1.9	–0.3	0.3
Denmark	3.6	6.4	–0.5	3.8	–1.9	4.1	–4.9	1.9
Germany (West)	1.7	0.5	–3.8	–5.5	–4.3	–6.6	–5.5	–8.6
Greece	NA	NA	–10.2	–15.6	NA	NA	–10.8	–13.4
France	7.9	13.3	3.3	7.2	3.1	8.1	1.7	5.1
Ireland	6.4	35.7	1.3	27.9	–0.6	26.6	–1.9	23.6
Italy	–3.0	–7.0	–6.4	–9.8	11.1	5.7	8.2	4.6
Netherlands	1.5	5.2	–1.4	1.9	–2.6	2.1	–3.9	0.1
	ERM entry[c]–August 1992				ERM entry[c]–December 1992[d]			
Spain	–2.1	–7.5	–8.1	–13.8	4.2	–2.2	0.5	–6.2
Portugal	NA	–4.6	NA	–6.9	NA	–9.5	NA	–9.5
United Kingdom	–1.7	–0.4	–4.0	–1.7	8.3	13.2	8.7	13.2

Source: Bank for International Settlements, except for the Spanish and Italian data, which were provided by the respective central banks.

Notes: Negative numbers indicate losses.

[a] Excluding Greece.

[b] Manufacturing sector.

[c] Spain: June 1989; Portugal: April 1992; United Kingdom: October 1999.

[d] Estimates.

whose citizens shared many of the same reservations and which in any case was not yet a member of the EC.

The turbulence that erupted in June mounted through the summer. On 16 July, citing concern that its money supply targets were being overshot, the Bundesbank raised its discount rate. This ratcheted up the pressure on weak-currency central banks, eliciting further complaints about German policy. When the Federal Reserve then cut rates in an effort to prod the U.S. economy out of recession, tensions in the EMS mounted further, as yet more capital flowed into the mark. On 26 August sterling fell to its ERM floor, where it was joined by the lira. There was then an attempt at an informal ECOFIN Council meeting in Bath to coordinate a response. This would have involved devaluing other ERM currencies against the deutschmark and the Dutch guilder and supplementing this with a cut in German interest rates. But the negotiations went badly wrong. German officials were badgered by an aggressive Norman Lamont, the British chancellor, who chaired the meeting. Preoccupied by inflation, German officials stubbornly refused to cut interest rates. British and French officials, fearing the consequences of association with Italy, discouraged talk of a general realignment.[42]

When Finland depreciated the markka on 8 September, speculators concluded that the façade was crumbling. They trained their sights on Sweden, which resembled its Nordic neighbor and, not being a member of the EMS, did not enjoy automatic support lines. Massive sales of krona forced the Riksbank to raise its marginal lending rate to 75 percent annualized, truly astounding levels in a period of single-digit inflation. Speculators next turned their fire on Italy. A second effort to negotiate a general realignment coupled with a German interest-rate cut again failed to produce results. Following bilateral negotiations with Germany, Italy devalued by 7 percent on

[42] The Major government had made the ERM peg the linchpin of British monetary policy. A Treasury paper circulated in the summer warned that devaluing—even in the context of a general realignment of ERM currencies—would deal a terrible blow to confidence and only foster expectations of further depreciation. And the French government had again been following a *franc fort* policy designed to so heighten confidence in the currency that Paris rather than Frankfurt might be able to set the tone for monetary conditions systemwide.

13 September, and the Bundesbank grudgingly lowered its Lombard rate by 25 basis points.[43]

George Soros's massive positions against sterling were then revealed in the financial press, an event whose timing was probably not a coincidence. On Wednesday, 16 September, four days prior to the French referendum, the German newspaper *Handelsblatt* published an interview with the Bundesbank president Hans Schlesinger in which he made the unfortunate observation that "further devaluations cannot be excluded."[44] Schlesinger's remarks ratcheted up the pressure on sterling, since it was thought that the Major government and the Bank of England had limited stomach for further interest-rate increases. Indeed, the view had already developed that such measures were unlikely to succeed. As Stephens put it, "officials believed an increase would have served only to heighten the tension between the domestic economy and the ERM. The financial markets would have recognized an increase as an act of desperation. In the words of one Bank official, 'There was a huge overkill even with base rates at 10 percent. Increasing rates would have been incredible.'"[45]

At the height of the speculative attack, on 16 September, the Bank of England raised its minimum lending rate from 10 to 12 percent. It announced a second increase to 15 percent to take effect the following day. But the first increase had no impact on currency markets. The Riksbank had been forced to raise marginal rates to 75 percent, as noted, and had still failed to dispel speculative pressure. Investors understood that the British government lacked the stomach for such policies. Recognizing that the game was up, Lamont rescinded the second increase. That evening the Monetary Committee accepted Britain's request to take the pound out of the ERM and did the same for Italy. It rejected, however, Lamont's face-saving request to suspend the ERM entirely.[46]

---

[43] The Bundesbank generally kept interest rates within a corridor, of which the discount rate formed the floor and the Lombard rate the ceiling.

[44] Schlesinger may not have been attempting to precipitate a blow-up, but he was no fan of monetary union. And he was not pleased by the pressure that had been brought to bear on the Bundesbank to relax its strict anti-inflationary stance, which only reinforced his skepticism about the monetary union project.

[45] Stephens (1996), p. 217.

[46] In addition, the Monetary Committee authorized a 5 percent devaluation of the peseta.

Given this evidence that governments had limited tolerance for harsh measures, French voters' razor-thin approval of the Maastricht Treaty on 20 September failed to reassure the markets. The Irish pound was pushed toward its ERM floor, reflecting worries about how the economy would be affected by sterling's depreciation; it was supported there only with the help of emergency controls.[47] Sweden was forced to abandon its peg on 19 November after the intolerable strain of raising marginal lending rates to 500 percent.[48] Spain and Portugal devalued by 3 percent. Norway abandoned its peg to the European Currency Unit on 10 December. Ireland devalued by 10 percent within the ERM on 30 January 1993. With the release of disappointing Spanish unemployment figures for the final quarter of 1992, attention turned back to Spain and Portugal, and their currencies were devalued again.

Speculators now had the French franc, the ultimate prize, in their sights. Given the high level of unemployment, the French government hoped that pressure on the franc could be relieved by cutting German interest rates. Paris had some leverage, for even if Germany could proceed to Stage III of the Maastricht process with the cooperation of a small rump group (say, the Benelux countries), meaningful progress on deeper political integration could not proceed without the participation of France. Thus, on 24 June Edmond Alphandéry, France's economic minister, requested a meeting with his German counterpart, Theo Waigel, for purposes of negotiating a reduction in German interest rates. Not one to be cornered, Waigel declined, citing other business. On the last Thursday of July, the Bundesbank Council again refused to lower the discount rate, citing Germany's money supply figures and inflation concerns. Massive sales of francs followed, forcing unprecedented intervention by the French and German central banks. The Bank of France expended more than thirty-two billion dollars of reserves in the last week of

---

[47] The French franc was pushed toward its floor as well. France did not reimpose controls but could achieve much the same effect by applying moral suasion to the banks and promising them preferential access to its lending windows if they limited loans to speculators seeking to sell the currency short. See Eichengreen and Wyplosz (1993).

[48] Again, 500 percent is an annualized figure. Despite these extraordinarily high interest rates, reserve losses in the six days leading up to the devaluation were the equivalent of more than 10 percent of GNP.

July, 80 percent of this on 28 July alone. The Bundesbank's reserves rose by forty billion deutschmarks, some 33 percent, foreshadowing a sharp increase in the money supply.

In a crisis meeting over the last weekend in July, central bank governors and finance ministers finally bowed to the inevitable. Failing to agree on measures to save the existing system, they widened the ERM's bands from 2¼ percent to 15 percent. The old narrow-band EMS was no more. And the prospects for further integration were uncertain.

The Transition to Monetary Union

Now came the surprise. The surrender to market forces neither destabilized European financial markets nor derailed the monetary union project. Instead of falling sharply, the remaining ERM currencies continued to hover around their central parities. The volatile exchange-rate swings that many feared would elicit complaints of arbitrary and capricious exchange-rate changes and undermine support for both the single market and the single currency failed to materialize. There was no sudden acceleration of inflation. There was no rise in interest rates in response to weakening market confidence. There was no loss of discipline by central banks. To the contrary, in the wake of the decision to widen the ERM's bands more than sixfold, the markets settled down and the monetary union project got back on track.

Part of the explanation may have been the cyclical upswing. With the European economy expanding again, there was more reason to think that governments would be able to live with the constraints of the ERM. Widening its fluctuation bands to plus or minus 15 percent meant that speculators could now lose a substantial chunk of change if a currency moved back from its lower bound to its central parity. Only the United Kingdom had permanently left the ERM; for the rest, the system still provided a nominal anchor, albeit with a less taut anchor line.[49] Having experienced first-hand the fragility of currency pegs in a world without capital controls, monetary unification was rendered more appealing. Hence, there was no loss of policy discipline. With the United Kingdom out of the ERM and Denmark prepared to ratify the treaty in its second referendum, the two principal obstacles to moving ahead with monetary unification had been shunted aside. That by 1993 the Maastricht target date of 1999 was in sight and the majority of governments were committed to participating in Europe's monetary union from the outset is the best explanation for why the markets responded in stabilizing fashion.

Abandoning the currency peg that had anchored monetary policy, the United Kingdom substituted another operating strategy: inflation targeting. Within three weeks of leaving the ERM, Lamont announced a target range for inflation of 1 to 4 percent. The government and the central bank quickly worked out the details. The Bank of England would publish a quarterly *Inflation Report* with an inflation forecast, the new yardstick of policy. The chancellor, who still controlled monetary policy (the Bank not yet being independent), committed to doing so in a manner consistent with the inflation forecast.[50] The Bank would be responsible for evaluating the conduct of policy in meetings with Treasury officials and publicly. The chancellor and the governor of the Bank of England would meet regularly; beginning in 1994 the minutes of their meetings were released after six weeks.

The combination of an explicit target and a transparent operating procedure reassured the markets. Fears that loss of the exchange-rate anchor would lead to a resurgence of inflation were put to rest. As inflation expectations stabilized, there was no excessive wage push to produce a sharp rise in unemployment. From its two short but turbulent years in the ERM, many Britons drew the lesson

---

[49] Italy had also been ejected temporarily but was committed to rejoin, as it did in the second half of the 1990s. Recall that Sweden had not been a member of the EMS because it had not been a member of the EC.

[50] Operational independence for the Bank and the creation of a Monetary Policy Committee with full responsibility for policy decisions followed in 1997.

that monetary union was not for them. And inflation targeting was a perfectly workable alternative.

For the other member states, still committed to the goal of monetary unification, attention turned now to meeting the Maastricht conditions. The key criteria were fiscal: a consolidated public-sector deficit of less than 3 percent of GDP and a falling debt-to-GDP ratio.[51] With the exception of Greece, the member states made just enough progress to satisfy the Commission. General government deficits fell EU-wide from 6 percent of GDP in 1993 to 2.4 percent in 1997 and 1.5 percent in 1998. (See figure 11.2.) At that point the decision on participation in Stage III was made. Once more, recovery helped, since the least painful way of bringing down the deficit-to-GDP ratio was by growing the denominator.[52] Devaluation had enhanced Italian, Spanish, and Portuguese competitiveness, and the expansionary thrust imparted by a depreciated currency provided an important boost to growth in circumstances where the fiscal impulse was limited.[53] The fact that the United States was now expanding also made for a favorable international climate.[54] Of the fiscal consolidation not accounted for by the cyclical upswing, the largest part in 1992–1993 was explained by efforts to boost revenues. In 1994–1997, adjustment was more heavily expenditure-based; primary structural expenditure (excluding interest payments and the effects of the cycle) fell by two percentage points of GDP over the period.[55] There was a general tendency toward convergence: mem-

[51] Most of the other criteria, which concerned interest rates, exchange rates, and inflation rates, were heavily endogenous. That is, if progress was made on the fiscal criteria and confidence developed that a country would not be excluded from participation in Stage III on these grounds, the other criteria would respond favorably to the knowledge that a future of high inflation and currency instability might therefore be ruled out.

[52] The point is general: reviewing episodes of fiscal consolidation in the OECD from 1975 through 1995, Heylen and Everaert (2000) find that a favorable growth environment is critical for the success of consolidation efforts.

[53] See, for example, Perotti (1996).

[54] The importance of which is emphasized more generally for episodes of successful fiscal consolidation by Alesina and Perotti (1995) and McDermott and Wescott (1996).

[55] France relied principally on increases in revenues, the United Kingdom relied more on reductions in spending, Italy employed both, and Germany seemed to switch from the revenue-enhancing to expenditure-reducing camp as the period proceeded. For details on these country patterns, see European Commission (2000).

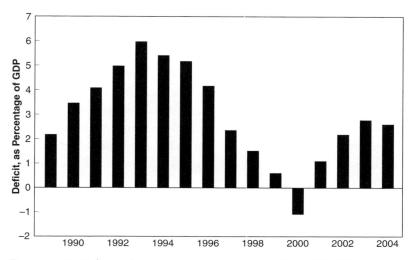

Figure 11.2. Deficit of general government, EU-15, 1989–2004. *Sources*: European Commission (2000); Eurostat. *Notes*: Figures are for EU-15 excluding Luxembourg.

ber states with unusually low revenues attempted to balance their budgets by boosting tax receipts, while those with unusually high spending sought to bring this down toward the EU average.

Insofar as Europe's problem was bloated public sectors and excessive taxes, cuts in spending were the more promising route. Thus, the fact that so much fiscal adjustment in the key period 1992–1997 was accomplished by tax increases did not bode well for the future.

The fact that which states qualified as founding members of the monetary union would be decided imminently meant that a short period of sacrifice might suffice to yield the desired result, it not being clear how tightly fiscal autonomy would be limited in Stage III. That this delicate decision would be reached by consensus suggested that it might be hard to exclude countries such as Italy that had cut their budget deficits to the neighborhood of 3 percent but had not yet succeeded in reducing their debt ratios to 60 percent. Fortunately for them, the Maastricht Treaty rewarded effort as well as achievement: the language concerning debt ratios contained a provision that recognized progress toward the goal.

369

Thus, the result was not a small monetary union centered on Germany, France, and the Benelux countries but a wide union that included also Ireland, Austria, and Finland (the latter two being new members that joined the EU in its third enlargement in 1995), together with the three "Club Med" countries (Italy, Spain, and Portugal).[56] The participation of these last three countries was a source of concern for Germany, which had doubts about their commitment to price stability. It encouraged skepticism among academics, who questioned the wisdom of consigning such a diverse set of countries to a single monetary policy.

EMU and Its Implications

The currencies of the eleven participating countries were irrevocably locked at the beginning of 1999.[57] The newly established ECB and its operating arms, the national central banks, exchanged currencies to meet demand. Henceforth, the relative price of francs and marks could no more vary than the relative price of nickels and dimes.[58]

ECB policy was neither the disaster warned of by the opponents of EMU nor the dramatic improvement promised by its champions. The policies of the new central bank, perhaps unsurprisingly, resembled those that would have been pursued by the Bundesbank in similar circumstances.[59] After running at 1 percent in 1999, inflation in the next five years hovered around 2 percent. The euro rose and fell against the dollar (actually, it first fell, by a bit more than 10 percent in the first half of 1999, before recovering and eventually rising about 10 percent from its inaugural levels by the end of 2004). There was nothing abnormal in this. A popular explanation for

---

[56] Sweden, the other participant in the third enlargement, having suffered the same fate as the United Kingdom in the 1992 currency crisis, now claimed the same right to opt out.

[57] Greece joined the monetary union in January 2001.

[58] The beginning of 2002 then saw the advent of the physical euro, as the national currencies of the twelve participating countries were replaced by euro notes and coins.

[59] Except, of course, that the ECB took conditions over the entire euro zone into account, whereas the Bundesbank would have limited its attention to Germany.

the euro's recovery against the dollar was that the Federal Reserve was quicker than the ECB to cut interest rates in response to recession in 2001. Some criticized the ECB for moving too slowly, owing to the unwieldy nature of its decision-making board, its inexperience, and its preoccupation with demonstrating its commitment to price stability. Others suggested that the ECB and the Fed in fact formulated policy using the same rule of thumb (the "Taylor rule" relating the level of the discount rate to deviations of inflation from target and the output gap), observing that the ECB had good reason to think that the output gap (the amount of unused capacity available to the economy) in Europe was smaller than in the United States, given the rigidity of European labor markets. Still others worried that the Fed overreacted to the bursting of the high-tech bubble in 1999–2000. They warned that the very low levels to which the Fed had cut interest rates only created problems for the future—when sharp increases would be needed even in the face of a relatively weak expansion—something that the ECB was wise to avoid. The ECB was derided as insufficiently transparent. Its founding president, Wim Duisenberg, was criticized as inconsistent. These debates were intense but obscure. Their technical nature is the best indication that the single monetary policy was functioning well at the aggregate level.

Where monetary union caused difficulties was in member states where economic conditions diverged markedly from the EU average. On the one hand, Ireland and Finland, which were booming, would have preferred a tighter policy to rein in inflation, house-price inflation in particular. Their fear was that what went up could come down, and if housing prices came down with a crash, they could devastate the banking system. On the other hand, Germany was suffering from slow growth reflecting high labor costs and the slump in its eastern *Länder*. It understandably preferred a looser monetary stance.

Fiscal policy was the obvious solution: Ireland could cut public spending or raise taxes to cool off its economy while Germany did the opposite. But Ireland was already running substantial budget surpluses, and there was popular resistance to raising taxes in this situation. Germany was up against the ceiling on deficits applied to members of the monetary union. Both there and in other countries, there had been a considerable relaxation of fiscal policies after 1999 despite the fact that the European economy was again expanding strongly. Having sucked in their guts to satisfy the Maastricht criteria, Germany, France, and Italy now loosened their belts. In part this was a backlash against the tax increases used to reduce deficits in the period leading up to the decision on who qualified for monetary union. In part it reflected the continued progress of the single market, now further invigorated by the single currency, which intensified tax competition and forced countries with high rates to bring them down or risk seeing footloose factors of production flee to lower-tax jurisdictions. Those concerned with the high level of taxes regarded this as healthy tax competition, but given limited scope for expenditure cuts it only contributed further to the growth of budget deficits in the short run.

These developments brought Germany, France, and Italy into conflict with the EU's fiscal rules, known as the Stability and Growth Pact (SGP) or Stability Pact for short.[60] There was no little irony in this fact, since in the early 1990s it had been German negotiators who had pushed to include an Excessive Deficit Procedure in the Maastricht Treaty. At the Dublin Summit in 1996 and the Amsterdam Summit in 1997, it had again been German negotiators who had forced through two regulations and a Council resolution to clarify the operation of that procedure. These specified exceptional and temporary circumstances under which member states participating in the monetary union could run budget deficits in excess of 3 percent of GDP without incurring penalties and fines.[61]

The expectation was that it would be the historically profligate Club Med countries that had to be restrained. No one anticipated that the big countries at the heart of Europe, and above all Germany, would be subject to the pact's strictures. What transformed the

[60] The reference to growth was added as a sop to French negotiators.
[61] Sanctions were to start as non-interest-bearing deposits in the amount of 0.2 percent of GDP that rise with the magnitude of the excess deficit and were then converted into nonrefundable fines in the absence of corrective action.

situation was exceptionally slow growth in Germany, even by European standards, in the first five years of monetary union. Slow growth meant stagnant tax revenues and calls for increased public spending on unemployment benefits, welfare, training, and other public programs.

It was already evident that the Stability Pact had two flaws. First, it provided only weak incentives for fiscal restraint in good times. Member states were supposed to maintain budgets close to balance in expansions, but the EU's mutual surveillance procedure could do little more than remind them of the desirability of this norm. This meant that when growth turned down, deficits might already be bumping up against their 3 percent ceiling, leaving little room for further stimulus. Fiscal policy would become dangerously procyclical, aggravating rather than damping fluctuations.

Second, taxation and public spending, even more than monetary policy, were delicate national prerogatives. Telling a member state to cut spending or raise taxes had political and distributional implications. The Excessive Deficit Procedure tacitly acknowledged this: whereas the anonymous technocrats of the Commission were supposed to issue the warning of an excessive deficit, it was the national officials constituting the Council who decided whether to accept the Commission's determination and thereby initiate the phase leading to sanctions and fines. This was not problematic so long as the subject was a small country such as Portugal that might usefully be made an example of, as happened in 2001. But when Germany and France were warned by the Commission in 2003–2004, the realism of expecting the EU's most consequential members to punish themselves was called into question.

The predictable result was exceptions for Germany and France and discussions of reforming the pact to allow more flexibility. An agreement reached in 2005 relaxed the definition of a "severe economic downturn" in whose presence countries are exempt from the SGP's 3 percent ceiling.[62] It stretched out to five years the period

---

[62] A country can now claim that it is the victim of a severe downturn when growth turns negative, not merely when output falls by 2 percent.

over which a country potentially in violation could correct its excessive deficit without incurring sanctions and fines. It placed more emphasis on debt sustainability, implying differential treatment of countries with debt ratios higher and lower than 60 percent. Finally, it gave special consideration—and potential exemption from SGP limits—to three kinds of public spending: costs associated with productivity- and employment-friendly structural reforms, costs incurred in conjunction with European integration (including German reunification), and the costs of foreign aid.

But none of these reforms addressed the pact's fundamental weaknesses. They did not compel countries to run balanced budgets in good times. They did not give enforcement powers to the Commission or another EU body independent of governments, which was an even larger problem than before insofar as the new provisions gave national authorities any number of additional grounds on which to dispute the Commission's recommendations.

In all, this revision of the SGP considerably reduced the likelihood that its warnings, sanctions, and fines would ever be imposed on one of the large member states. This was not obviously bad, since there had never been a particularly compelling rationale for why, having forsaken their national monetary autonomy, member states participating in the monetary union should now limit their fiscal autonomy. EU officials warned that if governments continued running excessive deficits and incurring excessive debts, financial markets might take fright. The ECB might be forced to buy up their debt, with inflationary consequences. But the ECB might equally leave the offending country to stew in its own juices. Even if an unsustainable debt threatened financial stability and the ECB felt impelled to inject credit into European financial markets, it was not certain that inflation would follow. The Fed had intervened in 1998 in response to the difficulties of the mega investment fund Long-Term Capital Management, but it had drained the additional liquidity once the crisis passed, preventing an increase in inflation. Although the SGP might be dead, in this view it should be allowed to rest in peace.

374

What about the other effects of monetary union? In product markets there was some reduction in the dispersion of prices, for example in the case of automobiles.[63] In labor markets there was a recognition that monetary union required greater flexibility. Thus, the need for flexibility-enhancing labor-market reforms was emphasized at the Lisbon meeting of the European Council in March 2000 and enshrined as the so-called Lisbon Agenda. But the need for reform is not the same as reform itself. Significant changes in the structure of European labor markets were slow in coming, monetary union or not.

Two places where the impact was immediately visible were finance and politics. The advent of the single currency led to explosive growth and rapid consolidation in European securities markets. By eliminating currency fluctuations within the euro area, the single currency eliminated the exchange risk that had previously segmented Europe into a dozen corporate bond and commercial paper markets, none of which possessed the scale and liquidity necessary to offer borrowers an attractive alternative to bank intermediation. Now, with monetary unification, the German *bund* (the Federal Republic's ten-year bond) became the benchmark on whose basis corporate debt was priced euro-area-wide. No longer worried by the risk of currency fluctuations between member states, investors began searching out attractive corporate debt securities regardless of the national market in which they were issued. Assets under management by bond funds pursuing Europe-wide investment strategies grew explosively starting in 1999.[64] The result was a larger and more liquid market. In 1999 the value of new euro-denominated corporate bond issues more than tripled relative to the amounts that had been issued in the "legacy" currencies in 1998.[65] A larger market enabled high-grade corporate credits to float larger issues. New issuers found

[63] See Goldberg and Verboven (2004).

[64] Especially if those bond funds catered to clients resident in France, Germany, and Austria. For evidence see Baele et al. (2004).

[65] That there was no comparable increase in bonds issued by European countries outside the euro area is further consistent with the idea that the single currency made the difference. The term *legacy currencies* refers to the currencies that were replaced by the euro.

it attractive to enter the market. Nearly 50 percent of all corporate bond issues in 1999 had A ratings, in contrast to earlier years when European bond markets had been dominated by AA and AAA rated issues. Further down the rating scale, the share of new corporate bonds in the junk-bond category rose from 4 percent to 15 percent.

Almost immediately, then, the euro began erasing the competitive handicap of Europe's lack of U.S.-style bond markets. Funding costs for European corporations declined as corporate credits grew explosively. Easier access to debt markets in turn helped to finance a wave of mergers and acquisitions that promised to strengthen Europe's corporate sector. Although these extraordinary early growth rates tailed off subsequently, debt issuance by nonfinancial corporations continued to outpace the growth of other sources of capital. To be sure, there were losers as well as winners. Europe's banks, faced with fiercer competition from the bond market, saw their profits squeezed.

In 2003–2004, the EU then convened an unprecedented constitutional convention. It is hard to imagine that this extraordinary exercise would have been undertaken except for the perceived need to create an effective political counterweight to the ECB and the other economic policy-making entities of the EU. After a painful gestation period, the delegates came forth with a document designed to strengthen the powers of the Parliament and the Council, providing a more effective counterweight to technocratic institutions such as the new central bank. The draft constitution was controversial. Although some saw it as a step toward streamlining the EU, others decried it as a 265-page bureaucratic nightmare. In a pair of hotly contested referenda, French and Dutch voters rejected the draft in the spring of 2005. This was not the first time, of course, that Europe's citizens had expressed their reservations about the erosion of national sovereignty. Still, by highlighting the long-standing tension between the advantages of economic integration and resistance to political integration, the controversy over the constitution stirred doubts about the viability of the euro and even the EU itself. This was a reminder that, however conducive the context and however powerful the forward momentum, there was nothing inevitable about the further progress of European integration.

Adjustment and Growth

By the end of the twentieth century, as a result of the integration initiatives of the preceding fifty years, Europe's economic landscape had been very considerably transformed. The Single Market Program had fused a set of segmented national markets into an integrated economic space. Product-market competition had intensified. Integration had operated as a powerful motor for financial deregulation. There were even glimmerings of increased labor mobility.

To be sure, critics could point to the continued reluctance of governments to extend comparable treatment to domestic and foreign firms. They could cite the range of subtle policies pursued to frustrate the Commission's efforts to ensure an equal footing.[66] Still, studies of the single market by official bodies and independent experts alike detected a noticeable impact.[67] The single market having created an incentive for firms to extend their reach, the intra-European share of mergers and acquisitions tripled between 1985–1987 and 1991–1993, reaching 30 percent.[68] Consolidation helped producers to reap economies of scale and scope without limiting competition; price–cost margins declined markedly over the period, suggesting a rise in competitive intensity. And rather than creating a Fortress Europe, the single market stimulated a further increase in Europe's trade with the rest of the world. To the extent that the single market initiative had been prompted by the desire to remove obstacles to the achievement of minimum efficient scale and ratchet up competitive pressure, this was evidence of its achieving its goal. Monetary union was still too recent to support a firm evaluation of its effects, but the early signs, especially in financial markets, pointed in the same direction, namely, toward efficiency gains through consolidation and growing competition.

---

[66] See, for example, Nicoletti and Scarpetta (2003).

[67] See European Commission (1996) and Allen, Gasiorek, and Smith (1998).

[68] Admittedly, most mergers and acquisitions activity was among competing producers within countries, not yet across borders, reflecting the obstacles that governments continued to place in the way of foreign acquisitions.

Capitalizing on these opportunities required structural change. Simply acquiring a rival was not enough; the newly merged entities had to reorganize their operations. Where there was duplication of capacity, enterprises had to be downsized. Where there was scope for exploiting economies of scale and scope, activity needed to be ramped up. Confronted with the need to adapt, firms and governments pursued expedients such as early retirement and part-time contracts to circumvent the obstacles posed by Europe's structured and regulated labor markets.

Still, the feeling was widespread that Europe was incurring the costs of adjusting to this new environment without as yet reaping the full benefits. With the deregulation and adaptation of some markets proceeding faster than others, there were worries that the larger economic system was operating less efficiently. In addition, there was a sense in which it was not entirely productive to delegate the initiative for difficult reforms to the institutions of the EU. Doing so diminished domestic "ownership" of reforms. It fueled complaints that national values were being trampled by faceless technocrats responsible to no one. One logical response to these objections was to strengthen the European Parliament as a way of creating a political body at the EU level capable of holding the Commission responsible for its actions. But transferring political prerogatives from governments to the EU sat uneasily with Europeans' deep-seated national identities protected by the vestiges of national sovereignty. Only time would tell how this tension would play out.

- TWELVE -

EUROPE AT THE TURN OF THE TWENTY-FIRST CENTURY

For more than thirty years, GDP per capita in Europe has been stuck at barely two-thirds of U.S. levels. By this measure, America continues to maintain its technological and organizational lead. At the same time, however, output per hour worked in Europe has risen to the point where it is now within spitting distance of the United States. Measured this way, Europe's labor productivity is almost 95 percent of U.S. levels. It is actually higher in France, Germany, Ireland, the Netherlands, Norway, Belgium, and Luxembourg than in the United States. Should labor productivity in Europe therefore be regarded as stagnating at 70 percent of the American level or really as on a par with that in the United States?

Another way of putting the point is that although Americans receive more take-home pay, Europeans enjoy vastly greater amounts of leisure time. The statistics on per capita income also disguise higher levels of earnings inequality in the United States. In Europe more people have health insurance. Infant mortality rates are lower. Poverty rates are lower. Rates of violent crime are lower. The number of prisoners incarcerated is only 87 per 100,000 of population versus 685 in the United States. All this suggests that relative welfare may be rather higher than suggested by simple comparisons of per capita GDP.

To be sure, Europe has serious unemployment problems. Hovering as they do in the high single digits, rates of joblessness are almost twice American levels. Burdened by high labor costs, Europe is challenged to maintain its international competitiveness. Yet, excluding Germany, job creation since the middle of the 1990s has been as fast in the euro area as in the United States. And although complaints about the inflexibility of European labor markets are rife, those rigidities have not stood in the way of rapid export growth. European exporters continue to dominate international markets in precision manufactures ranging from luxury sedans to dialysis machines. It is the United States, not Europe, whose auto companies and airlines are on the ropes owing to low productivity and poor product quality and which has massive trade and current-account deficits.

Such observations have not reassured those who worry about Europe's ability to maintain its international competitiveness, expand its exports, and grow in the face of competition not just from the United States but from China and the rest of the developing world. Moving further into the production of high-technology products in which developing countries have relatively little presence is one potential source of insulation from this competition, but here observers worry about the bureaucratic obstacles to new firm formation and prohibitive hiring and firing costs discouraging high-tech start-ups. The counterargument is that the stronger hand of government in setting product standards has given European firms producing high-tech products a leg up on their American competitors. After all, for much of the 1990s it was not some U.S. high-tech giant but Nokia, from tiny Finland, that dominated the global cell-phone market. The point is general: European firms continue to compete successfully in a wide range of high-tech products, from pharmaceuticals to high-speed trains.

Another widely cited U.S. advantage is the country's market-based financial system. America's well-developed securities markets allow investors to take bets on the emerging technologies that proliferate in periods of technological dynamism and uncertainty. The country's market-based financial system enables it to capitalize on the opportunities for financial business created by the ongoing process of securitization. On the other hand, Europe has not been subjected to the kind of scandals and malfeasance that brought down Enron and WorldCom. In light of these excesses, it is not easy to make unconditional statements about which financial system is better.

How are we to understand these contrasts? Is there really a crisis of economic performance in Europe?

Employment and Growth

Any comparison of output and productivity growth must acknowledge that annual hours worked per employed person are only 1,500 in Europe versus more than 1,800 in the United States. In addition, the share of the working-age population employed is 7 percent higher in the United States, with the largest gaps for women and older workers. (See table 12.1.) The result is that roughly one-third of the difference in per capita GDP between the two economies can be attributed to Europe's lower output per hour worked, one-third to fewer hours worked per employed member of the labor force, and one-third to lower employment rates.[1]

These divergences opened up only after 1975; prior to that, the participation rates of men and hours worked per employee had been roughly comparable.[2] Although hours had been falling since the mid-1960s, they had moved in tandem in the two economies, reflecting the common desire of workers to take some of their increased income in the form of leisure. After 1975, however, hours worked per employee stabilized in the United States, but in Europe they continued falling.

Europe's performance in the last quarter of the twentieth century therefore looks better when gauged in terms of GDP per hour than GDP per person. GDP per hour worked rose from less than two-thirds of U.S. levels in 1970 to more than 90 percent in 2000.[3]

---

[1] See Nickell (2003a) and table 2.3 in this book.

[2] Except in the Netherlands and the Nordic countries, where participation rates and hours worked per employee were already lower.

[3] These are figures for the EU-15.

TABLE 12.1

Employment rates by gender and age group, 1970–2003,
selected years (Percent of relevant working-age population)

	1970	1980	1990	2003
	EU-15			
Total	59	60	62	64
By gender				
Men	80	78	74	73
Women	39	43	49	56
By age group				
15–24	51	45	45	40
25–54	65	70	73	77
55–64	47	44	39	42
	United States			
Total	64	67	72	71
By gender				
Men	83	80	81	77
Women	46	55	64	66
By age group				
15–24	53	59	60	54
25–54	70	74	80	79
55–64	60	54	54	60

Source: Organisation for Economic Co-operation and Development Labor Force Statistics Database.

(See figure 12.1.) On this basis, it does not look as though Europe has a productivity problem.

Whether GDP per capita or GDP per hour is a more appropriate basis for comparison depends on how one interprets Europe's shorter hours. One set of observers, what we might call the MIT school, regards Europe's shorter hours as matter of cultural preference.[4] Shorter hours are not forced on European workers by inadequate demand or confiscatory taxes; they are simply the preference of those workers themselves, spoken for by organizations such as IG Metall, the German engineering union that has been pushing for shorter hours since the mid-1980s, and by the continent's Socialist parties, which have made the thirty-five-hour workweek a plank of their electoral platforms.

[4] See Blanchard (2004).

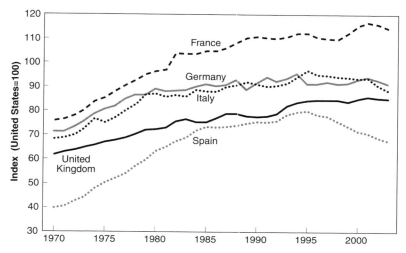

Figure 12.1. Gross domestic product per hour worked, 1970–2003. *Source*: Groningen Growth and Development Centre Database, www.ggdc.net/dseries.

Europeans, in this view, simply "enjoy their leisure more than their U.S. counterparts."[5] And if Europeans' shorter hours are simply a matter of different preferences, then their labor and leisure are equally valuable on the margin. This makes GDP per hour worked the appropriate value to impute to leisure time and the appropriate basis for welfare comparisons.[6]

Unfortunately, preferences for labor and leisure are not something on which there is convincing experimental evidence.[7] Also

[5] Blanchard (2004), p. 10.

[6] To be sure, personal characteristics differ between the employed and the nonemployed. Since the nonemployed tend to be less skilled, average earnings overstate the value of the time of the nonemployed. But McKinsey Global Institute (2002) makes the relevant correction and shows that it leads to only a relatively modest change in U.S.–European productivity comparisons. In addition, to the extent that labor costs are higher in Europe, firms will substitute capital for labor, boosting labor productivity at the expense of investment and therefore of consumption forgone. But, as Blanchard (2004) shows, if European capital–labor ratios are 30 percent higher than the comparable American ratios (which seems like a plausible upper bound), this raises European total factor productivity by only 10 percent, assuming a capital share of one-third.

[7] And the fact that behavior was so similar before 1975 but so different thereafter sits uneasily with the idea that Europeans simply have different tastes leading them to attach more value to leisure. It could, of course, be that Europeans have a higher income elasticity of demand for leisure, but this would then mean that the argument hinges not just on different preferences but on a different nonhomogeneity of preferences, evidence for which is more elusive still.

troubling is the fact that a nonnegligible portion of the shorter hours worked per capita in Europe reflects lower activity (labor-force participation) rates, something that is hard to ascribe to preferences. Although a somewhat higher preference for leisure might encourage some substitution of leisure for labor on the margin, in other words, it is hard to see that it should cause individuals to withdraw from the labor force entirely. Lower participation rates are particularly evident among women and older men. Among older men, the main determinants of cross-country variations appear to be social security provisions that subsidize early retirement and penalize those who work beyond the standard retirement age.[8] These policies were typically implemented after 1975 in the belief that removing older workers from the labor force would reduce unemployment.[9] Similarly, tax systems seem to be the most important factor explaining differences across countries and over time in the participation rates of women.[10]

This is the emphasis of a second set of observers, the members of what we might call the Minnesota school, who argue that Americans work more hours because lower taxes make doing so worth their while.[11] The sum of payroll, income, and consumption tax rates is 55 percent in Europe but only 45 percent in the United States.[12] Coincident with growth in the hours-worked differential, European tax rates have increased by 10 to 15 percent over the last quarter century while rising by only 8 percent in the United States.[13] Prescott (2004) has calibrated a model of a utility-maximizing household

[8] See Nickell (2003a).

[9] In fact, encouraging higher participation rates turned out to be a way to reconcile the demand for generous social services with the need for lower, employment-friendly tax rates, as the experiences of the Netherlands and Ireland, considered later in this chapter, demonstrate.

[10] For details on the Dutch and Irish cases, see the discussion later in this chapter. Freeman and Schettkat (2005) also ascribe part of the difference to the more limited availability of marketed services (child care, for example) in Europe. Though there may be something to the point (high minimum wages may increase the cost of supplying and purchasing such services), this association may also be picking up causality running in the other direction (lower rates of labor force participation reduce the demand for child care, etc.).

[11] See Prescott (2004).

[12] These figures, averages for the period 1988–1995, are constructed as unweighted averages for the EU-15 minus Luxembourg and Greece, for which comparable data are not available. See Nickell et al. (2002).

[13] See table 9.7.

and used it to argue that differences in taxes can account for virtually all of the difference in hours worked between the United States and Germany.

If this is right, then Europeans' greater consumption of leisure is simply a reflection of the different relative prices they face. The values of labor and leisure as they accrue to the household are again equalized on the margin. But the value of an hour of leisure is now less than the value of the output that can be produced in that hour, since part of the latter is lost to taxes before the household can transform it into consumption. Accordingly, imputing the value of leisure on the basis of output per hour worked will overstate European welfare.

A problem for the Minnesota school is that explaining variations in hours worked on the basis of the sum of income, payroll, and consumption taxes requires one to assume a much larger labor-supply elasticity than is consistent with the microeconomic evidence.[14] Moreover, in some European countries, such as Ireland, labor taxes are lower than in the United States and have barely risen for three decades, yet hours worked have nevertheless fallen in line with European trends.[15] Although tax rates vary across countries, in other words, they bear only a loose association with hours worked.[16] (See figure 12.2.)

Another problem for those who believe that Europe is suffering significant welfare losses from high taxes is to explain how the continent allowed itself to get into this mess in the first place. Perhaps

---

[14] See Eissa (1996) for a survey of this literature.

[15] Thus, Irish taxes on labor first rose in the 1980s and then declined, while hours worked trended down steadily.

[16] Thus, any model that purports to explain variations in hours worked exclusively on the basis of the sum of income, payroll, and consumption taxes is too flexible for its own good. Employment is also affected by the generosity of unemployment benefits, the structure of employment protection legislation, laws limiting weekly hours and part-time work, and the efforts of unions with market power to bid up wages. In addition, Americans may work more hours than Europeans because of greater occupational mobility. Ask a U.S. worker why she or he is in the office in the evening or on the weekend and a typical answer will be "to get a raise or a promotion." In Europe's more structured and regulated labor markets, there is less scope for exceptional rewards offering upward mobility to workers who invest extra effort in the form of additional hours on the job.

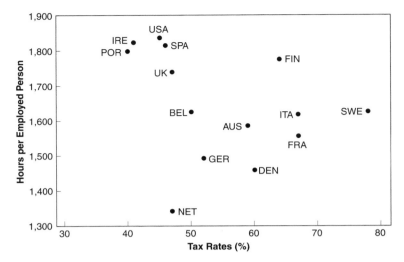

Figure 12.2. Tax rates versus average annual working hours per employed person. *Sources:* Nickell et al. (2002); Organisation for Economic Co-operation and Development, *Labor Force Statistics* (various years).

European policy makers did not realize that additional labor taxation would discourage labor-force participation. Once they started raising taxes and saw participation rates decline, they were forced to raise taxes still further in order to provide the same level of public services, which depressed participation even more.[17] If so, then tax rates can now be scaled back without requiring significant reductions in public services, since lower rates will elicit additional labor supply, broadening the tax base and thereby sustaining revenues. But this explanation requires one to assume considerable ignorance on the part of both European leaders and those who vote for them.

[17] This is essentially the model of Baily and Kirkegaard (2004). Alternatively, if Europeans do in fact have a stronger taste for collective goods, requiring the imposition of additional distortionary taxes to finance them, then it really is not a difference in tastes that explains the difference in hours worked, but rather a difference in the utility attached to collective goods. In this case, welfare comparisons need to be adjusted for the higher "shadow price" that Europeans attach to public goods. There is then nothing particularly inefficient about the European solution. A higher level of public-good provision inevitably entails a lower supply of private goods. And if all taxation is distortionary, then there may be additional costs of supplying public goods, which take the form of distorting the margin between leisure and market work. But there are no unexploited gains left on the table. I return to this point in chapter 13.

If neither tastes nor taxes can wholly explain the decline in hours worked, then what can? One answer is that advanced by Alesina, Glaeser, and Sacerdote (2005). They observe that, compared with the United States, Europe has powerful unions and low levels of labor mobility. Faced with supply shocks such as those that hit the advanced economies starting in the mid-1970s, which lowered labor productivity in some sectors but raised it in others, the United States was able to reallocate labor from sectors where productivity had fallen to sectors where it had risen. In these circumstances, labor productivity economy-wide will increase and with it compensation, eliciting additional labor supply. But in an economy such as Europe's, where labor is not free to move, aggregate productivity and compensation will not rise. To the contrary, average labor productivity may fall, and with it labor supply. In addition, unions in the declining sectors, concerned to maintain membership, may encourage work-sharing and therefore shorter hours. The fact that some people are working shorter hours and taking more days off will then encourage other people to prefer shorter hours and more days off because of coordination externalities—that is, because it may be much harder to get anything done if other people are not at work at the same time. If these coordination externalities are general, then the change in behavior will affect the entire economy and not just the heavily unionized declining sectors.

Although this hypothesis is provocative, the evidence for it is indirect. In support of coordination externalities, the authors cite the fact that most Europeans take their holidays in August, whereas in principle they could do so in any month. Most Europeans, similarly, do not work on Saturdays and Sundays, whereas in principle they could take off any day of the week. These patterns are obviously open to alternative interpretations that have nothing to do with the pattern of supply shocks hitting the economy since 1973.[18] Nor is this story of membership-maximizing unions in declining sectors

---

[18] For example, it might simply be that many people feel that the weather is especially conducive to vacationing in August. Or perhaps the preference for taking Saturdays and Sundays off is rooted in past religious practice.

combined with coordination externalities necessarily incompatible with the tax- and culture-centric interpretations. A complete explanation for differences in hours between the United States and Europe will almost certainly admit a role for all these factors.

Reducing Unemployment

A short workweek need not imply high unemployment; the two phenomena are distinct.[19] Yet unemployment remains a problem throughout much of Europe. At the same time a few successful stories such as the Netherlands and Ireland provide hints about how those high rates of joblessness might be brought down.[20]

Unemployment first rose to double digits in the Netherlands in the early 1980s, reflecting rapidly rising labor costs. Society's response was the Wassenaar Agreement reached in late 1982.[21] Union officials, employer representatives, and government leaders agreed to freeze minimum wages in nominal terms and to eliminate the indexation of other wages to inflation.[22] Given the inflationary climate of the time, the intent was to cut labor costs.[23] To make the freeze palatable and to limit the erosion of take-home pay, the government cut social security and other labor taxes, reducing the tax wedge (the difference between what employers pay to employ a worker and that worker's take-home pay) by half for minimum-wage workers.[24] With private-sector unions on board, the government

[19] Since wages and other factors, including productivity, can adjust.

[20] Two other cases that are sometimes considered in this context are Denmark and Sweden, where similar combinations of macroeconomic and structural reforms worked to stimulate growth from the early to mid-1990s (see Edin and Topel 1997).

[21] Wassenaar, a town near the Hague where the agreement was reached, was the home of the head of the leading union federation.

[22] The minimum wage had been indexed to prices back in 1974, when inflation rates accelerated, and escalator clauses were incorporated into virtually all private-sector wage contracts.

[23] Since the real cost would fall as prices continued to rise. Indeed, this was the effect; in the case of the minimum wage, the fall came to 22 percent in inflation-adjusted terms by 1997.

[24] Ultimately, from 30 to 15 percent. Generalizing this point, Garibaldi and Mauro (2002) find that the size of the tax wedge is one of the more robust determinants of the growth of employment across OECD countries in the 1980s and 1990s.

could then propose reducing public-sector compensation by 3.5 percent, as it did in 1983, and secure 3 percent reductions over the objections of the public-sector unions.

These measures kept average gross real wages stable through the 1980s and into the 1990s—in contrast with their 25 percent increase in the 1970s. Profitability surged as labor's share of national income declined. Buoyed by the improvements in competitiveness induced by the devaluation of the guilder in 1982 and the decline of European currencies against the dollar in the mid-1980s, strong employment gains followed.

These measures were then supplemented by structural reforms. Rules limiting part-time work were relaxed, facilitating women's labor-force participation.[25] In 1973 the labor-force participation rate of women had been less than 30 percent. By the mid-1990s it had risen to 60 percent. In 1982 the employment rate, at 52 percent, was the lowest of any OECD country. By 2000, the employment–population ratio had risen to 72 percent, eight points above the European Union (EU) average. Although this reflected mainly the increased labor-force participation of women, employment rates also rose among older men. In the mid-1980s nearly 10 percent of Dutch men aged fifty-five to sixty-four were drawing disability benefits, and a comparable fraction were drawing unemployment benefits.[26] The 1986–1987 reform of the unemployment insurance system then cut income replacement rates and reduced the duration of benefits for younger workers from thirty to six months.[27] Disability insurance was scaled back by reducing the maximum benefit from 80 to 70 percent of previous earnings and tightening qualification requirements. Beginning in 1987, partially disabled workers were required to find employment consistent with their diminished capa-

[25] Women working part-time in the service sector accounted for more than half of the total increase in employment between 1983 and 1997, according to Garibaldi and Mauro (2002).

[26] In contrast with most other countries, partial disability, including less than 50 percent disability, was supported by the scheme. Nor was it necessary to demonstrate that disability was work-related. Indicative of the generosity of the scheme, the stock of recipients of disability benefits was about twice as high as in other Western European countries.

[27] For details, see Visser and Hemerijck (1997), chapter 2.

bilities. In the early 1990s, further reform of the disability system was pushed through.[28]

These measures worked to raise employment and participation rates. Increased participation in turn broadened the tax base. It allowed essential social protections to be maintained even while tax rates were cut. By 1990, Dutch unemployment had been halved to 5 percent. The country then benefited from the demand stimulus spilling over from reunified Germany. Over the course of the 1990s unemployment continued to fall, reaching 2½ percent at the turn of the twenty-first century.

In Ireland, unemployment rose to 18 percent in 1987, reflecting the severity of the recession in neighboring Britain and the destabilizing effects of Irish fiscal policy.[29] Inspired partly by the Netherlands' success, the country adopted a Programme for National Recovery in 1988. Trade unions and employers agreed to limit annual wage increases to 2.5 percent per year for three years.[30] Employers were understandably enthusiastic about the offer of wage moderation, though skeptical that the agreement would hold. For their part, the unions, enfeebled by declining membership and rising unemployment, were in no position to resist.[31] As in the Netherlands, the government helped to bring the parties together. In addition it

[28] In particular, the 1992 reforms entailed bonuses for firms engaging partially disabled individuals and fines for those whose employees became disabled. The 1993 reforms tightened the criteria for qualifying as partially disabled, required potential recipients to take action to claim payment rather than offering it automatically, and provided for reduced payment following the initial period of disability. The number of new recipients peaked in 1991 and the stock of those receiving disability payment peaked in 1993. See Beljaars and Prins (2000).

[29] Irish fiscal policy was expansionary in the late 1970s, when the economy was already recovering (this was the so-called dash for growth—at some point, every country that fell behind seemed to adopt this hopeful terminology), and then contractionary in the mid-1980s, when growth was weak but the debt–income ratio threatened to spiral out of control.

[30] That the close coordination characteristic of continental corporatism was never attempted reflected the fragmented nature of the union movement and the absence of cohesive peak associations. But aspiring reformers were aware of the successes of coordinated capitalism on the European continent in the postwar period of catch-up and convergence. Seeking to end the thirty-plus-year delay in Irish convergence, they now sought to emulate the continental model. See Ó Gráda and O'Rourke (2000).

[31] Indeed, "the much-weakened unions were glad of the life-line thrown to them by social partnership," as Walsh (2002, p. 15) puts it. They welcomed face-to-face negotiations in a corporatist setting.

supported the bargain by cutting income and social security taxes, especially for low-wage workers, narrowing the tax wedge from 35 percent in 1987 to 29 percent in 1996. At the same time, the authorities maintained spending on education and unemployment relief, something that was possible without aggravating the fiscal position by raising participation and employment rates and thus broadening the tax base.[32] Hardiman (2000) refers to the result as "an experiment in competitive corporatism" in which employer concerns about competitiveness were met in return for a public commitment to maintain social spending and minimum welfare standards.

The 1988 program was then followed by four others, each covering three or four years. These agreements provided for modest wage increases (generally 2–3 percent per year), sought to ensure industrial peace, and addressed a range of social concerns. Bolstered by devaluations of the Irish pound in 1986 and 1993 and by the strong expansion of the OECD economies (note, once again, the parallel with the Netherlands), the balance between productivity and labor costs improved.[33]

From this flowed an enormous expansion of employment. After having stagnated for three decades, numbers at work now grew at an average rate of 3.3 percent per year between 1989 and 2003.[34] Investment and new hiring did little to drive up wages since labor supply was augmented by declining emigration, return flows from abroad, and eventually the highest rate of immigration in the EU.[35]

[32] In addition, the ratio of benefits to wages was scaled back in 1994, and recipients of assistance were eventually required to participate in public employment or training schemes in order to continue receiving benefits after six months on the rolls. To secure agreement on these concessions, the Irish government increased its spending on so-called active labor-market policies (financial support for job creation and activities such as job search, training, and education for the unemployed) to 1½ percent of GDP.

[33] The expansion was then sustained—and, in the view of some, stimulated excessively—by Ireland's participation in Europe's monetary union as a founding member in 1999, which conferred low interest rates on a booming economy.

[34] Walsh (2005), p. 1. The fact that the additional jobs were predominantly full-time—in contrast with the Netherlands—makes this expansion more impressive still.

[35] Labor supply was further augmented by the entry into the labor force of women, whose participation rates had been exceptionally low (just over one-third) at the start of the period. This trend was facilitated by the growth of part-time employment, a development also evident in the Netherlands and a number of other European countries. And, from the late 1990s, there were nonnegligible amounts of foreign migration into the country.

Labor costs rose by only 24 percent between 1988 and 1995, compared with 40 percent in Europe as a whole.[36] Here was an echo—or, to put it another way, much delayed emulation—of the post–World War II Western European strategy of growth based on elastic supplies of labor. An ample supply of numerate, literate, and English-speaking labor, reflecting reforms of the education system put in place in the 1960s, made Ireland an attractive production platform for U.S. companies seeking to sell into the EU.[37] The concentration of foreign information technology (IT), pharmaceutical, and health-care companies in the vicinity of the universities in Dublin, Cork, Galway, and Limerick is indicative of this fact. That education was more general and less vocational than in most of the countries of the continent also may have given Irish labor the skills needed to adapt flexibly to the challenges of the computer age, heightening the attractions of Ireland for IT-oriented multinational firms.[38] Low corporate tax rates also encouraged inward foreign direct investment (FDI), although they were applied across the board; in other words, the authorities did not favor underrepresented industries or depressed regions to any significant extent.[39]

Irish companies, seeing their profits boosted by productivity growth, similarly stepped up investment. The growth of the capital stock accelerated from 2–3 percent per year in the mid-1980s to 5–6

[36] O'Connell (2000), p. 81. Authors as diverse as Blanchard (2000), Glyn (2002), and Walsh (2002) agree that the stability of wages (relative to productivity) was the key factor in the Irish employment miracle.

[37] That the Irish reforms followed on the second enlargement of the EC in 1986, which rendered the European market more attractive, and coincided with the initiation of the Single Market Program promising more of the same was helpful from this point of view.

[38] Adequate infrastructure and efficient public administration further encouraged foreign firms to locate in the Republic. Here was where EU Structural Fund receipts played a role. They helped to support public investment, in infrastructure in particular, in the face of strong fiscal consolidation, especially after the signing of the Maastricht Treaty in 1992. That said, many Irish economists argue that other Europeans (the donors) have tended to exaggerate their role in Ireland's transformation. Consensus estimates ascribe to their impact no more than an additional ½ percent of annual growth.

[39] In addition, these tax-related inducements had been in place for many years before the surge of inward FDI in the 1990s (indeed, some of them were adopted as early as the 1950s). This suggests that favorable tax policies were at most a necessary but not sufficient condition for attracting FDI (Walsh 2002, Honohan and Walsh 2002).

percent in the 1990s. The result was nothing less than the wholesale transformation of the Irish economy. By 2000, unemployment had fallen below 4 percent. Although this was labor-rich growth, it also involved productivity advance and technical change. Between 1989 and 2003, GNP expanded half again as fast as employment, reflecting rising labor productivity.[40] Firms moved up the value-added chain, out of computer assembly into IT support, for example, capitalizing on the availability of skilled graduates. Between 1987 and 2003, GDP per capita rose from 62 percent to 115 percent of the EU-15 average, making Ireland the third richest member of the group, so measured.[41]

Implications for European Unemployment

Might the same approach be taken in the large countries of the continent where unemployment remains pervasive? To be sure, comparable volumes of inward FDI are not likely to be available to large countries where the lingua franca is not also the international scientific and commercial language.[42] Nor do other countries share the favorable demographics that contributed to Ireland's growth spurt. Currency depreciation as a device for jump-starting growth also is not available, since the countries in question are now members of a monetary union whose central bank is decidedly averse to inflation.[43] And the good luck that the Netherlands and Ireland enjoyed in the form of favorable currency movements and robust economic growth cannot be taken for granted.

[40] Walsh (2005), p. 3.

[41] Ireland's relative performance is somewhat less impressive when the comparison is based instead on GNP per person (netting out the returns to foreign investment). In addition there is the fact that about 17 percent of Irish GDP consists of profits of multinational corporations that are ultimately remitted abroad.

[42] Moreover, many of the FDI-supporting financial measures deployed by Ireland may no longer be permitted by EU regulations.

[43] This explains why currency depreciation may not be available to the members of the monetary union as a group, at least absent progress on the fiscal front to reassure the monetary authorities, as suggested later.

If these are all reasons for thinking that other countries might find it more difficult to bring down unemployment, this does not mean that they will find it impossible. Labor costs can be cut. Wages can be brought into line with productivity. Governments can encourage labor's cooperation by guaranteeing essential social protections and reducing distortionary taxes that place a wedge between labor costs and take-home pay. By investing in education and training, they can enhance occupational mobility and render more palatable the increased wage dispersion needed for a fluid, innovation-based economy. They can pursue structural reforms that encourage labor-force participation, thereby broadening the tax base and ensuring that the provision of social services does not threaten fiscal solvency or unnecessarily inflate nonwage labor costs. They can require the recipients of unemployment benefits to enroll in programs designed to impart training and enhance skills and revoke the benefits of those failing to participate.[44]

These supply-side reforms can then be complemented by demand-side stimulus, support for aggregate demand making structural reform easier to swallow. Currency depreciation not being available at the national level, this means a more expansionary stance on the part of the European Central Bank (ECB). Fiscal reforms that narrow public-sector deficits can make the ECB more comfortable with responding in this way. The resulting shift toward a looser monetary policy and a tighter fiscal policy would then make for a more investment-friendly policy mix.

If the nature of these steps is straightforward, their political economy is not. Employment protection measures benefit those presently at work while making it more difficult for the unemployed to be hired.[45] Thus, legislation scaling back these restrictions tends

[44] Such programs might include work experience stints, supplementary education, and training courses. This is a capsule description of how Denmark manages its labor-market programs, which are frequently held up as a paragon of efficiency.

[45] The effects of these measures are in fact disputed. Unlike reductions in social charges, which lower the cost of labor and raise labor demand, the effect of reductions in employment protection on labor demand is ambiguous theoretically. Hiring should be encouraged, since firms are less fearful of incurring costs if the hire does not work out. But firing also should be encouraged, since firms are also less fearful of incurring separation costs. This balance of effects does not suggest that stronger employment protections increase unemployment, at least in

to favor the unemployed at the expense of the employed, who therefore have an incentive to resist the relevant reforms. Similarly, agreement to moderate the growth rate of wages encourages firms to create additional jobs while reducing the take-home pay of those with the most seniority and job security.

Reform will also require solving the coordination problem created by the existence of multiple unions.[46] Each union will be reluctant to agree to wage moderation unless it knows that other unions will also agree. The Dutch and Irish cases suggest that this problem is most easily addressed in economies where agreement on moderating wages can be obtained simultaneously from the entire spectrum of unions and employers.[47] Although Ireland is not widely portrayed as a coordinated economy, the country "moved towards a corporatist system [after 1987]," as Barry puts it, "and labour market outcomes are undoubtedly vastly improved."[48] In particular, the intervention of the government, and specifically its provision of side payments in the form of cuts in taxes on low-wage workers and active labor-market policies, helped to facilitate the coordination of wage negotiations.

Similarly, the Netherlands saw a sharp increase in the coordination of wage bargaining at the time of the Wassenaar Agreement.[49]

---

the short run (Verick 2004). In contrast to this view, Caballero and Hammour (1998) have suggested that increases in separation costs may also encourage firms to substitute capital for labor in the medium run. Time-series analyses such as Lazear (1990), Scarpetta (1996), and Garibaldi and Mauro (2002) find some empirical evidence of this effect. Some of these authors have also suggested that in countries with extensive employment protection, the incentive to adopt new technologies may be lower.

[46] This is not unlike the coordination problem described in chapter 4.

[47] This case can also be made for Denmark and, arguably, for Sweden. The other way of accelerating the adjustment of wages to market-clearing levels, according to the "hump-shape hypothesis," is by significantly reducing union power and moving to a more atomistic labor-market structure, the approach taken by the United Kingdom under Prime Minister Thatcher. See Calmfors and Driffill (1988).

[48] Barry (2002), p. 195. Neocorporatist coordination is not the entire story, of course. In addition, the chastening effect of high unemployment may have simply heightened the unions' appreciation of the need for wage moderation, as Walsh (2002) observes.

[49] Although the standard numerical indicators (for example, those in table 9.4) put the country around the middle of the pack of European countries in terms of coordination of bargaining, Nickell and van Ours (2000, p. 173), among others, characterize Dutch wage bargaining in this period as "highly coordinated." These differences likely reflect the rapid changes in the degree of concertation occurring around this time, which make generalizations difficult.

The Dutch system had been highly corporatist in the 1950s and 1960s, although cooperation then declined in the face of low un-employment.[50] Still, "the whole institutional structure had always been there to allow a return to the consensual nature of industrial relations that is typical of the Dutch situation," as Hartog (1999) notes. There was a long-standing tradition of cooperation and con-sensus decision making stretching back to the practice of *polder*, the Dutch habit of working together to reclaim land from the sea. (Hence references in the 1980s and 1990s to the "*polder* model.") The Wassenaar Agreement thus built on a Dutch legacy of close cooperation that had fallen into abeyance, now developing more decentralized agreements that accommodated the need for greater wage flexibility while also acknowledging the need for economy-wide wage restraint. What was essential was not the strong central-ization of negotiations, which was in any case no longer feasible, but the corporatist mindset that valued solidarity and encouraged cooperative responses to crisis.[51]

In addition, agreement to scale back the generosity of job pro-tections and unemployment benefits may simply be easier in small countries. It may be easier there to put across the message that every-one is in the same boat and to get the relevant interest groups to-gether around the negotiating table. The benefits of reform may also

---

[50] The turning point was the 1970 Wage Act, objections to which provoked two major union federations to organize protest strikes and withdraw from the Labor Foundation and the Social and Economic Council. There was also an unauthorized but highly visible strike in the port of Rotterdam in 1970. The central organizations then tried to reach a series of agreements governing economy-wide wages, but in each case negotiations broke down in the face of strong inflationary pressure and the failure of union federations to agree. Wage negotiations became decentralized and chaotic.

[51] Wilensky (2002) generalizes the point, showing that more corporatist economies, as he defines them, exhibited superior performance in terms of unemployment outcomes in the period 1990–1996 (as well as, to a more limited extent, in the immediately preceding period), a success that he attributes to agreement to restrain wage growth in return for social security and related welfare benefits. The challenge, of course, is to reap the benefits of coordinated labor relations, in the form of agreement on moderating wages in the interest of competitive-ness and investment, without at the same time being saddled with sharp wage compression and other measures limiting labor-market flexibility, whose costs become increasingly burden-some in a dynamic high-tech economy. In other words, what is required is not the traditional model of European corporatism but a revision tailored to the circumstances of the twenty-first century.

be greater insofar as small countries may then find themselves on the receiving end of massive FDI inflows from a much larger world, as in the Irish case.

Here European integration may be having some of the same effects on the continent's larger economies. The more extensive the economic integration, the greater the scope for producers to relocate to lower-cost countries and regions within the EU, and the greater the incentive to reform in order to become a beneficiary rather than a victim of that process. Although enlargement of the EU to the east is clearly having this effect, the tendency is more general.[52] Already European integration has facilitated product-market integration by hastening the removal of border controls and discriminatory product standards. The creation of the euro, by further reducing transaction costs and making finance and production even more mobile, is an important step in this direction. More than ever, measures that push up labor costs or impose more restrictive work rules threaten to push jobs abroad, whereas measures moderating wages and making labor markets more flexible promise to attract employment from other countries.

Finally, in both Ireland and the Netherlands, reform may have been made easier by the perception that the rise of unemployment constituted a crisis. Already in 1979 there was a perception that Dutch growth was stagnating; in response, the government took the extraordinary step of bypassing existing institutions and appointing an ad hoc committee chaired by Gerrit Wagner, the president of Royal Dutch Shell, that bluntly recommended essentially the entire catalog of reforms adopted subsequently. Hartog (1999) cites as a key factor in the Wassenaar Agreement the fact that "unemployment had skyrocketed in the early 1980s, creating a strong sense of urgency." Similarly, in her discussion of Ireland, Hardiman (2000) refers to the "real sense of crisis" pervading the economy. Not only

---

[52] Thus, in the spring of 2005, General Motors' Opel subsidiary essentially ran a competition between Sweden and Germany for production of its midsize Saab models. Germany won as a result of workers agreeing first to freeze their wages, then to accept a series of nominal wage cuts, and finally to welcome the introduction of flexible work schedules linked to fluctuations in demand.

was unemployment well into double digits in both countries, but the share of the working-age population that was either unemployed or not in the labor force had risen to nearly 50 percent.[53] These outsiders, whose job prospects brightened when the government engineered a social pact to moderate the rate of growth of wages and agreed to relax employment protection measures, may not have constituted a political majority, but they came close. Their numbers may thus have compelled the government to adopt employment-friendly reforms in the interest of its own survival.[54] This perspective suggests that the widespread perception that the unemployment problem has reached crisis proportions is reason to hope that European societies are finally prepared to embrace fundamental change.[55]

Productivity Growth

Productivity growth, after running at rates nearly double that of the United States between 1980 and 1995, slowed in the subsequent seven years to barely three-quarters of the U.S. rate.[56] (See table

[53] Half again as high as the European Community average. See Tille and Yi (2001), p. 2.

[54] Unions' attention may also have been galvanized by the Thatcher revolution in the United Kingdom and the prospect that their failure to cooperate in reaching a solution might lead to radical political changes with even more unfavorable consequences for their position. Scharpf (2000), p. 60, argues this for the Netherlands, and much the same argument can be made for Ireland.

[55] At the same time, it suggests that some of the measures devised by European countries to address their unemployment problems may not be conducive to thoroughgoing reform. Limited-term contracts have been used, for example, to reduce the cost of employing new entrants to the labor force. Typically, individuals hired under these contracts do not enjoy the entire range of job protections until they have been employed for at least twelve months. In France, the share of employees on limited-term contracts rose from essentially zero in the mid-1980s to more than 10 percent at the end of the 1990s. In Spain, workers on temporary contracts accounted for virtually the entire increase in employment over the two decades. In many cases, the social charges required of firms are less for limited-term workers. Insofar as these measures reduce costs for employers, they are likely to create some additional demand for labor. This is why they were adopted, after all. But if, indeed, crisis breeds reform, then half-measures that reduce unemployment slightly may at the same time weaken support for more thoroughgoing measures.

[56] This comparison is based on the rate of growth of output per hour worked. Figures for output per capita show the same thing, because from the mid-1990s the rate of growth of hours was no longer slower in Europe than in the United States. Thus, the controversy over

TABLE 12.2

Sources of labor productivity growth, United States and EU-15, 1980–2001
(Average annual percentage increase)

	1980–1995	1995–2001
EU-15		
Average labor productivity	2.33	1.37
Contribution of capital deepening	1.21	0.90
Information technology	0.32	0.42
Noninformation technology	0.88	0.48
Total factor productivity	1.13	0.46
Production of IT		0.27
Other		0.19
Total IT contribution		0.69
U.S.		
Average labor productivity	1.37	1.85
Contribution of capital deepening	0.67	1.05
Information technology	0.48	0.72
Noninformation technology	0.19	0.32
Total factor productivity	0.70	0.80
Production of IT		0.44
Other		0.36
Total IT contribution		0.62

Source: van Ark and Smits (2004), table 6.

Note: The contribution of total factor productivity includes the contribution of labor quality.

12.2.) It is tempting to ascribe this to America's comparative advantage in intensive growth. But this hypothesis cannot explain why productivity growth slumped relative to the United States so suddenly after 1995. To explain this it is necessary to add another element, such as rising returns to investment in innovative information and communications technologies (ICT). The share of ICT investment in GDP has been consistently higher in the United States, despite Europe's higher overall investment rates.[57] What is true of ICT inputs has been true of ICT outputs as well: eleven of the world's twenty-five most popular Web sites ranked in terms of

whether the rate of growth of output per hour or per capita is a better measure of performance is not relevant to the narrow issue under discussion here.

[57] Circa 2001, ICT investment as a share of GDP was 4.2 percent in the United States versus 2.6 percent in Europe, as calculated by Timmer, Ypma, and van Ark (2003).

traffic are based in the United States, for example, whereas not one is in Europe.[58]

Extrapolating from a short period is risky. The second half of the 1990s was when a number of European governments sought to counter long-term unemployment by cutting payroll taxes for low-skilled workers, substitution toward whom could have depressed productivity growth. In addition, U.S. productivity growth was goosed by rapid demand-driven expansion and high capacity-utilization rates, while European productivity growth was slowed by the fiscal retrenchment pursued in countries seeking to meet the Maastricht criteria. Still, data postdating the late 1990s, when the U.S. economy was not artificially stimulated by a stock-market boom and Europe was not held back by fiscal stringency, seem to confirm that productivity growth has accelerated in the United States relative to Europe.[59]

Although it is not certain that the capacity to develop and apply ICT is responsible for this divergence, there are reasons for thinking that this may be the case. R&D spending, which is crucial for the development of these new technologies, continues to lag in Europe. In 2003, the United States spent 2.8 percent of its GDP on R&D, compared with 1.9 percent EU-wide. In Europe, limited cooperation between industry and academia makes it difficult to tailor research to commercial needs. In addition, the small, newly established firms that tend to pioneer new information technologies have the greatest difficulty coping with the complexities of European regulation.[60] Where it may take one or two weeks to complete the paperwork necessary for setting up a new business in the United States, the same process can take months in Italy and Spain.[61] Europe's immi-

---

[58] The other fourteen were based in China (seven), Korea (six), and Japan (one).

[59] Thus, data from the Sapir Report suggest that the gap between the United States and Europe in the rate of growth of output per hour again doubled between 2000–2001 and 2002–2003. See Independent High-Level Study Group (2003).

[60] Revealingly, Nicoletti and Scarpetta (2003) find that the adoption of best-practice technology in manufacturing is fastest in countries and sectors where entry barriers to new firms are lowest. The Single Market has gone some way toward harmonizing and thereby simplifying these regulations, but the rate of convergence to the EU standard continues to differ widely among member states.

[61] In the Spanish case, as many as fourteen different steps involving six different agencies were required in the mid-1990s.

gration-unfriendly policies make the continent less attractive for high-tech specialists hailing from Asia. Its emphasis on vocational as opposed to university education makes for a labor force less attuned to radical new technologies.[62] Lower hiring and firing costs make it easier for U.S. entrepreneurs to gamble on unproven technologies of great promise but uncertain commercial potential.[63] In Europe, where companies taking on employees also take on financial liabilities in the event of subsequent separation, it makes sense for start-ups to ramp up more slowly.

Similarly, although Europe's financial system is well suited to mobilizing saving and deploying it for investment by incumbent firms, much of this investment is poorly allocated now that technology is in flux. It does not go to the start-ups and small firms that are the motors of output and productivity growth.[64] Europe's tradition of bank-based finance makes for conservative investment, banks preferring to lend to enterprises using familiar technologies and possessing tangible collateral in the form of equipment and buildings. Venture capital and securities markets are less developed than in the United States, making it harder for enterprises developing and applying radical new technologies first to obtain seed money and then to go public.[65] Low levels of investment in distribution-related

[62] Thus, in 1991, 79 percent of upper secondary students in West Germany and 71 percent of Italian students were enrolled in vocational or apprenticeship programs. The EU average was 58 percent. In the United States, there is no separate stream of vocational training, and the share of students who completed 30 percent or more of all credits in specific labor-market preparation courses was just 7 percent in 1990 (Krueger and Kumar 2002). Only 14 percent of those enrolled in postsecondary education in 1991 were working toward a vocational associate's degree. On the other hand, 52 percent in the United States but only 28 percent in Germany and 33 percent in France of the relevant cohorts entered universities.

[63] Caballero et al. (2004) attempt to quantify these costs and demonstrate their negative correlation with productivity growth in a panel of industry-level data for a variety of countries. In their results, Belgium, France, and Italy stand out as having relatively high labor-force adjustment costs and relatively low productivity growth.

[64] One indication of this is that Germany possesses an incremental capital–output ratio of 4, whereas the comparable ratio in the United States is a more efficient 2.5.

[65] Although banks and other institutional investors have been moving into the provision of early-stage risk capital, such finance averaged only 0.05 percent of GDP in Europe as against 0.17 percent in the United States between 1999 and 2001. See Independent High-Level Study Group (2003), p. 38. Bottazzi and Da Rin (2002) find only a weak association in Europe between access to venture capital and exceptional growth of jobs and sales. This may reflect the functional underdevelopment of European venture capital, which works mainly to relax the credit constraints imposed on small firms and start-ups by the existence of a bank-based

IT services by small and medium-sized European firms are widely ascribed to the conservatism of bank lenders and to the difficulty of accessing alternative, market-based sources of finance.[66]

At the level of the individual, the compression of relative wages blunts the incentive for risk taking. The high taxes applied to upper incomes and Europe's reluctance to lavish U.S.-style rewards, including stock options, on successful entrepreneurs work in the same direction. So do high bankruptcy costs. In the United States an individual can declare bankruptcy and start over with a clean slate while protecting personal assets such as the family home, but bankrupts in the Netherlands, Spain, and Sweden must settle their debts in full, out of future earnings if necessary.

This pessimism should not be overdone. Europe has many successful universities actively seeking to foster business collaboration. Efforts are under way to ease the immigration of skilled workers from other continents. Labor-market reforms have included efforts to limit hiring and firing costs. The venture-capital industry is growing, and financial markets are slowly but surely being remade along Anglo-Saxon lines. Loans now account for only a minority of European banks' asset portfolios; much of the rest is in the form of securities, including the securities of smaller, more speculative companies that are increasingly able to access European bond markets in the wake of the euro. Were all this not true, it would be impossible to understand how Europe has so many successful companies and such dynamic export growth.

These arguments need the discipline of numbers. Unfortunately, efforts to measure returns to investment in IT are complicated by the fact that the relative prices of the relevant inputs and outputs are changing rapidly. Moore's Law suggests that computation capacity doubles every eighteen months; its corollary is that the observed price of a machine incorporating this capacity should be reduced by

financial system rather than providing the entire package of financial and quasi-managerial services offered by U.S. venture capital firms.

[66] See Rammer (2004). Thus, in 2002, the Neuer Markt, Germany's Frankfurt-based equivalent of the Nasdaq intended as a source of initial public offering–derived finance for high-tech companies, was shut down for lack of interest.

half when calculating inputs into production. Timmer, Ypma, and van Ark (2003) have gone partway, correcting IT inputs for quality change.[67] They find that although America's faster rate of growth of labor productivity in the period 1995–2001 reflects both a larger contribution of capital deepening (giving labor more capital with which to work) and faster total factor productivity (TFP) growth (that part of output growth that cannot be accounted for by the growth of capital and labor inputs), most of the differential is accounted for by the more rapid growth of TFP.[68] Greater capital deepening, which is entirely in the form of higher levels of investment in ICT (3 to 4 percent of GDP in the United States, compared with 2 to 3 percent in the EU—see table 12.3), explains only one-quarter of a percentage point of America's labor productivity growth advantage over Europe. In contrast, 70 percent of the measured difference in the growth of labor productivity is accounted for by America's faster rate of TFP growth.

The IT-producing sector is where the United States excels, for all the reasons enumerated earlier. But at 6 percent of GDP, that sector is too small to explain economy-wide differences in productivity trends.[69] Studies have found that America's productivity advantage since the mid-1990s has been centered in retail trade, wholesale trade, and financial services. Europe, in contrast, has enjoyed faster productivity growth in telecommunications, reflecting the effects of privatization and uniform product standards imposed at the EU level.[70] (See table 12.4.)

Retail trade, wholesale trade, and financial services are ICT-using activities. Banks use computers to provide back-office services.

---

[67] In principle, one would also want to apply the same correction to IT outputs.

[68] To return to an earlier question, the dominance of TFP over capital deepening suggests that it was not merely differences in business-cycle and demand conditions that accounted for faster labor productivity growth in the United States in the second half of the 1990s, although there may be methodological problems that lead researchers to falsely attribute to TFP some part of the productivity growth really associated with demand.

[69] Even in order to get a number as high as 6 percent it is necessary to adjust for changes in relative prices (reducing the price and thus increasing the volume of IT-related production).

[70] Thus, the EU adopted a common European standard, the Global System for Mobile Communications (GSM), for second-generation mobile telephony in the mid-1990s.

TABLE 12.3
Information and communications technology
investment as a percentage of gross domestic
product, 1980–2001 (Current prices)

	1980	1990	2001
Sweden	1.6	2.7	4.7
Finland	1.1	1.9	4.3
Belgium	1.7	3.1	3.6
Denmark	1.5	2.9	3.6
Greece	0.7	1.3	3.3
United Kingdom	0.8	2.3	3.0
Netherlands	1.6	2.4	2.9
Germany	1.3	2.4	2.5
Italy	1.5	2.3	2.5
Austria	1.3	1.9	2.4
Portugal	1.2	1.8	2.1
Spain	0.9	2.5	2.1
France	1.0	1.5	2.1
Ireland	0.9	1.2	1.9
EU-15	1.2	2.2	2.6
United States	2.5	3.3	4.2

Source: van Ark and Smits (2004), table 5.
Note: European countries ranked in descending order
of shares in 2001.

They use voice-recognition systems and the Internet to interact more efficiently with their customers. IT limits inventory carrying costs for retailers by providing real-time links between the point of sale and assembly facilities. Thus, although the explanation for faster TFP growth in the United States does not reside mainly in the ICT-producing sector, faster take-up of ICT may be at its heart.[71]

European companies have incentives to adopt these same labor-saving technologies, more so given the high cost of labor. Anyone who has had to master the intricacies of an automatic payment ma-

[71] This is not to say that IT is entirely responsible for the exceptional productivity performance of these sectors. For example, observers of the retail sector cite also improvements in distribution logistics and the advent of big-box stores (which spread more quickly in the United States than in Europe as a result of more accommodating land-use regulations). At the same time, it is hard to imagine that these other changes could have taken place absent advances in IT. This example thus points to the fundamental difficulty of separating out the roles of IT and other factors contributing to productivity growth.

TABLE 12.4

Labor productivity by sector in the euro area and the United States, 1986–2000
(Per person employed; percentage change per year)

	Euro area		United States	
	1986–1995	1996–2000	1986–1995	1996–2000
Manufacturing	2.8	2.7	3.2	5.6
Of which:				
High-technology industries	3.1	3.6	5.1	11.1
Utilities	3.3	6.9	3.0	2.4
Business-sector services	1.4	0.9	1.1	4.2
Of which:				
Wholesale and retail trade	1.8	0.5	1.3	7.6
Telecommunications	5.2	13.8	3.9	4.6
Finance and insurance	1.6	3.7	1.2	6.5

Source: European Central Bank, *Monthly Bulletin* (July 2004).

chine in a public parking garage in Europe will appreciate this fact. That such investment has not produced faster TFP growth may reflect the higher cost of computer hardware in Europe, itself a function of residual barriers to imports and competition.[72] It may reflect obstacles to downsizing and changing workplace rules and conventions and thus the difficulty of reorganizing the labor force to work more efficiently with this new technology.[73]

A half percentage point per year difference in labor productivity growth, much less one-sixth of a percentage point per year difference in the contribution of TFP growth outside the IT-producing sector, is not an economic disaster waiting to happen. And even if rigid labor markets are a problem for firms seeking to reorganize and reap the productivity benefits of IT, help is on the way in the form of

[72] Baily and Kirkegaard (2004) report that the cost of computer hardware is 20 percent higher in Europe than in the United States.

[73] It may also reflect the expansion of unskilled employment in these sectors in response to cuts in payroll taxes on low earnings adopted by governments to address long-term unemployment, as discussed earlier. Gust and Marquez (2002) find that ICT investment is lower in OECD countries with relatively stringent employment protection legislation, suggesting that high firing costs are an obstacle to the reorganization of work practices that is essential to reaping benefits from ICT investment. Similarly, critics of European land-use policy suggest that regulations in this area may also have slowed the reorganization of retailing to take advantage of IT by limiting the construction of big-box stores in urban centers. See, for example, Gordon (2004).

labor-market reform. Europe has the advantages of abundant human capital and strong regulatory institutions. Although there are no grounds for complacency, there are good reasons for not taking Europessimism too far.

Eastern European Prospects and Western European Implications

In the last four decades, the economic and political center of the United States has shifted to the South. This reflects not just the cooling influence of air-conditioning but also lower levels of unionization, more flexible labor markets, and competitive wages, factors that attracted New England textile firms and, more recently, European automobile and tire producers to the region in the first place. It reflects the South's liberal land-use policies, which facilitate the construction of greenfield plants and subdivisions. The American economy has benefited enormously from the South's dynamism and flexibility. It is fair to ask whether the EU's expansion to the East could have a similarly invigorating effect.

Like the American South after World War II, the EU's new Central and Eastern European members have relatively low labor costs and liberal land-use policies. As of 2003, their per capita incomes were still only about half of the EU-15 average. (See table 12.5.) This implies even more scope for catch-up than that available to Greece, Portugal, and Spain when they joined the EU in the 1980s, that trio's per capita incomes having been nearly two-thirds the EU average. Similarly, although the accession economies are behind Western Europe in the quality of their infrastructure, that gap is no greater than the one that separated Greece, Portugal, and Spain from incumbent EU members in the 1980s. The accession economies also compare favorably with the Mediterranean countries in the 1980s in terms of the quality of their human capital.[74] Re-

---

[74] A report by the Boston Consulting Group published in 2004 concluded that labor productivity in Central European factories matched that in Western Europe at comparable levels of capital investment and technology, reflecting comparable levels of human capital in Europe's West and East. See *Economist* (2004).

flecting the more extensive privatization of enterprise and liberalization of finance as well as a more favorable global environment, they are receiving more FDI than Greece, Portugal, and Spain did in the 1980s (3–6 percent of GDP as opposed to 1–3 percent). It costs only one-sixth as much to employ an autoworker in Slovakia as in France or Germany. Labor productivity is also lower, to be sure, but not by enough to offset these advantages. As a result, Slovakia has now collected virtually the entire set—one each—of the assembly plants of the principal Western European automotive producers.

In effect, the accession economies are applying the postwar Western European formula of wage moderation, exports, and high investment. Investment rates in the region are running at 24–25 percent, significantly above the EU-15 rate of 18 percent. The accession economies thus have scope for growing rapidly by pursuing the same extensive-growth strategy employed by Western Europe for a quarter century after World War II.

Nor is the quality of institutions obviously inferior to that in poorer members of the EU-15, not now and certainly not when the latter were first admitted to the union. As a precondition for gaining admission to the EU, the new members were compelled to adopt an *acquis communautaire* enumerating a long list of requirements regarding their public administration, judicial systems, and social policies. As members of the EU they also inherit the EU's competition policy and, eventually, its stable money in the form of the euro. To be sure, there is slippage between the letter and the application of the law. Judicial systems are easier to design than are competent judges to train. There is no shortage of complaints about the quality of public administration in the accession economies, and uncertainties about the administration of laws and regulations are widely invoked to explain why Central and Eastern Europe is not receiving even larger amounts of FDI.[75]

Although these problems have not been eliminated, their severity has been significant reduced. Opinions about the quality of institutions circa 2002 suggest few significant differences between the

---

[75] Again, see *Economist* (2004).

CHAPTER 12

TABLE 12.5
Income disparities in the enlarged European Union, 2004

Country	GDP per capita (in PPP) (EU-25 = 100)
Luxembourg	230
Ireland	136
Denmark	119
Austria	113
Belgium	108
Finland	106
Netherlands	106
United Kingdom	105
Germany	104
Italy	102
Sweden	102
France	101
Spain	85
Greece	73
Portugal	69
Average, EU-15	**102**
Slovenia	73
Cyprus	71
Malta	70
Czech Republic	66
Hungary	56
Estonia	55
Slovakia	54
Lithuania	47
Poland	44
Latvia	43
Average, new member states	**54**
Average, EU-25	**100**

Source: European Commission, AMECO database.

accession economies and, say, Greece, the latter being another country that was well behind the incumbents in terms of per capita income at the time of accession but then began to close the gap.[76] For example, World Bank surveys of the reliability of rule of law and control of corruption place Greece just below the seventy-fifth per-

---

[76] Employing essentially the same data, Weder (2001) examines the correlation between per capita income and the quality of institutions, finding that the accession economies are situated squarely on the regression line. That is, to the extent that the quality of their institu-

centile of the hundred-plus countries for which investigators solicited them.[77] (See figure 12.3.) Standard cross-country growth regressions predict that, given this level of institutional quality, there should be scope for an additional 1 to 1½ percentage points of growth per year over and above the EU average until the gap is substantially closed.[78] Convergence would proceed even faster, of course, were the high-income countries of Western Europe to permit free labor mobility. But this bumps up against fears of immigration. The incumbent member states in their wisdom have insisted on a transitional period of up to seven years, during which the freedom of the citizens of the new members to work in the West will continue to be constrained.

All this assumes that obvious policy mistakes, fiscal mistakes prominent among them, will be avoided. Political pressure for public spending is intense, and capital inflows make financing it seem deceptively easy. This means one important ingredient of the Irish recipe for convergence, fiscal discipline, may be difficult to replicate in Central and Eastern Europe.

In addition, the accession economies will be required to hold their exchange rates stable for at least two years as a precondition for acceptance into the euro area. Adopting the euro is a logical aspiration for economies already so closely linked to the euro area, but combining fiscal laxity with pegged exchange rates can be a

---

tions is not yet up to Western European standards, this is entirely explicable by their lesser stage of economic development. The tempting inference to draw from this finding is that the remaining discrepancy will disappear as living standards and levels of development catch up with those in the West.

[77] Data here and in the rest of this paragraph are from Kaufmann, Kraay, and Mastruzzi (2003). Confidence intervals around this point estimate range from about 70 to 80. (Italy is just ahead of Greece, while the other members of the EU-15 are in the eightieth and ninetieth percentiles.) The point estimates in figure 12.3 for the eight Central and Eastern European accession economies are quite close to those for Greece, and the confidence intervals overlap, suggesting no significant difference in opinions regarding the quality of institutions.

[78] This is the implication of the regressions in Eichengreen and Ghironi (2002), table 15.1. The regression analysis in Crafts and Kaiser (2004) points to similar conclusions; the authors conclude that the accession economies could grow by 3.5 percent a year (compared with rates slightly in excess of 2 percent exhibited by Western Europe). They also use an alternative growth-accounting approach, which suggests slightly faster convergence (depending on what is assumed about investment and TFP growth rates).

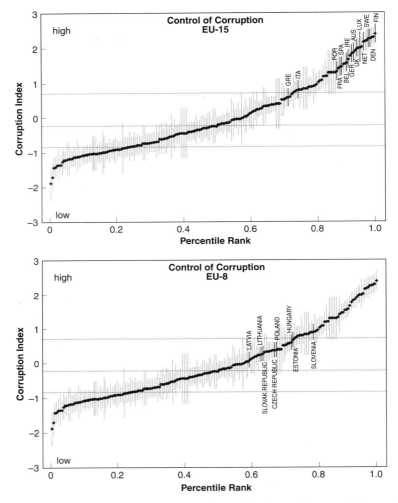

Figure 12.3. Control of corruption, 2002. *Source*: Kaufmann, Kraay, and Mastruzzi (2003).

recipe for disaster. The high interest rates associated with the combination of tight monetary policy and loose fiscal policy are a magnet for portfolio capital from abroad. As a result of these capital inflows, the currency will tend to become overvalued. Eventually, investors will question its sustainability, causing capital flows to turn around and the whole house of cards to come crashing down.

There is a real risk that the convergence of Eastern European with Western European living standards will be disrupted by this sequence of events.

Then there is the danger that the new member states will be forced by the incumbents, seeking to establish a "level playing field," to raise corporate tax rates above the levels appropriate for late-developing capital-scarce economies seeking to attract FDI. To this point, such pressure for "tax harmonization" has been successfully resisted by a coalition of new member states and some of the more free-market-oriented incumbents such as the United Kingdom. One hopes that this will remain the case.

How will the EU's eastward enlargement affect economic performance in the West? Most obviously, the flow of FDI to the East intensifies the pressure on Western firms and workers to cut costs or risk their livelihoods. There is a growing body of evidence of their willingness to act on this fact. In the summer of 2004, workers at two Siemens plants in Germany agreed to work five additional hours per week without extra pay in order to prevent their jobs from being relocated to Hungary. Similar concessions were then extended by French workers at a Bosch factory near Lyons in response to the threat that their jobs would be exported to the Czech Republic.[79]

In the same way, Slovakia's adoption of a flat 19 percent tax on capital, half of German levels, creates pressure for other countries to cut their rates of capital taxation or lose out in the competition for investment.[80] Austria, which borders on Slovakia, responded in 2005 by cutting its corporate tax rate from 34 to 25 percent.[81] In turn this created pressure for Germany to follow.[82]

[79] To be sure, French responses were more limited; in the case of Bosch, workers agreed only to one additional hour per week without extra compensation. And in both instances, concessions were limited to those necessary to prevent existing jobs from migrating to Eastern Europe, not of a scope sufficient to create new ones.

[80] Poland likewise lowered its corporate tax rate steeply, by 8 percentage points to 19 percent. Romania, soon to be an EU member as well, adopted a 16 percent flat tax in 2005.

[81] Finland cut its corporate tax rate from 29 to 26 percent, and Greece cut its from 35 to 32 percent.

[82] As noted earlier, there is also a backlash in the form of demands from some of the high-income countries that the EU be given authority to mandate the upward convergence of tax rates. In mid-2004, the French finance minister Nicolas Sarkozy objected that tax rates in the

Economic Prospects

Popular accounts portray Europe as either an economic phoenix or a basket case. The phoenix view observes that output per hour worked has risen from barely 50 percent of U.S. levels after World War II and two-thirds of those levels in 1970 to nearly 95 percent today and that labor productivity so measured is actually running above U.S. levels in a substantial number of Western European countries. Since the turn of the twenty-first century, the euro zone has created more new jobs than either the United States or the United Kingdom. Its exports have grown faster than those of the United States. It provides more of its citizens with health insurance, efficient public transportation, and protection from violent crime.

The basket-case view observes that the growth of aggregate output and output per hour have slowed relative to the United States since the mid-1990s. Between 1999, when EMU began, and 2005, euro-zone growth averaged just 1.8 percent, less than two-thirds the 3.1 percent recorded by the United States. Productivity growth has trended downward since the early 1990s, owing to labor-, product-, and capital-market rigidities, inadequate R&D spending, and high tax rates—in contrast to the United States, where productivity growth has been rising. The growth of the working-age population has fallen to zero and is projected to turn significantly negative in coming years. High old-age dependency ratios imply large increases in the share of national income devoted to health care, lower savings rates, potentially heavier fiscal burdens, and an aversion to risk taking. All these are reasons to worry about Europe's competitiveness and economic performance.

One way of reconciling these views is to distinguish the distant from the recent past and the past from the future. Comparing the European economy at the midpoint and the end of the twentieth century, there is no disputing the phoenix view. Economic performance over this half century was a shining success both absolutely

---

EU's new Eastern European member states were too low. See Patten (2004) for a critical view of these comments.

and relative to the United States. More recently, however, Europe has tended to lag. Although this does nothing to put the past in a less positive light, it creates doubts about the future.

One way of understanding these changing fortunes is in terms of the transition from extensive to intensive growth. Europe could grow quickly for a quarter century after World War II and continue doing well relative to the United States for some additional years because the institutions it inherited and developed after World War II were well suited for importing technology, maintaining high levels of investment, and transferring large amounts of labor from agriculture to industry. Eventually, however, the scope for further growth on this basis was exhausted. Once the challenge was to develop new technologies, and once growth came to depend more on entrepreneurial initiative than on brute-force capital accumulation, the low rates of R&D spending, high taxes, conservative finance, and emphasis on vocational education delivered by those same institutions become more of a handicap than a spur to growth. Consistent with this view is the fact that Europe's economic difficulties seem to have coincided with the ICT revolution and the opportunities it affords to economies with a comparative advantage in pioneering innovation, as well as with globalization and growing competition from developing countries such as China that are moving into the production of the quality manufacturing goods that have been a traditional European stronghold.

The question is what to do about it. Is it necessary for Europe to remake its institutions along American lines? Or is there still a future for the European model?

- THIRTEEN -

THE FUTURE OF THE
EUROPEAN MODEL

W riting the history of the future is harder than writing the history of the past. One manifestation of this is the familiar tendency of futurists to extrapolate trends. Output and productivity growth in the United States having surpassed that in Europe for the last decade, there is a tendency to assume that this gap will persist, leaving the European economy still further behind and creating a crisis for the European model that will ultimately force the continent to remake its institutions along Anglo-Saxon lines.

A longer view gives grounds for questioning whether recent trends will persist. In the 1980s it was fashionable to argue that a vibrant Japan would overtake the United States and that the United States urgently needed to remake its institutions along Japanese lines. In the first half of the 1990s, when productivity grew faster in Europe, it was argued that the United States needed to remake its economy along European lines, paying less attention to impatient financial markets and placing more emphasis on vocational training and industrial policy. Today both of these examples of "systems envy" have fallen out of fashion. For anyone encountering forceful statements of American triumphalism and Eurosclerosis, history is a reminder that this too shall pass.

Rather than proceeding by extrapolating from recent events, a more illuminating approach may be to apply the concept used in chapter 1 to explain postwar economic growth, namely the "fit" between an economy's institutions and the economic and technological imperatives of the day. The structures and institutions inherited from earlier periods and elaborated after World War II were better suited to incremental than to radical innovation and to periods when the challenge for growth was to fine-tune and apply existing technologies rather than to fashion new ones out of whole cloth. They were tailored to a world in which international competition was limited and foreign investment was regulated, not to one of seamless integration and intense cross-border competition. The institutions of European integration were designed for a handful of countries, not for a European Union of more than two dozen members with diverse political cultures and very different visions of the future. They were devised to achieve limited economic goals—the expansion of heavy industry, the liberalization of trade, the deregulation of product markets—not to push through wide-ranging and socially invasive structural reforms. For better or worse, these are the institutions that have been handed down to the present.

The implication is that one's view of how Europe will do relative to the United States should be conditioned by one's forecast of technological and organizational developments going forward. If coming years will be marked by radical innovations in information technology, biotechnology, and nanotechnology comparable to the innovations of the last decade, then an institutional inheritance more conducive to incremental than to radical innovation will not favor economic and productivity growth. If, on the other hand, the last decade was exceptional and future growth opportunities will instead favor countries with the capacity to apply, refine, and elaborate existing technologies, then Europe's inheritance will be less of a burden; indeed, it may be an advantage. Similarly, one can argue that global integration has further to go or else that a backlash is coming, again with different implications. One can conclude that European integration has developed irresistible momentum or that the process has reached its limit. Since forecasts of these developments are uncertain, so too, inevitably, are forecasts of Europe's economic performance.

415

My own conjecture is that coming decades will continue to be characterized by rapid, discontinuous advances in science-based, production-relevant technical knowledge. The basic-science content, pace, and discontinuities of technical change all trended upward over the course of the nineteenth and twentieth centuries.[1] To the extent that the basis for economic growth is cumulative, this may be even truer in the future than in the past.[2] Similarly, I suspect that the dual processes of regional integration and economic globalization will continue to be driven by technological changes reducing the costs of transacting across borders and that the results are unlikely to be rolled back. If these assumptions are correct, then it follows that Europe will have to adapt.

But Europe's response will differ from that of the United States owing to its different institutional inheritance. Europe has evolved a network of institutions whose components fit together in complementary ways. This makes it difficult to replace one without simultaneously replacing others, since replacing only one may result in problems of compatibility with the rest, depressing efficiency and productivity growth rather than raising them. These negative side effects create a predictable resistance to change. The result may then be to lock the economy into a structure that is not well suited to new conditions.

Here too, however, it can be misleading simply to extrapolate from the past. Institutions and practices do change despite the existence of network effects. In the present context one can point to any number of potential catalysts, the most obvious being the existence of a single integrated European market for merchandise, capital, and labor. Competition within the single market ratchets up the pressure to undertake productivity-enhancing structural reforms or risk losing business to neighboring countries. Enlargement of the EU to include the countries of Eastern and Central Europe further

[1] For the requisite nuance, see Mowrey and Rosenberg (1998).
[2] Here I can be accused of falling into the futurist's trap of extrapolating recent trends. I plead guilty.

intensifies the pressure to cut costs and raise productivity. And if this is not enough, there is also the pressure of globalization—competition from not just the United States and Japan but now also China and other developing countries.

There have been at least the glimmerings of a response for the past decade. In 1996, Viessmann, the manufacturer of heating technology, secured a two-and-a-half hour per week increase in working hours with no increase in pay from its German workers when it warned that it was considering moving production to a lower-wage European country. In the late 1990s, Belgium introduced legislation stipulating that nominal wage increases should not exceed a weighted average of those in neighboring countries and contemplated a number of farther-reaching structural measures coincident with Renault's decision to close a Belgian plant and expand another in Spain. In 2004, the Christian Democrat–led coalition governing the Netherlands proposed sharp reductions in welfare benefits and labor-market restrictions, having concluded that the *polder* model of collaboration and consensus decision making had become too costly for a world of intense international competition. In 2005, in response to BMW's threat to locate its new manufacturing plant in Eastern Europe, German unions agreed to allow line workers to toil on Saturdays for regular (rather than increased) wages and the company to increase the use of its plant and equipment by 40 percent without incurring overtime charges. In an effort to reduce costs and enhance labor-market flexibility more broadly, Germany adopted the so-called Hartz IV reforms replacing lifetime payments indexed to the worker's last pay slip with a means-tested flat-rate benefit, abolished income support for disabled recipients deemed capable of working at least three hours per day, cut benefits for unemployed persons rejecting an offer of work or training from the Federal Labor Agency, and raised the threshold firm size above which restrictions on layoffs apply. The French government overcame union resistance to relaxing rules limiting the workweek to thirty-five hours, permitting employees to work extra hours for extra pay, a modest reform but reform nonetheless. Pressure for reform has also found reflection

417

in the policies of the European Commission, which has advanced the principle of mutual recognition, discouraged anticompetitive mergers and state aids, and fostered deregulation. Markets where the effects are evident include those for everything from motor vehicle sales, where barriers to consumers buying abroad have been eliminated, to retail trade, where restrictions on opening hours have been relaxed and big-box stores have proliferated on the outskirts of European cities.

Indeed, some of the high-profile schemes of the Commission and the Council, such as the Lisbon Agenda intended to make Europe the world's most competitive economy by 2010, are precisely attempts to solve the coordination problem hindering reform and to overcome institutional inertia. Whether they will succeed is yet to be seen. The vested interests that develop around existing institutions are a source of resistance to change. More important, in my view, is the first-mover problem. Since reforms in one area will pay only if accompanied by reforms in other areas, whatever entity goes first will experience falling productivity and welfare until it has company—that is, until others undertake complementary reforms. This creates understandable fears that institutional reform and structural change may have fewer immediate benefits than costs. These fears in turn strengthen the hand of those with the most to lose from generalized reform. And there is no higher authority—certainly not the European Commission—with the power to mandate changes in all the relevant areas.

Comprehensive reform is necessary, but changes to some elements of the economic and social model will inevitably precede others, disrupting the operation and diminishing the efficiency of the system as a whole. For this reason, European growth is likely to disappoint in the short run. In the medium term Europe should perform better, since there then will have been the opportunity to adapt the entire constellation of complementary institutions to twenty-first-century conditions. As for the long run, there is no reason to foresee a crisis of European competitiveness, since the basic foundations on which competitiveness depends—a numerate, literate, and well-trained labor force, reliable contract enforcement, sound corporate governance, effective competition policy, efficient prudential supervision and regulation, and stable macroeconomic policies—remain in place.

Battle of the Systems

Over time, Europe developed and maintained highly structured and regulated labor markets because these complemented its cohesive employers associations, bank-based financial systems, and elaborate institutions of vocational education. Employees with well-developed skills and expectations of employment stability worked to identify and implement incremental improvements in existing technologies. Europe's bank-based financial systems provided patient finance for firms cultivating the skills of their workers. Vocational and apprenticeship training facilitated investment in sector-specific skills, while cohesive employers associations prevented firms from poaching experienced workers from their competitors. These arrangements were complementary. The effectiveness of one enhanced the effectiveness of the others. Europe's social model, entailing low levels of labor turnover and strong job protections, was a source of competitive strength. So too were the continent's bank-centered financial system and encompassing employers associations. For a half century and more, they enhanced the economy's capacity to deliver high-quality manufactured products, stable employment, incremental innovation, and an equitable distribution of income.

Two things have changed. First, technical progress has become more discontinuous, tipping the balance in favor of a U.S.-style system more capable of radical innovation. Second, financial globalization has become an irreversible fact that threatens to kick one of the essential props out from under the European model. In the face of growing competition from global securities markets, the share of bank loans in total financing declined from 74, 80, and 75 percent in 1989 in France, Germany, and Italy, respectively, to 42, 52, and

47 percent at the beginning of the twenty-first century.[3] A simple caricature of the European model is of a patient bank-based financial system that supplies finance to long-standing corporate customers providing on-the-job training to workers, the payoffs from which accrue over time. Competition from securities markets has now ratcheted up the pressure on banks to produce quick results. This leaves them less willing to patiently finance investments by their corporate clients in, inter alia, on-the-job training of their workers—investments that will pay off only down the road. With less patient finance, there will be more pressure on CEOs to focus on the current quarter's profit-and-loss statement. Firms will be less able to offer employment stability to their workers. With less employment stability there will be less investment in firm-specific training. If financial globalization really is inevitable and irresistible, forcing banks to give way to securities markets, then not simply one but ultimately all of the elements of the European model of the social market economy will have to change to prevent Europe from falling behind.

Taken to an extreme, this view suggests that the European model will have to converge to that of the United States. If the financial component of the European model comes to resemble that of the United States, then other components will have to come to resemble those of the United States as well, since only that one set of arrangements complements one another efficiently. If Europe instead maintains a combination that is second best, its economy will fall further and further behind, until at some point there is crisis sufficient to dissolve remaining resistance to adoption of the Anglo-Saxon model.

This conclusion is too strong, for at least two reasons. First, there may be more than one way to crack a nut. There may be more than one combination of labor-market, product-market, and public-sector institutions, in other words, capable of producing the same level of productive efficiency. Starting from different points, Europe and the United States may converge on different equilibria that are equally

[3] Data are from the World Bank Financial Structure Database, 2004.

420

efficient at delivering the economic goods. Perhaps. Economists and economic historians are tantalized by situations characterized by multiple equilibria. The challenge for proponents of this view is to formulate it precisely and marshal evidence in its support.

Second, if preferences differ, sustainable institutions can differ. Imagine that strong wage compression creates a sense of solidarity among citizens in European countries that is not felt equally by Americans and that this in turn produces greater effort on the part of European workers. Then Europe's labor-market institutions, which give rise to smaller income differentials than in the United States between the skilled and the unskilled, blue- and white-collar workers, and laborers and CEOs, will elicit a higher level of sympathetic effort. One can imagine a variety of other specific instances of this general phenomenon. All of them depend on Europeans' culture, preferences, attitudes, and history as the fundamental factors explaining persistent differences in institutions. As we saw in chapter 12, where there was an analysis of explanations for differences in hours worked between Europe and the United States hinging on differences in culture and preferences, the fundamental problem of validation is that culture and preferences are unobservable. They must be taken on faith. Be that as it may, this story certainly resonates with many observers, those impressed by the enduring influence of history in particular, in that it points to past experience as a factor contributing to distinctive features of European attitudes in the present.

Notwithstanding these caveats, competition between the models is bound to become ever more intense. Europeans may be willing to pay for inefficiencies in the production of private goods in order to support a higher level of public-good provision, but the costs of those inefficiencies, measured in terms of output and income, will rise as firms find it easier to source inputs abroad and consumers find it easier to purchase goods and services produced in other countries. There will be growing pressure for European countries to deliver their preferred mix of public and private goods more efficiently. The Scandinavian countries are widely cited as examples of societies that have already begun moving in this direction by successfully

maintaining essential social protections while enhancing the efficiency of their provision. Belgium and France are cited in this connection for moving away from a focus on minimum wages toward a
negative income tax as a more efficient way of supporting the living
standards of low-income persons. Over much of Europe, reforms
have been targeted at providing essential support for those separated
from their previous jobs without at the same time subsidizing unemployment. Reductions in hiring and firing costs have been more limited, but even here some countries, Italy and now Germany, have
made progress on this front. These reforms are not a dismantling of
the European model but rather an attempt to deliver its services
more efficiently.

Europe is not a perfect society. Unemployment is too high. Fiscal
discipline is too weak. It is unclear whether France and Germany
are willing to embrace market deregulation, not just in goods but
also in factor services, and to accept the further intensification of
product-market competition. Looking further ahead, a major challenge will be to cope with an aging population. The share of the
elderly in the population of the EU will double by 2050, reflecting
a combination of continuing increases in longevity and low birth
rates.[4] These may be global trends, with people living longer everywhere, but they are especially pronounced in Europe.[5] In 2050, the
ratio of the population older than sixty-five relative to those aged
fifteen through sixty-four will be nearly half again as high as in the
United States.[6] Inevitably, a substantially larger share of European
savings will have to go to support health care and retirement benefits, implying higher tax rates insofar as these programs are mostly
financed on a pay-as-you-go basis.

The United States deals with these problems partly by embrac-
ing immigrants, who are disproportionately of working age. It has

---

[4] Enlargement from fifteen to twenty-five member states will have only a brief rejuvenating
effect, since by 2020 the share of older people in the ten new EU members will approach that
in the original EU-15.

[5] As they are in Japan.

[6] In some countries, such as Spain and Italy, the ratio of pensioners to workers is projected
to reach one to one.

higher labor-force participation rates. In principle, Europe could do likewise. It could change its tax and pension laws to discourage early retirement. It could admit Turkey to the EU and extend full freedom of labor mobility to its residents. But Europe is less tolerant of immigrant cultures than the United States is. Its lower participation rates plausibly reflect culture and norms as well as tax laws, as discussed in chapter 12. Thus, it is not clear that Europe will display the cultural and economic flexibility needed to cope easily with its demographic future. How these tensions play out will have major implications for its economic performance going forward.

The Shadow of History

Europe today could not be more different from Europe fifty years ago. Following World War II the continent embarked on a process of extensive growth centered on heavy industry, driven by expanding inputs of labor and capital, and sustained by a backlog of unexploited technologies. Today Europe has converged to the technological frontier, and its growth derives from internally generated innovation. Fifty years ago the European economy was balkanized into closed national economies and riven by an unbridgeable East–West gap. Europe today has coalesced into an integrated economic zone. With the collapse of the Soviet bloc, the East–West divide has dissolved, incorporating the countries of Central and Eastern Europe into the Western European economy and leaving them to emulate the economic system of their Western neighbors.

Fifty years ago governments developed national economic strategies, implemented them by directing the flow of credit, and relied for macroeconomic governance on the close collaboration of union federations and employers associations. Today the market has escaped the shackles in which it emerged from World War II, diminishing the leverage of the social partners. In this brave new world of footloose finance and nationless production, governments are more limited in their options for shaping market outcomes. In Europe they have responded by adopting more market-acquiescent policies

423

but also by vesting additional power in the EU in the hope that by superseding the nation-state they can recapture a modicum of control. The parallel with the beginning of our period, when countries invested in the development of institutions of European integration so that the nation-state could regain mastery of its economic and political destiny, should not go unremarked.

For more than a half century, regional integration has been European policy makers' instinctual response to whatever problems they faced. The stage was set after World War II by an unusual conjuncture: nationalism had been discredited, there existed a venerable strand of integrationist thought, and there was support from the United States. The institutions of European integration that developed on this basis were designed to meet a specific set of postwar challenges. The European Coal and Steel Community allowed ceilings on German industrial production to be lifted, restoring the natural division of labor between producers of consumer and capital goods. The Common Market encouraged countries such as France that had been slow to restructure along export-oriented lines to capitalize on the opportunities for extensive growth. These institutions were then adapted, with reasonable facility, to meeting the challenges posed by the end of the golden age. The Bretton Woods System of pegged but adjustable exchange rates having broken down, European governments created the European Monetary System. Intensive growth implying a more intensely competitive environment, they adopted the Single Market Program to foster the deregulation of product markets and the euro to heighten price transparency.

These successive initiatives had an internal logic. The Coal and Steel Community created institutions with the capacity to manage a customs union. The Common Market, by increasing the volume of intra-European trade, created a constituency for the Single Market. The Single Market, which entailed the removal of capital controls, created pressure for the creation of a common currency. It is tempting to take this logic one step further and argue that the growing powers of the European Commission and the European Central

Bank have now created the need for a political counterweight to hold those in positions of authority in these institutions accountable for their actions. Advocates of a federal Europe harbored this idea from the start. But the majority of Europeans have always resisted the notion of transferring significant political powers from the national to the European level. This has made it problematic to employ the EU as an agent of social change when the changes involved threaten to undermine long-standing socioeconomic conventions and deeply held social values. Periodically, it has fueled reactions against the EU, as in the case of French and Dutch voters' rejection of the draft EU Constitution in their referenda in 2005. But the longer history of European integration reminds us that there is nothing particularly new or novel about this reaction. It suggests that recent proclamations of the death of the EU are premature. But it also suggests that the tension arising out of the unbalanced economic and political development of the European project will not be resolved anytime soon. Whether the EU can be an effective agent of economic reform under these conditions remains to be seen.

If at one level Europe today could not be more different from what it was fifty years ago, at another it remains strikingly similar. The institutions of tripartism and the welfare state, grounded in deep-seated Christian Democratic and Social Democratic values, display remarkable continuity. As networks of social relations, they are slow to change. At the same time, these institutions, which were ideally suited to a period of extensive growth, must now be adapted to a new era. In Western Europe, where there exists an articulated market system, the shift to intensive growth has been safely navigated, if not without difficulty and some decline in rates of productivity growth along the way. In Eastern Europe, where incentives were lacking, the inability to respond led to nothing less than the collapse of central planning and the end of the socialist experiment.

In political economy, as in physics, every action provokes a reaction. Globalization and the growth of impersonal markets have caused European politicians to complain of financial "locusts" drain-

ing European society of its lifeblood.[7] Expansion of the EU bureaucracy has provoked a sharp negative reaction from those who feel
their autonomy threatened. Optimism about Europe's innovative
capacity has succumbed to doubts about the continent's ability to
match the United States in the development of new technologies.
All that can be said with confidence is that this too shall pass.

[7] In the spring of 2005, Franz Müntefering, the chairman of Germany's Social Democratic
Party, characterized hedge funds as "swarms of locusts that fall on companies, stripping them
bare before moving on."

APPENDIX

SOURCES OF GROWTH

This appendix discusses in more detail the data and methods used in the growth decompositions in chapters 2, 4, and 9. Output per worker is decomposed into the portions accounted for by factor accumulation (increases in stocks of physical and human capital) and technical change (increases in the efficiency with which inputs are transformed into outputs). A long line of studies has adopted this approach. Its strength is its ability to place patterns of growth in bold relief. Some countries are shown as engaging primarily in catch-up—as starting out with capital–labor ratios below steady-state levels and growing via high investment. Others are shown as relying on technological progress—as maintaining their lead by boosting levels of technical efficiency. The weakness of this approach is the need for restrictive assumptions. One must assume a form for the aggregate production function through which inputs of capital and labor are translated into outputs.[1] One must assume values for the key parameters.[2] One must assume a weighting scheme for the components of capital and labor supplies.[3] One must assume, typically, that technical change is disembodied. Such assumptions are conten-

---

[1] Including the form in which technical change enters the production function.

[2] Notably for the elasticities of output with respect to capital and labor. Although these are typically taken to equal capital's and labor's respective factor shares, this is appropriate only under the assumption of, among other things, perfect competition.

[3] For example, one must assume that supplies of skilled and unskilled labor should be weighted by their respective wages, or that workers with different levels of education should be weighted by a factor based on estimated returns to years of schooling.

tious. They are easily criticized. But without such assumptions it is impossible to shed further light on the sources of growth.

The approach here builds on the work of Caselli and Tenreyro.[4] The change in aggregate labor productivity (output per worker), denoted y, is decomposed into the share due to the change in physical capital per worker k, the change in human capital per worker h, and the change in total factor productivity (technical efficiency) A.

$$D \log y = \alpha\, D \log k + (1 - \alpha)\, D \log h + D \log A \qquad (1)$$

where D is the difference operator. α the elasticity of output with respect to physical capital, is set to 0.33, as in most of the growth-accounting literature. GDP per worker y in purchasing power parity terms is taken from the Penn World Tables Version 6.1, except for Germany, where some splicing with earlier versions is needed.[5] The Penn World Tables also provide annual time series for investment but not for the capital stock. Wherever possible, I take capital stocks for 1950 (or the earliest subsequent year) from national sources, and extrapolate forward and backward adding real investment and netting out depreciation.[6] As in most of the modern growth-accounting literature, estimates of the stock of human capital h are based on average years of schooling s, where $h = \exp(\beta s)$. Years of schooling are taken from de la Fuente and Doménech (2002) for the period 1960–1990/5, and extrapolated forward and backward on the basis of Barro and Lee (2001).

Barro and Lee provide estimates of years of schooling in 1950 for only a subset of European countries. Their data for the rate of growth of average years of schooling in the 1950s are essentially

---

[4] In particular, Caselli and Tenreyro (2004).

[5] Version 5.6, covering the period 1950–1990, is spliced with version 6.1, covering the period 1991–2000.

[6] This differs from Caselli and Tenreyro (2004), who assume that investment up to 1950 had been the same as the observed level of investment between 1950 and 1955. Thus, they initialize the capital stock in 1950 by taking the level of investment in 1950 and dividing it by the sum of the investment growth rate between 1950 and 1955 and the depreciation rate (assumed to equal 6 percent). Although this procedure has been used elsewhere in the growth literature, it is problematic for the 1950s, when levels of investment were known to be much higher than in the earlier period and to have risen to different extents in different countries.

identical to those in Organisation for Economic Co-operation and Development (1974), which reports these for nine European countries and the United States. I therefore use the OECD figures for the ten countries concerned. For the others, I estimate years of schooling in 1950 using the following procedure. I take enrollment rates in primary and general secondary school from Flora (1983), who provides them for the beginning of each decade and each decennial midpoint (i.e., every five years). I regress de la Fuente and Doménech's measures of schooling starting in 1960 on primary and secondary school enrollment rates lagged (typically, secondary school enrollments lagged five years and primary school enrollments lagged ten years). These simple equations generally yield an R^2 on the order of 0.98–0.99 (which is not surprising since lagged enrollment rates are among the principal inputs used by de la Fuente and Doménech to construct their schooling figures). I then use lagged values of the independent variables to impute schooling levels in 1950. The rate of return to an additional year of schooling β is set at 0.10, following Caselli and Tenreyro (2004). A can then be calculated as a residual.

The variables in equation (1) can also be expressed relative to the United States. In this case y would be labor productivity in a European country, say Germany, relative to labor productivity in the United States, and similarly for k, h, and A. Each variable now indicates the extent of convergence to U.S. levels.[7]

Table A.1 shows output per worker relative to the United States in fifteen European countries over the period 1950–2000. (Figure A.1 graphs the same data.) The convergence of the European economies toward U.S. levels of productivity is evident in the positive values in the first column. But the rate of convergence was much faster for some countries than for others; for example, it was much faster for Ireland, which started out far behind and then successfully closed much of the gap, than for the United Kingdom, which was among the technological leaders at the start of the period but whose subsequent productivity performance was disappointing. Similarly,

[7] Caselli and Tenreyro (2004) undertake a similar exercise but use France rather than the United States as the basis for comparison.

TABLE A.1

Convergence decomposition relative to the United States, 1950–2000

Country	Total	Physical capital	Human capital	tfp
Austria	0.84	0.95	0.01	−0.12
Belgium	0.38	0.23	0.01	0.15
Denmark	0.22	0.33	−0.10	0.00
Finland	0.63	0.25	0.10	0.28
France	0.48	0.36	0.03	0.09
Germany	0.51	0.36	0.02	0.14
Greece	0.71	0.31	0.09	0.31
Ireland	0.94	0.21	−0.02	0.74
Italy	0.81	0.24	0.06	0.51
Netherlands	0.15	0.17	0.03	−0.06
Norway	0.30	0.19	−0.08	0.18
Portugal	0.92	0.31	0.02	0.60
Spain	0.84	0.18	0.07	0.59
Sweden	0.02	0.25	0.00	−0.23
United Kingdom	0.06	0.36	−0.03	−0.27

Source: See text.

the rates of growth of the three contributing factors—physical capital, human capital, and total factor productivity, all tended to be faster in Europe than in the United States, although some exceptions are evident in the last three columns of the table.

The three panels of table A.2 report the results of the same exercise for the 1950s, the fifteen years of high growth from 1960 to 1975, and the final quarter of the twentieth century. The first two panels show how all European countries exhibited a tendency to catch up with the United States in the 1950s and then in the period 1960–1975, although the sources of their performance differed. In the final quarter of the century, not surprisingly, the picture is much more heterogeneous. Only Ireland and to a lesser extent Portugal show a strong tendency to catch up with the United States in terms of output per worker, in Ireland's case owing to stellar rates of TFP growth and in Portugal owing to a combination of factors.

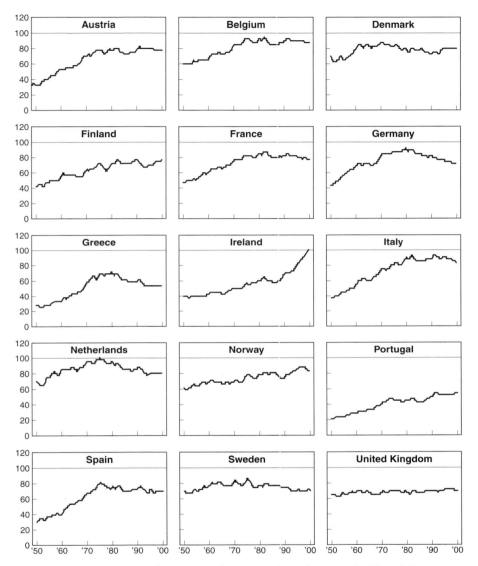

Figure A.1. Real gross domestic product per worker relative to the United States, 1950–2000. *Source*: See text.

TABLE A.2

Convergence decomposition relative to the United States, 1950–2000, various subperiods

Country	1950–1960				1960–1975				1975–2000			
	Total	Physical capital	Human capital	tfp	Total	Physical capital	Human capital	tfp	Total	Physical capital	Human capital	tfp
Austria	0.40	0.15	-0.03	0.28	0.43	0.26	-0.03	0.20	0.02	-0.01	0.08	-0.05
Belgium	0.11	0.14	-0.02	-0.01	0.31	0.15	0.00	0.17	-0.04	-0.05	0.03	-0.01
Denmark	0.23	0.20	-0.02	0.06	0.04	-0.02	-0.04	0.10	-0.05	-0.13	-0.03	0.11
Finland	0.30	0.28	-0.01	0.03	0.28	0.19	0.03	0.06	0.05	-0.04	0.08	0.01
France	0.24	0.17	-0.03	0.10	0.31	0.22	0.02	0.07	-0.07	-0.03	0.05	-0.08
Germany	0.45	0.28	-0.04	0.21	0.25	0.23	0.03	-0.01	-0.18	-0.15	0.03	-0.07
Greece	0.23	0.08	0.02	0.14	0.70	0.37	-0.01	0.34	-0.22	-0.13	0.08	-0.17
Ireland	0.09	0.02	-0.04	0.11	0.28	0.08	-0.03	0.22	0.57	0.11	0.06	0.41
Italy	0.40	0.12	-0.02	0.30	0.39	0.17	0.00	0.22	0.03	-0.05	0.08	0.00
Netherlands	0.21	0.16	-0.03	0.08	0.15	0.14	0.00	0.00	-0.21	-0.13	0.06	-0.13
Norway	0.11	0.17	-0.04	-0.02	0.12	0.07	-0.04	0.09	0.07	-0.04	0.00	0.11
Portugal	0.31	0.03	-0.01	0.28	0.43	0.19	-0.02	0.25	0.19	0.08	0.04	0.06
Spain	0.31	0.00	0.01	0.30	0.70	0.23	-0.04	0.51	-0.17	-0.05	0.11	-0.22
Sweden	0.10	0.21	-0.05	-0.07	0.11	0.14	-0.01	-0.02	-0.20	-0.11	0.06	-0.15
United Kingdom	0.06	0.23	-0.04	-0.13	0.02	0.17	-0.02	-0.13	-0.02	-0.05	0.03	-0.01

Source: See text.

REFERENCES

Abelschauser, Werner. 1975. *Wirtschaft in Westdeutschland, 1945–1948.* Stuttgart: Deutsche Verlags-Anstalt.

Abramovitz, Moses. 1986. "Catching Up, Forging Ahead, and Falling Behind." *Journal of Economic History* 46: 385–406.

Acemoglu, Daron, Simon Johnson, and James Robinson. 2001. "The Colonial Origins of Comparative Development: An Empirical Investigation." *American Economic Review* 91: 1369–1401.

Adams, William James. 1989. *Restructuring the French Economy.* Washington, D.C.: Brookings Institution.

Aitken, Norman D. 1973. "The Effect of the EEC and EFTA on European Trade: A Temporal Cross-Section Analysis." *American Economic Review* 63: 881–892.

Akerlof, George, Andrew Rose, Janet Yellen, and Helga Hessenius. 1991. "East Germany in from the Cold: The Economic Aftermath of Currency Union." *Brookings Papers on Economic Activity* 1: 1–87.

Aldcroft, Derek H., and Steven Morewood. 1995. *Economic Change in Eastern Europe since 1918.* London: Routledge.

Alesina, Alberto, Edward Glaeser, and Bruce Sacerdote. 2005. "Work and Leisure in the U.S. and Europe: Why So Different?" NBER Working Paper no. 11278 (April).

Alesina, Alberto, and Roberto Perotti. 1995. "Fiscal Expansions and Adjustments in OECD Countries." *Economic Policy* 21: 205–248.

Alexopoulos, Michelle, and Jon Cohen. 2003. "Centralized Wage Bargaining and Structural Change in Sweden." *European Review of Economic History* 7: 331–364.

Allen, Chris, Michael Gasiorek, and Alasdair Smith. 1998. "The Competition Effects of the Single Market in Europe." *Economic Policy* 27: 441–486.

Allen, Franklin, and Douglas Gale. 2000. *Comparing Financial Systems.* Cambridge, Mass.: MIT Press.

Allen, Kevin, and Andrew Stevenson. 1974. *An Introduction to the Italian Economy.* New York: Barnes and Noble.

Allsopp, Christopher. 1983. "Inflation." In *The European Economy: Growth and Crisis,* ed. Andrea Boltho, pp. 72–103. Oxford: Oxford University Press.

Alogoskoufis, George, and Ron Smith. 1991. "The Phillips Curve, the Persistence of Inflation, and the Lucas Critique: Evidence from Exchange Rate Regimes." *American Economic Review* 81: 1254–1275.

Amann, Ronald, Julian Cooper, and Robert William Davies, eds. 1977. *The Technological Level of Soviet Industry.* New Haven, Conn.: Yale University Press.

Anderson, Charles W. 1970. *The Political Economy of Modern Spain: Policy Making in an Authoritarian System.* Madison: University of Wisconsin Press.

Armstrong, Philip, Andrew Glyn, and John Harrison. 1991. *Capitalism since World War II: The Making and Breakup of the Great Boom.* London: Fontana.

Åslund, Anders. 2002. *Building Capitalism: The Transformation of the Former Soviet Bloc.* Cambridge: Cambridge University Press.

Åslund, Anders, Peter Boone, and Simon Johnson. 2001. "Escaping the Under-Reform Trap." *IMF Staff Papers* 48 (special issue): 88–108.

Atkeson, Andrew, and Patrick Kehoe. 1997. "Industry Evolution and Transition: A Neoclassical Benchmark." NBER Working Paper no. 6005 (April).

Ausch, Sandor, and Ferenc Bartha. 1968. "Theoretical Problems Relating to Prices in Trade between Comecon Countries." *Soviet and East European Foreign Trade* 2: 35–71.

Baele, Lieven, Annalisa Ferrando, Peter Hordhal, Elizaveta Krylova, and Cyril Monnet. 2004. "Measuring Financial Integration in the Euro Area." ECB Occasional Paper no. 14 (April).

Baily, Martin Neil, and Jacob Funk Kirkegaard. 2004. *Transforming the European Economy.* Washington, D.C.: Institute for International Economics.

434

Balassa, Bela. 1965. "Tariff Protection in Industrial Countries: An Evaluation." *Journal of Political Economy* 73: 573–594.

———. 1975. "Trade Creation and Diversion in the European Common
Market." In *European Economic Integration*, ed. Bela Balassa, pp. 79–118.
Amsterdam: North Holland.

Balcerowicz, Leszek. 1995. *Socialism, Capitalism, Transformation*. Budapest:
Central European University Press.

Balogh, Thomas. 1949. *The Dollar Crisis: Causes and Cure*. Oxford: Basil
Blackwell.

Barro, Robert, and Jong-Wha Lee. 2001. "International Data on Educational Attainment: Updates and Implications." *Oxford Economic Papers*
53: 541–563.

Barry, Frank. 2002. "Economic Policy, Income Convergence and Structural
Change in the EU Periphery." In *Europe and Globalization*, ed. Henryk
Kierzkowski, pp. 185–206. London: Palgrave-Macmillan.

———. 2003. "Integration and Convergence in the Cohesion Countries."
Journal of Common Market Studies 41: 897–922.

Baum, Warren C. 1958. *The French Economy and the State*. Princeton, N.J.:
Princeton University Press.

Bayoumi, Tamim, and Barry Eichengreen. 1994. "Macroeconomic Adjustment under Bretton Woods and the Post–Bretton Woods Float: An
Impulse-Response Analysis." *Economic Journal* 104: 813–827.

———. 1997. "Is Regionalism Simply a Diversion? Evidence from the EC
and EFTA." In *Regionalism in East Asia*, ed. Takatoshi Ito and Anne
Krueger, pp. 141–168. Chicago: University of Chicago Press.

Beckerman, Wilfred. 1962. "Projecting Europe's Growth." *Economic Journal*
72: 912–925.

Beljaars, Pim, and Rienk Prins. 2000. "Disability Programme Reforms and
Labour Market Participation in the Netherlands, 1990–2000: Principles,
Measures and Outcomes in a Decade of Combatting High Disability
Rates." Manuscript, Netherlands Social Security Agency and AS-Tri
Research & Consultancy Group (September).

Benner, Mats. 1997. *The Politics of Growth: Economic Regulation in Sweden,
1930–1994*. Stockholm: Arkiv Forlag.

Berend, Ivan. 1996. *Central and Eastern Europe, 1944–1993: Detour from
the Periphery to the Periphery*. Cambridge: Cambridge University Press.

435

Berend, Ivan, and Gyorgy Ranki. 1986. *The Hungarian Economy in the Twentieth Century*. London: Croom Helm.

Berger, Helge, and Albrecht Ritschl. 1995. "Germany and the Political Economy of the Marshall Plan: A Re-Revisionist View." In *Europe's Postwar Recovery*, ed. Barry Eichengreen, pp. 199–245. Cambridge: Cambridge University Press.

Bergson, Abram. 1983. "Technological Progress." In *The Soviet Economy: Toward the Year 2000*, ed. Abram Bergson and Herbert Levine, pp. 34–78. London: George Allen & Unwin.

Bernanke, Ben. 1985. "Employment, Hours and Earnings in the Depression: An Analysis of Eight Manufacturing Industries." *American Economic Review* 76: 82–109.

Berstein, Serge, and Jean-Pierre Rioux. 2000. *The Pompidou Years, 1969–74*. Cambridge: Cambridge University Press.

Bismans, Francis. 1992. *Croissance et Régulation: La Belgique 1944–1974*. Brussels: Académie Royale de Belgique.

Bispham, John, and Andrea Boltho. 1982. "Demand Management." In *The European Economy: Growth and Crisis*, ed. Andrea Boltho, pp. 289–328. Oxford: Oxford University Press.

Blanchard, Olivier. 2000. "The Economics of Unemployment." Manuscript, Massachusetts Institute of Technology.

———. 2004. "The Economic Future of Europe." *Journal of Economic Perspectives* 18: 3–26.

Blanchard, Olivier, and Justin Wolfers. 2000. "Shocks and Institutions and the Rise of European Unemployment: The Aggregate Evidence." *Economic Journal* 110: 1–33.

Bohi, Douglas. 1991. "On the Macroeconomic Effects of Energy Price Shocks." *Resources and Energy* 13: 145–162.

Boltho, Andrea, ed. 1982. *The European Economy: Growth and Crisis*. Oxford: Oxford University Press.

———. 1989. "Did Policy Activism Work?" *European Economic Review* 33: 1709–1726.

———. 2001. "Reconstruction after Two World Wars: Why the Difference?" *Journal of European Economic History* 30: 429–456.

Bottazzi, Laura, and Marco Da Rin. 2002. "Venture Capital in Europe and the Financing of Innovative Companies." *Economic Policy* 34: 229–269.

Bradley, John. 2004. "Committing to Growth: Experiences in Small European Countries." Manuscript, Economic and Social Research Institute, Dublin.

Broadberry, Stephen. 1997. "Anglo-German Productivity Differences, 1870–1990: A Sectoral Analysis." *European Review of Economic History* 1: 247–267.

Broadberry, Stephen, and N.F.R. Crafts. 1990. "The Implications of British Macroeconomic Policy in the 1930s for Long-Run Growth Performance." *Rivista di Storia Economica* 7: 1–19.

———. 2003. "UK Productivity Performance from 1950 to 1979: A Restatement of the Broadberry-Crafts View." *Economic History Review* 56: 718–735.

Broadberry, Stephen, and Sayantan Ghosal. 2002. "From the Counting House to the Modern Office: Explaining Anglo-American Productivity Differences in Services, 1870–1990." *Journal of Economic History* 62: 967–998.

Broadberry, Stephen, and Albrecht Ritschl. 1995. "Real Wages, Productivity, and Unemployment in Britain and Germany during the 1920s." *Explorations in Economic History* 32: 327–349.

Broadberry, Stephen, and Karin Wagner. 1996. "Human Capital and Productivity in Manufacturing during the Twentieth Century: Britain, Germany and the United States." In *Quantitative Aspects of Postwar European Economic Growth*, ed. Bart van Ark and Nicholas Crafts, pp. 244–270. Cambridge: Cambridge University Press.

Brown, William Adams, Jr., and Redvers Opie. 1953. *American Foreign Assistance*. Washington, D.C.: Brookings Institution.

Bruno, Michael. 1982. "World Shocks, Macroeconomic Response, and the Productivity Puzzle." In *Slower Growth in the Western World*, ed. R.C.O. Matthews, pp. 83–104. London: Heinemann.

Bruno, Michael, and Jeffrey D. Sachs. 1985. *The Economics of Worldwide Stagflation*. Cambridge, Mass.: Harvard University Press.

Brus, Wlodzimierz. 1986. "1953 to 1956: 'The Thaw' and 'The New Course.' " In *The Economic History of Eastern Europe, 1919–1975*, ed. Michael C. Kaser, pp. 3–39. Oxford: Clarendon Press.

Brus, Wlodzimierz, and Kazimierz Laski. 1989. *From Marx to the Market: Socialism in Search of an Economic System*. Oxford: Clarendon Press.

Buchheim, Christof. 1993a. "The Currency Reform in West Germany in 1948." In German Society for Business History, *Yearbook on Business History 1989–92*, pp. 85–120. Munich: Sauer.

———. 1993b. "Marshall Plan and Currency Reform." In *American Policy and the Reconstruction of West Germany, 1945–1955*, ed. Jeffry A. Diefendorf, Axel Frohn, and Hermann-Josef Rupieper, pp. 69–83. Cambridge: Cambridge University Press.

Buigues, Pierre, and Philippe Goybet. 1989. "The Community's Industrial Competitiveness and International Trade in Manufactured Products." In *The European Internal Market: Trade and Competition*, ed. Alexis Jacquemin and André Sapir, pp. 227–247. New York: Oxford University Press.

Buiter, Willem, Giancarlo Corsetti, and Paulo Pesenti. 1998. *Financial Markets and European Monetary Cooperation: The Lessons of the 1992–93 Exchange Rate Mechanism Crisis*. Cambridge: Cambridge University Press.

Buiter, Willem, and Marcus Miller. 1981. "The Thatcher Experiment: The First Two Years." *Brookings Papers on Economic Activity* 3: 315–380.

Burg, Steven L. 1983. *Conflict and Cohesion in Socialist Yugoslavia: Political Decision Making since 1966*. Princeton, N.J.: Princeton University Press.

Caballero, Ricardo J., Kevin Cowan, Eduardo Engel, and Alejandro Micco. 2004. "Effective Labor Regulation and Microeconomic Flexibility." NBER Working Paper no. 10744 (September).

Caballero, Ricardo J., and Mohamad Hammour. 1998. "Jobless Growth: Appropriability, Factor Substitution, and Unemployment." *Carnegie Rochester Conference Series on Public Policy* 48: 51–99.

Cairncross, Alec. 1996. *Managing the British Economy in the 1960s*. London: Macmillan.

Calmfors, Lars, and John Driffill. 1988. "Bargaining Structure, Corporatism, and Macroeconomic Performance." *Economic Policy* 6: 12–61.

Carew, Anthony. 1987. *Labour under the Marshall Plan*. Manchester: Manchester University Press.

Carr, Raymond, and Juan Pablo Fusi. 1979. *Spain: Dictatorship to Democracy*. London: Allen & Unwin.

Carré, Jean-Jacques, Paul Dubois, and Edmond Malinvaud. 1975. *French Economic Growth*. Stanford, Calif.: Stanford University Press.

Carreras, Albert, and Xavier Tafunell. 1997. "Spain: Big Manufacturing Firms between State and Market." In *Big Business and the Wealth of*

Nations, ed. Alfred Chandler, Franco Amatori, and Takashi Hikino, pp. 246–276. Cambridge: Cambridge University Press.

Casella, Alessandra, and Barry Eichengreen. 1993. "Halting Inflation in Italy and France after the Second World War." In *Monetary Regimes in Transition*, ed. Michael Bordo and Forrest Capie, pp. 312–345. Cambridge: Cambridge University Press.

Caselli, Francesco, and Silvana Tenreyro. 2004. "Is Poland the Next Spain?" Public Policy Discussion Paper no. 04-8, Federal Reserve Bank of Boston (December).

Chandler, Alfred. 1990. *Scale and Scope: The Dynamics of Industrial Capitalism*. Cambridge, Mass.: Belknap Press of Harvard University Press.

Committee for the Study of Economic and Monetary Union. 1989. *Report on Economic and Monetary Union in the European Community* [Delors Report]. Luxembourg: Office of Publications of the European Communities.

Committee on the Working of the Monetary System [Radcliffe Committee]. 1959. *Report*. London: H.M. Stationery Office.

Crafts, N.F.R. 1992. "Was the Thatcher Experiment Worth It? British Economic Growth in a European Context." In *Explaining Economic Growth: Essays in Honor of Angus Maddison*, ed. Adam Szirmai, Bart van Ark, and Dirk Pilat, pp. 327–352. Amsterdam: North Holland.

Crafts, N.F.R., and Kai Kaiser. 2004. "Long-Term Growth Prospects in Transition Economies: A Reappraisal." *Structural Change and Economic Dynamics* 15: 101–118.

Crafts, Nicholas, and Terence C. Mills. 2004. "TFP Growth in British and German Manufacturing, 1950–1996." Manuscript, London School of Economics and Loughborough University (June).

de Cecco, Marcello, and Francesco Giavazzi. 1993. "Inflation and Stabilization in Italy, 1946–1951." In *Postwar Economic Reconstruction and Lessons for the East Today*, ed. Rudiger Dornbusch, Wilhelm Nölling, and Richard Layard, pp. 57–83. Cambridge, Mass.: MIT Press.

de Grauwe, Paul. 1994. *The Economics of Monetary Integration*. Oxford: Oxford University Press.

de la Fuente, Angel, and Rafael Doménech. 2002. "Human Capital in Growth Regressions: How Much Difference Does Quality Data Make?" CEPR Discussion Paper no. 3587 (October).

Denison, Edward F. 1967. *Why Growth Rates Differ: Postwar Experience in Nine Western Countries*. Washington, D.C.: Brookings Institution.

Denitch, Bogdan Denis. 1976. *The Legitimation of a Revolution: The Yugoslav Case*. New Haven, Conn.: Yale University Press.

Denny, Kevin, and Stephen J. Nickell. 1992. "Unions and Investment in British Industry." *Economic Journal* 102: 874–887.

Deutsch, Karl W., Sidney A. Burrell, Robert A. Kann, Maurice Lee Jr., Martin Lichterman, Raymond E. Lindgren, Francis L. Loewenheim, and Richard W. Van Wagenen. 1957. *Political Community and the North Atlantic Area*. Princeton, N.J.: Princeton University Press.

Dewatripont, Mathias, and Gerard Roland. 1995. "The Design of Reform Packages under Uncertainty." *American Economic Review* 85: 1207–1223.

———. 1997. "Transition as a Process of Large-Scale Institutional Change." In *Advances in Economic Theory*, ed. David Kreps and Kenneth Wallis, pp. 240–273. Cambridge: Cambridge University Press.

Diebold, William. 1952. *Trade and Payments in Western Europe: A Study in Economic Cooperation, 1947–1951*. New York: Published for the Council on Foreign Relations by Harper.

Donges, J. B. 1976. *La Industrialización en España*. Barcelona: Oikos-Tau.

Dornbusch, Rudiger. 1976. "Expectations and Exchange Rate Dynamics." *Journal of Political Economy* 84: 1161–1176.

———. 2001. "A Primer on Emerging Market Crises." NBER Working Paper no. 8326 (June).

Dornbusch, Rudiger, and Holger Wolf. 1994. "East German Economic Reconstruction." In *The Transition in Eastern Europe, Volume 1: Country Studies*, ed. Olivier Blanchard, Kenneth Froot, and Jeffrey Sachs, pp. 155–190. Chicago: University of Chicago Press.

Dow, J.C.R. 1965. *The Management of the British Economy, 1945–1960*. Cambridge: Cambridge University Press.

Duchêne, François. 1994. *Jean Monnet*. New York: Norton.

Dunning, John. 1997a. "The European Internal Market Programme and Inbound Foreign Direct Investment: Part I." *Journal of Common Market Studies* 35: 1–30.

———. 1997b. "The European Internal Market Programme and Inbound Foreign Direct Investment: Part II." *Journal of Common Market Studies* 35: 189–223.

Dyson, Kenneth. 1994. *Elusive Union: The Process of Economic and Monetary Union in Europe*. London: Longman.

Dyson, Kenneth, and Kevin Featherstone. 1999. *The Road to Maastricht: Negotiating Economic and Monetary Union*. Oxford: Oxford University Press.

Economist. 2004. "Cheap Allure: Central Europe's Economies." *Economist*, 2 October, p. 52.

Edelman, Murray, and Robben Wright Fleming. 1965. *The Politics of Wage-Price Decisions: A Four-Country Analysis*. Urbana: University of Illinois Press.

Edin, Per-Anders, and Robert Topel. 1997. "Wage Policy and Restructuring: The Swedish Labor Market since 1960." In *The Welfare State in Transition: Reforming the Swedish Model*, ed. Richard B. Freeman, Robert Topel, and Birgitta Swedenborg, pp. 155–202. Chicago: University of Chicago Press.

Edinger, Lewis J. 1965. *Kurt Schumacher: A Study in Personality and Political Behavior*. Stanford, Calif.: Stanford University Press.

Eichengreen, Barry. 1994. *Reconstructing Europe's Trade and Payments: The European Payments Union*. Manchester: Manchester University Press.

Eichengreen, Barry, and Fabio Ghironi. 2002. "EMU and Enlargement." In *EMU and Economic Policy in Europe: The Challenge of the Early Years*, ed. Marco Buti and André Sapir, pp. 381–408. Cheltenham: Edward Elgar.

Eichengreen, Barry, and Pablo Vasquez. 2000. "Institutions and Economic Growth in Postwar Europe: Evidence and Conjectures." In *Productivity, Technology and Economic Growth*, ed. Bart van Ark, Simon Kuipers, and Gerard Kuper, pp. 91–129. Dordrecht: Kluwer.

Eichengreen, Barry, and Charles Wyplosz. 1993. "The Unstable EMS." *Brookings Papers on Economic Activity* 1: 51–143.

Eissa, Nada. 1996. "Tax Reforms and Labor Supply." *Tax Policy and the Economy* 10: 119–151.

Ellerman, David. 1998. "Voucher Privatization and Investment Funds: An Institutional Analysis." Manuscript, Development Economics Unit, World Bank (May).

Emminger, Otmar. 1977. "The D-Mark in the Conflict between Internal and External Equilibrium 1948–75." Essays in International Finance

441

122, International Finance Section, Department of Economics, Princeton University.

Esposito, Chiarella. 1994. *America's Feeble Weapon: Funding the Marshall Plan in France and Italy, 1948–1950*. Westport: Conn.: Greenwood Press.

Estrin, Saul, and Peter Holmes. 1983. *French Planning in Theory and Practice*. London: Allen & Unwin.

European Bank for Reconstruction and Development. 1999. *Transition Report 1999: Ten Years of Transition*. London: European Bank for Reconstruction and Development.

European Commission. 1985. *Completing the Internal Market: White Paper from the Commission to the European Council*, COM(85) 310 final. Brussels: European Commission (14 June).

———. 1995. *Annual Economic Report*. Brussels: European Commission.

———. 1996. *Economic Evaluation of the Single Market*. European Economy, Reports and Studies 4. Luxembourg: European Commission.

———. 2000. *Public Finances in EMU—2000*. European Economy, Reports and Studies 3. Luxembourg: European Commission.

———. 2001. *The Economic Impact of Enlargement*. Enlargement Papers 4. Brussels: European Commission.

Fauri, Francesca. 1996. "The Role of Fiat in the Development of the Italian Car Industry in the 1950s." *Business History Review* 70: 167–206.

Fischer, Stanley, and Ratna Sahay. 2004. "Transition Economies: The Role of Institutions and Initial Conditions." Paper presented at the Conference in Honor of Guillermo Calvo, International Monetary Fund (15 April).

Flanagan, Robert J., David W. Soskice, and Lloyd Ulman. 1983. *Unionism, Economic Stabilization, and Incomes Policies: European Experience*. Washington, D.C.: Brookings Institution.

Flanders, Allan. 1952. "Industrial Relations." In *The British Economy, 1945–1950*, ed. G.D.N. Worswick and Peter H. Ady, pp. 101–124. Oxford: Clarendon Press.

Fligstein, Neil, and Peter Brantley. 1995. "The 1992 Single Market Program and the Interests of Business." In *Politics and Institutions in an Integrated Europe*, ed. Barry Eichengreen, Jeffry Frieden, and Jürgen von Hagen, pp. 120–143. Berlin: Springer.

Flora, Peter. 1983. *State, Economy, and Society in Western Europe, 1815–1975: A Handbook in Two Volumes*, volume 1. Frankfurt: Campus Verlag.

Frankel, Jeffrey A. 1986. "The Implications of Mean-Variance Optimization for Four Questions in International Macroeconomics." *Journal of International Money and Finance* 5: 53–75.

Frankel, Jeffrey A., and David Romer. 1999. "Trade and Growth: An Empirical Investigation." *Quarterly Journal of Economics* 89: 379–399.

Fratianni, Michele, and Jürgen von Hagen. 1990. "German Dominance in the EMS: The Empirical Evidence." *Open Economies Review* 1: 67–87.

Freeman, Richard, and Ronald Schettkat. 2005. "Marketization of Household Production and the EU-US Gap in Work." *Economic Policy* 41: 5–50.

Friedman, Alan. 1988. *Agnelli: Fiat and the Network of Italian Power*. New York: New American Library.

Fuà, Giorgio. 1964. "The Contribution of Public Finance to the Formation of Demand in Italy 1955–63." Document DES/NL64.10, Organisation for Economic Co-operation and Development.

Furubotn, Eirik, and Svetozar Pejović. 1970. "Property Rights and the Behavior of the Firm in a Socialist State: The Example of Yugoslavia." *Zeitschrift für Nationalökonomie* 30: 431–454.

García Delgado, José Luis. 1987. "La Industrialización y el Desarrollo Económico de España Durante el Franquísimo." In *La Economía Española en el Siglo XX: Una Perspectiva Histórica*, ed. Jordi Nadal and Jaime Torras, pp. 164–189. Barcelona: Ariel.

Garibaldi, Pietro, and Paolo Mauro. 2002. "Anatomy of Employment Growth." *Economic Policy* 34: 67–114.

Garvin, Tom. 2004. *Preventing the Future: Why Was Ireland So Poor for So Long?* Dublin: Gill and Macmillan.

Gavin, Francis J. 2004. *Gold, Dollars, and Power: The Politics of International Monetary Relations, 1958–1971*. Chapel Hill: University of North Carolina Press.

Geroski, Paul A., and Alexis Jacquemin. 1988. "The Persistence of Profits: A European Comparison." *Economic Journal* 98: 375–389.

Gerschenkron, Alexander. 1962. *Economic Backwardness in Historical Perspective*. Cambridge: Harvard University Press.

Giavazzi, Francesco, and Alberto Giovannini. 1989. *Limiting Exchange Rate Variability: The European Monetary System.* Cambridge, Mass.: MIT Press.

Giavazzi, Francesco, and Luigi Spaventa. 1990. "The New EMS." In *The European Monetary System in the 1990s,* ed. Paul de Grauwe and Lucas Papademos, pp. 65–85. London: Longman.

Giersch, Herbert, Karl-Heinz Paque, and Holger Schmieding. 1992. *The Fading Miracle: Four Decades of Market Economy in Germany.* Cambridge: Cambridge University Press.

———. 1993. "Openness, Wage Restraint, and Macroeconomic Stability: West Germany's Road to Prosperity, 1948–1959." In *Postwar Economic Reconstruction and Lessons for the East Today,* ed. Rudiger Dornbusch, Wilhelm Nölling, and Richard Layard, pp. 1–28. Cambridge, Mass.: MIT Press.

Gillingham, John. 1991. *Coal, Steel and the Rebirth of Europe, 1945–1955: The Germans and French from Ruhr Conflict to Economic Community.* Cambridge: Cambridge University Press.

Gimbel, John. 1976. *The Origins of the Marshall Plan.* Stanford, Calif.: Stanford University Press.

Glyn, Andrew. 2002. "Labour Market Success and Labour Market Reform: Lessons from Ireland and New Zealand." CEPA Working Paper 2002-03, Center for Economic Policy Analysis, New York University (January).

Goldberg, Pinelopi Koujianou, and Frank Verboven. 2004. "Cross-Country Price Dispersion in the Euro Era: A Case Study of the European Car Market." *Economic Policy* 40: 483–522.

Gordon, Robert J. 2004. "Why Was Europe Left at the Station When America's Productivity Locomotive Departed?" NBER Working Paper no. 10661 (August).

Gospel, Howard F. 1992. *Markets, Firms, and the Management of Labour in Modern Britain.* Cambridge: Cambridge University Press.

Grabher, Gernot. 1991. "Rebuilding Cathedrals in the Desert: New Patterns of Cooperation between Large and Small Firms in the Coal, Iron, and Steel Complex of the German Ruhr Area." In *Regions Reconsidered: Economic Networks, Innovation, and Local Development in Industrialized Countries,* ed. Edward M. Bergman, Gunther Maier, and Frank Tödtling, pp. 59–78. London: Mansell.

Gramer, Regina Ursula. 2004. "From Decartelization to Reconstruction: The Mixed Legacy of American-Led Corporate Reconstruction in Germany." In *The United States and Germany in the Era of the Cold War, 1945–1990*, ed. Detlef Junker, volume 1, pp. 286–292. Cambridge: Cambridge University Press.

Gros, Daniel, and Niels Thygesen. 1992. *European Monetary Integration from the European Monetary System to the European Monetary Union*. London: Macmillan.

Grossman, Sanford, and Oliver Hart. 1981. "Implicit Contracts, Moral Hazard and Unemployment." *American Economic Association Papers and Proceedings* 71: 301–307.

Grubb, David, Richard Layard, and James Symons. 1984. "Wages, Unemployment and Incomes Policies." In *Europe's Stagflation*, ed. Michael Emerson, pp. 57–88. Oxford: Clarendon Press.

Gust, Christopher, and Jaime Marquez. 2002. "International Comparisons of Productivity Growth: The Role of Information Technology and Regulatory Practices." International Finance Discussion Paper no. 727, Board of Governors of the Federal Reserve System (May).

Haas, Ernst B. 1958. *The Uniting of Europe: Political, Social and Economic Forces, 1950–1957*. Stanford, Calif.: Stanford University Press.

Hackett, John. 1965. *Economic Planning in France: Its Relation to the Policies of the Developed Countries of Western Europe*. Bombay: Asian Publishing House.

Hall, Peter, and David Soskice, eds. 2001. *The Varieties of Capitalism: The Institutional Foundations of Comparative Advantage*. New York: Oxford University Press.

Hamilton, James. 1988. "A Neoclassical Model of Unemployment and the Business Cycle." *Journal of Political Economy* 96: 593–617.

Hansen, Bent. 1969. *Fiscal Policy in Seven Countries, 1955–1965*. Paris: Organisation for Economic Co-operation and Development.

Hansen, E. Damsgaard. 2001. *European Economic History from Mercantilism to Maastricht and Beyond*. Copenhagen: Copenhagen Business School.

Hardiman, Niamh. 2000. "Social Partnership, Wage Bargaining and Growth." In *Bust to Boom? The Irish Experience of Growth and Inequality*, ed. Brian Nolan, Philip J. O'Connell, and Christopher T. Whelan, pp. 286–309. Dublin: Institute of Public Administration.

Harrison, Joseph. 1978. *An Economic History of Modern Spain*. Manchester: Manchester University Press.

Harrison, Joseph, and David Corkill. 2004. *Spain: A Modern European Economy*. Aldershot: Ashgate.

Hartog, Joop. 1999. "Whither Dutch Corporatism? Two Decades of Employment Policies and Welfare Reforms." *Scottish Journal of Political Economy* 46: 458–487.

Hartog, Joop, and Jules Theeuwes. 1993. "Post-war Unemployment in the Netherlands." *European Journal of Political Economy* 9: 73–112.

Helliwell, John, Peter Sturm, and Gerard Salou. 1985. "International Comparison of the Sources of the Productivity Slowdown, 1973–1982." *European Economic Review* 28: 157–191.

Hellmann, Rainer. 1979. *Gold, the Dollar and the European Currency System: The Seven-Year Monetary War*. New York: Praeger.

Hemerijck, Anton, Brigitte Unger, and Jelle Visser. 2000. "How Small Countries Negotiate Change: Twenty-Five Years of Policy Adjustment in Austria, the Netherlands, and Belgium." In *Welfare and Work in the Open Economy*, volume 2, *Diverse Responses to Common Challenges*, ed. Fritz W. Scharpf and Vivien A. Schmidt, pp.175–263. New York: Oxford University Press.

Hennings, Klaus Hinrich. 1982. "West Germany." In *The European Economy: Growth and Crisis*, ed. Andrea Boltho, pp. 472–501. Oxford: Oxford University Press.

Herrigel, Gary B. 1989. "Industrial Order and the Politics of Industrial Change: Mechanical Engineering." In *Industry and Politics in West Germany*, ed. Peter J. Katzenstein, pp. 185–220. Ithaca, N.Y.: Cornell University Press.

Herring, Richard J., and Richard C. Marston, eds. 1977. *National Monetary Policies and International Financial Markets*. Amsterdam: North Holland.

Heylen, Freddy, and Gerdie Everaert. 2000. "Success and Failure of Fiscal Consolidation in the OECD: A Multivariate Analysis." *Public Choice* 105: 103–124.

Hill, T. P. 1979. *Profits and Rates of Return*, Paris: Organisation for Economic Co-operation and Development.

446

Hogan, Michael. 1987. *The Marshall Plan: America, Britain, and the Reconstruction of Western Europe, 1947–1952*. Cambridge: Cambridge University Press.

Holmes, Martin. 1985. *The First Thatcher Government, 1979–1983*. Brighton: Wheatsheaf.

Honohan, Patrick, and Cormac Ó Gráda. 1998. "The Irish Macroeconomic Crisis of 1955–56: How Much Was Due to Monetary Policy?" *Irish Economic and Social History* 25: 52–80.

Honohan, Patrick, and Brendan Walsh. 2002. "Catching Up with the Leaders: The Irish Hare." *Brookings Papers on Economic Activity* 1: 1–78.

Horowitz, Daniel L. 1963. *The Italian Labor Movement*. Cambridge, Mass.: Harvard University Press.

Hulten, Charles, James Robertson, and Rank Wykoff. 1989. "Energy Obsolescence and the Productivity Slowdown." In *Technology and Capital Formation*, ed. Dale Jorgenson and Ralph Landau, pp. 255–258. Cambridge, Mass.: MIT Press.

Independent High-Level Study Group. 2003. *An Agenda for a Growing Europe: Making the EU Economic System Deliver*. Brussels: European Commission.

International Monetary Fund. Various years. *Direction of Trade Statistics*. Washington, D.C.: International Monetary Fund.

———. Various years. *International Financial Statistics*. Washington, D.C.: International Monetary Fund.

———. Various years. *Primary Commodity Prices*. Washington, D.C.: International Monetary Fund.

Irwin, Douglas A. 1995. "The GATT's Contribution to Economic Recovery in Post-war Western Europe." In *Europe's Postwar Recovery*, ed. Barry Eichengreen, pp. 127–150. Cambridge: Cambridge University Press.

Jackson, Julian. 2003. *De Gaulle*. London: Haus Books.

Jacobsson, Per, and Alec Cairncross. 1950. *The Position of Germany in the European Payments Union*. Basel: EPU (13 November).

James, Harold. 1996. *International Monetary Cooperation since Bretton Woods*. Oxford: Oxford University Press.

Janossy, Ferenc. 1972. *La Fin des Miracles Economiques: Apparences de Réalité du Développement Economique*. Paris: Seuil.

447

Jeffries, Ian. 1993. *Socialist Economies and the Transition to the Market*. London: Routledge.

Johansen, Hans Christian. 1987. *The Danish Economy in the 20th Century*. London: Croom Helm.

Kaldor, Nicholas. 1966. *Causes of the Slow Rate of Economic Growth of the United Kingdom*. Cambridge: Cambridge University Press.

Katzenstein, Peter. 1984. *Corporatism and Change*, Ithaca, N.Y.: Cornell University Press.

———. 1985. *Small States in World Markets*. Ithaca, N.Y.: Cornell University Press.

Kaufmann, Daniel, Aart Kraay, and Massimo Mastruzzi. 2003. "Governance Matters III: Governance Indicators for 1996–2002." World Bank Policy Research Paper no. 3106 (August).

Kendrick, John. 1990. "International Comparisons of Productivity Trends and Levels." *Atlantic Economic Journal* 18: 42–54.

Kennedy, Ellen. 1991. *The Bundesbank: Germany's Central Bank in the International Monetary System*. London: Royal Institute of International Affairs.

Killick, John. 1997. *The United States and European Reconstruction, 1945–1960*. Keele: Keele University Press.

Kindleberger, Charles P. 1967. *Europe's Postwar Growth*. New York: Oxford University Press.

Kornai, János. 1990. *The Road to a Free Economy: Shifting from a Socialist System—The Example of Hungary*. New York: Norton.

———. 1992. *The Socialist System: The Political Economy of Communism*. Princeton, N.J.: Princeton University Press.

Köves, András. 1985. *The CMEA Countries in the World Economy: Turning Inwards or Turning Outwards*. Budapest: Akadémiai Kiadó.

Krueger, Dirk, and Krishna Kumar. 2002. "Skill-Specific Rather than General Education: A Reason for US–Europe Growth Differences?" NBER Working Paper no. 9408 (December).

Krugman, Paul. 1994. "Past and Prospective Causes of High Unemployment." *Economic Review*, Federal Reserve Bank of Kansas City (January): 23–43.

Labrousse, Agnès, and Jean-Daniel Weisz, eds. 2001. *Institutional Economics in France and Germany: German Ordoliberalism versus the French Regulation School*. Berlin: Springer.

Lamfalussy, Alexander. 1961. *Investment and Growth in Mature Economies: The Case of Belgium*. London: Macmillan.

Lane, Frederic Chapin. 1951. *Ships for Victory*. Baltimore: Johns Hopkins University Press.

Lange, Oscar. 1958. *The Political Economy of Socialism*. The Hague: Van Keulen.

Layard, Richard, Stephen Nickell, and Richard Jackman. 1991. *Unemployment: Macroeconomic Performance and the Labour Market*. Oxford: Oxford University Press.

Lazear, Edward. 1990. "Job Security Provisions and Unemployment." *Quarterly Journal of Economics* 105: 699–726.

Lewis, W. Arthur. 1954. "Economic Development with Unlimited Supplies of Labour." *Manchester School* 22: 139–191.

Lieberman, Sima. 1995. *Growth and Crisis in the Spanish Economy, 1940–93*. London: Routledge.

Lindbeck, Assar. 1994. "Overshooting, Reform and Retreat of the Welfare State." *De Economist* 142: 1–19.

Lindert, Peter H. 2004. *Growing Public*. Cambridge: Cambridge University Press.

Ljungqvist, Lars, and Thomas Sargent. 1998. "The European Unemployment Dilemma." *Journal of Political Economy* 106: 514–550.

Lundberg, Erik. 1968. *Instability and Economic Growth*. New Haven, Conn.: Yale University Press.

Lynch, Frances M. B. 1997. *France and the International Economy: From Vichy to the Treaty of Rome*. London: Routledge.

Machlup, Fritz. 1950. "Elasticity Pessimism in International Trade." *Economia Internazionale* 3: 117–141.

Maddison, Angus. 1991. *Dynamic Forces in Capitalist Development*. Oxford: Oxford University Press.

———. 2001. *The World Economy: A Millennial Perspective*. Paris: Organisation for Economic Co-operation and Development.

Maier, Charles. 1978. "The Politics of Productivity: Foundations of American International Economic Policy after World War II." In *Between Power and Plenty: Foreign Economic Policies of the Advanced Industrial States*, ed. Peter J. Katzenstein, pp.23–50. Madison: University of Wisconsin Press.

Marczewski, Jean. 1974. *Crisis in Socialist Planning*. New York: Praeger.

Marglin, Stephen A. 1990. "Lessons of the Golden Age: An Overview." In *The Golden Age of Capitalism*, ed. Stephen A. Marglin and Juliet Schor, pp. 1–38. Oxford: Clarendon Press.

Marsh, David. 1994. *Germany and Europe: The Crisis of Unity*. London: Heinemann.

Marrese, Michael, and Jan Vanous. 1983. *Soviet Subsidization of Trade with Eastern Europe*. Research Series no. 52, Institute of International Studies, University of California, Berkeley.

McArthur, John H., and Bruce R. Scott. 1969. *Industrial Planning in France*. Boston: Graduate School of Business Administration, Harvard University.

McDermott, John, and Robert Wescott. 1996. "An Empirical Analysis of Fiscal Adjustments." IMF Working Paper no. WP/96/59 (June).

McKinsey Global Institute. 2002. *Reaching High Productivity Growth in France and Germany*. New York: McKinsey Global Institute.

Meltzer, Allan H. 1991. "US Policy in the Bretton Woods Era." *Federal Reserve Bank of St. Louis Review* 73 (May/June): 54–83.

Mendershausen, Horst. 1949. "Prices, Money and the Distribution of Goods in Postwar Germany." *American Economic Review* 39: 646–672.

Mendis, Lionel, and John Muellbauer. 1983. "Has There Been a British Productivity Breakthrough? Evidence from an Aggregate Production Function for Manufacturing." Manuscript, London School of Economics (July).

Merigó, Eduardo. 1982. "Spain." In *The European Economy: Growth and Crisis*, ed. Andrea Boltho, pp. 544–580. Oxford: Clarendon.

Mierzejewski, Alfred C. 2004. *Ludwig Erhard: A Biography*. Chapel Hill: University of North Carolina Press.

Milward, Alan. 1984. *The Reconstruction of Western Europe, 1945–1951*. London: Methuen.

———. 1992. *The European Rescue of the Nation-State*. London: Methuen.

450

Milward, Alan, Frances M. B. Lynch, Federico Romero, Ruggero Ranieri, and Vibeke Sørensen. 1993. *The Frontier of National Sovereignty: History and Theory, 1945–1992*. London: Routledge.

Molitor, Michel. 1978. "Social Conflicts in Belgium." In *The Resurgence of Class Conflict in Western Europe since 1968*, ed. Colin Crouch and Alessandro Pizzorno, volume 1, pp. 21–52. New York: Holmes & Meier.

Moravcsik, Andrew. 1998. *The Choice for Europe: Social Purpose and State Power from Messina to Maastricht*. Ithaca, N.Y.: Cornell University Press.

Mowrey, David, and Nathan Rosenberg. 1998. *Paths of Innovation*. Cambridge: Cambridge University Press.

National Institute of Economic and Social Research. 1962. "Policies for Faster Growth." *National Institute Economic Review* 22 (February): 55–56.

Neves, João. 1994. *The Portuguese Economy in the Nineteenth and Twentieth Centuries*. Lisbon: Universidad Católica Editora.

———. 1996. "Portuguese Postwar Growth: A Global Approach." In *Economic Growth in Europe since 1945*, ed. Nicholas Crafts and Gianni Toniolo, pp. 329–354. Cambridge: Cambridge University Press.

Newell, Andrew, and James Symons. 1990. "The Passing of the Golden Age." In *Labor Relations and Economic Performance*, ed. Renato Brunetta and Carlo dell'Aringa, pp. 353–377. New York: New York University Press.

Nicholls, Anthony J. 1994. *Freedom with Responsibility*. Oxford: Oxford University Press.

Nickell, Stephen. 2003a. "Employment and Taxes." Paper prepared for the conference "Tax Policy and Employment" organized by CESifo, Venice (July).

———. 2003b. "Labour Market Institutions and Unemployment in OECD Countries." *CESifo DICE Report* 2: 1326.

Nickell, Stephen, Luca Nunziata, and Wolfgang Ochel. 2005. "Unemployment in the OECD since the 1960s: What Do We Know?" *Economic Journal* 115: 1–27.

Nickell, Stephen, Luca Nunziata, Wolfgang Ochel, and Glenda Quintini. 2002. "The Beveridge Curve, Unemployment and Wages in the OECD from the 1960s to the 1990s." CEP Discussion Paper no. 0502 (May), Centre for Economic Performance, London School of Economics.

Nickell, Stephen, and Jan van Ours. 2000. "The Netherlands and the United Kingdom: A European Employment Miracle?" *Economic Policy* 30: 137–180.

Nicoletti, Giuseppe, and Stefano Scarpetta. 2003. "Regulation, Productivity and Growth: OECD Evidence." *Economic Policy* 18: 9–72.

Nicoletti, Giuseppe, Stefano Scarpetta, and Olivier Boyland. 2000. "Summary Indicators of Product Market Regulation with an Extension to Employment Protection Legislation." Economics Department Working Paper no. 226, Organisation for Economic Co-operation and Development.

Nordhaus, William. 1972. "The Worldwide Wage Explosion." *Brookings Papers on Economic Activity* 2: 431–464.

North, Douglass. 1990. *Institutions, Institutional Change, and Economic History.* Cambridge: Cambridge University Press.

O'Connell, Philip J. 2000. "The Dynamics of the Irish Labour Market in Comparative Perspective." In *Bust to Boom? The Irish Experience of Growth and Inequality,* ed. Brian Nolan, Philip J. O'Connell, and Christopher T. Whelan, pp. 58–89. Dublin: Institute of Public Administration.

Ó Gráda, Cormac, and Kevin O'Rourke. 1996. "Irish Economic Growth, 1945–88." In *Economic Growth in Europe since 1945,* ed. Nicholas Crafts and Gianni Toniolo, pp. 388–426. Cambridge: Cambridge University Press.

———. 2000. "Living Standards and Growth." In *The Economy of Ireland: Policy and Performance of a European Region,* ed. John O'Hagan, pp. 178–204. Dublin: Gill and Macmillan.

O'Mahony, Mary, and Karin Wagner. 1994. *Changing Fortunes: An Industry Study of British and German Productivity Growth over Three Decades.* London: National Institute of Economic and Social Research.

Olson, Mancur. 1982. *The Rise and Decline of Nations.* New Haven, Conn.: Yale University Press.

———. 1996. "The Varieties of Eurosclerosis: The Rise and Decline of Nations since 1982." In *Economic Growth in Europe since 1945,* ed. Nicholas Crafts and Gianni Toniolo, pp. 93–94. Cambridge: Cambridge University Press.

Olsson, Anders, and Tom Burns. 1987. "Collective Bargaining Regimes and Their Transitions: The Rise and Decline of the Swedish Model." In

The Shaping of Social Organization, ed. Tom R. Burns and Helena Flam, pp. 176–212. London: Sage.

Orcutt, Guy. 1950. "Measurement of Price Elasticities in International Trade." *Review of Economics and Statistics* 32: 117–132.

Organisation for Economic Co-operation and Development. 1974. *Educational Statistical Yearbook*. Paris: Organisation for Economic Co-operation and Development.

———. 1983. *Flows and Stocks of Fixed Capital, 1955–1980*. Paris: Organisation for Economic Co-operation and Development.

———. 1992. *Employment Outlook*. Paris: Organisation for Economic Co-operation and Development.

———. 2002. "Product Market Competition and Economic Performance." *OECD Economic Outlook* 72: 155–162.

———. 2004. *Benefits and Wages: OECD Indicators*. Paris: Organisation for Economic Co-operation and Development.

———. 2005. *Employment Outlook*. Paris: Organisation for Economic Co-operation and Development.

———. Various years. *Labor Force Statistics*. Paris: Organisation for Economic Co-operation and Development.

———. Various years. *National Accounts*. Paris: Organisation for Economic Co-operation and Development.

Overy, Richard, 1995. *Why the Allies Won*. London: W.W. Norton.

Padoa-Schioppa, Tomasso, with Michael Emerson, Mervyn King, Jean-Claude Milleron, Jean Paelinck, Lucas Papademos, Alfredo Pastor, and Fritz Scharpf. 1987. *Efficiency, Stability and Equity: A Strategy for the Evolution of the Economic System of the European Community*. Oxford: Oxford University Press.

Paish, Frank. 1962. *Studies in an Inflationary Economy: The United Kingdom, 1948–61*. London: Macmillan.

Parsons, Craig. 2003. *A Certain Idea of Europe*. Ithaca, N.Y.: Cornell University Press.

Patten, Chris. 2004. "What Sarkozy Can Learn from Eastern Europe." *Financial Times*, 23 September, p. 17.

Perotti, Roberto. 1996. "Fiscal Consolidation in Europe: Composition Matters." *American Economic Association Papers and Proceedings* 86: 105–110.

Pfister, Thierry. 1985. *La Vie quotidienne à Matignon au temps de l'Union de la gauche.* Paris: Hachette.

Pick, Franz. Various years. *Pick's Currency Yearbook.* New York: Pick Publishing.

Piore, Michael, and Charles Sabel. 1984. *The Second Industrial Divide.* New York: Basic Books.

Podbielski, Gisèle. 1974. *Italy: Development and Crisis in the Post-War Economy.* Oxford: Clarendon Press.

Portes, Richard. 1993. "From Central Planning to a Market Economy." In *Making Markets,* ed. Shafiqul Islam and Michael Mandelbaum, pp. 16–52. New York: Council on Foreign Relations.

Prados, Leandro, and Jorge Sanz. 1996. "Growth and Macroeconomic Performance in Spain 1939–93." In *Economic Growth in Europe since 1945,* Nicholas Crafts and Gianni Toniolo, pp. 355–387. Cambridge: Cambridge University Press.

Pratten, C. F. 1976. "Labor Productivity Differentials within International Companies." Occasional Paper no. 50, Department of Applied Economics, University of Cambridge.

Prescott, Edward. 2004. "Why Do Americans Work So Much More Than Europeans?" *Federal Reserve Bank of Minneapolis Quarterly Review* 28 (July): 2–13.

Rammer, Christian. 2004. "Slowdown in the Pace of Innovation" In *ZEW News* 3, pp. 1–2. Mannheim: Zentrum fur Europakische Wirtschaftsforschung GmbH.

Rodrik, Dani. 1995. "Getting Interventions Right: How South Korea and Taiwan Grew Rich." *Economic Policy* 20: 53–107.

———. 1997. *Has Globalization Gone Too Far?* Washington, D.C.: Institute for International Economics.

———. 1998. "Why Do More Open Economies Have Bigger Governments?" *Journal of Political Economy* 106: 997–1032.

Roesler, Jörg. 1991. "The Rise and Fall of the Planned Economy in the German Democratic Republic, 1945–1989." *German History* 9: 46–61.

Roland, Gerard. 2001. "Ten Years After . . . Transition and Economics." *IMF Staff Papers* 48 (special issue): 29–52.

Roland, Gerard, and Thierry Verdier. 1997. "Transition and the Output Fall." CEPR Discussion Paper no. 1636 (May).

Romero, Federico. 1993. "Migration as an Issue in European Interdependence and Integration: The Case of Italy." In *The Frontier of National Sovereignty: History and Theory 1945–1992*, ed. Alan Milward, Frances M. B. Lynch, Federico Romero, Ruggero Ranieri, and Vibeke Sørensen, pp. 33–58. London: Routledge.

Rosenstein-Rodan, Paul. 1943. "Problems of Industrialisation in Eastern and South-Eastern Europe." *Economic Journal* 53: 202–211.

———. 1966. "Notes on the Theory of the Big Push." In *Economic Development for Latin America; Proceedings of a Conference Held by the International Economic Association*, ed. Howard Sylvester Ellis and Henry C. Wallich, pp. 57–81. New York: St. Martin's Press.

Ross, George. 1982. *Workers and Communists in France*. Berkeley and Los Angeles: University of California Press.

Ross, Stewart Halsey. 2003. *Strategic Bombing by the United States in World War II*. Jefferson, N.C.: McFarland Company.

Saint-Paul, Gilles. 2004. "Why Are European Countries Diverging in the Unemployment Experience?" *Journal of Economic Perspectives* 18: 49–68.

Sanderson, Michael. 1994. *The Missing Stratum: Technical School Education in England, 1900–1990s*. London: Athlone Press.

Sapir, André. 1992. "Regional Integration in Europe." *Economic Journal* 102: 1491–1506.

Sautter, Christian. 1982. "France." In *The European Economy: Growth and Crisis*, ed. Andrea Boltho, pp. 449–471. Oxford: Oxford University Press.

Scarpetta, Stefano. 1996. "Assessing the Role of Labour Market Policy and Institutional Settings on Unemployment: A Cross-Country Study." *OECD Economic Studies* 26: 4–98.

Scharpf, Fritz W. 1991. *Crisis and Choice in European Social Democracy*. Ithaca, N.Y.: Cornell University Press.

———. 2000. "Economic Changes, Vulnerabilities, and Institutional Capabilities." In *Welfare and Work in the Open Economy*, ed. Fritz W. Scharpf and Viven A. Schmidt, pp. 21–124. New York: Oxford University Press.

Schuman, Frederick L. 1951. "The Council of Europe." *American Political Science Review* 45: 724–740.

Schumpeter, Joseph A. 1942. *Capitalism, Socialism, and Democracy*. New York: Harper and Brothers.

Servan-Schreiber, Jean-Jacques. 1967. *Le Défi Américain*. Paris: Editions Denoël.

Shonfield, Andrew. 1965. *The Changing Balance of Public and Private Power*. New York: Oxford University Press.

Siebert, Horst. 1995. "Eastern Germany in the Fifth Year—Investment Hammering in the Basement?" Kiel Discussion Paper 250, Kiel Institute for World Economics.

Simonian, Haig. 1985. *The Privileged Partnership: Franco-German Relations in the European Community, 1969–1984*. Oxford: Clarendon Press.

Sinn, Gerlinde, and Hans-Werner Sinn. 1992. *Jumpstart: The Economic Unification of Germany*. Cambridge, Mass.: MIT Press.

Sinn, Hans-Werner. 2000. "Germany's Economic Unification: An Assessment after Ten Years." NBER Working Paper no. 7568 (March).

Sleight, Deborah Alpert. 1993. "A Developmental History of Training in the United States and Europe." Manuscript, Michigan State University (December).

Smith, Alan H. 1983. *The Planned Economies of Eastern Europe*. London: Croom Helm.

Solomon, Robert. 1977. *The International Monetary System, 1945–1976*. New York: Harper & Row.

Stephens, Philip. 1996. *Politics and the Pound: The Conservatives' Struggle with Sterling*. London: Macmillan.

Stiglitz, Joseph. 1999. "Whither Reform? Ten Years of the Transition." In *Proceedings of Annual Bank Conference on Development Economics*, pp. 1–32. Washington, D.C.: World Bank.

Streeck, Wolfgang. 1991. "On the Institutional Conditions of Diversified Quality Production." In *Beyond Keynesianism: The Socio-Economics of Production and Full Employment*, ed. Egon Matzner and Wolfgang Streeck, pp. 21–61. Cheltenham: Edward Elgar.

Surrey, Michael. 1982. "United Kingdom." In *The European Economy: Growth and Crisis*, ed. Andrea Boltho, pp. 528–553. Oxford: Oxford University Press.

Svennilson, Ingvar. 1954. *Growth and Stagnation in the European Economy*. New York: United Nations.

Swain, Geoffrey, and Nigel Swain. 1993. *Eastern Europe since 1945*. New York: St. Martin's Press.

Swain, Nigel. 1992. *Hungary: The Rise and Fall of Feasible Socialism*. London: Verso.

Temin, Peter. 1995. "The 'Koreaboom' in West Germany: Fact or Fiction?" *Economic History Review* 48 (second ser.): 737–753.

———. 2002. "The Golden Age of European Growth Reconsidered." *European Review of Economic History* 6: 33–22.

Tew, J.H.B. 1978. "Policies Aimed at Improving the Balance of Payments." In *British Economic Policy, 1960–74*, ed. F. T. Blackaby, pp. 304–359. Cambridge: Cambridge University Press.

Tille, Cedric, and Kei-Mu Yi. 2001. "Curbing Unemployment in Europe: Are There Lessons from Ireland and the Netherlands?" Federal Reserve Bank of New York, *Current Issues in Economics and Finance* 7 (5): 1–6.

Timmer, Marcel P., Gerard Ypma, and Bart van Ark. 2003. "IT in the European Union: Driving Productivity Divergence?" Research Memorandum GD-67, Groningen Growth and Development Centre, University of Groningen (October).

Toniolo, Gianni. 2005. *Central Bank Cooperation at the Bank for International Settlements*. Cambridge: Cambridge University Press.

Tortella, Gabriel. 2000. *The Development of Modern Spain*. Cambridge, Mass.: Harvard University Press.

Triffin, Robert. 1947. "National Central Banking and the International Economy." *Postwar Economic Studies* 7: 46–81.

———. 1957. *Europe and the Money Muddle*. New Haven, Conn.: Yale University Press.

———. 1960. *Gold and the Dollar Crisis: The Future of Convertibility*. New Haven, Conn.: Yale University Press.

Turner, Henry A. 1985. *Big Business and the Rise of Hitler*. New York: Oxford University Press.

Ulman, Lloyd, and Robert J. Flanagan. 1971. *Wage Restraint: A Study of Incomes Policy in Western Europe*. Berkeley and Los Angeles: University of California Press.

United Nations. 1962. *Economic Survey of Europe in 1961, Part 2: Some Factors in Economic Growth in Europe during the 1950s*. Geneva: United Nations.

———. 1972. *Economic Survey of Europe in 1971, Part 1: The European Economy from the 1950s to the 1970s*. New York: United Nations.

United Nations. 1980. *Economic Survey of Europe in 1979: The European Economy in 1979*. Geneva: United Nations.

Urwin, Derek W. 1994. *The Community of Europe: A History of European Integration since 1945*. London: Longman.

U.S. Department of State. 1947. *Occupation of Germany: Policy and Progress, 1945–46*. Washington, D.C.: Government Printing Office.

van Ark, Bart, and Jan Pieter Smits. 2004. "A Comparative Perspective on Technology Regimes and Productivity in Europe and the U.S." Paper presented to the Conference on the Development of the U.S. and European Economies in Comparative Perspective, Berkeley, Calif. (9–10 September).

van Brabant, Jozef M. 1980. *Socialist Economic Integration: Aspects of Contemporary Economic Problems in Eastern Europe*. Cambridge: Cambridge University Press.

van der Wee, Herman. 1986. *Prosperity and Upheaval: The World Economy, 1945–1980*. New York: Viking.

van Ryckeghem, Willy. 1982. "Benelux." In *Europe: Growth and Crisis*, ed. Andrea Boltho, pp. 581–609. Oxford: Oxford University Press.

van Zanden, Jan L. 1998. *The Economic History of the Netherlands, 1914–1995*. London: Routledge.

Verick, Sher. 2004. "Threshold Effects of Dismissal Protection Legislation in Germany." IZA Discussion Paper no. 991, Institute for the Study of Labor, Cologne (January).

Visser, Jelle, and Anton Hemerijck. 1997. *"A Dutch Miracle": Job Growth, Welfare Reform and Corporatism in the Netherlands*. Amsterdam: Amsterdam University Press.

von der Groeben, Hans. 1987. *The European Community: The Formative Years*. Brussels: Commission of the European Communities.

von Hagen, Jürgen, Rolf R. Strauch, and Guntram B. Wolff. 2002. "East Germany: Transition with Unification—Experiments and Experiences." ZEI Working Paper no. B19 (April).

Wallich, Henry. 1955. *Mainsprings of German Revival*. New Haven, Conn.: Yale University Press.

Walsh, Brendan. 2002. "When Unemployment Disappears: Ireland in the 1990s." Manuscript, University College, Dublin (December).

458

———. 2005. "The Transformation of the Irish Labour Market, 1980–2003." Manuscript, University College, Dublin (May).

Wang, Zhen Kun, and L. Alan Winters. 1991. "The Trading Potential of Eastern Europe." CEPR Discussion Paper no. 610 (November).

Weder, Beatrice. 2001. "Institutional Reform in Transition Economies: How Far Have They Come?" IMF Working Paper no. 114 (August).

Werner, Pierre. 1970. "Report to the Council and the Commission on the Realisation by Stages of Economic and Monetary Union in the Community." *Bulletin of the European Communities* supplement 11: 1–65.

Whitaker, Thomas Kenneth. 1958. *Programme for Economic Expansion.* Dublin: Stationery Office.

Wilensky, Harold L. 2002. *Rich Democracies: Political Economy, Public Policy and Performance.* Berkeley and Los Angeles: University of California Press.

Williams, Charles. 1993. *The Last Great Frenchman: A Life of General de Gaulle.* New York: John Wiley and Sons.

World Bank. 1963. *The Economic Development of Spain.* Baltimore: Johns Hopkins University Press for the World Bank.

Zauberman, Alfred. 1964. *Industrial Progress in Poland, Czechoslovakia and East Germany, 1937–1962.* London: Oxford University Press.

INDEX

Abramovitz, Moses, 205
Acheson, Dean, 66–67
Adenauer, Konrad, 77, 163, 167, 170, 173, 175
Afghanistan, 301
Agartz, Viktor, 64
Agreement for Intra-European Payments and Compensations, 76
agriculture: and Belgium, 129; and British free trade area, 175; in Central Europe, 142; and central planning, 135, 136, 300; collectivized, 134, 138; and Council on Mutual Economic Assistance, 157; and Eastern enlargement of European Union, 333; in Eastern Europe, 131–32, 137–38, 141, 142, 146; and East Germany, 149; and European Economic Area, 13; and Finebel Plan, 79; in France, 46, 61–62, 104, 110, 200; in Germany, 58, 70; and growth deceleration of 1960s, 223; and growth in 1950s, 104, 110, 112, 116, 119, 120, 122, 129; in Hungary, 150; in Ireland, 86, 119, 120; and Italy, 112, 116; labor output in 1950s in, 88; labor shift from, 28, 88–89, 116, 129, 138, 139, 205, 216, 218, 252, 413; and monetary integration, 188; 1960s employment in, 217–18; in Poland, 142, 150n; in Portugal, 205, 206; postwar, 60; postwar hoarding in, 61; postwar recovery of, 56; in Spain, 208, 215, 216; and transition from central planning, 317;

and United Kingdom, 122. *See also* Common Agricultural Policy (CAP)
Ahlen Program, 64
Albania, 137, 147, 156
Alesina, Alberto, 387
Algerian conflict, 102
Allen, Kevin, 114
Alphand, Hervé, 76
Alphandéry, Edmond, 365
Anglo-American Loan, 75
apprenticeship training, 5, 19, 26, 27n, 260–61, 401n. *See also* education; vocational education
assembly line, 2, 23, 76, 115, 257, 261
Association for Monetary Union, 352
atomic energy, 172. *See also* Euratom
Austria: banks in, 100; and Central and Eastern European transition economies, 333; complementary investment in, 92; coordination of wage bargaining in, 269; corporatism in, 99–100; currency devaluations of 1949 by, 77; employers associations in, 100; employment protection in, 273; and European Free Trade Association, 176–77; and European Payments Union, 81; and exports, 25, 99, 100; and French growth in 1950s, 100; growth in, 17, 19, 21, 99–100, 199, 204; and Hungary, 303; income per person in, 408; industry in, 99; inflation in, 277; and information technology, 404; interest rates in, 100; investment in, 33, 92, 99, 100, 404; labor in, 88, 255, 262,

Agreement on Multilateral Monetary Compensation, 75; and food, finance, and transshipment services, 165; and France, 128, 239; and free trade zone, 174; and Germany, 127, 128, 129; government in, 128; growth in, 17, 21, 126–29, 201, 202; imports in, 128; income per person in, 408; industrial relations in, 127, 128; industry in, 127, 128; inflation in, 282–83; information technology investment in, 404; infrastructure in, 129; investment in, 127, 128, 202; and Italy, 127; labor in, 88, 95, 128, 255, 262; labor costs in, 98, 127; labor markets in, 126–27; labor market unrest in, 127, 222; and Maastricht Treaty, 370; monetary policy in, 128; and Netherlands, 127, 128; 1950s investment in, 86; and political aspect of integration, 173; postwar exports from, 38; and postwar trade, 73, 74; prices in, 128; research and development in, 129; and Snake in the Tunnel, 249; social security in, 33; steel industry in, 74; taxes in, 274, 422; unemployment in, 264, 266; unemployment benefits in, 271; unions in, 127; wages in, 33, 127, 222, 269, 417, 422; wartime destruction in, 55; worker output in, 128

Bentham, Jeremy, 41
Bérégovoy, Pierre, 288, 341
Berlin Wall, 28, 87
Beyen, Jan Willem, 172
Bidault, Georges, 69, 168
Bismark, Otto von, 42
Bismarkian welfare state, 42
Bissell, Richard, 75
Blanchard, Olivier, 272
Blum, Léon, 163–64, 287
BMW, 417
Bolsheviks, 43
bond markets, 375–76
Brandt, Willy, 192, 193
Brandt government, 197

Bretton Woods System: breakdown of, 11, 30, 48–49; collapse of, 189–90, 242–45, 246, 252, 256, 284; European alternative to, 192; and France, 242; and monetary union, 194; of pegged but adjustable rates, 11, 30, 40, 49, 220, 225–26, 242, 243, 246, 424; regional recreation of, 247–48; and Smithsonian Agreement, 194; and Snake in the Tunnel, 247–48; and sterling, 235; and United Kingdom, 242; and United States, 244, 246–47; weakening of, 220
British Commonwealth, 126, 166, 175, 183, 231
British Empire, 126, 166, 175, 183, 231
British Employers' Confederation, 123
Brussels Treaty (1948), 170
Bucharest Formula, 159
budget(s): in Central and Eastern European transition economies, 311; and European Central Bank, 355; and French growth in 1950s, 111; and German growth in 1950s, 94–95; and Maastricht Treaty, 355, 372; and Marshall Plan, 66; and postwar decontrol of prices, 64, 68; in Spain, 209; and Stability and Growth Pact, 374; surveillance of, 352; and transition from central planning, 317
Bulgaria: and central planning, 134, 135; and Council on Mutual Economic Assistance, 156, 157; growth in, 17, 19, 139, 140; inflation in, 308; investment in, 137; labor in, 138; reform in, 147; transition economy of, 308, 310, 311, 314, 315
Bundesbank, 240, 284, 285, 286; and EMS crisis, 363; and European Central Bank, 353, 370; and European Monetary System, 348, 350; and German reunification, 319, 320, 323; and interest rates, 365; and monetary integration, 351, 354, 355; and recession of 1991, 358

469

Germany *(cont.)*
240, 241, 242, 248–49, 290; current account of, 81; and customs union, 163,
171, 174; decontrol of prices in, 66;
and Delors Report, 353; deregulation
in, 422; and dollar devaluation, 245;
and Eastern Europe, 132; and East Germany, 148; East-West split, 71; Economic Administration of, 71; as economic center of Europe, 58, 73;
employment protection in, 272, 273;
and EMS crisis, 363; and European
Central Bank, 355; and European Coal
and Steel Community, 36, 37, 168–69;
and European collective security, 170;
and European Community, 179, 197,
339; and European Defense Community, 169; and European integration,
10, 166, 167, 241, 338–39; and European Monetary System, 251, 283–86,
287, 348, 349, 350; and European Payments Union, 79, 80, 81, 83, 84; and
exchange rates, 83; and exports, 25,
38, 93, 94, 240; and Finebel Plan, 79;
and fiscal policy, 29, 94, 371, 372; follow the leader wage negotiations in,
34, 44; foreign-policy autonomy for,
169, 171, 197; and France, 57, 58, 69,
70, 73, 100, 101, 102, 109, 112, 172,
173, 187, 240, 246, 283–85, 289, 351,
354; free-market orientation of, 93,
125; and free trade zone, 174, 175; government in, 95; gross domestic product
in, 18; growth in, 17, 19, 21, 90, 93–
97, 199, 204, 223; Hartz IV reforms in,
417; and housing, 96; and immigration, 87, 96; income per person in,
408; and industry, 10–11, 20–21, 56–
58, 59, 63–64, 69, 70, 87, 93, 94, 95,
174, 338–39; inflation in, 43, 96, 220,
277, 282–83, 348, 358, 363; information technology investment in, 404; innovation in, 259–60; insurance in,
339; and interest rates, 365; interfirm
relations in, 259, 260; investment in,
22, 58, 87, 93, 94, 95, 128, 199; and

Italy, 115; joint-stock companies in,
268; and Korean War, 81, 168; labor
in, 87–88, 89, 96–97, 252, 255, 262,
268; labor costs in, 87; labor force in,
28; labor-management co-determination in, 32–33; law in, 319; legitimacy
of, 164, 197; and Level of Industry
Plan, 58, 70; as locked into Europe,
69, 112, 339, 353, 354; and Maastricht
Treaty, 356, 359, 370; market in, 93,
422; and Marshall Plan, 66; as monetary center, 250; and monetary integration, 197, 347, 350, 352, 354, 354–55,
357; monetary policy in, 68, 94, 350;
and monetary union, 193, 246, 371; nationalization in, 63–64, 70; and
NATO, 170, 172; and neocorporatist
wage stabilization, 268; and Netherlands, 99; occupation of, 57, 69–70,
169, 354; and ordo-liberalism, 94; and
Ostpolitik, 192; pensions in, 34, 95;
and political parties, 67, 94; postwar
output of, 70–71; postwar policy uncertainty in, 63–64; postwar reconstruction of, 56–58; and price-cost margins,
93; prices in, 66, 68, 93, 220, 284; producer durables from, 199; public ownership in, 95; public spending on worker
benefits in, 271; rationing in, 71; recession in, 289–90; regulation in, 339; reparations from, 69; research and development in, 258; reunification of, 318–
28, 353–54, 359; and savings in 1950s,
95; and Single European Act, 338; and
Snake in the Tunnel, 248, 249; and so-
cialized industry, 64; social market
economy in, 95; sovereignty of, 169;
and Soviet Union, 56–57, 68, 70–71;
and Spain, 213; and Stability and
Growth Pact, 372–73; steel industry
in, 33; stockpiled earnings in, 71–72;
taxes in, 33, 83, 95, 274, 411; technology in, 88; telecommunications in,
339, 341; and trade, 60, 84; transportation in, 95–96, 339; unemployment in,
87, 96, 218–19, 264, 417; unemploy-